Advance Praise for
Making Space for Indigenous Feminism, 3rd Edition

This volume offers a view of the development and expansion of Indigenous feminisms as theory and praxis, reaffirming the validity of our respective Indigenous epistemologies to guide us into the future.

—JENNIFER NEZ DENETDALE (DINÉ), University of New Mexico

Multiplying are the calls for transformative healing issued by Indigenous feminism, which is, at its core, about Indigenous sovereignty, solidarity, and liberatory justice for all. The diverse and incisive essays in this book expose ongoing cis-heteropatriarchal settler colonialism; anti-Indigenous racism; the erasure of gender and sexual diversity (including by Indigenous people ourselves); and their impacts upon minds, bodies, lived experiences, and relationships. Resistance and hope abound in the re-centring of (queer) Indigenous feminist futurisms: world-building that honours the self-determination of Indigenous women, girls, Two-Spirit, and trans folks and promotes wellbeing for all of Creation.

—CHANTAL FIOLA, University of Manitoba

This third edition continues to fulfill the promise of the title to make space for feminist interventions in Canadian Indigenous studies. Each author is committed to relational ethics and transformative praxis in addressing the most pressing issues that create epistemic and material injustices. From the heart, rendering an intimate state-of-the-field assessment from pillars in the field — from the politics of gender, policy, and violence manifested in Canada currently to latter chapters that open up new spaces by continuing to press for just Indigenous futures, in which decentring binaries of gender and sexuality is necessary — we see the importance of Indigenous feminist theorizing and praxis. Confronting gendered violence, heterosexism, disciplinary regimes, and colonialism with honesty and truthtelling, *Making Space* generously offers us new paths to materialize a decolonial world.

—MISHUANA GOEMAN, author of *Mark My Words: Native Women Mapping Our Nations*

Making Space for Indigenous Feminism provides us with powerful voices emerging from and incorporating past, present, and future. Each chapter continues to make space for the power of Indigenous feminisms, as women, femme, Queer, LGBTQS+ and Mad think together in a powerful analysis of our now. This latest edition of a classic, newly edited by Gina Starblanket, includes Elders and youth and brings us back to why Indigenous feminisms are the embodied, lived and felt knowledges that will inform our struggles going forward.

—DIAN MILLION, author of *Therapeutic Nations: Healing in an Age of Indigenous Human Rights*

This collection is all feast, no fluff. It covers foundational elements of Indigenous feminism with depth and breadth and engages issues of national and international importance with considerable insight. Due to its readability and smart use of theory, this book is eminently teachable. I haven't highlighted this much in a long time.

—MARGARET ROBINSON, Canada Research Chair in Reconciliation, Gender, and Identity

Clear, hopeful, fierce, and focused, this volume teaches us why Indigenous feminisms are needed, what they make possible now and for Indigenous futures. Attending to the theories, actions, movements, and conditions of Indigenous feminisms, this book provides readers with affirmation for the kinds of projects they are already doing and what they might create to bring about the change we want to see in the world.

— EVE TUCK, New York University

MAKING SPACE for
INDIGENOUS FEMINISM

3RD EDITION

MAKING SPACE for
INDIGENOUS FEMINISM

3RD EDITION

edited by Gina Starblanket

FERNWOOD PUBLISHING
HALIFAX & WINNIPEG

Copyright 2024 © Gina Starblanket

All rights reserved. No part of this book may be reproduced or transmitted in any form by any means without permission in writing from the publisher, except by a reviewer, who may quote brief passages in a review.

Copyediting: Lisa Frenette
Cover image: used with permission from the artist, Christi Belcourt
Cover design: Evan Marnoch
Text design: Lauren Jeanneau
Printed and bound in Canada

Published by Fernwood Publishing
Halifax and Winnipeg
2970 Oxford Street, Halifax, Nova Scotia, B3L 2W4
www.fernwoodpublishing.ca

Fernwood Publishing Company Limited gratefully acknowledges the financial support of the Government of Canada through the Canada Book Fund and the Canada Council for the Arts. We acknowledge the Province of Manitoba for support through the Manitoba Publishers Marketing Assistance Program and the Book Publishing Tax Credit. We acknowledge the Nova Scotia Department of Communities, Culture and Heritage for support through the Publishers Assistance Fund.

Library and Archives Canada Cataloguing in Publication
Title: Making space for Indigenous feminism / edited by Gina Starblanket.
Names: Starblanket, Gina, editor.
Description: 3rd edition. | Previous editions were edited by Joyce Green. | Includes bibliographical references and index.
Identifiers: Canadiana (print) 20240338537 | Canadiana (ebook) 20240338626 | ISBN 9781773635507
(softcover) | ISBN 9781773636719 (EPUB) | ISBN 9781773636702 (PDF)
Subjects: LCSH: Indigenous women—Political activity. | LCSH: Indigenous women—Social conditions. |
LCSH: Indigenous women—Civil rights. | LCSH: Women's rights. | LCSH: Feminism. | LCSH: Women
political activists.
Classification: LCC HQ1161 .M34 2024 | DDC 305.48/8—dc23

This book is dedicated to its readers, who will be transformative. It is dedicated to the Indigenous feminists who stood with us in the early days and have now left the physical world;

to Indigenous women and 2SLGBTQIA+ people globally who are fighting for their lives, their lands, and their relatives, on their own and together; to those resisting enclosures and crossing borders so that movements and solidarities can flow;

to all who suffer gendered violence, all working to eradicate it, and those who had to walk away from worlds for it to end;

to the Indigenous parents creating beautiful families in all their forms, and to their children, who will know and carry forward expansive understandings of love;

to everyone who has had their story taken from them, and who continues to honour themselves on their own terms;

to the generation of Indigenous feminists bringing forward new terms of change, and those who will follow.

Contents

SECTION I: Home | Identity | Legacies 1

1. Extending our Accounts of Indigenous Feminism
   Gina Starblanket and Joyce Green 2

2. Always Coming Home: Indigenous Identity, Indigenous Feminism, Scholarship, and Life
   Joyce Green 27

3. Why Am I a Feminist?
   Emma LaRocque 52

4. Settler Colonialism in Canada: Making "Indian" Women Disappear
   Mary Eberts, Shelagh Day and Sharon McIvor 72

SECTION II: Institutions | Representation | Resistance 99

5. Red Ticket Women: Revisiting the Political Contributions of the Indian Rights for Indian Women's Movement
   Gina Starblanket 100

6. Perpetual State of Violence: An Indigenous Feminist Anti-Oppression Inquiry into Missing and Murdered Indigenous Women and Girls
   Robyn Bourgeois 121

7. Gender Reveals That Matter: Cis-Heteropatriarchy, Settler Colonialism, and Child Welfare
   Megan Scribe 146

SECTION III: Land | Relationality | Love 167

8   Towards an Anti-Colonial Feminist Care Ethic
    Eva Jewell 168

9   Our Movements Need Some Love as Well:
    Indigenous Land Defence and Relationality
    Isabel Altamirano-Jiménez 193

10 Mana Wahine and Mothering at the Loʻi:
    A Two-Spirit/Queer Analysis
    Hōkūlani K. Aikau 214

SECTION IV: Decoloniality | Movement | Futurities 237

11 Decolonization Is a Queer Desire: Poetics, Politics, Negativity
    Billy-Ray Belcourt 238

12 Mad Indigenous Womanhood: The Psycho-Politics of
    Settler Colonialism
    Cara Peacock 251

13 On Black and Indigenous Relationality: A Conversation
    *Robyn Maynard, Leanne Betasamosake Simpson
    and Gina Starblanket* 269

14 Decolonization Is Also Metaphorical: Indigenous Feminist
    and Queer–Two-Spirit Storywork Matters
    Kelly Aguirre 286

About the Contributors 311

Acknowledgements 315

Index 318

SECTION I

HOME | IDENTITY | LEGACIES

ONE

Extending our Accounts of Indigenous Feminism

Gina Starblanket and Joyce Green

THIS BOOK IS ABOUT INDIGENOUS FEMINISM. While it focuses particularly on the Canadian legal and political context, Indigenous feminism exists wherever states have displaced and subordinated Indigenous Peoples. Indigenous feminism troubles the imposition and manifestation of racialized and gendered structures of power in colonial and Indigenous contexts, taking up and informing resistance to colonialism, racism, and sexism. When the first edition of this book was published in 2007, there was little scholarship on or activism mobilized by Indigenous[1] feminism, and very few Indigenous activists self-identified as feminist. Yet, those few voices have incrementally made space for more work about Indigenous feminism, in the form of foundations, echoes, and new Indigenous feminist articulations. That space has produced better analysis of the conditions that affect Indigenous women's lives; in particular, of distinctly gendered experiences of colonialism and attending violence.

The first edition of this book was conceptualized following a Symposium on Aboriginal Feminism in 2002 at the University of Regina organized by Joyce Green. The symposium was attended by self-identified Aboriginal feminists and some Indigenous women who were interested in women's issues but did not take the label of feminist. The conceptualization, organization, and execution of the symposium was an exercise in feminist solidarity. With the support of a politically focused affinity group, the Kitchen Table Collective, and of some non-Indigenous and Indigenous feminist bureaucrats in the BC Region division of Status of Women Canada, Green was able to secure a grant to hold a Symposium on Aboriginal Feminism. The presentations and discussions at the symposium impelled the inaugural edition of *Making Space for Indigenous Feminism* (2007).

While all participants were important contributors to the symposium, perhaps none was more helpful than Shirley Bear, a Maliseet (Wolastoqiyik) activist, feminist, and Elder, who spoke of the importance of feminism to her and to many sisters around the world (Green 2007, 26). Her participation was especially powerful because so many of us had been told that feminism was untraditional and incompatible with Indigenous cultures; indeed, a couple of participants had been told their feminism was proof that they were not Indigenous. Bear told the group that she had come to challenge the prohibition on doing healing ceremonies with women when they were menstruating because of a particular woman's need for help at that time; she said no one had ever been hurt by her ceremonies, but many had been helped. That experience led her to question other prohibitions on women. She was also a fierce advocate for Indigenous women's equality of Indian Act status recognition. She was a traditional ceremonialist, but not a fundamentalist who insisted on mindless conformity, without regard for the critiques that feminism has raised. She prayed with and for us, laughed with us, and joined with us in claiming feminism for Indigenous women. Following her 2022 passing, we want to take the space to honour Shirley Bear and her contribution to Indigenous feminist knowledge and activism in Canada, to the search for status justice for Indigenous women, and to the intellectual genealogy of the *Making Space* volumes.

In 2007, when the first edition of *Making Space for Indigenous Feminism* was published, there was virtually no explicit writing on Indigenous feminism in Canada, although there was some work critiquing feminist solidarity across racial and colonial lines[2] and some work claiming there was no such thing as Indigenous feminism. In the Indigenous ("Native") studies, English, and politics areas, there were also groundbreaking accounts both biographical and activist, as well as a number of works on identity regulation in particular.[3] This work took up two central themes — Indigenous women's experiences with colonialism and racism, and the identity problematic, policed as it has been by the settler state and then by Indian Act bands and other Indigenous political formations. The identity and status problematic has been central in the Canadian context because it is an effective part of the unending desire of the state to eliminate many in the state-recognized status category of Indian Act bands, including through the enforcement of European and Christian formulations of patriarchy (Eberts 2014, 2017).

The literature gap pointed to the invisibility of Indigenous women in feminist movements and in academia, and to the unthinking racism that has enabled some to fail to see Indigenous women in our full historical and contemporary contexts: as contemporary persons living in the context of colonial and gender oppression by the occupying state and populations of, for example, Canada, the US, Aotearoa/New Zealand, Sápmi, and Australia, with their racist mythologies, institutions, and practices. That gap also allowed male-dominated settler governments and some equally male-dominated Indigenous governments and lobby groups to say they spoke for women, while ignoring women in their vision, politics, and budgets. Thus, the impetus behind the 2002 Symposium on Aboriginal Feminism and then *Making Space for Indigenous Feminism* was the need to make some space in the academic and popular literature on women and liberation for Indigenous feminist voices.

When the second edition came out in 2017, much had changed, and space for Indigenous feminist analysis was being carved out in Indigenous and non-Indigenous contexts. While anti-feminist sentiment remained intact in many Indigenous communities, an increasing number of scholars and activists were taking up the feminist label and deploying explicitly feminist analyses. Contributors to the second edition examined applications of Indigenous feminist theory and practice, honing the movement's scope and intervention as a form of social and political critique. There was a growing body of theoretical, analytical, and creative writing relevant to Indigenous feminism, and within the Canadian academy, Indigenous feminism was beginning to be taken up in disciplines beyond the fields of law, politics, women's and gender studies and Native studies. There was more lip service within some Indigenous and non-Indigenous political organizations to the need for gendered analysis, for political legitimacy, and for sound policy and strategy, even if commitment and action lagged. A number of prominent Indigenous scholars also began recognizing the significance of feminist analyses and theories, naming them in their own work. Dene scholar Glen Coulthard, for example, wrote of gendered analysis that "the crucial interventions of Indigenous feminist scholarship and activism over the years have made it *impossible* for any credible scholar ... to ignore the impact that colonial patriarchy continues to have on our national liberation efforts" (2014, 157; emphasis in original).

At this point, there was a body of critical feminist anti-racist writing that framed Canada as a colonial settler state infused with racist conceptions about Indigenous Peoples and other non-white people (see, for example, Thobani 2007; Dhamoon and Abu-Laban 2009; Mawani 2009; Schick 2009; Razack 2002, 2016). Much important work was also done by non-Indigenous scholars tilling the fields of feminist, anti-racist, and post-colonial theory. A number of Indigenous scholars contributed work critical of settler colonialism that, while not always explicitly or even implicitly feminist, provided important insights for Indigenous and other feminist scholars. Thus, the scholarly literature became more robust, and the theoretical contributions more likely to take up gendered and raced accounts of Indigenous Peoples, and of colonialism's distinctive impacts on them.

These additional theoretical and empirical tools have been useful for both scholars and activists. The fear and marginalization that Indigenous feminists felt so keenly because of explicit hostility to the presence and analyses of Indigenous feminists were somewhat mitigated (though not erased) by 2017. More Indigenous women took the label, used the analyses, and worked for liberatory objectives consistent with Indigenous feminism. Yet, sexism, misogyny, and racism continued to afflict Indigenous women, and serious engagement with these factors had not yet become consistent or routine in either Indigenous or settler governments and communities. Thus, the second edition illuminated the need for consistent application of the analyses and tools provided by Indigenous feminism while providing some first-rate scholarship about matters impacting Indigenous women.

Two decades after the first symposium on Aboriginal feminism, Gina Starblanket and some feminist colleagues from the University of Victoria and the Yellowhead Institute organized a conference on Indigenous feminism at the University of Victoria. The purpose of this gathering was to engage a broad, interdisciplinary community-engaged dialogue considering how Indigenous feminism has grown as an area of study and practice in the past two decades; to workshop papers that would ultimately lead to the development of this third edition of

Making Space for Indigenous Feminism; and to bring together Indigenous feminist colleagues from across institutions to reflect upon Joyce Green's scholarly legacy and her contributions to the study of Indigenous feminism. This symposium also heard expressions of gratitude and indebtedness to Green, which incisively reflected the enormity, interdisciplinarity, and longevity of her influence across generations.

Now in its third edition, *Making Space* continues to advance Indigenous feminist theory and activism through new or extended applications of Indigenous feminist methods and theories, and through reflection and conversation about the movement's ideas, concepts, and approaches. In their invitations to write for this volume, contributors were asked to contemplate the future horizons of Indigenous feminism as it advances beyond the foundational phase of the movement. Some authors from the first and second editions were invited to provide updated chapters with an eye towards new social, legal, and political developments, and space was reserved for new chapters, solicited from leading and emergent voices across disciplines. Several new contributions are from authors who have the privilege of being trained by the first generation of scholars to call themselves Indigenous feminists; their experiences offer important insights into how Indigenous feminist tools, methods, and practices are being taken up in a range of theoretical, applied, and creative contexts. They also demonstrate the importance of having scholars legitimize Indigenous feminist analysis and practice through their teaching and research — scholarly and political invisibility renders discussion difficult.

This edition recognizes the intellectual genealogy of Indigenous feminism as well as the importance of tracing change, facilitating ongoing conversations between generations and cohorts, and pushing our horizons forward. At this juncture it was particularly important not to approach difference as a weakness meant to cultivate critique or divisiveness, but as a reflection of the diverse ways in which we encounter, respond, and live through different contexts from our own locations. Intergenerational, stylistic, and interdisciplinary differences in this volume were approached as generative, indicating a diversity of identities, thought, and language within the growing Indigenous feminist movement.

While this new edition reflects the fact that the content and form of some existing Indigenous feminist concerns have changed in relation to the political terrain, it also demonstrates that other preoccupations remain intact, indicating a continuity of structures of oppression. We have now had the time to gain the benefit of hindsight with respect to many matters, and this experience allows us to hone our approaches and analyses. And, moving beyond the inaugural phase of Indigenous feminism has opened space for us to engage in greater contemplation of our relationships, which are also changing. There are more alliances between Indigenous and non-Indigenous activists and academics, and with other feminist, queer, and liberatory movements, united by convergences in our goals, analyses, and solidarities. Trans and Two-Spirit inclusivity is now a significant consideration across feminist spaces, with all feminists being prompted to give closer attention to and reflect on how they approach and engage with gender and sexual identity.

Alongside these changes, certain constants remain. There is still a fundamental hostility toward feminism in many communities, public and political spaces, and universities. Some Indigenous women who identify as feminists remain cautious about claiming the label and explicitly invoking the analysis, and the Canadian feminist movement's coloniality and whiteness continue to attract significant critique in Indigenous academic and community contexts. Specific and structural colonialism, racism, and heteropatriarchy relegate our scholarly and activist contributions to the margins of dominant intellectual and political worlds. Thus, our work continues, as we must still convey, theorize, and validate our experiences and analyses to both non-Indigenous and Indigenous forms of knowledge production.

Continuing to "make space," in this context, means engaging critical questions about the theoretical and practical foundations and advances of Indigenous feminism over past decades, while also recognizing that our own encounters with the movement's central categories and concepts are varied, differently informed, and changing. Indeed, "making space" comprises a continuous project of being in conversation with one another about our shared *and* our different understandings and contexts, which in turn might enable new openings for potentially transformative conversations and relationships within our own movement, and with other movements and actors.

THE FINGERPRINTS OF INDIGENOUS FEMINISM

Women have been subjected to oppression arising from heteropatriarchy and misogyny in many cultural and political contexts, because of power relations in which men dominate and hold cultural, economic, political, and social privileges relative to women. The way this relationship has evolved has not been identical everywhere, but its existence is predominant. It is in this context that feminist theory and activism emerge, according to specific conditions, and envisioned by feminists who seek greater measures of autonomy, dignity, opportunity, respect, contextual equality, inclusion, and agency for women in all our diversity. Feminist theory and empirical work shed a bright light on power relations wherever they occur, and foreground women's voices and experiences with the heteropatriarchal assumptions and power relations that produce other forms of subordination, such as colonialism, racism, homophobia, and transphobia. This focus on power relations and oppression also contributes to other politics of resistance, such as ecofeminism and Indigenous ecological positions, both of which focus on protecting the earth and its creatures from the ongoing assault by human and corporate activity. It includes the activities of land and water protectors, and of what we can call "all our relations" — all life forms.

Indigenous feminism is all of this and more, for it is framed by the realities and histories of Indigenous experiences in the context of colonialism, as well as by the sexism, racism, and racially motivated misogyny that infects the settler state's populations and cultures. Indigenous feminists draw on and sometimes critique our own cultural contexts, which leads to particular insights and objectives. Indigenous feminism is a liberatory movement grounded on theoretical foundations. It is premised on rejecting oppression of Indigenous women, Indigenous Peoples, and the lands and waters that we hold responsibilities towards and from which we have been dispossessed by the settler states.

Indigenous feminism is a mode of critique, but it also entails a resurgent, future-oriented politic. Starblanket writes of three dimensions of resurgence significant to Indigenous feminism: the temporal dimension, with which resurgence illuminates present and future theoretical work; the land-based dimension, which considers land as a source of culture, education, and inspiration; and the "everyday" nature of acts of resurgence in our relationships (2017, 23–24). Ingrid Waldron provides a useful summary of Indigenous feminism and its resurgence politics:

> An Indigenous feminist politics is a political, social, and cultural theory and movement premised on transformative change through Indigenous forms of governance, actions

to combat gender discrimination and the social erasure and marginalization of Indigenous women, the repudiation of patriarchy in Indigenous communities, white supremacy and colonialism within mainstream white feminism, the decolonization of Indigenous men and women, and equality and sovereignty for Indigenous people globally. (2022, 98)

Indigenous feminists find themselves in the context of colonialism and resistance; of personal, collective, structural, and environmental racism and sexism; of genocides, territorial displacements, cultural repression or annihilation; and of ongoing economic exploitations. Like other feminisms, Indigenous feminism is a broad and deep category with different strands. The broad parameters sketched here are true for the majority of these strands. Indigenous feminism is also unique as a form of grounded and transformative critique: the signal distinction between other feminisms and Indigenous feminism lies in our simultaneous preoccupation with land, with histories of land theft and oppression, with the consequent cultural and material losses, and with the denial by the Canadian state (or other states) and by some First Nations bands (and other Indigenous communities) of our identities. These matters fuel our feminism just as much as the myriad forms of sexist, misogynist, and racist oppression that afflict our lives.

Thus, in addition to confronting gendered oppression, Indigenous women's liberation entails liberation from colonialism and the corollary practices of particularly extractivist capitalism because, as Rauna Kuokkanen writes, "the exploitation of Indigenous women and their bodies has been inextricably tied to the process of ongoing exploitation and dispossession of Indigenous lands and resources since the first contact" (2019, 191) and thus, "gender violence [is] a self-determination issue" (214). An Indigenous feminist analysis commends the withdrawal of the settler state from spaces of Indigenous sovereignty and jurisdiction; and remediation of the violence, deprivation, and dislocation imposed by the state and its corporate clients on Indigenous communities and nations. It challenges the logic of imperialism and re-centres Indigenous women (Stewart-Harawira 2007). It requires reclamation of territory, which has been stolen for settlement, state sovereignty, and "Crown lands," and for capitalist exploitation. These deprivations require reparations for colonial injuries inflicted on specific nations, communities, families, and individuals — and on the land itself. Those injuries are often a consequence of extractive industries supported by the state's legislative and enforcement powers (for example, see Hall 2022; Waldron 2022).

Indigenous feminist analyses of colonialism require confronting the systemic and specific forms of racialized sexism and misogyny that settler state citizens and institutions project on Indigenous women and girls. And yes, it requires demanding respect, equality, and non-violence from Indigenous governments and Indigenous men. That includes policy decisions from the former, and a consensus on the need for cultural and behavioural changes for some who are, frankly, appallingly violent, disrespectful, and dominating in their relationships. It includes the need for confronting gender oppression in contemporary self-government regimes which deploy gendered practices "that create hierarchies and exclusions that negatively affect Indigenous women more than men" (Kuokkanen 2019, 175; see also 2014) and to also confront forms of traditionalism "deployed to discipline and morally police Indigenous women" (Craft 2023, 101).

Indigenous feminism remains relevant in the context of ongoing gendered relations of power and cultures infected with masculinist and white supremacist practices and privileges. We continue to require methods and tools that allow us to form complex analyses and accounts of how power operates in society. We are in neither a post-feminist nor a post-colonial order. We have none of us attained our goals, even if we have advanced our struggles. Heteropatriarchy and misogyny, often fused with racism, continue to circumscribe and sometimes to obliterate the lives of women (Anderson, Campbell, and Belcourt 2018; Bourgeois 2017; Eberts 2007, 2017; Kuokkanen 2014, 2017; Thobani 2007, 2020; Rebick 2005; Razack 2002; Government of Canada 2019). Moreover, misogyny functions to enhance Indigenous women's oppression, as has been well demonstrated by Rauna Kuokkanen's study of Indigenous government in Canada, Greenland, and Sápmi (2019) and by Mary Eberts's important theorizations about the Victorian-inspired impositions Canada has and continues to apply to Indigenous women (2014, 2017).

Colonialism, the Canadian Constitution and federal division of powers, and the capitalist class, which works with government support to secure and "develop" resources on Indigenous lands, are perennial concerns for Indigenous feminists because "gender regimes are part of institutional design" (Kuokkanen 2019, 139). Aedan Alderson writes,

"The goal of gaining and maintaining a monopoly over Indigenous land, people, and natural resources has been an explicit part of the Crown's colonial aspirations" (2022, 50). In this, sexism writ large works with colonialism, as corporations and both constitutional orders of Canadian government appropriate Indigenous lands and resources.

Indigenous people are relationally connected to our territories. The misuse, destruction, and appropriation of Indigenous lands is a profound injury to our nations and to the women of those nations; moreover, male dominance in extractive industries' workforces — combined with their remoteness from other employment options and from women's support and protection services, as well as the gendered, sexist, and often racist ethos in the "man camps" — creates security liabilities for Indigenous women on our own territories (LAWS 2021; Waldron 2022).

These matters shape Indigenous feminist politics, scholarship, and priorities.

INDIGENOUS FEMINIST THEORY

The theoretical basis of Indigenous feminism is continuously being developed in relation to Indigenous feminist advocacy and activism. The contributions to the literature and activism signal what make it distinct from other feminisms. This includes its theoretical characteristics; its response to colonialism; specific Indigenous and gendered critiques and analyses; the shared terrain with other feminisms and feminists, and with other Indigenous people; its commitment to 2SLGBTQIA+ rights and voices; and solidarities with other movements towards justice and liberation from related forms of oppression.

Political theory is a set of tools that reveals phenomena, relationships, and foundations, and points to frameworks of analysis. Indigenous feminist theory does precisely that but is neither entirely separate from other feminist theory nor entirely consistent with it. Its distinctions are anchored in the social and political context of Indigenous women in particular communities; in oppressive, sexist, racist, and exploitative colonial relationships. It is concerned with the violence of classification, regulation, and representation of gendered, racialized identities. It is embedded in histories that dispute the stories of settler communities and institutions, histories which frame the wounds of intergenerational trauma, and the problems of intergenerational subjugation to colonial narratives, institutions, priorities, and privileges. Like other feminisms, it is *always* focused on praxis — on theoretically informed political action for transformative purposes.

The signal characteristic of Indigenous feminism to date has been its attention to the impacts of colonialism, racism, sexism, and misogyny both in private and public life, individually and systemically. This is not to deny other liberatory movements with which Indigenous feminism may ally, but to assert that there is a fundamental socially constructed, politically imposed power relationship at the core of gender- and sex-based oppression that requires analysis and resistance. Feminism employs a gendered, relational, and critical analysis of the relationships between men and women; sometimes of gender categories themselves; of male-dominated institutions and practices; and of gendered power in social and political contexts. Feminism, like resurgence, and like other critical social movements, is theoretically informed but also is directed at transformative action. It is a political as well as an intellectual exercise. Feminists have been on the front lines of political action in communities, movements, politics, and services to and protections for women and for trans and non-binary people. Feminism is not an armchair preoccupation.

In its organization and politics, feminist praxis relies on feminist processes. These have included engagements with internal movement structures and processes, with community members, and with the prioritization of specific political goals through consultation, advocacy, and often, through internal governance consensus practices. Following critiques within the Canadian feminist movement in the 1980s, the movement itself was prompted to address race and racism, sexual identity, class, and other forms of difference with political implications. The former premier Canadian national feminist organization, the National Action Committee on the Status of Women (NAC),[4] grappled with these on centre stage, as racialized women contested NAC's obliviousness to the power relations consequent to racism, colonialism, and privilege (Collier 2015, 26) and to its own structural and systemic racism. In the process, some white feminists in NAC demonstrated solidarity and awareness, while others refused the imputation of racism and some left the organization. Following Judy Rebick's 1990–93 NAC presidency, NAC engaged in an internal discussion about race and racism (Rebick 2005). Subsequently, more racialized women were elected to lead the organization: Sunera Thobani, of south Asian ancestry, in 1993; Joan Grant-Cummings, of Black ancestry in 1996; and Terri Brown, of Indigenous ancestry, in 2000.

Indigenous feminism is a unique position arising from the multiple forms of oppression layered onto Indigenous women, the overarching one of which is colonialism. That fundamental reality shapes Indigenous women's experiences — and that of all Indigenous people. It arguably also informs the lives of all other people, despite their general obliviousness to their privileges because of it. We contribute to theoretical development by revealing the parameters of gendered, racialized, and colonial relationships. Indigenous feminism is attentive to colonialism as a primary context for Indigenous and non-Indigenous people, in a way that has historically not been shared much by non-Indigenous feminism.

Indigenous women do not have the luxury of focusing only on gender oppression or only on issues of inclusion, access, and equality, or representation, because the fundamental colonial fact constructs and maintains a cascade of other oppressions for us. The first deprivation of colonialism is the theft of Indigenous land. Much of Indigenous feminist activism and theorizing focuses on the integral relationship between Indigenous people, particularly Indigenous women, and specific natural environments on particular territories. Many women are land and water protectors, and practitioners of ancient protocols for relationship with their territories. We are scholars who frame these activities as exercises of Indigenous law, of Indigenous title. Our theorizing is for our scholarly interests but also for our political emancipation and for the liberation of particular nations, communities, and individuals from the imposed strictures of the Canadian state. Increasingly, these theorizations are being extended to interrogate the impacts of colonial and heteronormative modes of thought at interpersonal, everyday levels, pointing to other lived and embodied layers of oppression impacting many Indigenous women.

The transformative character of Indigenous feminism arises from its intellectual and political foundations and aspirations. The personal is political, especially for feminists, because of the continuous denial by many men, the state, and a host of other governments, including Indigenous ones, that women's concerns and experiences are a priority. While Indigenous women may find themselves described as the centre of cultures and communities, this understanding is not generally reflected materially — not for men in our families and relationships, not for federal and provincial governments, and not for band governments or First Nations, Métis, Inuit, and other Indigenous organizations. Because they have been male dominated.⁵ Because men are accustomed to personal power and to being dominant. Because structural racism and sexism are inherent in state institutions. Because patriarchy and misogyny have infected colonized people — but also because, as Emma LaRocque noted, not all pre-contact Indigenous practices were benevolent for women (2010; 1993, 72–89; 2017, 75) and therefore we cannot afford the indulgence of romanticizing them.

To the extent that feminism is a theoretically informed, action-oriented social movement, it must in all its manifestations take into account Indigenous liberation in the conditions in which we have been oppressed, and in which we struggle now. For Indigenous feminists, there is no distinction between our resurgent, decolonial objectives and our feminism. Indigenous governance, self-determination, language recovery, land back, jurisdiction, and reparations for colonialism's racist encounter are essential goals for Indigenous feminists, even if we do not define and experience our struggles identically. Indigenous feminists share broader feminist terrain of seeking social and economic justice, freedom from male violence, personal autonomy, and measures of social, economic, and political equality and opportunity. Indigenous feminists are ecologically conscious and activist, concerned with the health and care of our territories and *all our relations,* not only human ones. Indigenous feminists are concerned with the perpetual struggles against national and provincial governments that are always imposing on Indigenous lands and communities and continuing with land theft and their justifications for it. In other words, these political issues are of primary concern to Indigenous feminists and to those who wish to understand and stand in solidarity with Indigenous feminists.

Intersectionality theory has informed the work of many Indigenous feminist scholars and activists in our engagements with overlapping, if often distinct, experiences of oppression. Kimberlé Crenshaw's powerful theory of intersectionality points to the importance of recognizing the multiplicity of identity categories that individuals occupy, highlighting how these inform the diverse experiences of individuals within them. Her analysis has provided important tools to analyze the ways in which location matters: it is not possible to consider power relations without accounting for the many ways socio-political locations shape experience, opportunity, and analyses (1989). Crenshaw observed that intersectionality is basically a lens, a prism, for seeing the way in which various forms of inequality often operate together and exacerbate each other. We tend to talk about race inequality as separate from inequality based on gender, class, sexuality or immigrant status. What's often missing is how some people are subject to all of these, and the experience is not just the sum of its parts. (Steinmetz 2020)

Rita Dhamoon writes that intersectionality reveals a single experience at the nexus of relations of dominance and subordination, of privilege and abjection; thus, intersectionality is a synergistic totality, not a set of additive singularities (2011, 230). Intersectionality can never be an invitation to consider Indigeneity as one factor and womanhood as another, which when read together produce an intersectional analysis, because we are simultaneously all of our subject positions and they produce a single experience for individuals and classes of individuals. It is this experiential singularity that is intersectional, that requires the nuanced analysis informed by the theoretical tool of intersectionality. Because we inhabit our identities diversely, and because oppressive structures can interact or collide in many different ways, we must account for how multiple axes of oppression encounter and operate in relation to one another to form distinct experiences of oppression.

Colonialism is a factor experienced by most Indigenous people, but not identically: gender, sexuality, location, class, cultural cohesion, and political consciousness frame and impact both actual experience and subjects' perceptions of and responses to their experience. And as Sherene Razack (cited in Dhamoon 2011, 232) argues, these positions are also produced relationally and must be considered in that context. One cannot engage Indigenous feminism without critically engaging the history, myths, and preoccupations of the Canadian state or of other settler states. Understanding how colonialism has created the conditions in which Indigenous women struggle, and thus, the conditions that have shaped the practice and discourse of Indigenous feminism, is essential to understanding the theory and practice of Indigenous feminism itself. It is an integral part of conceptualizing anti- and post-colonial aspirations for Indigenous people. Indigenous struggles are incomprehensible without understanding colonialism, an exploitive and racialized system of plunder that is ongoing on Turtle Island (Coulthard 2014; Thomas and Coburn 2022).

Theories of gender in the context of the un-hyphenated invisible and unconscious whiteness of settler society do not account for the context of most Indigenous people's lives. Colonialism, racism, economic class, and their consequences are largely invisible to the state's privileged white settler population but cannot be ignored by Indigenous women and men. One must be privileged to be oblivious to colonialism, racism, and sexism in Canada. Most Indigenous feminism takes this into account, producing powerful analyses and theory.

There are structural factors that privilege some at the expense of others. These factors are enjoyed particularly by white people, who need not see it or be conscious of it in order to benefit from it. Moreover, and most importantly, these factors are reproduced systemically, rendering them impervious to personal and individual frameworks of analysis. Thus, they persist and thrive even in the context of a rising chorus of political critique.

It is because of the oppression of colonialism that Indigenous women and men share, that Indigenous feminism is quite distinct from liberal feminism. It is because of the obliviousness of white privilege that the Canadian feminist movement has been challenged for its myopia, exclusion, and arrogance, notably in the 1980s and 1990s. It is the perennial, self-serving failure of the Canadian political class and academic elite to grapple with the structural and theoretical power of colonialism in the state that insulates Canadians from learning something about their privilege and our oppression. And because of these factors, it is premature to talk about state reconciliation, given the state does not take responsibility for or demonstrate an understanding of its own implication in and perpetuation of colonialism.

It is also because of the aspirational distinctions between settler and Indigenous women and gender-diverse people that our feminisms differ. Indigenous feminists, like other feminists, seek recognition and respect for the intrinsic value of women and girls — and increasingly, for gender-diverse and non-binary people. Like others, we seek safety in homes and in other spaces, and women-positive economic and social policy. We seek the elimination of male violence against women, girls, and 2SLGBTQIA+ people; we seek autonomy, legal and political rights, and personal self-determination over our bodies. But there is more, and it arises from Indigenous oppression by Canada and Canadians, from the structural conditions that shape our lives. It involves political self-determination, cultural authority and respect, language reclamation, and above all, the claim to traditional territory. It includes the right to *have* children, and to raise them in *our* families and communities, as well as the right to *not* become pregnant or reproduce. It takes up environmental exploitation that violates Indigenous relationships to lands and to the non-human beings that rely on them. These characteristics distinguish the grounds of our theoretical contributions and critiques, both identifying their distinctive qualities while also gesturing towards social and political convergences across theories and practices of change and liberation.

IDENTITY, INCLUSION, RECOGNITION, AND ERASURE

Indigenous identity, and particularly "Indian" status under the Indian Act, has been a major preoccupation of many Indigenous feminists because many Indigenous identities, and especially Indigenous women's identities, have been denied or compromised by the settler state, legislatively impaired by the Indian Act, and subsequently enforced by most "First Nations" (that is, Indian Act–defined bands) with terrible consequences. It is important to remember that non-Status Indigenous, Métis, and Inuit women are often afflicted by Indigenous identity denial by the state and sometimes by particular organizations, while simultaneously being subjected to the racism endemic in the state's populations, cultures, and institutions. Neither the lack nor the fact of a status card ever saved a single Indigenous woman from racism, violence, poverty, or marginalization. Indigenous women are identified and stigmatized as Indigenous by the dominant society regardless of their recognition by the state as "status." And too often the scholarly and political narratives are directed only at Status Indians, mostly on reserves, thus erasing at least two-thirds of Indigenous people and their experiences from consideration.

Indigenous feminists have long pushed back against the imposition, erasure, and policing of identity. We have revealed the forms of violence and dispossession that these can entail for diversely situated Indigenous women and have employed expansive understandings of Indigeneity in our theories and analyses. We have challenged the forms of marginalization and exclusion that arise from homogeneous constructions of Indigeneity within state legislation, and that are often reinforced in many Indigenous contexts. Many of our most prominent activists have relied on feminist methods and arguments to demand recognition of their identities and of the rights flowing from them, the state, the courts, and certain Indigenous communities (Beads and Kuokkanen 2007; Blaney and Grey 2017; Brodsky 2014; Glenn and Green 2007; Green in this volume and 2001, 1997, 1993, 1985; *Attorney General of Canada v. Lavell* 1974; McIvor and Kuokkanen 2007; Gehl 2021; Eberts et al. in this volume).

The Indigenous and non-Indigenous feminist movements have always included a contingent of women of diverse sexual orientations and diverse forms of association/identification with the category of woman. Indigenous women and Two-Spirit, queer, and non-binary folks in particular have troubled normative notions of gender and sexuality, advocating for fluid and non-binary understandings of gender identity, as well as more capacious grounds for conceptualizing individual identity. Just as identity remains a perpetual issue for Indigenous feminists, so too are questions of identity pointing to new conversations. For instance, Indigenous feminists are taking the lead in many contexts on questions of whiteness, privilege, appropriation/exploitation of Indigenous identities, and matters of accountability within our communities. Some are also reflecting on our own approach to, understanding of, and use of the category "woman" in our methods and analyses. We cannot yet characterize all Indigenous feminists as adequately inclusive of 2SLGBTQIA+ and gender-diverse members of our communities; neither can we claim that all Indigenous feminist accounts are centrally or substantially informed by their experiences. Still, there is some Indigenous feminist work that explicitly troubles and refuses normative constructions of sex and gender (Hunt 2018; Wilson 2015), and these questions and conversations are increasingly being engaged by activists and scholars within and in relation to Indigenous feminist thinking. The accounts offered by contributors in this volume, and their understandings of the category of "woman," are informed by diverse social, cultural, and historical contexts. They are also differently presented in terms of language and vocabulary surrounding gender constructs and gender and sexual identity. We regard these differences, gaps, or inconsistencies as important discursive spaces that require open, courageous, and accountable conversations into the future.

While some Indigenous scholars and activists proclaim liberation through an uncritical embrace of traditions and, particularly, traditionalist conceptions of Indigenous womanhood, Indigenous feminists do not all share the same reliance on a shared or overarching identity of woman typical of cultural fundamentalists from both Indigenous and settler communities. We are concerned with gender-specific forms of misogyny and oppression, particularly in the contexts of colonialism and with recovery of our territories and governance. We are concerned with re-animating our relationships with our territories and all our relations, not just human beings. We are concerned with re-animating our obligations to protect the land and water. Because we are concerned with our people's viability into the future, we insist on the rigorous evaluation of political and other important decisions for their impacts on us, on our territories, and on future generations. We are concerned for our families, communities, and networks of friends. We are concerned to recover our*selves*.

OVERVIEW

Conversations in *Making Space 3* illustrate varying avenues and approaches that Indigenous feminists have taken to contest sexism, colonialism, racism, and heteronormativity within Indigenous and non-Indigenous movements, communities, and institutions; to interrogate historical and contemporary constructions and representations of Indigenous identity; and to respond to and provide advocacy surrounding gender-based injustices, land dispossession, environmental degradation, and forms of gendered oppression at institutional, activist, and interpersonal levels. The first section looks at the trajectory of Indigenous feminist theories, analyses, and identities, exploring their historical and present-day significance and implications. Illustrating the intergenerational and transformative significance of Indigenous feminism, contributors to the early *Making Space* volumes sketch various intellectual and activist pathways ventured and demonstrate how they have circled those insights forward. Chapters model Indigenous feminist practices of critical self-reflection and long-term relationship building, demonstrating how the theories and analyses made possible by the first generation of Indigenous feminists have been animated, extended, and advanced across contexts and moments in time.

Section two explores the breadth of ways that Indigenous feminists are engaging, confronting, and resisting gendered violence and marginalization. Contributors examine various scales and forms of violence experienced by Indigenous women and girls ranging from physical violence to institutional violence against Indigenous children and families, to violence towards Indigenous Peoples' inter-subjective processes of being in relation. The third section then turns to matters of relationality with other living beings and the land. Here, contributors present the diverse ways Indigenous feminists are enacting relational ethics and practices to better care for and sustain our responsibilities to the living Earth and to other living beings. As the theorizing on relationality develops more in practice, Indigenous feminists are contemplating conditions that enable people to become active agents within new contexts, spaces, and relations of difference. Contributors point to different relational vocabularies that could be used to think through our political movements, interactions, and encounters across difference.

The last section explores the ways that binary, colonial, white, and heteronormative logics continue to configure many Indigenous and non-Indigenous social and political contexts, including in the construction of our own subjectivities and in how we understand our interrelations. Contributors explore the ways in which queer analytics and imaginaries can enable new visions of the political, prompting us to think beyond notions of decolonization that centre the reproduction of Indigenous bodies, traditionalist or essentialist notions of identity, and normative assumptions surrounding political action and change. Here, Indigenous feminism is put in conversation with other intellectual traditions and activist movements, drawing out associated influences, tensions, and entanglements and pointing to how these can be woven or braided to stitch a ground upon which to travel. Collectively, chapters point to a politics of the future that is refigurative in that it orients not just an abstract future but how we act in the present.

Intentionally, this edition presents a range of intellectual and creative production and presentation, including dialogues, non-academic essays, and untraditional formats. This diversity of style as well as viewpoint suggest the changing terrain in academic disciplines and research methodologies, and the significance of new discursive, intellectual, and activist spaces. Contributors prompt important reflections on central concepts and categories in Indigenous studies, politics, law, cultural studies, and women and gender studies, making space for extended and new applications of Indigenous feminist theory and praxis.

SPACES MADE AND COMING

Certain transformations have taken place over the years with respect to Indigenous feminism and its critiques of colonialism. A topic that was much maligned and seldom taken seriously in scholarly, political, or community discourses has now become a central concern for critical Indigenous and other scholars of colonialism, feminism, resurgence, and critical race theory. Indigenous feminism as both theory and praxis is essential to the project of Indigenous liberation from colonial oppression in Canada, and for Indigenous women's liberation from gendered oppression wherever we encounter it in our lives.

Indigenous feminists continue to employ critiques of gendered and sexualized harm and violence in multiple forms and registers, including critiques of our own governments, men, and communities. We continue making space for important conversations around Indigenous feminist practices, solidarities, and ethics that exceed commitments of inclusion, relationality, support, and solidarity. We can and should continue calling for accountability and justice among our Indigenous and non-Indigenous colleagues, peers, and relatives, and remain just as willing to examine our own roles in reproducing harmful, tokenistic, or extractive logics and/or power dynamics.

In the face of all this, we continue to provide support, solace, solidarity, encouragement, and recognition to one another. We enact modes of governance and of relationship through our own practices, as we move through the difficult, often isolating experience of deploying Indigenous feminist analyses, doing advocacy and support, calling for accountability in our relationships, and advancing transformative perspectives, theory, actions, and research. We enact them through the fraught process of having difficult discussions with one another.

The power of specific Indigenous feminist analysis lies in our overlapping experiences subjected to political analysis, solidarities, and action. Our analyses, like others, produce shifting political discourses over time. Our words centre and foreground the often-negated life, knowledge, and experience of our diverse ancestors and relatives, human and non-human. Our actions, like those of our Indigenous feminist aunties, transform the terrain of decolonial struggle now and for the future.

Unsurprisingly, this volume will not be the last word on these matters. We have not yet gained our liberation from colonialism, racism, and heteropatriarchy, although we have come some distance from the invisibility of these problematics a few decades ago. There is much room for activists and scholars to continue searching for measures of liberation, accountability, and consolation, while also contributing to the theories and empirical studies on the matters that preoccupy us.

NOTES

1. In this chapter we use the term "Aboriginal" within certain references to Indigenous Peoples, particularly those that refer to our constitutional status and rights. We use the two terms interchangeably.
2. This included Cherrie Moraga and Gloria Anzaldúa's *This Bridge Called My Back* (1981), Lee Maracle's *I am Woman* (1996), Haunani-Kay Trask's *From A Native Daughter: Colonialism and Sovereignty in Hawai'i* (1999), and several works by Trish Monture-Angus (1995; 1999), among others.
3. This included *Enough Is Enough: Aboriginal Women Speak Out* (Silman 1987), Maria Campbell's equally profound *Halfbreed* (1973), Bonita Laurence's powerful analysis of Indigenous and "Indian" identity in *"Real" Indians and Others* (2004), Kehaulani Kauanui's *Hawaiian Blood* (2008), and Pam Palmater's *Beyond Blood: Rethinking Indigenous Identity* (2011), among others.
4. Founded in 1971 to advocate for the recommendations in the 1970 Royal Commission on the Status of Women report, NAC functioned as an umbrella organization whose members were women's organizations and individuals across the country. It was a powerful political voice in the constitutional negotiations leading to the Canadian Charter of Rights and Freedoms in the 1982 Constitution Act. The organization relied on funding from the federal government and was punished for its opposition to the Charlottetown Accord with budget cuts by the Mulroney government; these were continued by the subsequent Chrétien government. After years of under-funding and increasing marginalization by the federal government, NAC dissolved in 2007.
5. AFN National Chief RoseAnne Archibald and Métis National Council President Cassidy Caron became, as of 2021, new women leaders who could potentially disrupt that male dominance — if they do not find the pressure from the institutions and their male counterparts to be unduly problematic. Troublingly, RoseAnne Archibald was deposed by the Assembly of First Nations on June 28, 2023 (Forester and Stefanovich 2023), becoming the first National Chief in the AFN–NIB's history to be ejected before the end of their term of office. For an Indigenous feminist critique of this, see Sy and Green 2023.

REFERENCES

Case Law/Legislation

Attorney General of Canada v. Lavell. 1974. S.C.R. 1349 (with Yvonne Bedard added to the appeal). Supreme Court of Canada.

Other

Alderson, Aedan. 2022. "An Abdication of Duty: Suppression of Indigenous Sovereignty in Canada's 'Consent-by-Default' Industry." In *Capitalism and Dispossession: Corporate Canada at Home and Abroad,* edited by D. Thomas and V. Coburn. Halifax and Winnipeg: Fernwood Publishing.

Anderson, Kim, Maria Campbell, and Christi Belcourt. 2018. *Keetsahnak: Our Missing and Murdered Indigenous Sisters.* Edmonton: University of Alberta Press.

Beads, Tina, and Rauna Kuokkanen. 2007. "Aboriginal Feminist Action on Violence Against Women." In *Making Space for Indigenous Feminism*, edited by J. Green. Halifax and Winnipeg: Fernwood Publishing.

Blaney, Fay, and Sam Grey. 2017. "Empowerment, Revolution and Real Change: An Interview with Fay Blaney." In *Making Space for Indigenous Feminism*, second ed., edited by J. Green. Halifax and Winnipeg: Fernwood Publishing.

Bourgeois, Robyn. 2017. "A Perpetual State of Violence: An Indigenous Feminist Anti-Oppression Inquiry Into Missing and Murdered Indigenous Women and Girls." In *Making Space for Indigenous Feminism,* second ed., edited by J. Green. Fernwood Publishing: Halifax and Winnipeg.

Brodsky, Gwen. 2014. "McIvor v. Canada: Legislated Patriarchy Meets Aboriginal Women's Equality Rights." In *Indivisible: Indigenous Human Rights*, edited by J. Green. Halifax and Winnipeg: Fernwood Publishing.

Campbell, Maria. 1973. *Halfbreed.* Toronto: McClelland and Stewart.

Collier, Cheryl N. 2015. "Not Quite the Death of Organized Feminism in Canada: Understanding the Demise of the National Action Committee on the Status of Women." *Canadian Political Science Review* 8, 2.

Coulthard, Glen. 2014. *Red Skin, White Masks: Rejecting the Colonial Politics of Recognition.* Minneapolis: University of Minnesota Press.

Craft, Aimée. 2023. "Thawing the Frozen Rights Theory: On Rejecting Interpretations of Reconciliation and Resurgence That Define Indigenous Peoples as Frozen in a Pre-colonial Past." In *Indigenous Resurgence in an Age of Reconciliation*, edited by H. Stark, H. Aikau, and A. Craft. Toronto: University of Toronto Press.

Crenshaw, Kimberlé. 1989. "Demarginalizing the Intersection of Race and Sex: A Black Feminist Critique of Antidiscrimination Doctrine, Feminist Theory and Antiracist Politics." *University of Chicago Legal Forum* 1, 8.

Dhamoon, Rita. 2011. "Considerations on Mainstreaming Intersectionality." *Political Research Quarterly* 64, 1.

Dhamoon, Rita, and Yasmeen Abu-Laban. 2009. "Dangerous (Internal) Foreigners and Nation-Building: The Case of Canada." *International Political Science Review* 30, 2.

Eberts, Mary. 2014. "Victoria's Secret: How to Make a Population of Prey." In *Indivisible: Indigenous Human Rights*, edited by J. Green. Halifax and Winnipeg: Fernwood Publishing.

___. 2017. "Being an Indigenous Woman Is a 'High-Risk Lifestyle.'" In *Making Space for Indigenous Feminism*, second ed., edited by J. Green. Halifax and Winnipeg: Fernwood Publishing.

Eberts, Mary, Sharon McIvor, and Teressa Nahanee. 2007. "Native Women's Association of Canada v. Canada." *Resources for Feminist Research* 32, 3–4.

Forester, Brett, and Olivia Stefanovich. 2023. "RoseAnne Archibald Ousted as Assembly of First Nations National Chief." *CBC News Online*, June 29, 2023. cbc.ca/news/indigenous/afn-archibald-removal-1.6891660.

Gehl, Lynn. 2021. *Gehl v. Canada: Challenging Sex Discrimination in the Indian Act*. Regina: University of Regina Press.

Glenn, Colleen, and Joyce Green. 2017. "Colleen Glenn: A Métis Feminist on Indian Rights for Indian Women." In *Making Space for Indigenous Feminism*, second ed., edited by J. Green. Halifax and Winnipeg: Fernwood Publishing.

Government of Canada. 2019. *Reclaiming Power and Place: The Final Report of the National Inquiry Into Missing and Murdered Indigenous Women and Girls*. Government of Canada, National Inquiry into Missing and Murdered Indigenous Women and Girls.

Green, Joyce. 1985. "Sexual Equality and Indian Government: An Analysis of Bill C-31 Amendments to the Indian Act." *Native Studies Review* 1, 2.

___. 1993. "Constitutionalising the Patriarchy: Aboriginal Women and Aboriginal Government." *Constitutional Forum* 4, 4 (Summer).

___. 1997. "Exploring Identity and Citizenship: Aboriginal Women, Bill C-31 and the Sawridge Case." PhD Thesis, University of Alberta.

___. 2001. "Canaries in the Mines of Citizenship: Indian Women in Canada." *Canadian Journal of Political Science* 34, 4: 715–738.

___ (ed.). 2007. *Making Space for Indigenous Feminism*. Halifax and Winnipeg: Fernwood Publishing.

Hall, Rebecca. 2022. "The Gendered Violence of Canadian Extraction." In *Capitalism and Dispossession: Corporate Canada at Home and Abroad*, edited by D. Thomas and V. Coburn. Halifax and Winnipeg: Fernwood Publishing.

Hunt, Sarah. 2018. "Embodying Self-Determination: Beyond the Gender Binary." In *Determinants of Indigenous Peoples' Health*, edited by M. Greenwood, S. de Leeuw, and N. Lindsay. Canadian Scholars Press: 22–39.

Kauanui, J. Kēhaulani. 2008. *Hawaiian Blood: Colonialism and the Politics of Sovereignty and Indigeneity*. Durham and London: Duke University Press.

Kuokkanen, Rauna. 2014. "Confronting Violence: Indigenous Women, Self-Determination and International Human Rights." In *Indivisible: Indigenous Human Rights*, edited by J. Green. Halifax and Winnipeg: Fernwood Publishing.

___. 2017. "Politics of Gendered Violence in Indigenous Communities." In *Making Space for Indigenous Feminism*, second ed., edited by J. Green. Halifax and Winnipeg: Fernwood Publishing.

___. 2019. *Restructuring Relations: Indigenous Self-Determination, Governance, and Gender*. New York: Oxford University Press.

LaRocque, Emma. 1993. "Violence in Aboriginal Communities." In *The Path to Healing,* RCAP: 72–89.
___. 2010. *When the Other is Me: Native Resistance Discourse 1850–1990.* Winnipeg: University of Manitoba Press.
___. 2017. "Metis and Feminist: Contemplations on Feminism, Human Rights, Culture and Decolonization." In *Making Space for Indigenous Feminism,* edited by J. Green. Halifax and Winnipeg: Fernwood Publishing.
Lawrence, Bonita. 2004. *"Real" Indians and Others: Mixed-Blood Urban Native Peoples and Indigenous Nationhood.* University of Nebraska Press and UBC Press.
LAWS (Liard Aboriginal Women's Society). 2021. *Response to the Yukon Mineral Development Strategy.* liardaboriginalwomen.ca/index.php/resources/about-3/news-releases/106-ymds-laws-feb-2021/file.
Maracle, Lee. 1996. *I Am Woman: A Native Perspective on Sociology and Feminism.* London: Global Professional Publishing.
Mawani, Renisa. 2009. *Colonial Proximities: Crossracial Encounters and Juridical Truths in British Columbia, 1871–1921.* Vancouver: University of British Columbia Press.
McIvor, Sharon, and Rauna Kuokkanen. 2007. "Woman of Action: An Interview with Sharon McIvor." In *Making Space for Indigenous Feminism,* edited by J. Green. Halifax and Winnipeg: Fernwood Publishing.
Monture-Angus, Patricia. 1995. *Thunder in My Soul: A Mohawk Woman Speaks.* Halifax and Winnipeg: Fernwood Publishing.
___. 1999. *Journeying Forward: Dreaming First Nations' Independence.* Halifax and Winnipeg: Fernwood Publishing.
Moraga, Cherrie, and Gloria Anzaldúa (eds.). 1981. *This Bridge Called My Back: Writings by Radical Women of Color.* New York: State University of New York Press.
Palmater, Pamela D. 2011. *Beyond Blood: Rethinking Indigenous Identity.* Saskatoon: Purich Publishing Ltd.
Razack, Sherene. 2002. *Race, Space, and the Law: Unmapping a White Settler Society.* Toronto: Between the Lines.
___ (ed.). 2016. "Gendering Disposability." *Canadian Journal of Women and the Law* 28, 2.
Rebick, Judy. 2005. *Ten Thousand Roses: The Making of a Feminist Revolution.* Toronto: Penguin Canada.
Schick, Carol. 2009. "Well-Intentioned Pedagogies that Forestall Change." In *I Thought Pocahontas Was a Movie,* edited by C. Schick and J. McNinch. Regina, University of Regina, Canadian Plains Research Centre.
Silman, Janet. 1987. *Enough Is Enough: Aboriginal Women Speak Out.* Toronto: Women's Press.
Starblanket, Gina. 2017. "Being Indigenous Feminists: Resurgences Against Contemporary Patriarchy." In *Making Space for Indigenous Feminism,* second ed., edited by J. Green. Halifax and Winnipeg: Fernwood Publishing.
Steinmetz, Katy. 2020. "She Coined the Term 'Intersectionality' Over 30 Years Ago. Here's What It Means to Her Today." *Time Magazine* 23.

Stewart-Harawira, Makere. 2007. "Practising Indigenous Feminism: Resistance to Imperialism." In *Making Space for Indigenous Feminism*, edited by J. Green. Halifax and Winnipeg: Fernwood Publishing.

Sy, Christine, and Joyce Green. 2023. "Shenanigans, Misogyny, and the AFN: This Is Not How We Are to Treat Each Other." *Windspeaker*, July 14, 2023. windspeaker.com/news/opinion/opinion-shenanigans-misogyny-and-afn-not-how-we-are-treat-each-other.

Thobani, Sunera. 2007. *Exalted Subjects: Studies in the Making of Race and Nation in Canada*. Toronto: University of Toronto Press.

___. 2020. *Contesting Islam, Constructing Race and Sexuality: The Inordinate Desire of the West*. Bloomsbury Publishing.

Thomas, David, and Veldon Coburn (eds.). 2022. *Capitalism and Dispossession: Corporate Canada at Home and Abroad*. Halifax and Winnipeg: Fernwood Publishing.

Trask, Haunani-Kay. 1999. *From a Native Daughter: Colonialism and Sovereignty in Hawai'i (Revised Edition)*. Honolulu: University of Hawai'i Press.

Waldron, Ingrid. 2022. "On the Shubenacadie River: The Grassroots Grandmothers and the Fight against Alton Gas." In *Capitalism and Dispossession: Corporate Canada at Home and Abroad,* edited by D. Thomas and V. Coburn. Halifax and Winnipeg: Fernwood Publishing.

Wilson, Alex. 2015. "Our Coming In Stories: Cree Identity, Body Sovereignty and Gender Self-Determination." *Journal of Global Indigeneity* 1, 1.

TWO

Always Coming Home

Indigenous Identity, Indigenous Feminism, Scholarship, and Life

Joyce Green

ASSERTING MYSELF

FOR MOST OF MY LIFE, OTHERS have told me who I am and who I am not. In this chapter, I tell my own story of learning and becoming who I am across my sixty-eight years. I comment on the problematic of Indigenous identity in the contexts of a white settler state and its universities; I write of my fragmented family history; and I gesture at my search for myself and for Indigenous liberation in the context of Canada's iterations of colonialism. I explore the subjects of identity, colonialism, and feminism through the prism of my own experience over some decades.

I have been on a lifelong walk, finding my way home despite many wrong turns. I bring with me the gifts of analyses, education, and relationships. I seek the stories and the knowledges that will instruct me in how to *be* in this phase of my life, as Ktunaxa, on part of ʔamakʔis Ktunaxa, the territory of the ancient Ktunaxa Nation.[1] I also comment on the experience of being an invisible Indigenous scholar in a white racist university context for the duration of my scholarly life. I object to this invisibility. That too is part of naming my own identities rather than letting others define me; it is part of being at home in my own skin, wherever I work and live.

I was born and raised in the beautiful territory of the Ktunaxa Nation. Then, we knew it only as the East and West Kootenay. My parents and we three children lived in a succession of small communities, as my dad followed the logging companies. We wound up on a farm in the Blaeberry, a rural area northeast of Golden, tucked against the massive Rockies in the east and with a view of the Purcell range to the west. That is where I spent most of my childhood. In all of this, we were well connected to both of my parents' families. My dad's parents had immigrated from Britain. My mom's parents were, on her father's side, Anglo-Americans, and on her mother's side, Cree-Scots Métis (or half-breeds) and Ktunaxa and English. We did not know much about my mother's family's Indigeneity. It was alluded to, but not really discussed. We children talked among ourselves, imagining and wanting so much more than we knew. We especially missed knowing our cousins. I know my mother and her siblings felt the same as children (Shirley Green 2017).

Early in life the disparity between men and women, girls and boys, became evident to me. In my rural community and family, boys did outside chores. Girls did domestic chores. Men were authoritative, while women were subordinate. Men and their wants and needs were privileged, while women's voices and ideas were largely dismissed as secondary and trivial. Popular humour mocked women. We've all heard the "jokes" and the put-down when we were unamused: "Can't you take a joke?" Men could be violent, women could get pregnant, and all of this was women's fault. Women were taught to compete for the scarce resource of male attention and that ultimate prize: a male spouse. Sexual activity by unmarried women was evidence of a lack of "morals" and of judgment; men could notch their belt buckles with every new liaison and suffer no ill regard.[2] We had never heard of gender fluidity, and gays and lesbians were subjected to unrestrained homophobia. Non-white people were viewed through racist lenses. What I've described above is fairly normal for the white rural redneck community in which I was raised and others like it. Much of it is also typical in Indigenous communities: as Rauna Kuokkanen (2019) has suggested, our institutions and societies are thoroughly gendered, even while we are racialized and oppressed as Indigenous. This all grated on me. Feminism offered me a way to understand these things, and later, political science, with its emphasis on power relations, was useful despite its predominantly white male and colonization-affirming canon.

IDENTITIES AND BEING

In my life, identity has been a challenging set of shifting relationships and conceptions. Thus, I spend a fair amount of energy contemplating the difference location makes in the colonial landscape, and working through the problematics of living together in the contexts we have. I have come to terms with at least some of the tensions in my identity, and I struggle to honour all of my ancestors, and to acknowledge and enjoy what they have left for me, even as I grieve the loss of so much that I do not have from some strands of my family.

I have spent much of my professional life in the university, although I have only recently begun claiming my Indigenous identities in the context of my scholarly work. There are reasons for my early reticence, and now, there are reasons for my public self-identification. First, I was raised in a context where my family's Indigenous identities and the knowledges associated with them were suppressed, and had been for a very long time. I did not feel I had the right to claim an Indigenous identity, although I always claimed my Indigenous heritages. Second, I have always believed that my ideas, scholarship, and political activism should speak for themselves, without reference to my personal location, which I viewed as private. The changing zeitgeist and my own changing analyses led me to rethink that. My ideas, scholarship, and political activism — my choices of what to study and teach, what to research and publish — have been driven by my personal context as well as my professional training.

I will say, though, that writing about these matters now still discomforts me — it is so personal, yet set forth for those who do not know me. I accept this discomfort to offer to others my own account of my scholarly, political, and personal formation in the contexts I describe. I hope it may be of help to others, who are doubtless engaged in their own walks home.

GREAT WHITE MISOGYNISTS

Sir George Simpson, a towering political and corporate figure in the early 1800s, called Indigenous women he consorted with, as well as the Indigenous wives of his white employees, "squaws," "bit(s) o' brown," "commodities," and "brown jugs" (Van Kirk 1980), and doesn't that say it all? His attitude was shared by many of his colleagues. Sylvia Van

Kirk writes that fur traders "increasingly looked upon native women as objects for temporary sexual gratification, not as wives. The women, on the other hand, now found themselves being judged according to strict Victorian standards of female propriety" (1980, 146; see also Eberts 2014, 2017).

This early white attitude toward Indigenous women is well engrained in Canadian culture, manifesting in the virulent racist misogyny that killed Helen Betty Osborne (see Megan Scribe's chapter in this volume) and so many others; that produced Robert Pickton and other killers; that frames the conditions for thousands of missing and murdered Indigenous women and girls; and that resides in the complacency of settler state populations, cops, and political elites toward these terrors of Indigenous life (Government of Canada 2019). I often think of Helen Betty; she would be four years older than me. Maybe she would have become a mother, a nurse, or a political scientist. She wasn't allowed to live her life and make those choices.

The routinized denigration of Indigenous life and history, and of Indigenous women in particular, infests the contemporary body politic of Canada. Despite inquiries and demonstrations, there is little concrete action and virtually no accountability by the state that thrives at the expense of those it has stigmatized, dispossessed, and de-historicized. Now, the elite political class, including the Catholic Church (Hilleary 2022), prattles on about "reconciliation," but has yet to acknowledge its sins in creating the matters for which it seeks to reconcile, or to commit to restitution (Green 2019; Green and Burton 2016). One cannot reconcile for sins one cannot acknowledge. I digress.

On my mother's maternal side, I come from a long line of women who have been voiceless, unnoticed, disregarded by their societies and by the men who should have loved and cared for them.[3] We suffer from the betrayals, the "disloyalty of kin and community in looking the other way, even blaming" (LaRocque 1990, xxix); and from "the loneliness that comes from so many places," and from "plodding through the maze of identity crises" inflicted on Indigenous women by the racist state and society we are in (1990, xxviii). Many of us lived under cones of silence, wrapped in cloaks of invisibility, unable to assert our identities, our*selves*. So many women have been voiceless, unable to advocate for their interests. Some of my relatives have lived with violence and with arbitrary deprivation of their children.

In my Sinclair family (which would have used the term "half-breed," not Métis), boys were historically sent off to Scotland for education (Lent 1963, 23; Sutherland 2008, 253–55), while girls were married off to spouses as white as possible (Peers 1999, 293). The terms "half-breed" and "Métis" are important, for they reveal the racial categories of the past and show how they shift into the present. But for that racism discharged in attitudes, policies, army and police actions, and in the Indian Act, many half-breeds, "non-Status" Indians, and Métis (or "m"etis) would be considered Indians — as many Status Indians are no different racially than many in these other Indigenous communities. Racism conflates Indigenous and other racialized identities with physical characteristics and white-ascribed stereotypical "traits."

Race is a socially constructed matter, always produced relationally. I find it interesting to observe the shifting nature of racial categories and consider their context of legitimacy and power relations. Jean Teillet (2019, 133, 141, 143) refers to my great-great-grandfather James Sinclair as Métis, including us in that great nation; many of my relatives consider themselves Métis as well. Historically, however, my ancestors would have used the term "half-breed" for their complicated location in Red River society and the fur trade economy of the 1800s. This was true for many non-French-related half-breeds and even for some French-related half-breeds. The evolution of our understanding of these terms is also a process of claiming who we are and rejecting the racist appellations of the past.

One ancestor, my great-great-aunt Betsey Sinclair, was the paramour of the racist (Ross 2007), sexist, and white supremacist Sir George Simpson[4] (he had many such liaisons), who, when he tired of her and while she was pregnant with his daughter (Lent 1963, 145–146), dumped her into a marriage with an underling who may also have had no choice (Lent 1963, 61–62; Sutherland 2008, 248). Many of my foremothers have been impoverished, controlled, and abused by the men who were supposed to care for them. Some of them have been deprived of their Indigenous cultures and languages, while others felt compelled to deny them — and thus they deprived their children of these also.[5] I use my voice for my own purposes, but I am also speaking because certain of my foremothers could not — bearing the burdens LaRocque wrote of.

In the situation where a certain non-Indigenous relative was both a violent abuser and a chronic pedophile, many in our family and in other families were subjected to his assaults, while silence was both maintained and enforced by family members. Nor was he the only abuser. Others in that family also preyed on and were protected from and sometimes by their victims. *Don't talk about private matters; never embarrass the family* was the implicit and explicit instruction to us all. And we didn't, fearing violence, perhaps death; fearing ostracization from the only family we had. Feeling *responsible* for it all.

The damage was compounded by our collective location as those who never fit in, who never belonged, who could not connect with our Indigenous communities and were not entirely accepted within white settler communities. You may imagine the consequences for people's psychological health and their own parenting abilities. They can be seen today in damaged seniors in my age cohort and older, who still feel the betrayal of childhood trust, who still have difficulty fitting in to the social communities that we are part of. Too many of us have difficulty in personal relationships, with boundaries, with trust, with autonomy and decision-making, with addictions.

Too often, we do not feel worthy of love or respect, and our collective experiences do not lead us to expect recognition and friendship. Faced with these kinds of conditions, is silence the best option, or should we sing like canaries? But who will listen to such canaries? My family's history shows that silence was both recommended and enforced as a condition of acceptance within the family, and perhaps, within the larger community. Silence created impunity for abusers. No one wanted to hear about these things, much less act on them. And the culture of fear and abuse, of silence as the price of acceptance, cultivated in many the psycho-social conditions for victimization.

CONSCIOUSNESS RAISING 101

I took a circuitous route to Indigenous feminism. I was living in Cranbrook in the early 1970s, still in my teens. The Cranbrook Women's Resource Group — comprised entirely of white settler women — organized a number of consciousness-raising groups. Each group was limited to about a dozen women. They met weekly, discussed issues in the context of a set topic, and after a number of months the groups dissolved. I was the youngest person in one of those groups, and the other members gave me support, kindness, and the gift of their insights. Mainstream feminism was unconsciously white dominant, and approaches ranged from radical to socialist and liberal, to ecofeminist and theological feminism. My group's context and structure were inflected by a generic and unspecific gentle feminism.

Still, thanks to the sense of solidarity and safety of the group, the sharing of analyses and some reading, I developed some confidence to question, to object, to shoot for goals other than those set by the redneck rural white community in which I had been socialized. I took those tools into my future and they served me well.

But those women could not offer me any insights into the problematic of Indigenous invisibility in the white and racist communities in which I had lived: they were oblivious to their privileges and to the immiseration and perhaps even to the existence of the Ktunaxa Nation. The sisters in my group did not relate to me as an Indigenous person and did not wonder why, in Ktunaxa Territory, the consciousness-raising groups were so white.

Nor did I understand the factors limiting my Indigeneity. Thus, I was largely oblivious, even as my family suffered from the deprivation of our Indigenous family, communities, and cultures. We did not know why this was so; we did not understand systemic oppression; we had no way to analyze or resist colonialism, racism, and sexism. Some of us internalized our intergenerational misery, projected our anger on each other, and struggled with the pain of never fitting in. And so, despite my Indigenous heritages, I was politically oblivious and had much to learn.

I left the East Kootenay in 1976 to attend the University of Lethbridge, majoring in Native American studies. Lethbridge was the biggest community I had ever lived in, and it was a shock to be away from all I knew and from the mountains which defined my home. I got a good education, but I learned that Indigenous students and professors — well, virtually all students and professors — had little use for feminist analysis. That puzzled and confused me. There was no discussion of women's concerns or of feminism in any course; the normative male focus was considered neutral and sufficient. I also struggled with identity despite asserting my Indigenous heritages, as the other Indigenous students and professors insisted on relating to me as a white woman. I found that painful and insulting, but I did not have the tools or courage to challenge it.

SURVIVING IN IVORY TOWERS

In my first years of studenthood, scholarship, and teaching, I was away from the territory where I was born and raised and distant from my family in more ways than spacially. As a young female scholar who studied Indigenous challenges — especially Indigenous women's challenges — I had a tentative voice. I was afraid of the criticisms that I inevitably got, and of the male — including Indigenous male — disapproval directed at me. That latter disapproval was more painful and more consequential, as I was then married to a Kainai man, and we were both dealing with the challenges by others to what was seen as a "mixed" marriage. I also was subject to criticisms of my feminist analyses and of my*self*, for the non-Indigenous traits attributed to me by those who thought they knew me.

I continued my studies sporadically over many years. I was a slow learner, making many life mistakes. Later, that experience helped me understand that we are not destined to always *be* our mistakes. We can learn, we can change, we can grow — and this too is a teaching of feminist process. Moreover, it is a fundamental part of my Indigenous communities' views of human frailty and potential, best epitomized by something Sophie Pierre, a respected Elder in my Ktunaxa community, said: "We don't have so many people that we can afford to throw even one away" (Sophie Pierre, personal communication, 2021, in the Ktunaxa Nation's Constitution Committee discussions). I try to remember this, given I sometimes wish to throw certain people overboard. I am not as patient and tolerant as Sophie, so I know I still have much to learn.

My much-interrupted studies produced an MA from the University of Calgary, and many years later, post-divorce and single parenting my daughter, a PhD from the University of Alberta, both in political science. Both courses of study were focused on Indigenous issues: self-government in the first, and the violence done to Indigenous women who were divided from their communities because of the sexist, racist Indian Act membership provisions in the second. I had moved away from the singular white feminist framework and for the remainder of my political and scholarly career, I focused primarily on Indigenous matters, particularly concerning Indigenous women.

It was during my doctoral work that my membership in the Blood Tribe, acquired upon my first marriage, was revoked. I received a letter that said I was being removed because I had "no Indigenous heritage" and "had shown no interest in Blood culture and language." I was shocked and replied that the first was not true and the second was not tested. I asked for a process to consider these things. The reply was essentially, "time for appeal is over." My daughter was also removed from that membership list, despite being herself Blackfoot (my daughter is adopted, and her birth mother was Peigan). I still remember her fear and anxiety when she came to me and said "Mom, what am I now — am I Métis?" I told her she was Piikani, and no one could take that truth away from her. But they would not recognize it, either; they have still not recognized it. My daughter was erased as a Status Indian, as a Peigan woman, as Blackfoot, as niitsitapi.

You can see how deeply personal all of this is for me. At the same time, the factors that plagued my own life have afflicted so many, because of racism and sexism encoded in cultures and in that putrid, racist, sexist Indian Act. I am quite aware that my removal from the Blood Tribe band list was done in solidarity with my former husband. The dissolution of our relationship was not amicable. And after all, he explained it to me — what he said, what the chief said, what the membership person said, and then he added: "Don't fight it, you'll just get hurt." That too is politics — the bare-knuckle variety well known to Indigenous women who are targeted by male power elites.

I cannot remember the year, but some time after I obtained my MA I was invited to present a paper at what was my first academic conference, organized by an Indigenous professor at the University of Lethbridge. I presented on the inequality of the infamous section 12.1.b of the Indian Act. I was shocked and embarrassed when two prominent older Indigenous women attacked me, insisting that Indigenous women wanted nothing to do with white feminist ideas. I did not have enough composure to tell them that *this* Indigenous woman certainly did want to consider feminist ideas. And therefore, they were effective in painting me and my presentation as both white and feminist and thus, as irrelevant to the conference and to the subject of Indigenous women's equality rights. I experienced these attacks several times in my career, even as my own scholarly competence became more respected.

This, I learned, was something that other Indigenous women had experienced also. Sharon McIvor, who led the Native Women's Association of Canada for a period and who fought sex discrimination in the Indian Act for decades, writes about being castigated for showing how un-Indigenous she was for pressing for Indian women's equal rights to status (McIvor and Kuokkanen 2007). The thing about this kind of discipline is how effective it is: women who are not attacked observe what happens when one is identified as feminist, and then avoid putting themselves in that situation. They avoid taking the label of feminist, and of taking positions that are evidently feminist. They self-censor. White and other marginalized women also do this, and some of you will recall the old homophobic labels attached to every woman who raised women's oppression as a topic of discussion or a political matter. No matter how diffident, it was rarely enough to protect the speaker from allegations of being a man-hating feminist and a lesbian, hurled like an epithet.

I learned during my academic training that there was little appetite in the academy for feminist, critical race, post-colonial, socialist, ecological, and other foundational critiques. I was often isolated and criticized by student colleagues and some members of the professoriate, who would not treat seriously my critiques of misogyny, colonialism, racism, capitalism, and Canada's whitewashing myths about its origins and practices. Yet, those critiques are directed precisely at the disciplinary canon — the literature — student scholars are required to learn. Of course, there is an assumption that senior scholars have something of worth to impart to younger ones, but it is deeply problematic when the scholarly processes of teaching and credentialization are hostile to thoughtful critiques directed at the very canon that sanctifies self-congratulatory perspectives and erases critiques (see also Wallace 2022).

I invite you to think about the complicity of the elite scholarly cadre of professors and universities in colonialism and in perpetuating male and white privilege. In so doing, they are mis-educating successive generations of student scholars, the very people who will replace them. There are systemic and intergenerational implications to this because universities produce elites who go on to form the backbone of political, corporate, and other powerful institutions. They carry with them their lack of comprehension of colonialism; their lack of responsibility for and engagement with racism and sexism; and they have power, which is exercised in favour of the status quo, not for women's nor Indigenous emancipation. I will return to this topic shortly.

GATEKEEPERS ARE NOT MENTORS

Post-graduation, as I interviewed for tenure track academic positions, I tried to suppress my views of patriarchy and imperialism lest they cost me a job offer. When I got the job, I had to be concerned about others' views of my work and political positions because of what LaRocque calls "promotion procedures as fair as war" (2017, 323), and about losing scholarly opportunities such as conference invitations, publications, and research grants. I found myself at odds with people who had power over me, who disapproved of me, who could and did affect my career trajectory. I learned that the university and its elites discipline us *as women, and as Indigenous women, Indigenous scholars,* into conformity, or place us at risk of reprisal.

To my sorrow, I know too many, mostly women, many racialized, still bear that burden. It stunts their joy in scholarship and their experience in the academy, as it did mine (see Thobani 2021 for a recent analysis of this). Much of my scholarly career was marred by active hostility on the part of certain colleagues who sought to discipline me in a variety of ways, from social isolation and denial of access to opportunities such as graduate supervision, to maligning me and my talents to other academic colleagues and to powerful actors in political and civil society circles; and by challenging my application for tenure because I was "uncollegial" (they lost that one). So often critical scholars and feminists are labelled uncollegial and difficult. I and others endured hostility and loneliness; we leaned on each other (thank you, Emma LaRocque, Darlene Juschka, Rita Dhamoon, Gina Starblanket, and others) to survive and thrive in the alienating and difficult, but also important and rewarding, context of the academy.

Like feminism, scholarship is a process of learning how to theorize and strategize for the changes we seek. Scholars must also research and produce original, excellent, and relevant peer-reviewed work that draws on or distinguishes itself from the existing work in a field — we are required to contribute to the body of knowledge in our fields. Feminist scholarship, critical Indigenous scholarship, and other critical approaches are essential for the production of important, interesting, generative knowledge. They are transformative for scholarship, for public policy and legal analyses, and for civil society perspectives. And sometimes our analyses and positions cost us, in a rigged process that relies on stale pale male canonical frameworks in a racist, sexist academy that does not share Sophie Pierre's important insight on tolerance and throwing people overboard.

IDENTITY AND NEUTRALITY

Long ago LaRocque wrote, "As a scholar, I am expected to remain aloof from my words; I am expected to not speak in my own voice" (1990, xxi). I too had assumed I needed a neutral academic persona and to restrain my own voice. But while I was professoring I came to realize that there is no neutral position in the academy or anywhere else, although not all are aware of their positionality, their privileges, and their responsibilities. Sometimes the best we can do is identify the ideologies, the experiences, the objectives, and the presumptions that we hold while executing our research and teaching, our politics and our relationships. All of this includes our personal locations. That realization, too, led me to claim my Indigeneity in the context of the university.

I decided that I needed to be more visible as an Indigenous scholar so that the academy would know I was there; so that my students would know they had an Indigenous professor; and so that my presence and my voice would speak about exclusions and omissions when the syllabus and canon did not. Because I am often "read" as white — I am fair skinned and have blue eyes — it was necessary for me to assert my identity, sometimes in the face of rejection by some who thought they knew what my background is better than me. Thus, I again encountered the politics of identity: who claims it and why; who validates it; the problematics of identity fraud; what the practices of gatekeeping perform, and for whom. And I grew weary of people telling me who I was *not*, telling others who I was *not*, or rejecting me without ever talking to me because they *assumed* I was not Indigenous. Such gossip is consequence-free for its purveyors.

Being labelled as an identity fraud has the potential to destroy one's professional reputation. And that is another reason why I am asserting my identity. I own my reputation. It was produced through decades of education, work, experience, mistakes, and successes. It is *me*. I am not inclined to let it be destroyed by innuendo.

None of us is only one thing (Said 1993, 336). Some people claim only part of their heritage, but I refuse to deny any of my family. My community recognizes me. I am a citizen of the Ktunaxa Nation and I am a member of Yaqı̓t ʔa·knuqɬiʔit (Tobacco Plains Indian Band). In both cases I am accepted because of my Ktunaxa lineage. I am also Métis: my Sinclair family is well known in the context of Métis history. My mother and my family know who I am. It is not for others to tell me who I am not.

Indigenous identity problematics include who has it, who endorses it, and who and what it serves. These claims construct a hierarchy of knowers, those with the social and political power to confirm or deny identity. Those judged to be authentic or traditional can say more without being challenged for their claims or for their authority. Those who do not fit the more visible, identifiable categories are at risk of being called out as imposters.

The fact that there really *are* imposters complicates this further: we all know of recent incidents of people being shown to not be who they claim to be, while they've built prominent and lucrative careers on their false or inflated claims to Indigeneity. Socially and politically significant institutions have participated in creating these imposters, building them up because it makes the institutions look good without doing the hard work of post-colonial anti-racist transformation. Thus, I fault the institutions at least as much as those who claim Indigeneity without sufficient factual basis, and I also deplore the cruelty and cupidity of these institutions, which, when they are called to account by Indigenous people for endorsing identity fraud, turn their backs on their marquee frauds while failing to take responsibility for their presences. As though so many smart people were fooled by a single person, rather than being complicit in the entire arrangement.

I suspect none of these imposters sees themselves as frauds — after all, they have been celebrated for epitomizing Indigeneity and naming Indigenous issues by powerful voices and lucrative careers and sometimes, for their significant intellectual contributions. And I agree that certain of these people have deployed dubious claims for professional and perhaps for personal benefit (that is, to support an identity formation which is a psychologically problematic self-conception) in a process which effectively denies access and recognition to "real" Indians and others — that is, to relationally, culturally, historically located Indigenous persons whose lives and histories are marked by experiences with colonialism.

I had kept my Indigeneity private. I had declined to name it for and require recognition of it from the institutions where I worked. But over time — much time — I came to believe that my search for scholarly integrity and neutrality and for privacy was, in fact, frustrated by my reticence about my personal location. At a minimum, people did not really know who I was — although I still feel that if we had genuine relationships, they would have gotten to know me; and in the absence of those relationships, none are entitled to the details of my family and my life. My reticence deprived me of certain solidarities and of recognition of my context. Moreover, there is no neutral position in the academy or anywhere else, and it is through making our position explicit that we avoid pretending we are "just" speaking facts into the universe. Facts are always curated for political context and implication.

My reticence also stifled my voice, masking it in citations and arguments with which the academy is most comfortable. Citations are important, of course — they are a form of recognition that we always are indebted to others, and they are a form of accountability. The citations were also a comfort — for it was not me speaking alone when others who had published were also taking positions that I shared. But I also grew more comfortable with my positions and with the fact of the opposition they attracted. I asserted my arguments, found some allies, and enjoyed the work of teaching and research. Still, the university and the political arena in which I laboured were lonely and unsupportive spaces. I find this line from LaRocque's poem "Long Way From Home" so very resonant: "I do my footnotes so well nobody knows where I come from" (2017, 322). While you will find scholarly citations in this chapter, I hope that you will also find me as who I am and where I am positioned at this point in my life. I am the authority on who I am, and I am telling you where I come from.

FEMINISTING IN THE UNIVERSITY

In 2002, I was a professor at the University of Regina and a Research Fellow with the Saskatchewan Institute of Public Policy. With the support of a small group of white feminists in our politically focused affinity group, the Kitchen Table Collective, and with the support of some white and Indigenous feminist bureaucrats in the federal civil service, I was able to obtain funding to hold a Symposium on Aboriginal Feminism. Some of the attendees there used a feminist analysis, though not many: some women attended to speak their feminism, while others said they were not comfortable with the feminist label. Still, we had some excellent conversations. Following the symposium, I pulled some other feminists into a project that became the 2007 book *Making Space for Indigenous Feminism*.

I read my introduction to that collection now and cringe: I was so tentative and so fearful of being attacked and discredited. We were all fearful — feminism meant so much to so many, most of it wrong. It meant man-hating women who didn't have children or value the family; it invited homophobia, repudiation, or mockery. But the book came out, and we weren't alone: more Indigenous feminists kept coming out of the woodwork. Also, over time the numbers of Indigenous women in universities increased, and their articulation of feminism and colonialism was sophisticated, compelling, and far less apologetic than mine had been.

By the time the second edition of *Making Space* was published in 2017, we were less fearful and clearer in arguing for the value of feminist analysis. The range of topics had increased and the analyses were more sophisticated. There are now many Indigenous scholars and activists who are comfortable with the feminist label, and even more scholars who accept feminist critiques. There are scholarly articles published, and books, both scholarly and popular; and there are new generations of Indigenous and settler women who take up the analytical tools of feminism in their work on the problematics of racialized, colonial, and settler state female experiences. We do not all agree, but we use a common recognizable critical discourse and theoretical corpus to locate our arguments. That is evidence of scholarly maturity. Indigenous feminism is here to stay. This third edition is quite different than the previous two, but it draws on its predecessors, because Indigenous feminism is generative, responsive, and liberatory.

IVORY TOWER COLONIALISM

My professional workplace has, for much of my life, been in the university. For Indigenous feminist academics, there is the enormous problematic of engaging in the production of knowledge (which the academy certifies and valorizes through its teaching, credentialing, recruitment, and recognition processes) while teaching and researching Indigenous knowledges, experiences, and critical analyses that contest the settler state's hegemony. One is forced to learn the colonial myths and lies and, while being "trained" and examined, to tug one's forelock in the direction of prominent colonial apologists and blatant racists whose stature in the academy renders their works canonical. Rebecca Wallace's 2022 research on how "comps lists" (the field lists of literatures that doctoral students must read and become proficient with) are formed, curated, and evaluated by a largely white male elite in political science illuminates how the discipline and universities replicate the elite racist and colonial status quo, cohort after student cohort.

Institutions tend to reproduce themselves and the structural and policy paradigms most familiar to them. In the settler state of Canada, public, private, and academic institutions are deeply imbued with the assumptions, expectations, and attitudes that valorize colonialism, denigrate Indigeneity, and mythologize the settler state that Indigenous people experience as violent, racist, and oppressive. For those of us who are privileged — who have elite education and labour in the university — the strictures of institutional hierarchies, of the deference paid to scholars who have done much to consolidate and celebrate the myths of the state's benevolence, innocence, and goodness; and the authority and authoritarian nature of scholarly canon, function to make our professional lives complicated at best, untenable at worst. I have struggled to deliver an excellent education to my students, which necessitated teaching against much of the canon of my discipline. Few racialized and Indigenous scholars thrive in such an environment (Tungohan 2022; Coburn et al. 2024). Combine our criticality with feminism, and academic institutions barely tolerate us (Thobani 2021).

As Edward Said argues, "the growth of knowledge is a process of selective accumulation, displacement, deletion, rearrangement and insistence within what has been called a research consensus" (1993, 176). Feminist, anti-colonial, anti-racist, and other critical work must displace and delete canonical work, foundational assumptions, in order to advance a different and better understanding of political matters. This kind of critical work in our professional and personal lives is akin to rolling boulders uphill while some colleagues push them back down again.

While working in the hostile context I've described, I, like so many of you, also had to manage my personal life: family and marital circumstances, deaths, single parenting, economic precarity, and the pressure to perform to a relentless neoliberal white settler state model of white male competence. Those of us who remain in the academy, who succeed despite the structures and processes, who are psychologically intact despite the continual assaults on our identities, our analyses, and our political contexts, are superheroes. Take a bow, all who recognize themselves in this account.

The academy has long been complicit with and an advocate for colonialism. In the words of Cindy Blackstock, "The highly educated have littered colonialism across the country ... [they] were not just bystanders — they deployed their knowledge and skills to abet colonialism and, in too many cases, continue to do so today" (Backhouse 2021, xv). Legal scholar Constance Backhouse writes:

> Academia's harms were at least threefold: complicity with the colonial regime even in the face of evidence of harms viewed by some people of the period to be immoral, if not criminal; ignoring of the situation of First Nations, Métis, and Inuit peoples; and direct engagement with colonial harms via experiments on children in the schools, legal efforts intended to strip Indigenous rights, and creation of conditions for the perpetuation of colonialism and discrimination in public policy. (2021, 5)

To this she could have added the policing, carceral, social work, and health care systems; the corporate elite so well supported by Canadian public governments with Indigenous lands and resources, and the "whole of government" assault on Indigenous Peoples and lands that continues today. An example of this phenomenon in operation is provided by Métis scholar Verna St. Denis, who writes of this "whole of government" assault on her family "through the forces of colonial structures on our communities and our families" (2022, 23).

POLITICAL SCIENCE AND COLONIAL TRIUMPHALISM

I am a political scientist located in the field of Canadian politics. The field is particularly invested in justifying colonialism, colonial mythology, settler state law and institutions, and in the policies and other mechanisms that have oppressed Indigenous Peoples since the inception of the Canadian settler state. The origins and emergence of the state are taught uncritically by too many members of the professoriate. They focus on great names, mostly men, in the Canadian political pantheon, many of whom were the authors, directors, and enforcers of oppression, dispossession, and genocide of Indigenous Peoples, while the remainder were complicit in this. Some of those great names were given honorary degrees for their contributions (for example, Duncan Campbell Scott — who had executed the residential school policy across the country, as well as committing other sins against Indigenous people — was granted honorary degrees that, at the date of publication of this book, still stand, by the University of Toronto and Queen's University) or had universities named for them (Ryerson University, now renamed Toronto Metropolitan University; Egerton Ryerson was one of the architects of the residential school effort). The majority of the scholarly cadre focus on Canadian institutions uncritically, failing to take up how they were designed by and for a privileged, mostly white citizenry, *at the expense* of Indigenous nations.

I recall that first awful conference experience, the public rebuke for deploying a feminist analysis, and the distress I felt. Now, however, there are so many more Indigenous feminist scholars producing brilliant work, and I am not alone when I speak. This transformation has been remarkable and is changing the character of the academy. Canadian universities have much to answer for because of their implication in colonialism and genocide, and the persistent racism in what is taught. But universities are worth struggling with and improving, as they are also perhaps the last place in contemporary society where independent scholarship and critical thinking is at the core of the job description. And the students I taught were always worth my discomfort with the canon, the institution, and its managerial elites.

Because of the power relations and dominant paradigms in the discipline, my experience also gestures at the place of Indigenous scholars, especially Indigenous feminist scholars, in the university. I include students in those categories. Our students also struggle with marginalization, in the context of relations of dominance and subordination, where their success often depends on approval of those who insist on intellectual conformity.

Political scientists and indeed, most scholars, study matters of *general* or majoritarian interest, excluding Indigenous interests. In Canada, that really means *white male* interests. They have not considered how Indigenous existence and oppression have been fundamental to the state's conception and implementation. When these scholars consider Indigenous Peoples, too many focus on the social and economic deficits in Indigenous communities without considering the contexts or the structural relationships. When they write their texts on the discipline, too often they throw in a token chapter on Indigenous people and on women, failing to take either seriously in their work. These scholars typically fail to conceive of Indigenous nations in their self-determined political forms both prior to and following colonial dispossession. The socio-political consequences of the imposition of colonialism, of the violence and the deprivations it entails, have been misrepresented as Indigenous deficits, intrinsic to underdeveloped cultures in need of governmental and corporate remediation though capacity building, education, and inclusion in the Canadian body politic. And thus, colonial oppression continues in and is disseminated from the academy. The work of such scholars is represented as authoritative in public policy and civil society debates.

These factors have made the discipline a particularly challenging place for Indigenous scholars. My own experience affirms this. From my student years to my professorial ones, I've struggled to assert Indigenous experiences into the canon, contesting misrepresentations of Canadian politics and history. I've chosen Indigenous and Indigenous feminist topics to study; some colleague reviewers have been remarkably disapproving of my work, including a two-line response to an entire scholarly paper submitted by me and another senior Indigenous colleague: "This is a screed. Do not publish." Were *they* worried about being neutral?

Patricia Monture-Angus wrote about this a very long time ago in the context of teaching in a faculty of law: "Our [Aboriginal professors'] participation was silently conditional on our acceptance of the already entrenched pedagogical structure" (2002, 170). Even the title of her piece says so much about Indigenous scholars' experiences: "On Being Homeless: Aboriginal Experiences of Academic Spaces." Those who teach against the crushing weight of colonial scholarship and institutional racism, and of sexism, homophobia, and other prevalent forms of domination, must often struggle. They struggle against colleagues, students, university officials in the academic hierarchy, research funding agencies, and processes ranging from peer evaluation to "rate my professor" that push back on critical scholarship critiquing the discipline and the university, the state, its elites, its foundation, and its privileged white citizens. Combine this with an Indigenous feminist analysis, and even Indigenous scholars are often unhappy with us.

This does not mean that we are wrong.

IDENTITY AND INDIGENOUS BELONGING

Having left the East Kootenay to get an education, I thought that I would never get to return home because home was a rural area, a bit of a backwater, and there would be no university job there for me.

Moreover, as many of you know, "home" is also a place in time and in one's imagination, and leaving home comes with no guarantee that there is home to return to.

Much later in life and suffering from pain and infirmity because of a compromised spine, I went on long-term disability leave from my professorship. That leave, and the support of my husband (I had remarried), allowed me to return to ʔamakʔis Ktunaxa, where I was born and raised. With that, I had the gift of proximity to what is left of some of my family (my father and my two brothers are dead), and through family connection, access to at least some part of my Indigenous heritages. My disability became a means to an opportunity, a gift that was a consequence of a problem.

Since I foregrounded my Indigenous identity and voice; since I was told by certain Elders, activists, and family members in the Ktunaxa Nation that I had the right to claim my identity because of my ancestry and my family, my scholarship feels more authentic and more relevant *to me*. It also seems to be interesting more readers and listeners. I am more comfortable with myself and my voice. Ironically, I've immersed myself in these matters after my departure from an active role in the university as part of long-term disability leave, and now, post-retirement.

Does recognition by others matter? As the prominent Indigenous feminist Sharon McIvor noted in her eponymous case against sex discrimination in the Indian Act, the absence of recognition is a form of erasure, a denial of who one is.[6] So many Indigenous women have felt and have been rendered invisible in law and by social practices. Recognition is important, and misrecognition has been deployed in the service of a virulent racism deeply embedded in Canadian history, institutions, and cultures. It has a particular lens for regarding Indigenous women. That lens has legitimated extraordinary gender-specific racist violence against Indigenous women, most recently documented as genocide by the National Inquiry into Missing and Murdered Indigenous Women and Girls (Government of Canada 2019). (Indigenous men have endured racist violence also, but not identically to that directed at women.)

As should be clear from my account earlier in this chapter about the historical roots of racism directed at us, there is a long trajectory of racist misogyny fuelling the marginalization and erasure of Indigenous women in Canada. We bear the burden identified by LaRocque as "a haunting and hounding sense of loss" and "the loneliness that comes from so many places: forced separation from one's children or parents, emotional and intellectual isolation, the experiencing of daily indecencies inherent in a racist society, the grieving that follows death" (1990, xxviii). Despite that pain, we organize, strategize, theorize, and fight for Indigenous women's rights, as Indigenous women in a settler state squatted on Indigenous territories. And we fight to be our authentic selves.

BEING MYSELF

So many feminists, especially Indigenous feminists, know well what I've written about in this chapter. Our social spheres, our work lives, and our opportunities are damaged by the disciplinary impulses of white and other male power directed against women. But we are transformative (Green 2001; 2002). We make space for others. We initiate changes, however slowly they come to pass (FAFIA 2021; Gehl 2019; Green 2014, 2017; McIvor, Palmater, and Day 2019). We are warrior women when we need to go to war.

Living as an authentic person in the conditions of political and personal contradiction and complexity is, for me, a life work still in progress. Perhaps that is a life work for all of us. My identity has been denied to me by colonialism and racism, and by those who assumed they knew me, for too long. I am able to claim all of my identity now, and it animates both my scholarship and my contemporary relationships. I will spend the rest of my life learning more about my Indigenous communities, learning about their particular gifts of knowledge, and trying to, finally, "fit in" as who I am.

I have emerged as an Indigenous feminist scholar; a political scientist in a racist white academy, in a white supremacist capitalist settler state on stolen Indigenous lands; and more recently, as a citizen of the Ktunaxa Nation, accepted because of my lineage; and as a member of Yaqit ʔa·knuqɬiʔit (the Tobacco Plains Indian Band), the reserve where a portion of the community from which a portion of my Ktunaxa family originated was forced to reside in 1884 (Tobacco Plains Indian Band 2017) while another portion declined that "option." And I am also English and Cree-Scots Métis. *I neither choose my ancestors, nor curate them. I recognize them.*

Those factors have shaped my thinking about my own Indigeneity, my feminism and scholarship, and the politics and problematics of identity. We are never done with this: we are all works in progress — learning, leaning on each other for support, drawing on the past, and looking to a better, more just and more authentic future for ourselves and all our relations.

Living out one's authentic identity is a process of commitment, engagement, and enactment; as Edward Said conceived of identity, it is "established by acts of self-representation that are always essentially political" (Ashcroft and Ahluwalia 1999, 13). I have a political analysis of Canada, and I pursue the political objective of revisioning the state and repositioning Indigenous people as the rightful owners of our territories.

ʔaɬ ʔa-kukpukam, hun ini Ktunaxa ȼ quɬ ʔini nintik[7] ȼ Cree-Scots Métis.[8] Hu qaki qaxi Yaqit ʔa·knuqɬiʔit.[9] Hu qawsaqaʔni ʔa·kiskaqɬiʔit.[10] I am a product of ʔamakʔis Ktunaxa, Ktunaxa Territory, where I drew my first breath and grew to adulthood. This territory has shaped me in foundational ways, and now, my Ktunaxa identity, always present but only recently animated through community recognition and through linguistic, political, and cultural engagement, is gifting me with insights into my past, our past, and our relationship to the world in the context we find ourselves in. I no longer allow others to tell me who I am and who I am not. I am an English — Ktunaxa — Cree-Scots Métis feminist, activist, and scholar, and I am finding my way home.

NOTES

1. In Canada, this includes the East and West Kootenay and eastern Columbia region of BC; Ktunaxa territory also extends across the Medicine Line and through three states. Interested readers may consult the Nation website at ktunaxa.org/wp-content/uploads/Traditional_Territory_Av2_02.png.
2. Sylvia Van Kirk's work on "mixed race" marriages of the 1800s' fur trade suggests these attitudes are as old as colonialism on Turtle Island (1980, 146).
3. See, for example, Donna Sutherland's (2008) discussion of my great-great-great grandmother Nahoway Sinclair's life; and my mother Shirley Green's discussion of her own life (2017, 291–293).
4. Lent notes that "he had not too much love for the half-breeds" (1963, 57), although she gives him a pass on this and generally takes the white settler view of colonial-Indigenous relations and colonization in her book.
5. Sylvia Van Kirk observes that this was commonplace in Red River society in the 1800s: mixed-blood children could pass as European, but not "without paying a price — that price being the suppression of every vestige of their Indian heritage" (1980, 236).
6. Sharon McIvor has been fighting this in court for most of her life and interested readers can look up each of her cases online on the Supreme Court of Canada website. See also her co-written chapter in this volume.

7   quł ʔini nintik, people from across the water, refers to both English and Scottish people. I thank Vi Birdstone, Elise McKay, Terrance Gatchalian, Sophie Pierre, Alfred Joseph, and ka nana Mara Nelson for their patient teaching of Ktunaxa to me.
8   I am (my roots are) Ktunaxa and English and Cree-Scots Métis. I can say this in any order, and I vary the order to make it clear that I am all these things, and I do not have to choose from or prioritize my ancestors.
9   I am from Yaqit ʔa·knuqłiʔit (Tobacco Prairie or Plains).
10 I am (staying) at ʔa·kiskaqłiʔit (Where two trails meet on the prairie — the Ktunaxa name for the Cranbrook area).

REFERENCES

Case Law/Legislation

Tobacco Plains Indian Band v. Her Majesty the Queen in Right of Canada SCTC 4 (2017) para. 22.

Other

Ashcroft, Bill, and Pal Ahluwalia. 1999. *Edward Said: The Paradox of Identity.* London and New York: Routledge.

Backhouse, Constance. 2021. "Introduction." In *Royally Wronged: The Royal Society of Canada and Indigenous Peoples,* edited by Constance Blackhouse, Cynthia E. Milton, Margaret Kovach, and Adele Perry. Montreal: McGill-Queen's Press.

Blackstock, Cindy. 2021. "Foreword." In *Royally Wronged: The Royal Society of Canada and Indigenous Peoples,* edited by Constance Blackhouse, Cynthia E. Milton, Margaret Kovach, and Adele Perry. Montreal: McGill-Queen's Press.

Coburn, Elaine, Rita Kaur Dhamoon, Joyce Green, Genevieve Fuji Johnson, Heidi Kiiwetinepinesiik Stark, and Gina Starblanket. 2024. "Anti-Racist Feminism and the Generative Power of Disruption." In *Feministing in Political Science: A Manifesta for Change in the Academy,* edited by Nisha Nath, Ethel Tungohan, Stephanie Paterson, Alana Cattapan, and Fiona MacDonald. Edmonton: University of Alberta Press.

Eberts, Mary. 2014. "Victoria's Secret: How to Make a Population of Prey." In *Indivisible: Indigenous Human Rights,* edited by Joyce Green. Halifax and Winnipeg: Fernwood Publishing.

———. 2017. "Being an Indigenous Woman Is a 'High-Risk Lifestyle.'" In *Making Space for Indigenous Feminism,* second ed., edited by Joyce Green. Winnipeg and Halifax: Fernwood Publishing.

FAFIA (Canadian Feminist Alliance for International Action). 2021. *Submission to United Nations Committee on the Elimination of Discrimination Against Women: Day of General Discussion on the Rights of Indigenous Women.* fafia-afai.org/en/submission-to-cedaw-on-the-rights-of-indigenous-women-2021/.

Gehl, Lynn. 2019. "Ending Sex Discrimination in the Indian Act Through '6(1) a All the Way.'" Rabble.ca, May 6, 2019. rabble.ca/feminism/ending-sex-discrimination-indian-act-through-61a-all-way/.

Government of Canada. 2019. *Reclaiming Power and Place: The Final Report of the National Inquiry into Missing and Murdered Indigenous Women and Girls.* mmiwg-ffada.ca/final-report/.

Green, Joyce. 2001. "Canaries in the Mines of Citizenship: Indian Women in Canada." *Canadian Journal of Political Science* 34, 4.

___. 2002. "Transforming at the Margins of the Academy." In *Women in the Canadian Academic Tundra*, edited by Linda Paul, Elena Hannah, and Swani Vethamany-Globus. Montreal: McGill-Queens University Press.

___ (ed.). 2007. *Making Space for Indigenous Feminism*. Winnipeg and Halifax: Fernwood Publishing.

___ (ed.). 2014. *Indivisible: Indigenous Human Rights*. Winnipeg and Halifax: Fernwood Publishing.

___ (ed.). 2017. *Making Space for Indigenous Feminism,* second ed. Winnipeg and Halifax: Fernwood Publishing.

___. 2019. "Enacting Reconciliation." In *Visions of the Heart: Issues Involving Indigenous People in Canada,* fifth ed., edited by Gina Starblanket & David Long. Toronto: Oxford University Press.

Green, Joyce, and Mike Burton. 2016. "Twelve Steps to Post-Colonial Reconciliation." In *Wrongs to Rights: How Churches Can Engage the United Nations Declaration on the Rights of Indigenous Peoples.* Winnipeg: Mennonite Church of Canada.

Green, Shirley. 2017. "Looking Backward, Still Looking Forward." In *Making Space for Indigenous Feminism,* second ed., edited by Joyce Green. Winnipeg and Halifax: Fernwood Publishing.

Hilleary, Cecily. 2022. "Indigenous North Americans Speak Out on Papal Apology." VOA, July 28, 2022. voanews.com/a/indigenous-north-americans-speak-out-on-papal-apology/6677898.html.

Kuokkanen, Rauna. 2019. *Restructuring Relations: Indigenous Self-Determination, Governance, and Gender.* Oxford, England: Oxford University Press.

LaRocque, Emma. 1990. "Preface." In *Writing the Circle: Native Women of Western Canada,* edited by Jeanne Perreault and Sylvia Vance. Edmonton: NeWest Publishers.

___. 2017. "Long Way From Home." In *Making Space for Indigenous Feminism,* second ed., edited by Joyce Green. Winnipeg and Halifax: Fernwood Publishing.

Lent, D. Geneva. 1963. *West of the Mountains: James Sinclair and the Hudson's Bay Company.* Seattle: University of Washington Press.

McIvor, Sharon, and Rauna Kuokkanen. 2007. "Sharon McIvor: Woman of Action." In *Making Space for Indigenous Feminism,* edited by Joyce Green. Winnipeg and Halifax: Fernwood Publishing.

McIvor, Sharon, Pamela Palmater, and Shelagh Day. 2019. "Equality Delayed Is Equality Denied for Indigenous Women." *Canadian Woman Studies/Les Cahiers De La Femme* 33, 1–2.

Monture-Angus, Patricia. 2002. "On Being Homeless: Aboriginal Experiences of Academic Spaces." In *Women in the Canadian Academic Tundra,* edited by Linda Paul, Elena Hannah, and Swani Vethamany-Globus. Montreal: McGill-Queens University Press.

Peers, Laura. 1999. "'Many Tender Ties': The Shifting Contexts and Meanings of the S BLACK Bag." *World Archaeology* 31, 2 (The Cultural Biography of Objects, October).

Pierre, Sophie. Personal communication, 2021, in the Ktunaxa Nation's Constitution Committee discussions.

Ross, Val. 2007. "Canadian Hero, or 19th-Century 'Sociopath'?" *Globe and Mail*, October 11, 2007. theglobeandmail.com/arts/canadian-hero-or-19th-century-sociopath/article1084203/.

Said, Edward. 1993. *Culture and Imperialism*. Vintage Books, Random House: New York.

St. Denis, Verna. 2022. "Living My Family Through Colonialism." In *White Benevolence: Racism and Colonial Violence in the Helping Professions*, edited by Amanda Gebhard, Sheelah McLean, and Verna St. Denis. Halifax and Winnipeg: Fernwood Publishing.

Sutherland, Donna G. 2008. *Nahoway: A Distant Voice*. Petersfield, MB: White Buffalo Books.

Teillet, Jean. 2019. *The Northwest Is Our Mother: The Story of Louis Riel's People, the Métis Nation*. Toronto: Patrick Crean Editions, HarperCollins Publishers.

Thobani, Sunera (ed.). 2021. *Coloniality and Racial (In)Justice in the University: Counting for Nothing?* Toronto: UTP.

Tungohan, Ethel. 2022. "The Ultimate Academic Auntie." *Academic Aunties*. academicaunties.com/episodes/the-ultimate-academic-auntie/.

Van Kirk, Sylvia. 1980. *Many Tender Ties: Women in Fur-Trade Society in Western Canada, 1670–1870*. Watson & Dwyer.

Wallace, Rebecca. 2022. "Beyond the 'Add and Stir' Approach: Indigenizing Comprehensive Exam Reading Lists in Canadian Political Science." *Canadian Journal of Political Science* 55, 3 (September).

THREE

Why Am I a Feminist?

Emma LaRocque

THROUGHOUT THE YEARS AS AN ENGAGED academic I have written a number of articles on gender inequality and Indigenous and non-Indigenous violence against women; I have also pondered on the role of tradition (be it European or Indigenous) in gender roles and expectations. Based on research, sociological observations, and personal/community experience I have strongly taken a feminist analytical approach. Often, we as academics express our views (whether we are feminist or not) with statistical, theoretical and/or traditional, cultural, and nationalist argumentations, much of which are probably threaded with political and ideological positions. Some of us, me included, have taken a positionality approach, which has included some sharing of personal stories and information. But few of us really ever share why exactly we are feminist. We know more about why many women, including Indigenous women, reject the label "feminist" but we know less why some of us accept feminism. In the new edition of this essay, I want to share more about what factors have contributed to my way of thinking about feminism, about women and girls' rights as human beings, as well as some thoughts on what may constitute gender liberation and decolonization.

To speak or write on matters of human rights for Indigenous Peoples, especially for women, is to be confronted with extraordinary challenges, in part because there are so many issues to address. I have struggled with what issues to foreground with respect to Indigenous women and feminism, reviewing a menu of socio-political items such as poverty, racism, sexism, violence and the culturalization of violence, the criminal justice system, self-government, exclusions of Aboriginal women in constitutional processes, and so forth. Yet, one feels compelled to offer a more positive portrait of the ways in which Aboriginal women live: as victims of colonization and patriarchy, yet as activists and agents in their lives; as oppressed, yet as fighters and survivors; and as among the most stereotyped, dehumanized, and objectified of women, yet as the strong, gracious, and determined women that they are. I also wondered whether I should just concentrate on Metis Nation women as their histories and contemporary concerns are frequently submerged, if not erased, under the umbrella terms and treatment of Aboriginal (now Indigenous)[1] women, which almost always means dealing exclusively with First Nations issues.

Perhaps a way to bring together some of these wide-ranging concerns is to offer reflections on my engagement with feminism as a scholar and educator, a writer and social critic, a human rights advocate, and, most pertinently, as a Metis woman who grew up with all the contradictions and burdens of a community wracked with the colonial situation, and in a society inured to this situation.

Many, perhaps even the majority, of Indigenous women do not identify with or readily use the label "feminist" (Green 1993, 2007; Ouellette 2002; Anderson 2010). Reasons for this are complex and include political, historical, cultural, and socio-economic factors, as well as some misunderstanding about feminism. The majority of Canadians do not understand feminism well, and disparaging feminism has been in vogue in the dominant as well as Indigenous communities. For some Aboriginal women, such misunderstanding reflects their disadvantaged socio-economic position and marginalization, which, among other things, deprives them of attaining adequate education. But there are also Native intellectuals who charge white feminism with having little or no understanding of colonial history, Indigenous Peoples, or race oppression (Stevenson 1993; Monture-Angus 1995; Ouellette 2002).

There is, however, a growing societal awareness about Indigenous women's issues in light of the relatively recent but substantial attention given to the missing and murdered Indigenous women reports, such as *Stolen Sisters* (2004, 2014) by Amnesty International, *Sisters in Spirit: What Their Stories Tell Us* (2010) by the Native Women's Association of Canada (NWAC), and *Reclaiming Power and Place* (Government of Canada 2019), the final report of the National Inquiry into Missing and Murdered Indigenous Women and Girls. It should be noted that the topic is not new, and information about the violence (in general) against Indigenous women has long been available. For several decades there have been public reports, provincial inquiries, and organizational outcries on the issue. For example, the Aboriginal Justice Inquiry of Manitoba (Government of Manitoba 1991) produced a special section on Helen Betty Osborne, the nineteen-year-old First Nations girl from The Pas, Manitoba, who was brutally killed by four white men. NWAC has been advocating for the well-being and legal and human rights of Aboriginal women since its inception in 1974 (also see Pearce 2013). And there is considerable Indigenous and non-Indigenous literature, both academic and popular, which addresses gendered violence, racism, and colonialism.[2] Feminist analysis has made important contributions to this literature. However, with the possible exception of university students who pursue research in this area, I am not sure that all of this has necessarily led to any greater appreciation for feminism or for feminist analysis within Indigenous communities. Since feminism and feminists are often stereotyped and associated with Western ideologies, it is important to review some basic assumptions, definitions, and understandings about feminism.

WHAT IS "FEMINISM"?

I understand feminism as a struggle to end sexism and gender-based inequality with the premise that "women are as capable and valuable as men" (Freedman 2002, 31). As Christine Overall (1998, 15) explains: "Feminism is comprised of the well-founded belief that girls and women are legally, politically and socially disadvantaged on the grounds of their sex; the ethical stance that this oppression is morally wrong; and the pragmatic commitment to ending injustice to all female human beings."

bell hooks (1984, 24) has a more comprehensive approach:

> Feminism is the struggle to end sexist oppression. Its aim is not to benefit any specific group of women, any particular race or class of women. It does not privilege women over men. It has the power to transform in a meaningful way all our lives. Most importantly, feminism is neither a lifestyle nor a ready-made identity or role one can step in to.

Feminism, then, does not belong to any particular group, and those who understand and practise the social idea of ending gender inequality and injustice are feminist. In this sense, men and women of all backgrounds can be feminists, and feminists should be among Indigenous Peoples' best allies, and many are. Indigenous writers, artists, scholars, and community activists resisting our dehumanization and our dispossession are doing work very similar to feminist principles and objectives. Feminist and Indigenous resistance entails both deconstruction and reconstruction. Indigenous, non-Indigenous, male, and female feminists will especially examine theories, portrayals, political positions, or social treatments of Indigenous women. Feminism provides us with theoretical tools that we can use to analyze historical realities such as patriarchy. Feminism is not so much about objecting to one particular man, event, or even piece of legislation (such as the Indian Act); rather, feminism is an analysis of how cultural, political, and social systems work to privilege men and disadvantage women. Feminism has an ethical component in that feminist analysis interrogates, confronts, and seeks to transform those realities that compromise women's well-being and human rights.

Given the seemingly innocuous and even grand principles and objectives for human rights embedded in feminism, I have often been surprised, at times even startled, at the negative reactions to this concept. Because the labels "feminist" or "feminism" carry such a negative or unclear meaning for many women, perhaps it is best not to fixate on terminology or on oppositional politics, but rather to focus on what is important to us as Aboriginal women. Here I outline what is important to me with the inference that what is important to me may also be important to other women.

I sometimes think I was born a feminist but I did not know much, if anything, about the history, the theories, or the label "feminism" until well into my twenties or thirties. Nor am I sure when or why I began to realize that women were to look, dress, and act differently from men, and that such material difference translated into different socio-economic standing within family units as well as in the larger community and in societal roles and expectations. As a child I took for granted that the roles my parents enacted on a daily basis were just "normal." As I grew older it became clearer that there was an expected division of labour, and that women's roles were more homebound and restrictive than men's. There were also expectations that men and women were to be distinct in terms of "masculinity" and "femininity," and that the distinction was to be made evident in appearance, dress, and behaviour. Interestingly, as children we were free or freer to behave and even dress similarly. In my small matrilocal Metis community in northeastern Alberta, boys and girls played together completely equal and yet as we grew a bit older, we just seemed to know the heteronormative ways of being. For me I probably began to feel intense pressure about gendered behaviour, dress, and appearance when I was about nine years old — which interestingly, was when I started school. But even before school I "knew" girls had to wear dresses at special events; I remember complying happily when preparing for Catechism and my First Communion. In various parts and in various degrees, and without much awareness, I had been influenced by the church, my home, in school, and popular culture.

I also saw that women and men were expected to function differently in the area of home life and work. For much of my childhood my parents fed, clothed, and sheltered us by living off the land, and by my father working as a labourer on a seasonal basis, eventually working every summer for a railroad company. When my father was working for wages, for which he had to leave our home, the division of labour and distinct gender roles was very apparent. But when my parents were on the land, they not only worked together, they often criss-crossed gender roles. They gardened together; they raked leaves together. They fetched water and wood together or equally. They cut and sawed wood and carried it in as required. My dad most always made breakfast and often helped with making lunches for us for school. They were both free to work outside as inside. Living off the land requires resourcefulness and interdependence. However, even here there was division of labour — like most women in our area my mom did the major portion of cooking, laundry, and tending to children. In the winters during trapping and hunting seasons men left the home to go to traplines and women were left to take care of children and fend for their families while the men were gone. But women could go with the men to their traplines, and some did, especially those who did not have small children or children who had to be in school.

METIS LIFE AND LOSSES

I do not come from any racially or economically equal, much less privileged, background (see LaRocque 1990b, 2016). The Metis in my community have been written up by some from an urban-centric bias as "bush people" living in "isolated" or "remote Indian" communities along a railroad line in northeastern Alberta (Garvin 1992). Although we spoke Plains Cree (with Michif) and lived off the land, legally we were/are not Status Indians and so never lived on reserves. We were/are Metis but never lived in the Alberta Metis Settlements, or "Colonies" as they were once called. We knew ourselves as Apeetowgusanuk (or "half-sons" in Cree) who were descended from both the Red River Metis and locally originated Metis[3] communities with deep kinship connections to both Status and non-Status Indian peoples. And although Metis do originate from the early fur trade era of First Nations and European peoples, both my maternal and paternal family histories are grounded in Metis Nation lineage with no remembrance of relational ties with non-Aboriginal people. My parents, aunts, and uncles all spoke of "scrip"[4] and how Apeetowgusanuk lost and were continuing to lose beloved domains of lands either through scrip or simply through urban, industrial, and farming encroachments. Legally, we did not own any land, but in those years we could still definitely live on, from, and with the land, for morally, it was our land. My younger brother has remained on our original land area but, like my father before him, can only lease the land as we have never had resources to purchase this land. But if there was any justice for Metis people the governments should simply transfer ownership to those Metis families who have loved and tended specific lands — and continue to do so — since long before Confederation. After all, my grandparents occupied, used, and loved this land long before Confederation, and my father was born before Alberta became a province.

My parents' generation made a living from the many resources of the land, including hunting and trapping, as well as from wage labour, wherever such could be found. And although most Apeetowgusanuk were hardworking, proudly independent, or Otehpayimsuak (people who own themselves) peoples, they/we were suffering from unimaginable poverty and racism, complete with layers and waves of both legal and social dispossession.

Among the multiple sites of dispossession, public schooling contributed significantly to my generation's sense of cultural dislocation and intellectual alienation. Not only did schooling aim to extract us from our mother language and our motherland with its re-settler[5] curriculum, but it also failed to teach us basic classroom reading and writing skills, thereby failing to prepare us for the new brave world of industrialization/urbanization, even as this world was fast overtaking us, especially after World War II. Undergirding this pedagogy was the colonialist version of history and the "National Dream," all equated with "progress." Not surprisingly, the vast majority of Metis students left school as fast as they could do so legally. In 1971, the average grade level for Metis people in Alberta was Grade 4. This and more have left many people of my generation and their children in a socio-cultural vacuum. This is the direct and continuing legacy of colonization, and it is the sociological after-effects of this colonial earthquake that have dislocated and disoriented many of our youth.

Two things have always followed me from my early years: on one hand, our richly woven cultural life based on our blended land and railroad line ways, textured with our Metized (my coin) Cree oral literature, language, and worldview; and on the other hand, our extreme poverty and alienation from the financial and material privileges of mainstream Canada. I do not speak of poverty in any abstract sense. Depending on seasons (trapping or non-trapping), wage labour employment or non-employment, we could also go without much food for months, for years. My parents typically struggled to outfit us with adequate or socially acceptable clothing, lunches, and other school supplies during school terms. Poverty in my family and community translated into social warfare on our bodies. As virtually penniless people of the land who spoke only Cree and often lived miles away from town, we had minimal access to doctors or hospitals throughout the 1900s, particularly and most relevant for my generation, during the 1940s–1970s. Consequently, many people died, often from tuberculosis (TB) or other diseases. Many of my relatives were sent away to sanatoriums due to TB, among them my older sister and brother. Some came back in coffins. We were lucky: my older brother and sister survived and came home. Some children were never returned from hospitals, and those who were orphaned (but were taken care of within extended kinship systems) were often confiscated by state welfare agencies. The now infamous Sixties Scoop, social welfare systems taking children away from Indian families, was also practised on northern Metis communities. Those who survived were left with bewilderment and broken hearts along with a wide array of medical and social problems. Some individuals and some families increasingly displayed fragmentation, depression, alcohol abuse, anger, and violence.

FAMILIAL STRUCTURES

Yet, remarkably, numerous Metis individuals and families kept body and soul together and, I hasten to add, many men including my father did not take to violence under any circumstances. In my home there was no physical violence (except for the rare disciplinary willow lashings from my mother); as a rule, I grew up safe and secure inside our home. But my mother (1918–81) did not grow up so safe. Somewhere, during the Depression, my maternal grandfather had been dispossessed of his scrip, store, land, and dairy farm, uprooting his large family. Apparently, he took to drinking and family violence. Overnight my mother's young life had become one of abject poverty, and she and her sisters suffered the most immediate consequences. As part of making ends meet, my grandfather pushed his many daughters out of the home as soon as they became "of age." In a patriarchal world, they were left to find men who could take care of them.

I cannot say whether my grandfather's treatment of his daughters was typical of Metis attitudes of those times, but I can say that patriarchy did not end with my grandfather. The Metis community of my generation was by no means free from patriarchal notions and practices. Take the name we had for ourselves: Apeetowgusanuk, or "half-son." Why not "half-daughters"? In my own family, all the men got two given names, and all the women had one name. This practice goes back to my grandparents and great-grandparents. There was also the typical double standard about male and female sexual behaviour. To put it in the vernacular, men could "run around," women could not. If women exercised sexual freedom they could expect censorship. In the Roman Catholic Church, boys could assist priests in the service, girls could not. In our home, however, my mother, who integrated Cree Metis traditions with Roman Catholic rituals, assumed spiritual leadership. She also led the way in many of our family decisions and activities.

Although my own parents allowed the girls as much freedom of expression as the boys, I do recall one incident that indicated they had been much influenced by male-favoured thinking. When I was quite young I was told by my mother not to walk over my father's and brothers' trapping/hunting supplies and preparations. I immediately asked why not? She explained that it would bring bad luck to their trapping/hunting. I do not remember her answer, if any, to my next "why?" but I called on natural justice — if my brothers could walk over them, so could I. I was left to my youthful logic, but the message was disturbing: girls are contaminated, girls bring bad luck, and girls can't do all the things boys can, simply because they are girls. I am aware that today people attach spiritual power to menstrual taboos, but I was premenstrual, indicating that this taboo reflected wider and deeper gender biases and could be invoked and generalized at will.

I should add that my mom was by no means sanguine about traditions that impacted her more directly. Although she was a remarkably resourceful woman who took exceptional care of us, she was not a happy homemaker. She most definitely did not romanticize motherhood (and neither did anyone else). Actually, no one romanticized motherhood or femaleness in our area. Not once did I ever hear anyone, male or female, associating motherhood or the feminine as sacred. In fact, as a child I heard mockery of womanhood even by women, but not of manhood. My own reading of this is that our community was deeply colonized, but that attitudes about gender also reflected some old beliefs and customs (apparent in some Wehsakehcha stories and other legends I grew up with). If anything, my mother resented the fact that responsibility fell on her to do the major portion of child-rearing and other home-related duties. This is all the more interesting because in retrospect I consider my father a feminist, for he eschewed violence and modelled respect for women. Unlike many other fathers, he assisted with many of the household chores, such as cooking, making our lunches for school and so forth, whenever he was home. Conversely, my mother enjoyed working outside alongside my dad. My mom was as free to trap and do many other so-called masculine-assigned tasks as my father was free to work in the home. Yet the key difference for my mom lay in the fact my father had a choice concerning childcare and kitchen work, whereas my mother did not. And she really had no other choice. Although highly gifted and creative, my mom, along with the vast majority of other Metis women of her generation (and even my older sisters' generation), never had any opportunity to go to school or to develop her many gifts, much less to have a career or even get a job. So, my mom lived with the frustration of remaining financially dependent on my father — something she viewed as an obstacle to her sense of freedom and an affront to her dignity.

TRAUMA AND LIMITED POWER

What is little known about many Metis homes — at least in my home and surrounding area when I was growing up — is the power of women in the family, if not community. Women made most of the decisions that had to do with daily family life; women did most of the teaching and disciplining of children, and women determined the religious life of the family. This was true whether we lived on the land or whether we lived with my dad's work schedule. What was not in women's control was money. As already noted, in our home it did not escape my mom's attention that my dad got paid for his labour but my mom's work, which was truly never done, was never recompensed. This situation was a key source of discontent for my mom; not only was "women's work" devalued (not in our home but certainly in town that we frequented), but she was completely financially dependent on my dad, something that she found very difficult. This industrial and capital-based economic system of separating work from home with compensation for "work" was also a key source of modelling heteronormative and patriarchal gender roles for children.

Accordingly, my parents, liberal as they were in many respects, expected the boys to find a good job so that they could take care of their families; and they expected my sister and me to find a good man to take care of us. My sister who had little opportunity to get an education did end up with a man and having children. Which was not a happy story at all. I would have none of this. Much to my parents' disappointment and fears for my future, as soon as I could I set out to make a life for myself such that I would not be financially dependent on anyone. I am sure my mother's highly vocalized unhappiness influenced me in that direction. She had also taught me to love learning. She was the one in our family who regaled us with stories, among them Wehsakehcha stories — all in Cree. She was the one who bought us comic books from town which motivated me to go to school so that I could read them. She was also the one who inspired in me a spiritual hunger and curiosity such that I spent a lot of my young life searching for that proverbial meaning of life. My mom was the religious person in our family; she read the Bible in Cree syllabics and she recited the rosary every evening as we all knelt by our homemade futons on the floor. At the same time she practised Cree beliefs; during thunder storms she would hastily grab tobacco, run out and talk to Pehehsoo (thunder spirit-being, often angry) as she pointed the tobacco-filled cigarette in four directions. And Pehehsoo always went away! Just like the night dancing spirits would swoop down on us when we whistled, and they would swoop back up when we cracked dry twigs at them. And seeing or hearing ghosts was routine.

My mom was also a haunted woman with many broken hearts. She suffered through many tragedies in her life. She was born in 1918 and died in 1981 from breast cancer. When she was a little girl, as explained earlier, her father who once had a thriving store and dairy farm lost everything almost overnight — with it scrip for the land. A white storekeeper from town got all of my grandfather's possessions as payment for what my grandfather owed him. This white storekeeper had been my grandfather's supplier for his little store in the country. He had accumulated a large debt due to his generosity to his Native clients and apparently his alcoholism. He and my grandmother had a very large family and when he no longer could feed all his children, he kicked out all the girls who had "come of age"; they were to find men who could take care of them. My mother found my dad — a man much older than she but a very steady, kind, and hardworking man. Together they eked out a living and had five children — all four to five years apart. My mother was still a teenager when she had her first girl — four years later she had her second girl, whose name was Josephine. When Josephine was four she died; my dad told me she died from some stomach ailment but my sister told me Josephine got sick after she had been sexually assaulted by one of my mom's deranged brothers. I was never able to confirm this story as my sister told me after our parents had passed. But it broke my heart even though my two brothers and I were not born yet when Josephine died.

This was in 1944. During the 1930s to 1940s in Alberta death and illness were common for poverty-stricken Metis people. My parents spoke only Cree (with some Michif) and there were no schools for Metis people of their generation so they did not read or write English (or French), and even though they lived about five miles from the local town, they did not have easy access to transportation for medical help as no one had vehicles in the community. Numerous Metis people throughout central and northern Alberta were dying, usually from tuberculosis or pneumonia. Access to health care was just not available. My community was not spared from all this. Nearly every family my parents knew lost parents, siblings, children, and other relatives or friends. People were walking in grief.

My mother never truly recovered from these traumas. Sadly, she and her many siblings took to drinking and they did not handle their drinking well at all. And as if my poor mother had not suffered enough, she herself was brutally attacked by her sister's son, one of my many male cousins who became predators in our communities. As one may understand, the oft repeated phrase "All My Relations" has never sat well with me. Of course, many of my relatives, especially aunts and uncles, were very nice people. They were generous, kind, wonderful storytellers who also loved to laugh. But what was disturbing was the extent to which they, along with most other people in the area, tolerated sexual and other forms of violence against women and girls. In fact, most people blamed the victims. Victims were shamed and silenced. Nor was there any elevation of womanhood. Or motherhood. There was no particular honour or respect; if anything, there was a tendency to denigrate femaleness, even by women. The worst insult one could level at another was to swear with words (in Cree) that referred pejoratively to female genitalia. There were no grand career expectations for girls either. A rather bullyish woman from the community once mocked me for declaring that I was going to be a teacher when I grew up — this woman just sneered at me and said, "Oh you are not going to be any different from anybody, you are going to get knocked up and have babies before you are fifteen."

It was my dad who seemed to be the only person in my life who never insulted women or me. He no doubt contributed to my feminism. My father was an unassuming amiable gentleman who modelled honesty, hard work, sobriety, respectfulness, and non-violence. He never mistreated my mom; he never harmed us in any way. Nor did he ever discipline us with violence. As I pointed out earlier, he worked alongside my mom, whether it was outdoors or indoors. He was not hung up with gender roles — he cooked, swept floors, washed dishes, as well as he laboured in traplines or railroad tracks. He never pressured any of us to get married or have children. He too had his heartbreaks and difficult times. He worked very hard for much of his life — and for very little pay. He found physical hard labour onerous whether on the railroad or out on the trapline. I remember once when he got home from the trapline saying: "What kind of God makes people plow through waist-deep snow in order to make a living?" I also remember him taking my one brother aside and telling him never to disrespect women, that "men would be nothing without women."

Was my dad a feminist? In some ways he definitely modelled feminism in that he eschewed macho attitudes and behaviour and he worked with my mom and most genuinely respected women. But he was a product of his times and like most families of the times, he did not think that school was of any use to girls because they would get married anyways. It was my mother who supported my desire to go to school. But once I did start my dad never tried to impede my wishes. In fact, he often walked me to school, made my lunches and worked hard to provide us with food and clothes.

FEMINISM AND INJUSTICE

So why am I a feminist? How could I not be a feminist? How could anyone not be a feminist after growing up with all these tragedies, contradictions, and the unremitting violence so many women, including my sisters and my mother, went through? And violence against women and girls was widespread in our area. Almost all my aunties, my grandmother, my female cousins were victims of violence — all sorts of violence from all sorts of men, be they police, priests, husbands, cousins, or wandering white men (sometimes teenage gangs) who were looking to find an "Indian girl" (or woman) to assault. Before I was born my mother's eighteen-year-old younger sister disappeared in the nearby town. Her name was Julie. Months later her body was found buried in a sawdust pile in this town. She was last seen walking with a white man but the police never bothered to investigate. In 1977 my sister-in-law's fourteen-year-old sister disappeared in Edmonton — days later her wounded body was found in some back alley. Her name was Cheryl. The police never bothered to investigate.

Violence against women and girls is the most enduring and most frequent violation of human dignity. It should be declared a crime against humanity, and not just for women caught in war. Violence against women is war. And it is a hate crime. War on our bodies, on our freedoms, on our dignities. And we are all vulnerable. Given this kind of violence is international in scope, given it happens in every culture, given men of all backgrounds — rich, famous, poor, colonized — are engaging in such misogyny and narcissism, one would think there would be worldwide efforts in the prevention of such behaviour. I was fourteen when my poor mom was brutalized (and had to be hospitalized); I was in my thirties when my surviving sister told me about Josephine. Hate crime against women and girls is a particularly egregious social and cultural illness that we have barely begun to address in our universe. How could I not be a feminist? Feminism is very personal to me.

But my feminism is not just personal. I was a feminist even before I learned about these horrible incidents. For that I owe it to both my parents who in each of their ways taught me independence, resourcefulness, determination, hard work, and the importance of dignity. Early in life I also gained a deep awareness of our inequality in society. I developed a fierce sense of justice — I truly hated injustice. Even in play as a child I insisted on absolute fairness. In schools I was bullied a lot and that deepened my awareness of injustice and vulnerability. All these experiences in my family history and the communities I have come to know directed me to learn and to try to understand this world so that I could change it.

Feminism is a way to best understand how and why women and girls have been subjected to violence and numerous other injustices and inequities that go back to the beginning of time. Feminism is important and integral to our well-being as women, certainly as Indigenous women. It is an analytical tool with a macro (structural) perspective for dealing with social, cultural, and political issues, including the ugly realities of colonial and patriarchal domination, misogyny, and racism. Feminism may be defined as a theoretical and yet practical movement to end all forms of injustice against women and girls, and to work for our rights to be safe, self-determining, and equal in this world. To be able to live, to thrive without fear or PTSDs shadowing us. For all women and girls everywhere. For that matter, for all people, including men.

COLONIZATION AND CHOICE

Since the early 1970s I have been writing, lecturing, and teaching about colonization. One of the questions I ask my graduate students is: "What is it that makes colonization wrong?" Students usually list a long string of socio-economic and cultural or political ailments. I usually answer with a related question: "What is it that makes us human, that distinguishes us from animals?" Generally, students remain quiet. According to Peter Puxley (1977) what makes us human is the capacity to make choices. And what makes colonization — or any other sort of oppression such as institutionalized misogyny including violence — so wrong is that it forcibly takes choice away from people. And force is dehumanizing and incapacitating. We can extrapolate from this that any oppression, be it individual or collective, is dehumanizing. Freedom is fundamental to being human. Such freedom includes freedom from want, fear, and personal or political violence. A positive way of saying this is the freedom to thrive, bodily and culturally; freedom to make political and personal decisions; freedom to vote, freedom to speak, to disagree, to worship (or not); to own our identities, to own our bodies; freedom to love — all these freedoms are fundamental to being human.

But no one should be free to cause harm to others. Colonization and patriarchy cause harm, not only to individuals but to societies. Indigenous feminist analysis has laid open the history and the powerful machinations of colonization and sexism. Frankly I do not know of one Indigenous individual in this country who is not affected in some way by the intersectional realities of historic dispossession, racism, poverty, marginalization, and/or gendered violence — realities born out of colonization that haunt many of us quite directly, no matter our own individual successes or journeys. Poverty also sets up social conditions that facilitate violence against women. In my mother's generation, white males, including police and priests, attacked Native women because they knew the women were in no position to bring them to justice. Similarly, homegrown predators in our communities targeted the most defenceless because they too knew they could get away with it. Generally, many women in our area were bullied, battered, or assaulted. Not that this was ever openly dealt with by anyone — silence, shame, and suppression ruled my parent's generation. Indigenous women's relocations to urban centres are in part a result of such poverty and violence.

Previously, I addressed the topic of violence against women within Native communities (1990a, 1993, 1997). I tried to place this troubling issue in the context of colonialism, yet at the same time emphasized that for many reasons, male violence cannot be fully explained by social or political conditions. In other words, neither colonization nor poverty explains everything about why or how Native men and boys (and societies) may assume sexist attitudes or misogynistic behaviours. This point has to be emphasized because male violence continues to be tolerated, justified, or virtually absolved by so many communities and political interests, criminal justice systems, and even academics (of all colours), usually in defence of cultural difference, community loyalties, or nationalist agendas, or out of reaction to white feminist critiques. Or to colonization. I am concerned that in our fairly unified criticisms of the systemic racism and sexism embedded in colonialism, we are overlooking issues such as personal responsibility and accountability. I am afraid that the historical consequences of colonization are being used in ways that mitigate what are extremely personal and violent crimes. This is not decolonization!

How should we address these issues? One commonly proposed answer to gender violence seems to centre around notions of Indigenous cultures being all about relatedness. The phrase "All Our Relations" is commonly used in both academic and popular works. Yazzie and Baldy (2018, as noted in Anderson 2021, 44) refer to it as "radical relationality." I remember my favourite auntie scolding me for being very angry at some male cousins about their violence, and her basis of chiding me was that we were all related. But she never scolded those cousins who were violent towards their relations, in this case, her very own sister! If relationality is to mean anything, at the very least it should mean that our male relatives be held accountable for their actions; our oppressions cannot give us the right to oppress our own relatives in our communities. Nor should it mean that we tolerate violent behaviour.

Even colonized and/or poor people still have moral capacity to make some choices. And obviously the majority of men in our communities have made choices against violence, such as my father and many others of his generation. We may not have the original lands or resources but we can still make choices, especially in the realm of what is right and what is wrong. In other words, to be human is to be accountable to others — which ought to be the basis and core of what it means to practise "radical relationality." To be human is to take personal responsibility for our behaviours. At some point our growth as human beings depends on our capacity to assume responsibility for our actions. Men must assume responsibility for their actions. And society must make men (or anyone else) accountable for violent behaviours. The justice system should include real justice for women and girls. And of course, we must also educate as much and as quickly as possible. Education should not just be in schools or universities; it should also be in our homes and communities.

I have found it disturbing the extent to which Indigenous and non-Indigenous spokespersons and agencies have come to blame colonization and/or intergenerational trauma for everything. Especially in the area of gendered violence. The part that is particularly disturbing is that so many agencies, including the legal community, have used historical factors to effectively absolve men who assault women. Or to treat them as if they are the victims! Poor Boy "explanations" have been used to excuse or modulate heinous assaults against women and girls. The source of such assaults is systemic (and seemingly universal) patriarchy, which has bred toxic masculinity with its muscular sense of entitlement. Of course, colonization is imprinted in our lives, but colonization does not answer everything, especially in the area of sexual violence. Neither do residential schools or any other oppressive institutions. And there are many. But they cannot and must not explain away every behaviour or all violence. For instance, in our community (and surrounding area) none of us went to residential school — yet, violence was quite pervasive. Studies often focus on women; for example, in the case of violence against women in the sex trade, reports have emphasized their "risky lifestyle." Or violence is reduced to "domestic violence" (now "intimate partner violence") and so forth. Indigenous organizations generally point to colonization and racism as sources of attacks against Indigenous women and girls. All this may be true — certainly they are all contributing factors. But what is often missing is analysis and focus on the men themselves.

So this takes me back to square one — sadly, violence against women, all women, has not really changed. Sometimes it looks like the more we expose the violence, the worse it gets. The scope of violence in Canada is wide and deep. And is not declining (Statistics Canada 2021).

I WAS BORN ASKING

Readers of this chapter may wonder or even assume that I must be a "man-hater" or ultra conservative. I am neither! Poverty as I have experienced it, and indeed, continue to experience in a myriad of "fall-out" ways, has in no small measure influenced me to view human behaviour with less than romantic eyes. However, and as I have written elsewhere ("Tides, Towns and Trains" 1990b), I was born asking. On the issue of violence against women and girls, so many more people need to start asking why this is so. Really asking. Not just assuming all there is to it is colonization or the proverbial "white man." Then working to do something about it. Critical thinking along with social activism is feminism in its wholeness.

Freedom from imperial, systemic, and personal dominations must remain the basis of our emancipatory efforts. As Indigenous feminists this also means that we assume a "voice" and political positionality. Not only may we speak in the first person but we also assume an anti-racism and post-colonial or de-colonial analysis. We must maintain our rights as human beings, and part of this involves asking what it is that makes us (men and women) human. And what empowers us. For me, freedom to choose, freedom to own our own bodies, and personal accountability feature large. I take consolation in the knowledge that whatever theoretical or political differences there are among Indigenous women about the label feminist/feminism, in the final analysis I believe we all share this one goal — to end systemic, racist, and misogynistic violence against women and girls.

NOTES

1. Colonial labelling and terminology are problematic. I use the umbrella terms Native, Aboriginal, and Indigenous interchangeably and inclusively, as they include First Nations, Metis, and Inuit.
2. Numerous and varied works analyzing violence against Aboriginal women as a systemic problem rooted in colonialism were available long before the fairly recent focus on the missing and murdered Indigenous women. See Campbell (1973), Maracle (1988), and McGillivray and Comaskey (1999). Popular works which feature violence against Indigenous women include plays and novels such as *The Ecstasy of Rita Joe* (Ryga 1970, which was performed for the Canadian centennial activities in 1967; published in 1970), *The Rez Sisters* (Highway 1988), and *Dry Lips Oughta Move to Kapuskasing* (Highway 1989), *In Search of April Raintree* (Culleton-Mosionier 1983), *Honour the Sun* (Slipperjack 1987), *Monkey Beach* (Robinson 2000) and so many more.
3. Some capitalize "Metis" to indicate those who originate from the Red River in order to make distinctions from other metis who do not have Red River lineage. See Peterson and Brown (1985).
4. Between 1870 and 1900, the federal government issued a series of tickets with monetary or land value (scrip) to "Halfbreed Heads of Families" as a form of recognizing Metis rights to land. However, in large part, the Metis were divested of the scrips by speculators, fraud, government legislation, and cultural processes alien to them (see RCAP 1996).
5. I prefer to use the term "re-settler." To call Euro-North Americans "settlers" (or "settler society") is to imply that Indigenous Peoples did not settle or have settlements. The justificatory colonial notion of settlement versus nomadism forms one of the key features to the ideological binary construct I have come to call Civ/Sav (LaRocque 2010, 37–58), a construct that rationalized the invasion, dispossession, and re-settlement of Indigenous lands. See also LaRocque 2015.

REFERENCES

Amnesty International. 2004. *Stolen Sisters: Discrimination and Violence Against Indigenous Women in Canada.* Ottawa: Amnesty International.

———. 2014. *No More Stolen Sisters: The Need for a Comprehensive Response to Discrimination and Violence Against Indigenous Women in Canada.* Ottawa: Amnesty International.

Anderson, Kim. 2001. *A Recognition of Being: Reconstructing Native Womanhood.* Toronto: Canadian Scholars Press.

———. 2010. "Affirmations of an Indigenist Feminist." In *Indigenous Women and Feminism: Politics, Activism, Culture,* edited by Cheryl Suzack et al. Vancouver: University of British Columbia Press.

———. 2020. "Multi-generational Indigenous Feminisms: From F Word to What Ifs." In *Routledge Handbook of Critical Indigenous Studies,* edited by Brendan Hokowhitu, Aileen Moreton-Robinson, Linda Tuhiwai-Smith, Chris Andersen, Steve Larkin. Routledge.

Campbell, Maria. 1973. *Halfbreed.* Toronto: McClelland and Stewart.

Culleton-Mosionier, Beatrice. 1983. *In Search of April Raintree.* Winnipeg: Pemmican Publications.

Freedman, Estelle. 2002. *No Turning Back: The History of Feminism and the Future of Women.* Ballantine.

Garvin, Terry. 1992. *Bush Land People.* Calgary: Arctic Institute of North America of the University of Calgary.

Government of Canada. 2019. *Reclaiming Power and Place: The Final Report of the National Inquiry into Missing and Murdered Indigenous Women and Girls.* mmi-wg-ffada.ca/final-report/.

Government of Manitoba. 1991. *Aboriginal Justice Inquiry.* Vol. 2.

Green, Joyce. 1993. "Constitutionalising the Patriarchy: Aboriginal Women and Aboriginal Government." *Constitutional Forum* 4, 4.

———. 2007. "Taking Account of Aboriginal Feminism." In *Making Space for Indigenous Feminism,* edited by Joyce Green. Halifax and Winnipeg: Fernwood Publishing.

Highway, Tomson. 1988. *The Rez Sisters.* Saskatoon: Fifth House.

———. 1989. *Dry Lips Oughta Move to Kapuskasing.* Saskatoon: Fifth House.

hooks, bell. 1984. *Feminist Theory: From Margin to Center.* Boston: South End Press.

LaRocque, Emma. 1990a. "Racism/Sexism and Its Effects on Native Women." *Public Concerns on Human Rights: A Summary of Briefs.* Ottawa: Canadian Human Rights Commission.

———. 1990b. "Tides, Towns and Trains." In *Living the Changes,* edited by J. Turner. Winnipeg: University of Manitoba Press.

———. 1993. "Violence in Aboriginal Communities." *The Path to Healing: Report of the National Round Table on Aboriginal Health and Social Issues.* Ottawa: Royal Commission on Aboriginal Peoples.

———. 1997. "Re-examining Culturally Appropriate Models in Criminal Justice Applications." In *Aboriginal and Treaty Rights in Canada: Essays on Law, Equity and Respect for Difference,* edited by M. Asch. Vancouver: University of British Columbia Press.

———. 2010. *When the Other is Me: Native Resistance Discourse 1850–1990.* Winnipeg: University of Manitoba Press.

___. 2015. "Foreword: 'Resist No Longer': Reflections on Resistance Writing and Teaching." In *More Will Sing Their Way to Freedom: Indigenous Resistance and Resurgence,* edited by E. Coburn (ed.). Halifax and Winnipeg: Fernwood Publishing.

___. 2016. "Colonialism Lived." In *In This Together: Fifteen Stories of Truth and Reconciliation,* edited by D. Metcalfe-Chenail. Victoria: Brindle & Glass Publishing.

Maracle, Lee. 1988. *I Am Woman.* Vancouver: Write-On Press Publishers.

McGillivray, Anne, and B. Comaskey. 1999. *Black Eyes All of the Time: Intimate Violence, Aboriginal Women, and the Justice System.* Toronto: University of Toronto Press.

Monture-Angus, Patricia. 1995. *Thunder in My Soul: A Mohawk Woman Speaks.* Halifax: Fernwood Publishing.

NWAC (Native Women Association of Canada). 2010. *What Their Stories Tell Us: Research Findings from the Sisters in Spirit Initiative.* Ottawa: Native Women's Association of Canada. nwac.ca/assets-knowledge-centre/2010_What_Their_Stories_Tell_Us_Research_Findings_SIS_Initiative-1.pdf.

Ouellette, Grace J.M.W. 2002. *The Fourth World: An Indigenous Perspective on Feminism and Aboriginal Women's Activism.* Halifax: Fernwood Publishing.

Overall, Christine. 1998. *A Feminist I: Reflections from Academia.* Peterborough: Broadview Press.

Pearce, Maryanne. 2013. "An Awkward Silence: Missing and Murdered Vulnerable Women and the Canadian Justice System." Diss. University of Ottawa.

Peterson, Jacqueline, and J. Brown (eds.). 1985. *The New Peoples: Being and Becoming Metis in North America.* Winnipeg: University of Manitoba Press.

Puxley, Peter. 1977. "The Colonial Experience." In *Dene Nation: A Colony Within,* edited by M. Watkins. Toronto: University of Toronto Press.

RCAP (Royal Commission on Aboriginal People). 1996. *Perspectives and Realities,* Volume 4. Ottawa: Supply and Services.

Robinson, Eden. 2000. *Monkey Beach.* Toronto: Alfred A. Knopf.

Ryga, George. 1970. *The Ecstasy of Rita Joe.* Vancouver: Talon Books.

Slipperjack, Ruby. 1987. *Honour the Sun.* Winnipeg: Pemmican Publications.

Stevenson, Winona, et al. 1993. "Peekiskwetan." *Commentaries/Commentaires Canadian Journal of Women and the Law/Revue Femmes et Droit* 6.

FOUR

Settler Colonialism in Canada
Making "Indian" Women Disappear

Mary Eberts, Shelagh Day and Sharon McIvor

THIS CHAPTER EXAMINES CANADA'S USE of discrimination against women under the Indian Act in an effort to reduce, and eventually eliminate, the population of "Indians," whose very existence challenged Canada's assertion of sovereignty over land once occupied and cared for by Indigenous Peoples. This discrimination started at Confederation and was a feature of the settler colonization of what is now Canada. The discrimination continued even after Canada adopted its own rights legislation and adhered to international covenants forbidding sex discrimination. It has not yet fully ended, despite vigorous litigation and law reform efforts over the last fifty years on the part of Indian women and their families. As Canada contemplates how it can bring into effect the United Nations Declaration on the Rights of Indigenous Peoples, the time has come for it to stop resisting the end of sex discrimination in the Indian Act, and to provide redress for women and their families who have lost their communities and cultures because of it.

SETTLER COLONIALISM SHAPES THE INDIAN ACT

Settler colonialism is a process in which settlers (Veracini 2010, 53) establish residency and multi-generation families, and engage in activities like farming, building, and resource development, which assert possession over the land. We see this purpose in the wording of section 91(24) of the Constitution Act (1867), which gives Canada jurisdiction over "Indians and lands reserved for Indians." In *Daniels v. Canada*

(2016, paras. 4–5), the majority of the Supreme Court affirms that the purposes of section 91(24) were "closely related to the expansionist goals of Confederation." It identifies those purposes as "to control Native peoples and communities where necessary, to facilitate the development of the Dominion, to honour the obligations to Natives that the Dominion inherited from Britain" and "eventually to civilize and assimilate Native people" (para. 353).

In order to confirm its sovereignty, title, and jurisdiction, the settler state tolerates no assertion of a right or interest in land by Indigenous Peoples. Indeed, it seeks to eliminate such peoples, either through outright killing, or by various means like assimilation, incarceration and institutionalization, or forceful removal from their traditional land (Veracini 2010, 33, 35, 37, 45). Indigenous Peoples "challenge with their very presence the basic legitimacy of the settler entity" (Veracini 2010, 33), and the settler state strives to establish that the land over which it asserted sovereignty was indeed terra nullius: land occupied by no one (Encyclopedia Virginia 1493; Holy See Press Office 2023; McNeil 2016; Tomchuk 2023).

The relationship between settler colonialism and genocide is inextricable. The Convention on the Prevention and Punishment of the Crime of Genocide (United Nations 1948) defines genocide as

> any of the following acts committed with intent to destroy, in whole or in part, a national, ethnical, racial, or religious group as such: killing members of the group; causing serious bodily or mental harm to members of the group; deliberately inflicting on the group conditions of life calculated to bring about its physical destruction in whole or in part; imposing measures intended to prevent births within the group; forcibly transferring children of the group to another group.

Rafael Lemkin, originator of the term genocide, explored the "constitutive and inherent" relationship between genocide and settler colonialism (Docker 2004, 3). In his unpublished writings he focused on the genocide perpetrated by English, French, and post-independence Americans: dispossessing Indigenous Peoples of their land, removal and deportation, removal or stealing of children, disease through overcrowding on reservations with inadequate food and medicine, self-destruction brought about by introduction of liquor, curtailing and deprivation of legal rights, and cultural genocide (Docker 2004, 9–14).

The Indian Act, a feature of Canadian law since Confederation, has been the repository of authority for the actions of the state — described in the Convention on the Prevention and Punishment of the Crime of Genocide and by Lemkin — designed to control, reduce, or eliminate the Indigenous population. The Indian Act is the largest single erasure of Indigenous Peoples in the history of Canada.

When it passed the Indian Act, Canada created a world it could define and tightly control. Canada created rules about who would be recognized as "Indian" (or, in other words, have Indian Status), and only those persons would participate in the world created by the Indian Act. Any benefits provided under the Act, like the right to inhabit reserve land, were available only to "Indians." Through the Indian Act, Canada created a small "official" Indigenous population that could be controlled and gradually eliminated through the rules about who would receive status.

THE INDIAN ACT: PATRIARCHAL AND COLONIAL DOMINANCE

Since Confederation, the Act identified the father as the only parent who could confer status on a child (*An Act providing for the organisation of the Department of the Secretary of State of Canada, and for the Management of Indian and Ordnance Lands* 1868, s. 15). This is one of the two most powerful types of sex discrimination in the Indian Act. That the Indian Act is legislation that embodies and enforces patriarchy has significant implications.

In a patriarchy, women's sexuality and reproductive capacity are not under their own control (Lerner 1986, 77). Their bodies and sexual services are at the disposal of their kin group, their husbands, and their fathers (80). The imposition of patriarchy thus totally undercut the social structures of those Indigenous Peoples organized on matriarchal principles, while it imposed Victorian patriarchy on all Indigenous Peoples, privileging Indian men, and it imposed patriarchal norms for relations between the powerful state and dispossessed Indigenous people. In settler Canada, white dominance over Indigenous Peoples is symbolized and accompanied by the exposure of Indigenous women to sexual assault from white men.

Sherene Razack (2016, 293) argues that the targeting of Indigenous women for sexualized violence is part of the "deeply embedded and systematized devaluing of Indigenous life in settler societies." In

Razack's analysis, Indigenous women suffer not only the dehumanization and disposability characterizing settler attitudes toward Indigenous people (293). In addition, sexual violence against them sends powerful messages about the hegemony of the white "race," and the ability of white men to assert dominance over Indigenous men and women. The violability of Indigenous women symbolically represents, as well, the vulnerability of lands once occupied by Indigenous Peoples. She states, "The visible signs of sexualized violence make it clear that Indigenous women are collectively sexually violable and that Indigenous lands are occupied" (293).

VOLUNTARY AND INVOLUNTARY ASSIMILATION

Enfranchisement

The first method of assimilation tried by Canada was enfranchisement, introduced before Confederation, and brought forward into post-Confederation Canada in 1869 (*An Act for the gradual enfranchisement of Indians* 1869). The purpose of enfranchisement was "to encourage the progress of Civilization among the Indian tribes of this province and the gradual removal of all legal distinctions between them and Her Majesty's Canadian subjects" (*Gradual Civilization Act* 1857, preamble). An enfranchised person would no longer have Indian Status.

Enfranchisement was primarily intended for men, although for a period voluntary enfranchisement was also available to single women. It was exploited by Indian agents, whose administration of it was declared illegal in the case of *Hele v. Attorney General of Canada* (2020).

A committee would examine a male candidate for enfranchisement to determine his language capacity, education, and moral character. Enfranchisement entitled a man to occupy a portion of reserve land to which he would ultimately receive title (*Gradual Civilization Act* 1857, III, IV). The wife and children of the enfranchised man were also enfranchised, but without their consent, and without the kind of inquiry into their capacity for "civilization" that men experienced (*Gradual Civilization Act* 1857, VIII). In 1951, the Indian Act added a provision that upon her marriage to a non-Indian, a woman could be enfranchised (*Indian Act* 1951b, s.108 (2)). Enfranchisement was unnecessary, given that women lost status upon such a marriage, but Canada imposed it nonetheless.

Kathleen Jamieson (1978) reports that between 1965 and 1975, 5,035 women and children were enfranchised following the woman's marriage to a non-status male. In the same period, there were 228 voluntary enfranchisements. That is, 95 percent of enfranchisements were of women who had no choice. In the period of 1973 to 1976, 99.32 percent of all enfranchisements were of women who had no choice. Following 1975, Jamieson notes, the Governor in Council ceased issuing enfranchisement orders in respect of women who married non-Indian men but continued to deprive them of status without taking the extra step of enfranchising them (65).

The enfranchisement of men had little success in lowering the number of male Indians because of opposition from Indigenous nations (Kirkby 2018, 3, 13–14, 17, 33–34). The failure of male enfranchisement means that Canada's principal statutory means of reducing the number of Status Indians has been discrimination against women and their children. One form of that discrimination has been mentioned already: the right of the male parent, but not the female, to confer Indian Status on a child. The only exception in the Act to the statutory preference for the status male as sole conveyor of status was that a status woman who had a child outside marriage could give the child status, as long as no one came forward to prove to the Registrar that the father was not a Status Indian (*Indian Act* S.C. 1951 c. 29, s.11(e)).

Loss of Indian Status Upon Marriage

The second powerful kind of discrimination against women was introduced by an 1869 statute: an Indian woman marrying anyone other than an Indian as recognized by the Indian Act would cease to be an Indian within the meaning of the Act. No children of that marriage would be considered Indian. Any Indian woman marrying an Indian of any other tribe or body of Indians would cease to be a member of her natal band and would become a member of her husband's band (*An Act for the gradual enfranchisement of Indians* 1869, s.6).

As witnesses before the Penner Committee (House of Commons 1982) proclaimed in 1982, this exile literally erased women's identity. They told MPs: "I am not recognized as an Indian person and I am not recognized as a white person," and "We are literally wiped off the face of the earth" (65).

COLONIZATION IN THE AGE OF RIGHTS

In the 1960s and 1970s, section 12(1)(b) (*Indian Act* S.C. 1951, c. 29) was the version of the statutory provision removing status from a woman who married a non-status male, and providing that the couple's children could not have status.

Mary Two-Axe Earley, a Kanien'kehá:ka woman from Kahnawa:ke (Brown 2017), had lost her status upon marriage to a non-status man. She founded Indian Rights for Indian Women in Quebec and co-founded its national counterpart. Mary Two-Axe Earley, and other women from the Kahnawa:ke reserve, presented a brief urging the repeal of section 12(1)(b) to the Royal Commission on the Status of Women, appointed by Canada in 1967. In its final report, in 1970, the commission recommended the repeal of section 12(1)(b) (Royal Commission on the Status of Women in Canada 1970).

The Canadian Bill of Rights

At around that time, Jeannette Corbiere Lavell, an Anishinaabekwe from Wikwemikong, and Yvonne Bedard, a Haudenosaunee woman from Six Nations, filed separate challenges to section 12(1)(b) of the Indian Act, which were heard together in the Supreme Court of Canada in 1973. Both had lost status because of marriage to non-status men and had been banished from their communities. In their challenges, they relied upon the guarantee of "equality before the law" in section 1(b) of the Canadian Bill of Rights (1960), which had been enacted by the Diefenbaker government to apply to federal statutes. Indian leadership was arrayed against the women. One of the main reasons was that they feared that the women's success might result in removal of the Indian Act, the link between Indians and the treaties that Canada's White Paper (Department of Indian Affairs and Northern Development 1969) had proposed to get rid of a short while before (Cardinal 1977; Weaver 1981).

In 1973, the Supreme Court issued a five-to-four judgment against the women. The majority stated that equality before the law under the Bill of Rights means that as long as the Indian Act discriminates against all Status Indian women, there was no inequality before the law (*Attorney General of Canada v. Lavell; Isaac et al. v Bedard* 1973, 1366–1373). However, Justice Laskin stated on behalf of the four dissenting judges that section 12(1)(b) amounted to "statutory excommunication" of Indian women from their communities (1386).

International Human Rights Covenants

International human rights treaties entered into by Canada beginning in the 1970s, particularly the International Covenant on Civil and Political Rights (ICCPR) (1966) and the Convention on the Elimination of All Forms of Discrimination Against Women (CEDAW) (1979) have been relied on by those protesting women's loss of status upon marriage. Both have an Optional Protocol (First Optional Protocol to International Covenant on Civil and Political Rights 1976; Optional Protocol to the Convention on the Elimination of All Forms of Discrimination against Women [1999]) allowing individuals to complain directly to the UN Human Rights Treaty Body overseeing that treaty, alleging violation of its terms. In addition, Canada is obligated to submit a periodic report to the Treaty Body for review, a process also allowing civil society organizations and individuals to comment on Canada's compliance with the treaty. The Treaty Body issues concluding observations after the review, with recommendations to ensure compliance with the treaty's provisions. The ICCPR is administered by the UN Human Rights Committee and CEDAW by the Committee on the Elimination of Discrimination Against Women.

Canada ratified the ICCPR (1966) and its First Optional Protocol in 1976. Sandra Lovelace, a Maliseet woman from the Tobique Reserve in New Brunswick, was the first to file a complaint about sex discrimination in the Indian Act under the ICCPR. Ms. Lovelace complained in 1977 that section 12(1)(b) of the Indian Act violated her right to equality on the basis of sex and her right to enjoyment of her culture.

Ms. Lovelace had lost her status at marriage to a non-status man, and upon separating from her husband was unable to return to the Tobique Reserve with her non-status children. The Human Rights Committee ruled in July 1981 that her right to equal enjoyment of her culture under Article 27 of the Convention had been violated: as long as section 12(1)(b) continued in effect, it denied her right to live in her community and share her culture with her family and kin (*Sandra Lovelace v. Canada* 1984).

Around the same time as it was signing on to the ICCPR, Canada deliberately excluded the Indian Act from the application of the Canadian Human Rights Act (Revised Statutes of Canada, c. H-6, c.33) passed in 1977. Canada did not make the Human Rights Act applicable to the Indian Act until 2011. Moreover, during this period Canada began its practice of ignoring the many recommendations to end sex discrimination in the Indian Act made by UN Treaty Bodies under several human rights covenants (Human Rights Committee 1999, 2006, 2015; CERD 2007, 2012; CEDAW 2003, 2008, 2015, 2016; Committee on Economic Social and Cultural Rights 2006, 2016; Human Rights Council 2013, 2018) and also the decisions of UN committees on individual complaints (CEDAW 2022b; Human Rights Committee 2019; McIvor and Grismer 2010, 2019; *Sandra Lovelace v. Canada* 1984; United Nations Human Rights Committee 2022).

PASSAGE OF BILL C-31

Canada's ratification of the Convention on the Elimination of All Forms of Discrimination Against Women (CEDAW) in 1981 and the coming into force of section 15 of the Canadian Charter of Rights and Freedoms in 1985, propelled Canada into revision of the Indian Act. Bill C-31, passed in 1985 (*Indian Act* 1985), no longer included provisions allowing enfranchisement of men or women. Nor did it include provisions removing status from an Indian woman for marrying a non-status male. However, Bill C-31 did not make women fully equal to their male counterparts or address all the inequities in the previous Indian Act. It also introduced new forms of sex discrimination.

It did this by ending the system where there was only one kind of legislated status and introducing a new system with two kinds of status, one superior to the other. Status under s.6(1)(a) of Bill C-31 (full status) was available to all those (mostly male) Indians and their descendants who already had full status prior to April 17, 1985. Status under section 6(1)(c) of Bill C-31 was provided to women whose status had been denied, or whose status had been removed because of marriage to a non-Indian, under the previous legislation. This woman and the non-status father of her child would have offspring with "half status," unable to transmit that status unless he or she parented with another status person.

Bill C-31 introduced the requirement that a child needs to have two status parents in order to acquire status under the Act. Canada held this out as being gender neutral, because it ended the requirement to have a male status parent to be eligible for status, and it applied to women and men equally. However, the requirement has differential effects because of the previous history of discrimination. The woman who had had her status restored by section 6(1)(c) of Bill C-31 had a spouse with no status. Through her reinstatement, her children became children with one Status Indian parent. Prior to this legislation, a wife who acquired status through marriage had been unable to pass status on to the couple's children, because of the general rule that status could pass only from a male parent. But since the non-Indian wife of a male Indian already had full status under section 6(1)(a), Bill C-31 ensured that she was considered an Indian parent and could pass on status. Consequently, the couple comprised of a status male and the wife who had acquired status through marriage could, as two status parents, pass status to their children. The woman restored to status and her husband with no status would not so qualify.

The corollary of the two-parent rule is the provision in section 6(2) of Bill C-31 that a person with only one status parent has status for her or his lifetime, but they cannot pass status on to a child unless the other parent of that child also has status. This rule has become known as "the second-generation cut-off." The cut-off results from the lesser kind of status possessed by the child of a woman restored to status under section 6(1)(c).

One further consequence of the two-parent rule is that the ability of the woman to pass status to a child she had had out of wedlock was no longer included in the Act. This was the only benefit she had had under the former legislation.

Under the two-parent rule the father is still in a controlling position with respect to conferring status. Although it is relatively easy to determine who is the natural mother of a child, establishing the identity of the father is more difficult. By withholding consent to being identified as the father, a man could prevent the child from being registered with two status parents. The two-parent rule also prejudices the child of a woman who feels constrained not to reveal the identity of the father, as in cases of incest or rape, or is unable to do so, as in cases of gang rape.

Bill C-31 brought about an immediate increase in the population of Status Indians, which exceeded predictions. By December 31, 2000, 114,512 people had gained Indian Status based on Bill C-31 (Furi and Wherrett 1996/2003, 5). In the five years after 1985, the Status Indian population rose by 19 percent as a result of the amendments, with women representing the majority of those who had gained or regained status (5). In 2000, registrants under Bill C-31 made up 17 percent of the Indian Register (5).

Actual experience and long-term projections, however, indicate that the result of Bill C-31 will be a decline in the number of Status Indians. From 1985 to 1999, thirteen thousand children were born to mothers with only 6(2) status and no other Indian parent. These children did not have the right to be registered as Status Indians (Gehl 2013). Government projections done before another amendment to the Indian Act made in 2010 show that by 2029 there will be 93,800 persons born on reserve who will be ineligible for registration, in contrast to about 4,300 in 2004. Persons born off reserve not entitled to registration will rise in 2029 to 144,800 from about 61,500 in 2004. Those disentitled to registration are expected to begin to outnumber those entitled to registration in about three generations and around the end of the fifth generation, no further children will be born with entitlement to registration (Hurley and Simeone 2010, 5).

BANGING ON A CLOSED DOOR: LITIGATION AFTER 1985

A tide of litigation challenged the inadequacies and inequities of Bill C-31. Madam Justice Masse of the Quebec Superior Court said that Canada preferred "to wait for the courts to rule on a case-by-case basis before acting and for their judgments to gradually force amendments so that statutes are finally consistent with the Constitution" (*Descheneaux v. Canada* 2015, 239).

The first court challenge to Bill C-31 was brought by Sharon McIvor of the Lower Nicola Band in British Columbia and her son Jacob Grismer. In 1985, McIvor applied unsuccessfully for s.6(1)(a) (i.e., "full") status under the revised Indian Act. Sharon and her brother, Ernie McIvor, had each married a non-status person and had a child, and each child married a non-status person and parented children with that person. Application of s.6(1)(a) of the Indian Act to Ernie and his wife ensured that both had status and could confer "full" status on their son. Because McIvor had lost her status upon marriage to a non-status man and regained it under s.6(1)(c), her son was the child of only one Status Indian and had the lesser kind of status conferred by s.6(2). Grismer could not pass status to the child he had with his non-status wife, whereas his cousin, Ernie's child, was able to do so.

In 1986, McIvor and Grismer began an action in the Supreme Court of BC to challenge the refusal of 6(1)(a) status to women who had married non-status men and their direct descendants who claimed entitlement through the female line of descent. This challenge was successful. Justice Carol Ross concluded that the registration provisions in the 1985 Act continue to prefer descendants who trace their Indian ancestry along the paternal line over those who trace their ancestry through the maternal line. The provisions thus continue the very discrimination that the amendments were intended to eliminate. She found that the amendments concerning transmission of status violate section 15 of the Charter as well as section 28, which guarantees the equality of men and women (*McIvor v. The Registrar, Indian and Northern Affairs Canada* 2007).

When ruling on Canada's appeal of this decision, the Court of Appeal of British Columbia acknowledged that there had been a violation of section 15 of the Charter but confined it very narrowly. The Court of Appeal did not compare descent through the female line with descent through the male line, as Justice Ross had done. Rather, it compared the treatment of Grismer under the Act with that of a child whose mother and grandmother had both received status by marrying a status male — the "double mother rule," which had only been a feature of the Indian Act for a short time. A child affected by the double mother rule under the previous Act would receive status only until the age of twenty-one, but under Bill C-31 they would receive status under s.6(1)(a) and keep it for life. That child could thus confer status on a child even if the child did not have another status parent. Grismer had status under s.6(2) of the Indian Act, and no status wife, and thus could not confer status at all. The Supreme Court of Canada denied McIvor and Grismer leave to appeal that same year (*McIvor v. Canada* 2009/2010).

In response to the Court of Appeal decision, Canada introduced Bill C-3 (*Gender Equity in Indian Registration Act* 2010). This bill kept the 6(1)(a) and 6(1)(c) hierarchy, but it gave children of women restored to status under s.6(1)(c) the ability to pass status on to a child even as the only status parent. Canada reported that 37,000 newly entitled individuals were registered from 2011 to 2017 through the implementation of Bill C-3 (Government of Canada 2018).

Bill C-3 was based on the Court of Appeal's narrow view about the basic problem. McIvor and Grismer decided to pursue at the UN Human Rights Committee a remedy for the core sex discrimination against the maternal line of descent still entrenched in the 6(1)(a)–6(1)(c) hierarchy. They filed their petition in 2010 (McIvor and Grismer 2009/2010), arguing that Bill C-31 violated their right to Indigenous identity and the right to enjoy their culture contrary to Article 27 of the ICCPR, and also the right to be free from sex discrimination contrary to Article 26.

In January 2019, the Committee held that despite revisions to the Indian Act, it still incorporated a distinction based on sex that was not founded on objective and reasonable grounds. This continuing distinction affected the right of McIvor and Grismer to enjoy their own culture together with other members of their group, free from sex discrimination (Human Rights Committee 2019).

Loss of the right to enjoy one's culture together with other members of their group was the basis of the Human Rights Committee decision in *Lovelace* in July 1981. That same human rights violation was found by the Human Rights Committee in *McIvor* in 2019. Despite adherence to international human rights instruments, and the entrenchment of its own Charter of Rights, Canada was still legislating and vigorously defending the deprivation of culture — a hallmark of the settler state and also of genocide.

In August 2015, Justice Masse of the Quebec Superior Court rendered a decision in a case brought by several plaintiffs who experienced sex discrimination that had not been remedied by Bill C-31 (*Descheneaux v. Canada* 2015). One of the plaintiffs, Stephane Descheneaux, had been denied status because his Indian lineage came through his Indian grandmother, who had lost her status when she married a non-status male. Had his grandparent been male, he would have had status and been able to confer it on his wife, children, and grandchildren. Justice Masse ruled in his favour and did not take the very narrow approach to the problem that Justice Groberman had done in the McIvor case.

Another plaintiff, Susan Yantha, was born out of wedlock to a Status Indian father. Under the pre-1985 Act, the father of a child born out of wedlock could confer status on his son, but not his daughter. Because of this sex discrimination, neither Yantha nor her daughter Tammy had status. Although this difference in treatment between male and female children was well known before passage of Bill C-31 (*Martin v. Chapman* 1983), the bill had not addressed it. Justice Masse found that this differentiation between the male and female children born out of wedlock to a status male father was contrary to the Charter.

The 1994 application for status of Dr. Lynn Gehl, an Algonquin Anishinaabekwe, was denied because the identity of her paternal grandfather had never been confirmed. Since only his mother had status, her father had status under section 6(2) of the Act and could not transmit it to Gehl because her mother was non-status. The Ontario Court of Appeal ruled in 2017 that the evidence presented by Gehl was sufficient to establish the Indian Status of her paternal grandfather (and thus the full status of her own father), although she had not been able to provide her grandfather's name. The Court decided that the Indian Act did not require Gehl to provide the name, and the Registrar had been incorrect in requiring her to do so (*Gehl v. Canada* 2017).

After the *Descheneaux* and *Gehl* cases, Canada introduced Bill S-3 (*An Act to amend the Indian Act in response to the Superior Court of Quebec decision in Descheneaux c. Canada* 2017). Bill S-3, as initially drafted by Canada, left in place the 6(1)(a)–6(1)(c) hierarchy, and still did not put Indian women on the same footing as their male counterparts with respect to eligibility for status and transmission of status.

An amendment to the bill introduced in the Senate was referred to colloquially as the "6(1)(a) all the way" amendment, because it gave full status under s.6(1)(a) to women and their descendants born before C-31 came into effect in 1985. The "6(1)(a) all the way" amendment was accepted by the Senate Committee, chaired by Senator Lillian Dyck, who herself had been affected by sex discrimination in the Act: her father was not a Status Indian and she had to claim her status after 1985. The bill as amended was then adopted by the full Senate.

When the bill with this amendment was sent to the House of Commons, it was voted down by the governing Liberals. However, the proceedings then returned to the Senate, and the Senate refused to back down on its amendment. The government accepted the amendment as long as it did not come into force at the same time as the other provisions of S-3, and only at a time to be decided by Cabinet. The bill's original provisions, responding to the *Gehl* and *Descheneaux* decisions, came into force in December 2017, and the "6(1)(a) all the way" amendment came into effect in August 2019, after a public campaign by First Nations women and their allies.

The 6(1)(a) all the way amendment provides to women and their descendants the same right to status and transmission of status as their male counterparts, with respect to the period 1876 to 1985. Bill S-3 does not cure the discrimination identified by the UN CEDAW Committee in its 2022 decision on the petition of Jeremy Matson. The Committee held that Bill S-3 carries forward the old sex discrimination by denying status, or full status, to matrilineal descendants born or married after 1985 (CEDAW 2022b).

The Parliamentary Budget Officer estimated that 670,000 persons had become newly entitled to status as a result of Bill S-3. He believed that 270,000 of these would actually register, and that they would probably not move back to reserves (Office of the Parliamentary Budget Officer 2017). Indigenous Services Canada estimated the number of women and their descendants benefiting from this amendment at between 270,000 and 450,000 (Government of Canada 2020).

As of January 2023, only about 40,000 people now entitled to status pursuant to Bill S-3 have actually been registered (Indian Act Discrimination Working Group 2023). The Indian Registrar has advised that an additional 57,000 persons who were already registered at the time Bill S-3 was passed have had their status "upgraded," an improvement that might well entitle more of their family members to registration. However, the Registrar has not advised these people of their status upgrades. Unless someone accidentally discovers the status upgrade, having such an improvement is unlikely to be of benefit to that person and their descendants (*Indian Act Discrimination Working Group 2022a*).

The inadequacies of the registration process are notorious and well documented (Indigenous Services Canada 2022a; Standing Senate Committee on Aboriginal Peoples 2022; Indian Act Discrimination Working Group 2022b). It takes from six months to two years, or more, to be registered as a Status Indian, much more time than getting a passport, which requires similar confirmations of identity. The registration process is cumbersome and demanding, and there are many complaints about lost documents, misdirection, and failure to communicate. Canada decides upon the resources allocated to registration and could have ensured that the Indian Registry would have what it needed to handle large numbers of new applications under Bill S-3, but it did not. By retaining a cumbersome and slow registration process, Canada can impede the growth in numbers of Status Indians, despite the changes to legislation that have removed legal barriers to registration.

In December 2022, Canada introduced Bill C-38 (*An Act to amend the Indian Act [New Registration Amendments]* 2022), to amend the Indian Act in response to a Charter challenge filed on behalf of members of the Haida Nation whose ancestors had involuntarily lost status because of the enfranchisement of their husband or father (Stefanovich 2021). Bill C-38 also addresses the transfer of women from their natal band to that of their husbands when they married a man from another band. These legislative corrections are both long overdue. This bill, however, has only passed first reading—the second reading is in progress.

Bill C-38 does not remove the bar to compensation that has been included in Bill C-31, Bill C-3, and Bill S-3 (*An Act to amend the Indian Act in response to the Superior Court of Quebec decision in Descheneaux c. Canada* 2017, ss. 10-10.1). Canada has explicitly barred any recovery of damages by women and their children who experienced the statutory excommunication of the Indian Act. Canada has provided financial settlements with respect to forced attendance at residential school and day schools, the child seizures during the "Sixties Scoop" by child welfare authorities, underfunded child welfare services (Choi 2022; Crown–Indigenous Relations and Northern Affairs Canada 2020, 2021a, 2021b, 2023a; Canadian Press 2023), and impure water supplies to reserves (Indigenous Services Canada 2022b). Yet Canada refuses to contemplate compensation for the intergenerational life-altering deprivations of status it has inflicted on women, ignoring the fact that it is a party to treaties that require it to provide effective remedies for discrimination, including compensation. José Francisco Calí Tzay, the UN Special Rapporteur on the Rights of Indigenous Peoples, in his March 2023 end of mission statement called on Canada to "create an affordable, reliable, timely, and accessible remedy to compensate those that have suffered the effects of discrimination" (McLeod 2023; Calí Tzay 2023).

Bill C-38 also leaves in place the second-generation cut-off and the two-parent rule, which extend the sex discrimination beyond 1985 and create a final extinction plan. Special Representative Claudette Dumont-Smith noted that the second-generation cut-off was the issue of paramount concern in her consultations among First Nations regarding Bill S-3 (Dumont-Smith 2019). The second-generation cut-off and the two-parent rule, she wrote, will see the gradual elimination of persons eligible to be registered as an Indian, with some communities feeling this impact in the next generation while most First Nations communities, regardless of location, will feel this impact within the next four generations. The end result, in the not-so-distant future, is that some communities will no longer have any registered Indians, or the number of registered Indians will have declined significantly. Since the government's funding allocations for services and programs are based on numbers of Status Indians, the viability, and the existence, of First Nations communities is threatened. So, too, is their ability to continue residing on reserve land.

THE WAY FORWARD

The United Nations Declaration on the Rights of Indigenous Peoples (UNDRIP) (2007) was adopted by the General Assembly on September 13, 2007, after decades of developmental work in which Indigenous leaders from Canada were deeply involved. In May 2016, Canada announced that it was accepting the Declaration unreservedly, reversing its earlier position (Fontaine 2016). In 2021, Canada passed the United Nations Declaration on the Rights of Indigenous Peoples Act (UNDA), the preamble of which states that "the rights and principles affirmed in the Declaration constitute the minimum standards for the survival, dignity and well-being of Indigenous peoples of the world, and must be implemented in Canada."

Article 8 of the Declaration (2007) provides that "Indigenous peoples and individuals have the right not to be subjected to forced assimilation or destruction of their culture." It requires that states provide effective mechanisms for prevention of, and redress for any action which has the aim or effect of depriving them of their integrity as distinct peoples or of their cultural values or ethnic identities; any action which has the aim or effect of dispossessing them of their lands, territories or resources; any form of forced population transfer which has the aim or effect of violating or undermining any of their rights; and any form of forced assimilation or integration.

In its draft Action Plan for the implementation of UNDRIP (Government of Canada 2023), required by the UNDA, Canada does not acknowledge its imposition of forced assimilation or the need to provide redress for the harms it has caused. In the draft plan, Canada recognizes that "the Indian Act is a colonial-era law designed to exert control over the affairs of First Nations, and as such, the Act will never be fully aligned with" UNDA. It states that for Canada's laws to fulfil the UNDA, the Indian Act must be repealed. The plan announces that "the government is seeking to make the Act's registration and band membership provisions more consistent with UNDA, until a clear consensus on a way forward on comprehensive change or the Act's repeal is possible."

It plans to "co-develop a collaborative consultation process on a suite of broader reform, relating to registration and band membership issues, prior to any transition away from the Indian Act" (22).

This is an exceedingly mild and self-forgiving description of the Indian Act and of Canada's settler colonialism. It may also be signalling that Canada is now prepared to give up using the Indian Act as a way of limiting the Indigenous population so that it will not, by its very existence, cast doubt on the validity of Canada's claims to sovereignty.

Indeed, it could be said that Canada has achieved about as much validation of its sovereignty claim as it can. In *Tsilhqot'in Nation v. British Columbia* (2014, para. 69), the Supreme Court of Canada said that the doctrine of terra nullius has never applied in Canada. It describes Aboriginal title to land as coming from the fact of Aboriginal occupancy of land at the time of European sovereignty. In *Haida Nation v. British Columbia (Minister of Forests)* (2004), Chief Justice McLachlin says,

> The process of reconciliation flows from the Crown's duty of honourable dealing towards Aboriginal peoples, which arises in turn from the Crown's *assertion of sovereignty over an Aboriginal people and de facto control of land and resources that were formerly in the control of that people.* (para. 32, emphasis added)

The italicized phrase represents a description of what has actually taken place in Canada: *assertion* of sovereignty and *de facto* control of land and resources.

Since the 1973 Supreme Court decision in *Calder* (*Calder et al. v. Attorney General of British Columbia* 1973) recognizing Aboriginal title, Canada has been negotiating comprehensive claim or self-government agreements, largely with Indigenous nations whose land had not been previously covered by a treaty. Canada reports that its first twenty-nine comprehensive claim or self-government agreements cover over 40 percent of Canada's land mass of 9,984,670 square kilometres. These instruments, by and large, are constructed so as to allow Canada to substantially fulfil its goals of furthering development and access to resources (Crown–Indigenous Relations and Northern Affairs Canada 2023b, 1–2).

As it contemplates leaving the Indian Act behind, however, Canada gives no sign of willingness to assume the burden of repairing the damage done by its use of the Indian Act as an instrument of colonization.

This burden should not be left unattended to and should not be left to others. Not only has Canada's use of the Indian Act deprived generations of Indian women and their descendants of their identity culture and community, Canada's way of changing the Indian Act to remove sex discrimination has emphasized a dichotomy between the individual rights of the woman and the group rights of the nation.

Canada's argument before the Court of Appeal in *McIvor* was repeated by Justice Groberman as a reason why very limited restoration of women and their children to status was "pressing and substantial" under section 1 of the Charter: "There were widespread concerns that the influx [of reinstated persons] might overwhelm the resources available to bands and that it might serve to dilute the cultural integrity of existing First Nation groups" (*McIvor v. Canada* 2009/2010, 129).

This position turns the truth on its head, ignoring Canada's long history of despoiling the culture of Indigenous Peoples through residential schools, sex discrimination, criminal prohibitions on cultural practices, and many other means, and its persistent underfunding of First Nations' basic needs.

Moreover, the position implies that the right to self-determination, collective rights, and cultural integrity are in competition with the individual rights of First Nations women. By contrast, the UN Human Rights Committee considering the cases of Sandra Lovelace, Sharon McIvor and Jacob Grismer recognized their right under the ICCPR to be included in the collectivity, and to practise and enjoy their culture in common with others and on an equal basis.

In its new General Comment, the Committee on the Elimination of Discrimination Against Women (CEDAW 2022a, para.19) has stated:

> Collective rights are indispensable for the existence, well-being and integral development of Indigenous Peoples, including Indigenous women and girls. The individual rights of Indigenous women and girls should never be neglected or violated in the pursuit of collective or group interests, as respect for both dimensions of their human rights is essential.

Many women and First Nations share the goal of establishing self-government. They recognize the harm that sex discrimination has done by reducing the numbers of Status Indians, to the point where the existence of First Nations is threatened in the not-so-distant future. And as

Dr. Pam Palmater (2011, 54) states, "There can be no rebuilding of our Nations without loyal citizens to carry forward our identity, culture, practices, traditions, beliefs, laws, and customs for future generations."

There already exists a way of upholding both the interests of women seeking restoration to status and those of First Nations. That is to restore status to the women and their families, ensuring that the Indian Act or any successor scheme will not use sex discrimination as a means of limiting the recognized Indigenous population. First Nations will need adequate resources to deal with the increase in numbers and associated dislocations such as the need for more housing, cultural integration, education, and other services. Importantly, women and their families must receive redress for the long exile from their communities, with all of the practical and spiritual consequences such exile entails. The Native Women's Association of Canada has described the costs to women as "immeasurable" in psychological, economic, social, cultural, and political terms, not to mention the denial of hundreds of millions of dollars in lost federal programs and services, loss of their share in band assets, and loss of homes and property interests on reserves (House of Commons 1982, 58, 17).

This proposed approach recognizes that Canada has created these problems and should not leave women or First Nations to deal with them without support (Government of Canada 2023, 10[ii]). The women thus restored would, as contemplated by Indian Rights for Indian Women, be present and able to participate in the development of self-government and its institutions, the protection of the land, and the restoration of culture. Women will not be excommunicated from their communities and First Nations will not be driven out of existence by statutory rules enacted to serve the discredited process of colonization.

REFERENCES

Case Law/Legislation

An Act for the gradual enfranchisement of Indians, the better management of Indian affairs, and to extend the provisions of the Act 31st Victoria, Statutes of Canada 1869, c.6

An Act providing for the organisation of the Department of the Secretary of State of Canada, and for the Management of Indian and Ordnance Lands, Statutes of Canada, 1868, c.42, s.15

An Act to amend the Indian Act, Statutes of Canada 1884, c.27, s.3
An Act to amend the Indian Act. Statutes of Canada 1922, c.26, s.1
An Act to amend the Indian Act in response to the Superior Court of Quebec decision in Descheneaux c. Canada (Procureur general). 2017. Statutes of Canada c.25 "Bill S-3"
An Act to amend the Indian Act (New Registration Amendments). 2022. Bill C-38 1st reading
Attorney General of Canada v. Lavell; Isaac et al. v Bedard. 1973. Supreme Court Reports 1849
Calder et al. v. Attorney General of British Columbia. 1973. 3 SCR 313
Canadian Bill of Rights, Statutes of Canada. 1960. c.44, Revised Statutes of Canada 1970, app.III
Canadian Human Rights Act. 1976–77. Revised Statutes of Canada chapter H-6, c.33 s.67. First passed by Statutes of Canada, 1976-77, c.33
Committee on Economic Social and Cultural Rights. 2006. *Concluding Observations of the Committee on Economic, Social and Cultural Rights*, E/C.12/CAN/CO/4 and E/C.12/CAN/CO/5. https://www.refworld.org/docid/45377fa30.html.
___. 2016. *Concluding Observations on the 6th Periodic Report of Canada*, E/C.12/CAN/CO/6. https://digitallibrary.un.org/record/831868?ln=en.
Constitution Act. 1867. United Kingdom, 30&31 Victoria, c.3
Daniels v. Canada (Indian Affairs and Northern Development). 2016. Supreme Court of Canada 12 (CanLII)
Descheneaux v. Canada. 2015. QCCS 3555
Gehl v. Canada (Attorney General). 2017. ONCA 319 (Court of Appeal) reversing Gehl v. Attorney General of Canada 2015 ONSC 3401
Gender Equity in Indian Registration Act. 2010. Statutes of Canada c.18 "Bill C-3"
Gradual Civilization Act. 1857. *An Act to Encourage the Gradual Civilization of the Indian Tribes in the Province and to amend the Laws respecting Indians*, c. XXVI
Haida Nation v. British Columbia (Minister of Forests). 2004. 3 SCR 511
Hele v. Attorney General of Canada. 2020. QCCS 2406
Human Rights Committee. 1999. *Concluding Observations of the Human Rights Committee: Canada.* CCPR/C/79/Add.105. refworld.org/docid/3df378764.html.
___. 2006. *Concluding Observations of the Human Rights Committee: Canada*, CCPR/C/CAN/CO/5. refworld.org/docid/453777a50.html.
___. 2015. *Concluding Observations on the 6th Periodic Report of Canada*, C/CAN/CO/6. digitallibrary.un.org/record/831868?ln=en.
___. 2019. "Views Adopted by the Committee under Article 5 (4) of the Optional Protocol, Concerning Communication No. 2728/2016." digitallibrary.un.org/record/3979204?ln=en.
Human Rights Council. 2013. "Report of the Working Group on the Universal Periodic Review, Canada, A/HRC/24/11." https://www.right-docs.org/doc/a-hrc-24-11/.
___. 2018. "Report of the Working Group on the Universal Periodic Review, Canada, A/HRC/39/11." http://daccess-ods.un.org/access.nsf/Get?Open&DS=A/HRC/24/11&Lang=E
Indian Act. 1985. Revised Statutes of Canada, c. I-5, Originally passed as An Act to amend the Indian Act, S.C. 1985, c. 27 ("Bill C-31")

Indian Act. 1951a. Revised Statutes of Canada 1951, c.I-5
Indian Act. 1951b. An Act respecting Indians, S.C. 1951.c.29 s.1
Martin v. Chapman. 1983. 1 SCR 365
McIvor v. Canada (Registrar of Indian and Northern Affairs). 2009/2010. BCCA, application for leave to appeal dismissed SCC Case Information Docket 33201
McIvor v. The Registrar, Indian and Northern Affairs Canada. 2007. British Columbia Supreme Court 827, BCJ 2569
Sharon McIvor and Jacob Grismer. 2010. "Communication Submitted for Consideration under the First Optional Protocol to the International Covenant on Civil and Political Rights." povertyandhumanrights.org/wp-content/uploads/2011/08/McIvorApplicantsPetition1.pdf.
Sharon McIvor and Jacob Grismer. 2019. "Petitioner Submission Regarding Implementation by Canada of the 11 January 2019 Decision of the Committee Concerning the Petition of Sharon McIvor and Jacob Grismer (CCPR/C/124/D/2020/2010)." povertyandhumanrights.org/wp-content/uploads/2022/05/Petitioners-Submission-Follow-up-Process-June-15-2021.pdf.
Parliament of Canada. 2022. *An Act to amend the Criminal Code (sterilization procedures)* First Reading.
Tsilhqot'in Nation v. British Columbia. 2014. Supreme Court of Canada 44 (CanLII) or 2014 SCC 44 (CanLII)
United Nations Declaration on the Rights of Indigenous Peoples Act, Statutes of Canada, 2021, c. 14
United Nations Human Rights Committee. 2022. "Follow-Up Progress Report on Individual Communications CCPR/C/134/4." https://digitallibrary.un.org/record/3988177?ln=en.

International Covenants, Decisions and Observations

Convention on the Elimination of All Forms of Discrimination against Women, G.A. res. 34/180, 34 U.N. GAOR Supp. (No. 46) at 193, U.N. Doc. A/34/46, *entered into force* Sept. 3, 1981.
Optional Protocol to the Convention on the Elimination of All Forms of Discrimination against Women, G.A. res. 54/4, annex, 54 U.N. GAOR Supp. (No. 49) at 5, U.N. Doc. A/54/49 (Vol. I) (2000), *entered into force* Dec. 22, 2000. https://www.ohchr.org/en/instruments-mechanisms/instruments/optional-protocol-convention-elimination-all-forms.
CEDAW. 2003. *Concluding observations of the Committee on the Elimination of Discrimination Against Women: Canada*, Report of 28th (13–31 January 2003) and 29th (30 June–18 July 2003) Sessions, A/58/38, at paras 325–389. http://daccess-ods.un.org/access.nsf/Get?Open&DS=A/58/38(SUPP)&Lang=E.
———. 2008. *Concluding observations of the Committee on the Elimination of Discrimination Against Women: Canada*, CEDAW/C/CAN/CO/7, 7 November 2008. https://www.ohchr.org/en/documents/concluding-observations/cedawccanco-concluding-observations.
———. 2016. *Concluding Observations on the Combined 8th and 9th Periodic Reviews of Canada.* CEDAW/C/CAN/CO/8-9. 25 November 2016. https://digitallibrary.un.org/record/3802136?ln=en#record-files-collapse-header.

———. 2015. *Report of the Inquiry Concerning Canada of the Committee on the Elimination of Discrimination Against Women under Article 8 of the Optional Protocol to the Convention on the Elimination of All Forms of Discrimination against Women*, CAN/CEDAW/C/O P.8/CAN/1.30 March 2015. digitallibrary.un.org/record/836103?ln=en.

———. 2022a. *General Recommendation No. 39 on the Rights of Indigenous Women and Girls*, CEDAW/C/GC/39, 26 October 2022. https://www.ohchr.org/en/documents/general-comments-and-recommendations/general-recommendation-no39-2022-rights-indigeneous

———. 2022b. *Views Adopted by the Committee under Article 7 (3) of the Optional Protocol, Concerning Communication No. 68/2014*, 11 March 2022. [Matson]. https://digitallibrary.un.org/record/3968023/files/CEDAW_C_81_D_68_2014-EN.pdf?ln=en

International Covenant on Civil and Political Rights. G.A. res. 2200A (XXI), 21 U.N. GAOR Supp. (No. 16) at 52, U.N. Doc. A/6316 (1966), 999 U.N.T.S. 171, *entered into force* Mar. 23, 1976. https://www.ohchr.org/en/instruments-mechanisms/instruments/international-covenant-civil-and-political-rights.

First Optional Protocol to the International Covenant on Civil and Political Rights. G.A. res. 2200A (XXI), 21 U.N. GAOR Supp. (No. 16) at 59, U.N. Doc. A/6316 (1966), 999 U.N.T.S. 302, *entered into force* March 23, 1976. https://www.ohchr.org/en/instruments-mechanisms/instruments/optional-protocol-international-covenant-civil-and-political.

Human Rights Committee. 1984. *Sandra Lovelace v. Canada*. Communication No. 24/1977, U.N. Doc. CCPR/C/OP/1 at 83.

———. 2010. *Sharon McIvor and Jacob Grismer v. Canada*. Communication Submitted for Consideration under the First Optional Protocol to the International Covenant on Civil and Political Rights, 24 November 2010. povertyandhumanrights.org/wp-content/uploads/2011/08/McIvorApplicantsPetition1.pdf [McIvor].

———. 2019. *Views Adopted by the Committee under Article 5 (4) of the Optional Protocol, Concerning Communication No. 2020/2010*, 20 November 2019. https://tbinternet.ohchr.org/_layouts/15/TreatyBodyExternal/Download.aspx?symbolno=CCPR%2FC%2F124%2FD%2F2020%2F2010&Lang=en [McIvor].

———. 2019. *Petitioner Submission Regarding Implementation by Canada of the 11 January 2019 Decision of the Committee Concerning the Petition of Sharon McIvor and Jacob Grismer* (CCPR/C/124/D/2020/2010), 15 June 2021. https://povertyandhumanrights.org/wp-content/uploads/2022/05/Petitioners-Submission-Follow-up-Process-June-15-2021.pdf [McIvor].

———. 1999. Concluding Observations of the Human Rights Committee: Canada. CCPR/C/79/Add.105, 7 April 1999. https://tbinternet.ohchr.org/_layouts/15/treatybodyexternal/Download.aspx?symbolno=CCPR%2FC%2F79%2FAdd.105&Lang=en.

———. 2006. Concluding Observations of the Human Rights Committee: Canada, CCPR/CAN/C/CO/5, 20 April 2006. https://tbinternet.ohchr.org/_layouts/15/treatybodyexternal/Download.aspx?symbolno=CCPR%2FC%2FCAN%2FCO-%2F5&Lang=en.

___. 2015. Concluding Observations on the 6th Periodic Report of Canada, C/CAN/CO/6, 13 August 2015. https://tbinternet.ohchr.org/_layouts/15/treatybodyexternal/Download.aspx?symbolno=CCPR%2FC%2FCAN%2F-CO%2F6&Lang=en.

International Convention on the Elimination of All Forms of Racial Discrimination, 660 U.N.T.S. 195, *entered into force* Jan. 4, 1969. https://www.ohchr.org/en/instruments-mechanisms/instruments/international-convention-elimination-all-forms-racial.

CERD (Committee on the Elimination of Racial Discrimination). 2007. Concluding Observations of the Committee on the Elimination of Racial Discrimination: Canada, CERD/C/CAN/CO/18, 25 May 2007. https://tbinternet.ohchr.org/_layouts/15/treatybodyexternal/Download.aspx?symbolno=CERD%2FC%2FCAN%2FCO%2F18&Lang=en.

___. 2012. Concluding Observations of the Committee on the Elimination of Racial Discrimination: Canada, CERD/C/CAN/CO/19-20, 04 April 2012. https://www2.ohchr.org/english/bodies/cerd/docs/cerd.c.can.co.19-20.pdf.

International Covenant on Economic, Social and Cultural Rights, G.A. res. 2200A (XXI), 21 U.N.GAOR Supp. (No. 16) at 49, U.N. Doc. A/6316 (1966), 993 U.N.T.S. 3, *entered into force* Jan. 3, 1976. https://www.ohchr.org/en/instruments-mechanisms/instruments/international-covenant-economic-social-and-cultural-rights.

CESCR (Committee on Economic Social and Cultural Rights). 2006. Concluding Observations of the Committee on Economic, Social and Cultural Rights, E/C.12/CAN/CO/4 and E/C.12/CAN/CO/5, 22 May 2006. https://tbinternet.ohchr.org/_layouts/15/treatybodyexternal/Download.aspx?symbolno=E%2FC.12%2FCAN%2FCO%2F4&Lang=en.

___. 2016. Concluding Observations on the 6th Periodic Report of Canada, E/C.12/CAN/CO/6, 23 March 2016. https://tbinternet.ohchr.org/_layouts/15/treatybodyexternal/Download.aspx?symbolno=E%2FC.12%2FCAN%2FCO%2F6&Lang=en.

United Nations Declaration on the Rights of Indigenous Peoples, G.A. Res. 61/295, U.N. Doc. A/RES/47/1 (2007). https://www.un.org/development/desa/indigenouspeoples/wp-content/uploads/sites/19/2018/11/UNDRIP_E_web.pdf.

Calí Tzay, José Francisco, Special Rapporteur on the Rights of Indigenous Peoples, Visit to Canada, 1–10 March, 2023, End of Mission Statement. https://www.ohchr.org/sites/default/files/documents/issues/indigenouspeoples/sr/statements/eom-statement-canada-sr-indigenous-2023-03-10.pdf

Convention Against Torture and Other Cruel, Inhuman or Degrading Treatment or Punishment, G.A. res. 39/46, annex, 39 U.N. GAOR Supp. (No. 51) at 197, U.N. Doc. A/39/51 (1984), *entered into force* June 26, 1987. https://www.ohchr.org/en/instruments-mechanisms/instruments/convention-against-torture-and-other-cruel-inhuman-or-degrading.

Convention on the Prevention and Punishment of the Crime of Genocide, 78 U.N.T.S. 277, *entered into force* Jan. 12, 1951. https://www.un.org/en/genocideprevention/documents/atrocity-crimes/Doc.1_Convention%20on%20the%20Prevention%20and%20Punishment%20of%20the%20Crime%20of%20Genocide.pdf.

Human Rights Council. 2013. Report of the Working Group on the Universal Periodic Review, Canada, A/HRC/24/11, 28 June 2013. https://documents.un.org/doc/undoc/gen/g13/152/42/pdf/g1315242.pdf?token=Gm9Dzfb47tjReTB-5jc&fe=true

———. 2018. Report of the Working Group on the Universal Periodic Review, Canada, A/HRC/39/11, 11 July 2018. ohchr.org/en/documents/reports/report-working-group-universal-periodic-review-canada.

Other

Brown, Wayne. 2017. "Mary Two-Axe Earley: Crusader Fought for Equal Rights for Aboriginal Women." *Windspeaker*, February 18, 2017. windspeaker.com/news/womens-history-month/mary-two-axe-earley-crusader-fought-for-equal-rights-for-aboriginal-women.

Canadian Press. 2023. "'Historic' $2.8B Class-Action Indigenous Court Settlement Approved." *CBC News*, March 9, 2023. cbc.ca/news/canada/british-columbia/indigenous-class-action-settlement- approved-1.6774186.

Cardinal, Harold. 1977. *The Rebirth of Canada's Indians*. Edmonton: Hurtig Publishers.

Choi, Joseph. 2022. "Canada Agrees to $31.5B Settlement Over Treatment of Indigenous Children." *The Hill*, January 4, 2022. https://thehill.com/policy/international/588212-canada-agrees-to-315b-settlement-over-treatment-of-indigenous-children/

Crown–Indigenous Relations and Northern Affairs Canada. 2020. "Are You Part of the Sixties Scoop Class Litigation?" rcaanc-cirnac.gc.ca/eng/1517425414802/1559830290668.

———. 2021a. "Federal Court of Canada Approved the Gottfriedson Settlement Agreement for Former Day Scholars at Indian Residential Schools." October 1, 2021. canada.ca/en/crown-indigenous-relations-northern-affairs/news/2021/10/federal-court-of-canada-approved-the-gottfriedson-settlement-agreement-for-former-day-scholars-at-indian-residential-schools.html.

———. 2021b. "Indian Residential Schools Settlement Agreement." rcaanc-cirnac.gc.ca/eng/1100100015576/1571581687074.

———. 2023a. "Agreement-in-Principle Reached to Resolve Percival Class Action Lawsuit." canada.ca/en/crown-indigenous-relations-northern-affairs/news/2022/12/agreement-in-principle-reached-to-resolve-percival-class-action-lawsuit.html#.

———. 2023b. "Modern Treaties." rcaanc-cirnac.gc.ca/eng/1677073191939/1677073214344.

Department of Indian Affairs and Northern Development. 1969. "Statement of the Government of Canada on Indian Policy (The White Paper)." publications.gc.ca/site/eng/9.700112/publication.html.

Docker, John. 2004. "Raphael Lemkin's History of Genocide and Colonialism." Washington DC: United States Holocaust Memorial Museum, Centre for Advanced Holocaust Studies.

Dumont-Smith, Claudette. 2019. *Annex A: Minister's Special Representative Final Report on the Collaborative Process on Indian Registration, Band Membership and First Nation Citizenship*. rcaanc-cirnac.gc.ca/eng/1561561140999/1568902073183.

Encyclopedia Virginia. 1493. "*Inter caetera* by Pope Alexander VI (May 4, 1493)." encyclopediavirginia.org/entries/inter-caetera-by-pope-alexander-vi-may-4-1493/

Fontaine, Tim. 2016. "Canada Officially Adopts UN Declaration on Rights of Indigenous Peoples." cbc.ca/news/indigenous/canada-adopting-implementing-un-rights- declaration-1.3575272.

Furi, Megan, and Jill Wherrett. 1996/2003. *Indian Status and Band Membership Issues*. Library of Parliament, Parliamentary Research Branch.

Gehl, Lynn. 2013. "Unknown and Unstated Paternity and the Indian Act: Enough Is Enough!" *Journal of the Motherhood Initiative for Research and Community Involvement* 3, 2.

Government of Canada. 2018. "Background on Indian Registration." rcaanc-cirnac.gc.ca/eng/1540405608208/1568898474141.

___. 2020. "The Final Report to Parliament on the Review of S-3: December 2020." sac-isc.gc.ca/eng/1608831631597/1608832913476.

___. 2023. "The Action Plan." justice.gc.ca/eng/declaration/ap-pa/index.html.

Holy See Press Office. 2023. "Joint Statement of the Dicasteries for Culture and Education and for Promoting Integral Human Development on the 'Doctrine of Discovery,' 30.03.2023." https://press.vatican.va/content/salastampa/en/bollettino/pubblico/2023/03/30/230330b.html.

House of Commons. 1982. "Minutes of Proceedings and Evidence of the Subcommittee on Indian Women and the Indian Act of the Standing Committee on Indian Affairs and Northern Development." library.law.utoronto.ca/sites/default/files/media/Issue%202%20%28September%209%2C%201982%29_0.pdf.

Hurley, Mary C., and Tonina Simeone. 2010. *Bill C-3: Gender Equity in Indian Registration Act*. Library of Parliament, Legislative Summary.

Indian Act Discrimination Working Group. 2022a. "Bill S-3: Goals and Timetables, Prepared for Minister of Indigenous Services Canada for Meeting January 21, 2022."

___. 2022b. "Briefing Note on Bill C-38."

Indigenous Services Canada. 2022a. "Evaluation of First Nations Individual Affairs." sac-isc.gc.ca/eng/1657191112753/1657191157646#chp7.

___. 2022b. "Implementation Underway and Claims Period Open under the Safe Drinking Water Settlement Agreement." canada.ca/en/indigenous-services-canada/news/2022/04/implementation-underway-and-claims-period-open-under-the-safe-drinking-water-settlement-agreement.html.

Jamieson, Kathleen. 1978. *Indian Women and the Law in Canada: Citizens Minus*. Advisory Council on the Status of Women, Indian Rights for Indian Women.

Kirkby, Coel. 2018. "Reconstituting Canada: The Enfranchisement and Disenfranchisement of 'Indians,' c. 1837–1900." *University of Toronto Law Journal* 69, 4.

Lerner, Gerda. 1986. *The Creation of Patriarchy*. Oxford: Oxford University Press.

McLeod, Marsha. 2023. "Advocate Pushes for More Work on Discrimination in Indian Act Status Provisions." *The Globe and Mail*, March 7, 2023. theglobeandmail.com/politics/article-advocate-pushed-for-more-work-on-discrimination-in-indian-act-status/.

McNeil, Kent. 2016. "The Doctrine of Discovery Reconsidered: Reflecting on Discovering Indigenous Lands: The Doctrine of Discovery in the English

Colonies, by Robert J Miller, Jacinta Ruru, Larissa Behrendt, and Tracey Lindberg, and Reconciling Sovereignties: Aboriginal Nations and Canada, by Felix Hoehn." *Osgoode Hall Law Journal* 53, 2 (Winter).

Office of the Parliamentary Budget Officer. 2017. "Bill S-3: Addressing Sex Based Inequities in Indian Registration." https://distribution-a617274656661637473. pbo-dpb.ca/de734931849e82cdc1962a4432020610fb1fae20741a65f3982d293f-36d53c06.

Palmater, Pamela D. 2011. *Beyond Blood: Rethinking Indigenous Identity*. Saskatoon: Purich Publishing.

Razack, Sherene. 2016. "Gendering Disposability." *Canadian Journal of Women and the Law* 28, 2.

Royal Commission on the Status of Women in Canada. 1970. *Report of the Royal Commission on the Status of Women in Canada*. Ottawa: Queen's Printer.

Standing Senate Committee on Aboriginal Peoples. 2022. "Make It Stop! Ending the Remaining Discrimination in Indian Registration." sencanada.ca/content/sen/committee/441/APPA/reports/2022-06-27_APPA_S-3_Report_e_FINAL.pdf.

Stefanovich, Olivia. 2021. "'Old Wounds': Descendants of Families Who Lost Indian Status Launch Charter Challenge." *CBC News*, July 5, 2021. cbc.ca/news/politics/charter-challenge-bc-supreme-court-status-enfranhisment-1.6088049.

Tomchuk, Travis. 2023. "The Doctrine of Discovery: A 500-Year-Old Colonial Idea That Still Affects Canada's Treatment of Indigenous Peoples." Canadian Museum for Human Rights. humanrights.ca/story/doctrine-discovery.

Veracini, Lorenzo. 2010. *Settler Colonialism: A Theoretical Overview*. New York: Palgrave Macmillan.

Weaver, Sally M. 1981. *Making Canadian Indian Policy: The Hidden Agenda 1968–1970*. Toronto, Buffalo and London: University of Toronto Press.

SECTION II

INSTITUTIONS | REPRESENTATION | RESISTANCE

FIVE

Red Ticket Women

Revisiting the Political Contributions of the Indian Rights for Indian Women's Movement

Gina Starblanket

"This is the story of a long battle. We created an organization called Indian Rights for Indian Women.... We made history when we challenged Section 12(1)(b) — the discriminatory section of the old Indian Act. People now have to understand what we were doing, and they are not really thinking about how that law affected them." (Carlson and Steinhauer 2013, xxii)

INDIGENOUS FEMINIST ANALYSIS AND ACTIVISM have revealed the asymmetry and heterogeneity of lived experiences of violence in Canada (Kuokkanen 2015; Razack 2016; Simpson 2016; Bourgeois 2017). Attending to the complex and diverse forms of violence and dispossession that characterize colonial contexts necessitates inquiry and action across sites and scales of violence (Hunt 2015). This includes forms of violence against bodies, lands, and waterways, but also manifestations of violence resulting from the representation and regulation of Indigeneity in colonial contexts. This chapter contemplates how gendered constructions of the "treaty Indian" in Canadian policy have actively produced and reinforced forms of violence disavowed by the liberal tradition as a characteristic of Canada's history of relations with Indigenous Peoples.[1]

In the general body of scholarship on Indigenous-Canadian political relations, the dominant narrative surrounding the creation and governance of a purportedly sovereign "Canada" holds that colonial settlement was negotiated and governed legally and fairly. In approaching questions of settlement in the territories claimed by Canada, the British Empire was said to be of a "liberal" mindset that purported to respect and cultivate ideals of human freedom and equality. Imperial approaches to Indigenous people and lands are said to have been grounded upon these ideals, employing treaty-making processes as mechanisms to enable the purportedly non-violent settlement of the prairie west. Such representations of treaty have always been contested by Indigenous people, who have long pointed to more expansive understandings of the relationships we entered with the Crown and have undertaken sustained critique of violations of this relationship. As I've demonstrated in other work, perception and representation of the treaty relationship play a significant role in configuring contemporary social and political conditions and interrelations in treaty territories (Starblanket 2019). Thus, there remains a need for critical inquiry into the myriad forms of violence that flow from misrepresentations and misapplications of treaty in colonial contexts.

It is imperative to note that all matters of colonialism and dispossession begin with an originary and overarching violence enacted upon Indigenous people through settler colonialism: the possessory claims of settlers to our ancestral lands, which, not least, impact our ability to live freely in relation to creation, and from which flow other limits on our ability to be self-determining. This brings me to what I attend to specifically in this chapter; that is, the harm that colonial constructions of treaty have wrought upon Indigenous Peoples' inter-subjective processes of being together, of making sense of the world, and of the roles and responsibilities of humans towards other living beings.

FRAMING MATTERS

To begin, I explore the question of *why* different approaches to the study of Indigenous politics matter. Through reference to the work of the Indian Rights for Indian Women's (IRIW) movement and to my own training, I examine the risks of applying disciplinary norms, principles, and frames, such as those that configure the study of Canadian politics, in intellectual engagements with Indigenous politics. Here I'm not merely interested in methodological risks, but how contemporary engagements with Indigenous politics entail a particular form of discursive and epistemological harm when they remain tethered to the past lineage of Canadian political science.

While Indigenous politics is beginning to gain more traction within the study of political science, in many contexts Indigenous politics scholars are still working to carve out space within the existing suite of subfields, which often involves the addition of "Indigenous content" or "Indigenous elements" into pre-established disciplinary approaches and structures (Wallace 2022; Ladner 2017; Ferguson 2016). This observation is not to discount the critical work that has already been and is being done in this area by both Indigenous and non-Indigenous political scientists. Many scholars have identified and problematized the forms of intellectual and epistemological containment placed upon Indigenous Peoples, both in the academy and in the design of colonial law and policy (Simpson 2007; Smith 1999). And there have been excellent analyses put forward by scholars of nationalism, pluralism, empire, settler colonialism, and Indigenous politics that have sought to interrogate Canadianist approaches from Indigenous positions and perspectives, demonstrating that not only does Indigenous politics entail a vision that exceeds Canadian theories and practices, but also represents a critique that lies outside of the horizon of Canadian politics (Nichols 2020; Coulthard 2014; Simpson 2017).

Many of the early and continuous works of Indigenous political scientists in Canada have been directed towards identifying the limits of Western terms, concepts, debates, and frames, such as the vocabulary of cultural difference, accommodation, and recognition (Green 2001; Turner 2006; Coulthard 2014). These entail important practices of dialogue, contestation, and reflection that have highlighted the historical and ideological specificity of Canadian political concepts, theories, and practices, as well as differences in Indigenous and Western understandings and meanings. They have demonstrated how Western political vocabularies and frames place unnecessary limits on Indigenous political life by allowing only selective engagement of dimensions of "the political" that are legible to non-Indigenous people, misrepresenting and distorting other dimensions, and rendering yet others invisible.

When referring to the frames that configure our understanding, I'm talking about the vocabulary of identity politics and central debates surrounding individual and collective rights, essentialisms and anti-essentialism, and other binary representations of Indigenous political action. Such frames tend to situate Indigenous feminist critiques as either marginal to (and potentially at odds with) decolonial and nationalist movements and/or as derivative of white feminism. For instance, many of the inquiries into Indigenous women's historical political activism interpret their movements as a struggle against gender discrimination in the Indian Act, rendering the breadth of political action undertaken by Indigenous women down to a universal struggle to gain recognition of their individual rights by a settler state. Their complex and diverse political visions, contestations, and actions are then viewed and sedimented within this predetermined frame. The frame, then, serves a narrowing function that threatens to detract from our ability to fully comprehend or appreciate the breadth and significance of Indigenous women's interventions, then and now. In the process, we risk overlooking the ways in which Indigenous feminist interventions stand to broaden the space for critical conversations beyond binary registers and perhaps point to broader modes of engagement and analysis.

I am of the perspective that Indigenous political practices and specifically the nature of our political conflicts are too context specific to be looked at in excessively general frames or universal terms. Indigenous Peoples are uniquely politically situated in relation to Canada compared to other minority or cultural groups, but we also differ substantially in nature from one another. Contextual approaches to defining, understanding, and theorizing political practices and conflicts can be challenging as they require adequate depth of engagement to establish the political vocabulary and concepts that will ground one's analysis. They necessitate an understanding of knowledge and experience as grounded in specific places and moments in time, along with a willingness to advance analyses and arguments that don't fit neatly within existing frameworks and that aren't necessarily appropriate to extract and apply onto other communities. The context informs the concepts, language, and norms that we build the category or frame of analysis from, rather than the other way around. This can help mitigate the potential for essentialist depictions of Indigeneity and Indigenous political life. Subsequent sections of this chapter will explore how the application of pre-established frames onto Indigenous Peoples and politics contributes to the ongoing misrecognition, distortion, and ultimately, marginalization of Indigenous politics generally, and of Indigenous women's political contributions in particular.

Attempting to bring forward a more contextual mode of inquiry, I turn to archival and historical records of the IRIW and attempt to listen with what Sara Ahmed (2022) calls a "feminist ear," that is, the process of focusing on what is "out of tune, those jarring notes, those awkward stirring sounds of not being accommodated." In the context of this research, a feminist ear is required to pick up on the sounds obscured by narrow representations that depict Indigenous women as doing little more than saying "no" to the supposedly broader political interests and assertions of male-led Indigenous organizations. Rather, a feminist ear equips us to detect Indigenous women's diverse political articulations that were not, indeed are still not, being heard in many of our communities, to hear the plural "yeses" in their political visions, to become attuned to the other worlds of politics that their critiques entail. As Audra Simpson writes on the many discourses of unfreedom that configure Indigenous lives in conditions of colonialism, the riot of noise that is colonialism requires "an ear, and a decipherment, an audibility but perhaps a willingness to listen" (2016, 2). If, like Simpson, I endeavour to think through the auditory mess of settlement, then my objective is to become attuned to the conversations and contestations that Indigenous women have with their Indigenous relations in a localized context. Here, I examine the social and political discourses that have historically proliferated about Indigenous women, with attention to their contextual scales and iterations. Specifically, I look to the layers of violence surrounding their political presence and practice in the aim of drawing out a broader account than that enabled by dominant frames of engagement in the discipline of political science.

In undertaking this inquiry, I turn specifically to the personal dimensions of the conflict. My research consists predominantly of primary sources, mostly newspaper clippings, notes, and communications that offer insight into the work of the IRIW and local responses from Indigenous nations and organizations located in the Provincial Archives of Alberta. In my examination of these documents, I am less interested in formally expressed political positions and stances, but in the interpersonal and often violent communications and exchanges between Indigenous men and women that surrounded the IRIW's labour. I focus on specific words, accusations, and vocabularies to better understand the contours of the conflict — the tensions, emotions, and stakes at hand. This mode of analysis builds upon intersectional approaches but also coheres with relational modes of inquiry and knowing that flow from Indigenous ways of knowing and being (Wilson 2008; Moreton-Robinson 2017).

LOCATING AND DECONSTRUCTING THE "RED TICKET" WOMAN

Between 1876 and 1951, an Indian woman who married a non-status man in Canada lost her Indian Status and could commute her financial connection with her community, such as her treaty annuities. If she did not commute her interest, she could continue to collect these monies indefinitely. Her name would remain on band lists, but she had no other rights as an Indian. During the '30s and '40s, these individuals were sometimes referred to as Red Ticket Women, after the red colour of the special treaty card issued to them. In later years, Indigenous women in similar positions came to be known as "exited Indian women," and even after many had their Indian Status re-instated in 1985, they became known as "Bill C-31 women." The Red Ticket Woman, then, is a treaty Indian but is not an Indian registered under the Indian Act, which creates an interesting subject position and political dilemma for her and her relations.

While the practice of issuing red treaty cards was not longstanding and much of the associated vocabulary has changed, the impact of the classifications and tensions surrounding the subject position of the Red Ticket Woman have endured. My interest is in the social and political implications of this classification and characterization of Indigenous women and in how they might impact our inter-subjective processes of relating to one another as Indigenous people. Figures such as the Red Ticket Woman and those who are similarly situated have social, political, and economic dimensions that can teach us a great deal about the lived and material implications of identity constructions as the classifications themselves, left unchecked, can contribute to the continuity of political divisions, negations, and exclusions. Alternatively, when deeply and critically interrogated, and perhaps troubled, these constructions can offer clarification over the nature of political activity being undertaken by Indigenous women, challenging the ways in which political differences and movements within our communities have been perceived and represented over time.

The '70s–'80s was a formative time in both the construction and contestation of Indigenous politics in Canada, and one that can offer great insight into the complexity of Indigenous political struggles as it's where we see new techniques and strategies of governance emerge, collide, and face critique from both within and outside of Indigenous communities. Up until the 1950s, the Indian Act imposed mechanisms to repress Indigenous political mobilization, but after the 1951 amendments the number and veracity of local and territorial Indigenous organizations grew exponentially as Indigenous people sought to engage direct challenges to structures and processes of colonial domination, with some groups, such as Indigenous women's organizations, also aiming to attend to our diverse experiences within them. The 1960s onwards constituted a particularly significant period of Indigenous political activity and contestation surrounding land, treaty, and self-government, and examination of this era can help contextualize the origins of the binaries, contradictions, and problematics within Indigenous political organizing that have reverberated across generations.

In dominant representations from this period in time, Indigenous men are typically celebrated for building new political relations and networks and for championing new techniques and strategies of governance. Indigenous women are not generally represented as contributing to the Treaty Rights movement in a substantial way, nor as contributing to or significantly informing the mainstream feminist movement. When they are represented, Indigenous women's historical political activities are commonly depicted as enacting challenges to male-dominated governance structures and positions but are rarely credited for undertaking forms of political activism grounded in treaty. I want to be clear that the focus of this project is not the historical period in which the practice of issuing red treaty cards occurred, nor is it the practice itself, though these are worthy areas of inquiry. I'm also not interested in solely looking at the way in which the figure of the Red Ticket Woman gets constructed in Canadian legislation, as there has already been a great deal of work done and that continues to be done on sex and gender discrimination in the Indian Act. There are many excellent existing analyses of the dedicated activism that Indigenous women have undertaken to end gender discrimination in the Indian Act (see Eberts, Day, and McIvor in this volume) that complement this work.

My inquiry looks to the accounts and records of the western chapter of the IRIW to trace out a reading of the political context, conflict, and objectives at play during this important era of political change. Many members of the IRIW were Red Ticket Women, who lost Indian Status but retained certain "Treaty Rights," or Indigenous women who lost both Indian Status and "Treaty Rights" and who engaged actively in political work outside of state institutions. Indeed, Nellie Carlson and Kathleen Steinhauer write of the IRIW, "The politics here is not the Ottawa kind so admired by patriarchal leadership. [It] is about kitchen work, which in the end always gets finished and is what *pimatisiwin* (the good life) is really all about" (2013, xvi). Much of the IRIW's activism work took place from the 1970s to the 1990s, during a time when Indigenous people were building their capacity to navigate Canadian political institutions and developing new political strategies and approaches, while also mobilizing within new political formations. It also represents a period marked by internal division and contestation among Indigenous political actors who comprised the Treaty Rights movement and, at a broader scale, the movement towards self-government.

I look to the Red Ticket Woman as a category of political identity to better understand the operations of gendered and racialized structures in colonial contexts but also the ways that difference within these structures of power is discursively interpreted and represented. The act of "marrying out" of one's community is not just a social choice; it has significant perceived economic, political, and cultural connotations that merit consideration. Red Ticket Women are often represented as having been deprived of a legitimate political location, as having little power of representation in either Indigenous or non-Indigenous communities. With no proper political arena of their own, they are perpetually constructed in relation to mainstream political movements, such as the Treaty Rights movement or the mainstream feminist movement, despite their marginality or wholesale erasure relative to each. Because of their disenfranchisement, they are read as political actors whose interventions are almost always framed as oppositional to those of the communities they are excluded from. To be more specific, their political interventions are generally represented as forms of disruption, grievance, and/or complaint *against* the Treaty Rights movement rather than as broad and future-oriented forms of political visioning and activism operating within it. Yet, when we look beyond hegemonic representations of Indigenous political activism and towards the real-world political goals and objectives of involved actors, the political aims of the IRIW and male-dominated movements were not as contradictory as depicted, even if those aims were differently pursued. Both shared the protection of Treaty Rights as their overarching goal, but differed in the Red Ticket Woman's desire to address the impacts of racist, gendered constructions of treaty and of Indigeneity on Indigenous women, seeking to advocate for treaty in ways that included both Indigenous men *and* women. In the aim of exploring the consequences and implications of this perceived difference, I will now turn to the political conflict surrounding the Red Ticket Woman's existence, with specific focus on the expectations and subsequent accusations levied upon her by her Indigenous relations.

UNPACKING THE EXPECTATION/ACCUSATION

Having "married out" of Indigenous communities, Red Ticket Women were frequently met with what the IRIW termed the "cultural recognition" position, which suggested that Indigenous women who married non-Indigenous men and their children should no longer be recognized by their cultural community. This argument was grounded in the position that Indigenous women frequently left their cultural communities when entering marriages or other forms of relationship prior to contact, and that discrimination in the Indian Act was in keeping with pre-contact tradition. The expectation, then, was that for Indigenous women to maintain the ability to live freely in relation to their homelands, historical and contemporary relations, and cultural traditions and practices, they should intentionally choose to enter intimate partner relations with Indigenous men. In one news article, for instance, a male chief from Alberta indicates that "these women were advised by elders and made to understand what would happen when they [married non-Indians]" (*Globe and Mail* 1985, 5). Statements such as this work to discipline and police Indigenous women's intimate relations, implying that such determinations should be made from a collective interest rather than at the level of the individual person and body. It signals the imposition of an ordering of social relations within some Indigenous communities through constructed, gendered, and racialized categories and expectations.

The IRIW conducted a great deal of historical research to challenge this argument, demonstrating that within pre-contact Indigenous communities, there was no necessary formula for where their members would reside with their intimate partners, nor were there punitive consequences for these choices (PAA PR2013.0313/356). Rather, they identified a significant degree of variation in family patterns and rules governing post-nuptial residence. The IRIW described the choice to raise children either in Indigenous or non-Indigenous communities as a fact of self-determination that was a matter of intention and desire. In so doing, they weren't just resisting dominant conceptions of self-determination, but were also articulating visions of self-determination that would allow them to maintain cultural involvement, continuity, and mobility as Indigenous people for themselves and their children.

The Red Ticket Woman, then, had a biopolitical dimension, demonstrating that self-determination did not only mean collective governing rights but the rights for individual people to be self-determining in terms of their own bodies and in choosing how to honour the many relations they inhabit. She sought an affirmation of her humanity *and* her Indigeneity, showing that these are not mutually exclusive, but that she was an agent with the capacity to make determinations for herself in relationships with others. This was true with respect to her own body, including her embodied gender expression, sexuality, and her intimate relationships. Refusing to sever treaty, Red Ticket Women challenged the suggestion that they had made their own beds by "marrying out," and that they should just lie in them and accept their exclusion.

For doing so, the Red Ticket Woman was critiqued as having as an objective the protection of her individual interests at the expense of collective rights. On account of this perceived individualism, the prospect of her returned presence to the reserve was described by some Treaty 8 chiefs as a direct threat to their own cultural rights:

> One cannot ignore the potential cultural impact which the Bill invites. Many, if not most, of the persons whom the Bill would allow to live on reserves have little, if any, appreciation of the concept of collective rights. These rights are a pillar of the way of life of Indian band communities. Crowding reserves with persons who are unfamiliar with or not committed to collective rights will undoubtedly have a deleterious effect upon, if not destroy, our communal lifestyle. (PAA PR2013.0313/359)

The Red Ticket Woman's political efforts and strategies extended far beyond binary interpretations of Indigenous political activity as primarily involving a struggle for either individual or collective rights, or as arguing for/against state intervention in the adjudication of cultural identity. Instead, she pointed to the limitations and violence inherent in processes of state recognition, the need for expansive approaches to the protection of Treaty Rights for all treaty people, and the urgent need to repair the relationships between Indigenous men and women at interpersonal and collective scales.

The Red Ticket Woman also illustrated the diverse and complex locations of Indigenous people relative to matters of cultural identity. As an Indigenous woman, she challenged the popular association between Indigenous women and the preservation of culture (Lavell and Memee Lavell-Harvard 2006; Valaskakis, Guimond, and Stout 2009; Brant 2019). This association suggests that Indigenous women's purportedly essential association with creation situates her with a central role in motherhood, social reproduction, and cultural continuity. From this expectation of Indigenous women as the keepers or central agents of cultural transmission, we gain a better understanding of the grounds of the expectations and accusations levied against the Red Ticket Woman, as well as the nature of the political conflict she is perceived to represent. Her identity is not essential; she was not born with innate characteristics warranting her exclusion. It does not represent an inherent threat; rather, her subjectivity only constitutes a threat in the moment she becomes an agential actor in ways that differ from essentializing and homogenous constructions. In doing so, she is perceived to be betraying a cultural and social expectation in addition to a political one.

A relational orientation that is attentive to context allows us to see that the Red Ticket Woman is treated differently from other "treaty Indians" because she married out, an act that male commentators depicted as narrow-sighted, ill-informed, and harmful to purportedly collective movements towards self-government. If the act of marrying out was said to warrant consequences of violence and exclusion, this was exacerbated when the Red Ticket Woman not only refused to accept that exclusion but retained treaty and undertook a broad range of activist and policy responses advocating for the equal application of Treaty Rights.

Many of the accusations advanced in local responses to the IRIW emphasized the importance of unity in Indigenous political organizing and charged the Red Ticket Woman with creating confusion surrounding collective movements towards self-government. Specifically, she was accused of spreading misinformation, creating distrust, and cultivating division within communities (PAA PR2013.0313/317). Here is where we can hear the activity of the Red Ticket Woman depicted through the essentialist/anti-essentialist frame, when she gets situated as someone who, in not passively accepting her exclusion, actively prevents or negates the unifying strategies depicted as necessary to move purportedly broader Indigenous interests forward. Yet, the records of the IRIW indicate that unity among Indigenous people was an overarching aim of the organization: "All of the Indian people of this land must work together to build an Indian unity.... Together we can become an invincible force for Peace and Justice" (Two-Axe Early 1994, 433). It appears that while both the male-dominated Treaty Rights movement and Indigenous women's movements had unity among Indigenous people as a key objective, they held different perspectives surrounding the cause of, and potential responses to, Indigenous political conflict and divisiveness. Where male-led organizations considered self-government to be a prerequisite to gender equality and sought unity through a form of strategic essentialism, the IRIW considered equal treatment of Indigenous men and women to be a prerequisite to bringing about greater strength and unity in advocating for Treaty Rights and addressing matters of poverty affecting all Indigenous people (Two-Axe Early 1994, 433).

The Red Ticket Woman's political interventions, however, were eclipsed by the act of marrying out, which was seen as bringing about negative economic consequences for communities already living with disproportionately high levels of poverty relative to non-Indigenous people. That is, reductions in the numbers of Status Indians often resulted in the further alienation of Indian lands. By marrying out and having children who would no longer be recognized as Status Indians, the Red Ticket Woman was seen as contributing to the community's loss of its own population and in turn, lands. Marrying out, then, also has a geopolitical implication, as settlers continue to expropriate Indigenous lands and inflict damage to creation and to Indigenous Peoples' abilities to enact our responsibilities towards creation. To her critics, the Red Ticket Woman's actions were contrary to liberation from colonial domination on account of her marriage to a white man; that is, her seemingly voluntary entry into the segment of society that benefits directly from our ongoing marginalization and dispossession, and her greater proximity to individuals who embody a position of gender, race, class, and colonial privilege.

This brings me to the next pillar of critique levied against her, which is an economic critique. The Red Ticket Woman's drive towards reinstatement was represented as a move among women who had married out to access the benefits of Indian Status and resources of Indigenous communities. The arguments advanced by critics of the Red Ticket

Woman suggested that, if she and similarly situated Indigenous women were to be reinstated, it would lead to the "flood" of white people to the reserves: "Non-native could take over the whole culture and could control the reserve's political, social and economic systems" (PAA PR2013.0313/362). What they meant, though, was the flood of white men to the reserve, since white women were already gaining Indian Status and associated rights, and this did not pose an evident concern for Indigenous men. The rise in numbers resulting from the presence of white women on reserves, and their access to status and membership, was not problematized by male-led Indigenous organizations. bell hooks (2015, 69) notes a similar response to inter-racial relationships in the Black women's movement, observing:

> In some instances black men who are themselves involved in inter-racial relationships act contemptuously towards black women who exercise the same freedom of choice. They see their own behavior as acceptable because they view white women as victims, while they see white men as oppressors.

Indeed, Indigenous men did not appear to regard white women as exercising degrees of agency and authority that would represent a threat to their own; what they seemed expressly intent on avoiding, however, was the possibility of non-Indigenous men gaining greater access to reserve lands, governance, and decision-making processes.

This position was relatively easy to unravel; after all, if male leadership were so concerned about cultural continuity, the IRIW interrogated why they did not problematize the allocation of Indian identities and rights to non-Indigenous women. They asked: "How can you sit there and watch these white women acting and trying so hard to be an Indian," and "what a disgrace it is to our native culture and our spiritual beliefs" (PAA PR2013.0313.114). The on-the-ground concern, then, appears to relate less to the inclusion of non-Indigenous people within the community generally, and more centrally to the potential impact of proposed changes on Indigenous men; when a white woman gained status, it did not require Indigenous men to relinquish their status or position relative to their community. The IRIW took ongoing issue with this asymmetry, arguing for the reinstatement of status and membership to Red Ticket Women and other exited Indigenous women but also proposing the denial of status to non-Indigenous women marrying Indigenous men with status.

In their responses, Red Ticket Women also pointed to the economic underpinnings of the political accusations levied against them. As Jenny Margetts of the IRIW wrote, "In Alberta, it's purely an economic issue.... If many of us were reinstated as Indians, they would have to share their oil wealth with us — they're afraid" (Goyette 1981). Indeed, archival records of newspaper articles capturing the reactions of Indigenous men's organizations illustrate that many positions against the reinstatement of Red Ticket Women were couched in the vocabulary of scarcity, particularly relating to land and monetary resources (PAA PR2013.0313/359). This language reflects the incorporation of Indigenous leaders within capitalist economies, as we see male leaders' political ideas and positions determined not by their ancestral and ongoing relational obligations, but by the availability of resources and parcels of land relative to individual and family units. For instance, in a *Globe and Mail* article, Saddle Lake Chief Eugene Steinhauer suggested that violence "might result" if the federal government approved legislation to end gender discrimination in the Indian Act (*Globe and Mail* 1985, 5). Steinhauer justified this assertion through reference to a housing shortage on his own reserve: "We have 200 people on waiting lists for housing and they say if they build houses for [those women who move back], they'll burn them down." He further defended this position by explaining that Indian leaders are "simply protecting their rights" against damage to "the social and cultural fabric of the Indian nations." Yet, the IRIW continually refused these logics by pointing instead to the high and long-term costs of exclusion upon the community: "This is the kind of violent thinking that will destroy us, not our blood being thinned out" (Carlson and Steinhauer 2013, xv).

While many male Indigenous leaders deployed notions of scarcity, most Indigenous communities across Canada were already living in under-resourced conditions, and for some time. Rather than advance an argument grounded in treaty for additional resources and funding to support reinstatement, Indigenous leaders sought to contain the exercise of "Indian benefits" and Treaty Rights to their purportedly legitimate bearers. The threat of the Red Ticket Woman seemed to centrally reside in the potential economic implications of her possible return to the reserve, but also in her proximity to colonialism and white male power and in the perceived mobility, resources, and privilege that she was potentially able to access through this relation. Recall that this is the context in which we were seeing a rapid creation of an Indian political elite navigating new forms of access to Canadian political processes and to resources and industry partnerships. If Indigenous communities were working to map out unified or cohesive parameters to gain state recognition, the Red Ticket Woman constituted the other who was seen as continually interrogating and interrupting that process.

This conflict helps shed light on the ways in which the shifting political and economic contexts, along with the internalization of Western conceptions of property and capital accumulation, have impacted the terrain and stakes of Indigenous governance and resistance. It also points to how the language of cultural unity and preservation has been mobilized to shield oppressive, exclusionary, and self-interested practices, particularly when questions of power and resources are involved. By complicating male leaders' claims, the Red Ticket Woman sought to highlight the urgency in addressing longstanding political matters such as ongoing forms of violence within our communities. She articulated a range of political critiques and visions grounded in her relational obligations to her kin, both born and to be born. She fought for a return to healthier modes of relating and sought to institute strategies for negotiating the present involvement of diverse members within the governance of their communities. This important call is rarely interpreted as identifying the need for generative and inclusive political process that may stand to advance, rather than detract from, the collective political aims of Indigenous people.

Responses to the Red Ticket Woman were notably violent and included a range of efforts to delegitimize and diminish her person and political interventions. As Nellie Carlson and Kathleen Steinhauer wrote in their book *Disinherited Generations*, members of the IRIW were "insulted, ridiculed, and humiliated. They were called 'Squaw Libbers' and threatened with beatings and threats, [and told] that they and their families would be shot if they tried coming back to their reserves" (Carlson and Steinhauer 2013, xv). These sorts of accusations indicate the presence of a particularly adversarial, individualistic, and paternalistic mode of political intimidation and communication. For instance, when describing their experience giving a 1984 report to the Standing Committee, Nellie Carlson indicated that:

> The IRIW made a submission but the chiefs flooded it. The chiefs were listening but laughing. Women were treated unfairly by the chiefs; they rattled chairs, booed and when

> Jenny [Margetts] said the women were getting unfair treatment the chiefs walked out. Judy Erola was booed and there was noise throughout her speech. (PAA PR2013.0313.114)

In their work, the IRIW continually pointed to these behaviours to highlight the need to address the high levels of violence in their communities, problematizing the ways in which Indigenous modes of engaging in dialogue and diplomacy across difference had deteriorated. For them, the revitalization of our modes of kinship and relationality would do much more for the community and for future generations than state recognition of a right to self-government would.

At its heart, the IRIW's work was grounded in a desire to repair Indigenous Peoples' modes of relating to each other. They pointed to the high costs of falling victim to state-sanctioned modes of engagement and of allowing these to configure our identities and lives even in attempts to oppose or navigate them. Rather, they intervened in the violent strategies employed by some male leaders and challenged the notion that self-determination was a prerequisite to addressing the violence and exclusions they faced. They highlighted the need for methods to address violence in their communities, among other significant and transformative political aims. As Maria Campbell observed of their work:

> You gave so much — all of you — and the benefit to your people, our people, for we are all relatives, has been immeasurable. Did you know that 170,000 First Nations people benefited from your struggle to restore an inheritance that is about identity, belonging and place? Ah-hay thank you for your strength, fortitude and love. Thank you for protecting the inheritance of the children and beginning the work of mending Wahkohtowina. Your actions were the beginning of real healing for our people. It is your courage that is the catalyst, which will one day end violence against Aboriginal women. (Carlson and Steinhauer 2013, 17–18)

Campbell's words highlight how the IRIW's work was grounded in a desire to reframe the terms of transformation and to repair the core of Indigenous governance: our ability to relate well to one another.

If we dig deeper into the expectations and accusations outlined in this section, it becomes evident that there is much more going on in this conflict than dominant representations would suggest, though many of those representations certainly tell us part of the story. What else can the existence and the struggle of the Red Ticket Woman teach us? Might she be exercising a vision of relationality in her political actions that we can learn something from? She's trying to make an intervention in her community, not in the service of detracting from, but of bettering the relations that constitute it. The political project that she is undertaking is an important and careful balancing act, carrying out her responsibilities to her children and her relations not yet born from a space of exclusion and possibility. In opening up the space to interrogate and hold dialogue surrounding the destructive and violent tendencies she is witnessing within her community, she is doing much more for her people than she is credited for.

The Red Ticket Woman is rarely taken up as a complex political actor who, through her critique, is also articulating a different vision of self-determination, freedom, and liberation. She demonstrates the harm in flattened representations of any perceived identity category, including hegemonic representations of Indigenous womanhood. She should be understood as not merely responding to or intervening in dominant Indigenous and non-Indigenous political systems and processes but as articulating a vision of a different type of politics; that is, she works to reshape the conditions of possibility for political life within and in relation to her community. Within the context of the IRIW in particular, the Red Ticket Woman's political energy and work was certainly directed against the state's attempts to regulate her identity, but it was also directed towards the numerous and competing power relations within Indigenous communities.

The work of the IRIW challenged the false dichotomy between individual and collective rights. Members called on their relatives to critically confront masculinist conceptions of what is politically significant, challenging the notion that Indigenous people must move in unison towards singular political goals (and particularly ones that held no future for their children). Far from only being motivated by women's self-interests, their work was informed by the spirit and intent of the treaty relationship. In their retrospective on the IRIW's work, Carlson and Steinhauer (2013, xxviii) ask their readers to "look deeply into the prairie treaties, to learn more about them and to protect them." They wonder "how much western Canadians of all backgrounds know about the promises in these documents," writing that "Treaty rights involve so much more than a treaty card in a wallet."

Rather than sacrificing day-to-day, community-level concerns in the name of treaty, Red Ticket Women pointed to the inadequacy in the everyday distribution of material conditions flowing from colonial representations of treaty — what they saw as their children's denial of the inheritance that are Treaty Rights — but perhaps even more importantly, the need for strategies to address violence and begin to repair relationships between Indigenous people in our own approach to treaty.

RE-FRAMING THE FOUNDATIONS OF INDIGENOUS POLITICAL ANALYSIS

In the context of the IRIW's work, the Red Ticket Woman can help us interrogate, deliberately unsettle, and broaden the longstanding frames and assumptions that have informed narrow representations of Indigenous governance and its primary actors in Canada. The Red Ticket Woman is a relational category, not an essential one; she allows us to see the actual structures of power at play vis-à-vis some Indigenous women who have historically been, and in many contexts continue to be, treated differently, and to gain greater insight into how and why they are treated in this way. She also allows us to see the conditions through which identity, culture, and tradition are politicized and deployed to legitimize violence within our own communities. The Red Ticket Woman has a significant relation to otherness because of the intense, overlapping, and public nature of the violence and exclusion she faces. But she also reminds us of the flattening nature of many of the popular frames and assumptions in the study of Indigenous politics. These classifications themselves represent a form of discursive violence that upholds and eclipses lived experiences of marginalization and exclusion and that continue to predetermine the ways in which Indigenous people can be understood as legible political actors in the present.

Recognition of the constraining function of representation in the study of Indigenous politics highlights the need for nuanced and contextual engagements, both historically and into the future. In light of the reductive function of dominant modes of representation, future analyses might attend to the question of how we might work to transform this terrain rather than further entrenching it. This is the part of the conversation that I think scholars are much less willing to have — the phase where we engage in critical, self-reflexive conversations over ways of broadening the assumptions and forms of intellectual containment that continue to hamstring many in our work. Acknowledgment of the limits of our canons and disciplinary premises and approaches is the first and important step. Yet this recognition does not necessarily facilitate the growth and advancement of the study of Indigenous politics, nor does it necessarily alter the primacy of existing theories and methods. As Indigenous Peoples continue to work towards political transformation, there is an associated need to create space to raise questions and concerns about the ways that relationships are currently being inhabited and the ways that relational conflict is perceived and understood within our own networks and communities. The Red Ticket Woman can help us better understand diversely situated Indigenous people as not only subjects, but also active agents, of political relationships with important experience and insight into theory and practice. This will allow us to ascertain and draw out more nuanced and deeper relational understandings of the specific form and content of Indigenous feminist political activity. Specifically, it will offer a more capacious understanding of the diversity and complexity of Indigenous women's political theorizations, formations, practices, and contestations, then and now.

NOTE

1 Earlier versions of this chapter were presented at the 2019 meeting of the American Studies Association and the 2021 meeting of the American Political Science Association. I extend my gratitude to Kevin Bruyneel for his helpful commentary at APSA 2021, along with Sagi Cohen, an old friend who contributed to my approach and thinking on these matters.

REFERENCES

Ahmed, Sara. 2022. "Feminist Ears." *feministkilljoys* (blog). June 1, 2022. feministkilljoys.com/2022/06/01/feminist-ears/.

Bourgeois, Robyn. 2017. "A Perpetual State of Violence: An Indigenous Feminist Anti-Oppression Inquiry into Missing and Murdered Indigenous Women and Girls." In *Making Space for Indigenous Feminism*, second ed., edited by Joyce Green. Halifax and Winnipeg: Fernwood Publishing.

Brant, Jennifer. 2019. "Indigenous Mothering: Birthing the Nation from Resistance to Revolution." In *The Routledge Companion to Motherhood*, edited by L.O.B. Hallstein, A. O'Reilly, and M.V. Giles. London: Routledge.

Carlson, Nellie, and Kathleen Steinhauer, with Linda Goyette. 2013. *Disinherited Generations: Our Struggle to Reclaim Treaty Rights for First Nations Women and Their Descendants*. Edmonton: University of Alberta Press.

Coulthard, Glen. 2014. *Red Skin, White Masks: Rejecting the Colonial Politics of Recognition*. Minneapolis: University of Minnesota Press.

Ferguson, Kennan R. 2016. "Why Does Political Science Hate American Indians?"

Perspectives on Politics 14, 4.

Globe and Mail. 1985. "Women Undeterred by Threats." March 25, 1985. ProQuest Historical Newspapers.

Goyette, Linda. 1981. "Federal Funding Bias 'Aiding Native Sexism.'" *Edmonton Journal*, March: B12.

Green, Joyce. 2001. "Canaries in the Mines of Citizenship: Indian Women in Canada." *Canadian Journal of Political Science* 34, 4.

hooks, bell. 2015. *Ain't I a Woman: Black Women and Feminism*. London: Routledge.

Hunt, Sarah. 2015. *Violence, Law and the Everyday Politics of Recognition: Comments on Glen Coulthard's Red Skin, White Masks*. Native American and Indigenous Studies Association Annual Meeting, Washington, DC.

Kuokkanen, Rauna. 2015. "Gendered Violence and Politics in Indigenous Communities: The Cases of Aboriginal People in Canada and the Sámi in Scandinavia." *International Feminist Journal of Politics* 17, 2.

Ladner, Kiera. 2017. "Taking the Field: 50 Years of Indigenous Politics in the CJPS." *Canadian Journal of Political Science* 50, 1.

Lavell, Jeannette Corbiere, and Dawn Memee Lavell-Harvard. 2006. *"Until Our Hearts Are on the Ground": Aboriginal Mothering, Oppression, Resistance and Rebirth*. Toronto: Demeter Press.

Moreton-Robinson, Aileen. 2017. "Relationality: A Key Presupposition of an Indigenous Social Research Paradigm." In *Sources and Methods in Indigenous Studies*, edited by C. Andersen and J. O'Brien. London: Routledge.

Nichols, Robert. 2020. *Theft Is Property! Dispossession and Critical Theory*. Durham: Duke University Press.

PAA (Provincial Archives of Alberta). PR2013.0313.114, Jenny Margetts Fonds, Important Correspondence, Box 6. "Letter to President of I.A.A., March 2, 1983."

___. PR2013.0313.114, Jenny Margetts Fonds, Important Correspondence, Box 6. "IRIW 16th Annual Meeting held at Rocky Mountain House — Friendship Centre, Oct 6, 1984."

___. PR2013.0313/317, Jenny Margetts Fonds, Indian Self-Gov't pre Bill C-31 Newspaper Articles, Box 12. "Top Indian Blasts 'Do-Gooders.'"

___. PR2013.0313/356, Jenny Margetts Fonds. 1982. Standing Committee on Indian Affairs and Northern Development Sub-Committee Submissions, Box 13. "Enfranchisement of Indian Women Pursuant to the Indian Act."

___. PR2013.0313/359, Jenny Margetts Fonds, General Bill C-31 Reaction Newspaper Articles 1995, Box 13, "Some People Think There Are Only Two Kinds of Indians: Victims and Villains."

___. PR2013.0313/362, Jenny Margetts Fonds, Pre Bill C-31 Native Mens Org. Reaction Newspaper Articles, Box 13. "Indians Want to Be Consulted Before Discrimination Ended," 1985.

Razack, Sherene. 2016. "Gendering Disposability." *Canadian Journal of Women and the Law* 28, 2.

Simpson, Audra. 2007. "On Ethnographic Refusal: Indigeneity, 'Voice' and Colonial Citizenship." *Junctures: The Journal for Thematic Dialogue* 9.

___. 2016. "The State Is a Man: Theresa Spence, Loretta Saunders and the Gender of Settler Sovereignty." *Theory & Event* 19, 4.

Simpson, Leanne. 2017. *As We Have Always Done: Indigenous Freedom Through*

Radical Resistance. Minneapolis: University of Minnesota Press.

Smith, Linda Tuhiwai. 1999. *Decolonizing Methodologies: Research and Indigenous peoples*. London: Zed Books.

Starblanket, Gina. 2019. "The Numbered Treaties and the Politics of Incoherency." *Canadian Journal of Political Science* 52, 3.

Turner, Dale. 2006. *This Is Not a Peace Pipe: Towards a Critical Indigenous Philosophy*. Toronto: University of Toronto Press.

Two-Axe Early, Mary. 1994. "Indian Rights for Indian Women." In *Women, Feminism, and Development,* edited by H. Dagenais and D. Piché. Montreal: McGill-Queen's University Press.

Valaskakis, Gail Guthrie, Eric Guimond, and Madeleine Dion Stout (eds.). 2009. *Restoring the Balance: First Nations Women, Community, and Culture*. Winnipeg: University of Manitoba Press.

Wallace, Rebecca Audrey. 2022. "Beyond the 'Add and Stir' Approach: Indigenizing Comprehensive Exam Reading Lists in Canadian Political Science." *Canadian Journal of Political Science* 55, 3.

Wilson, Shawn. 2008. *Research Is Ceremony: Indigenous Research Methods*. Winnipeg: Fernwood Publishing.

SIX

Perpetual State of Violence

An Indigenous Feminist Anti-Oppression Inquiry into Missing and Murdered Indigenous Women and Girls

Robyn Bourgeois

FOR DECADES, THOUSANDS OF INDIGENOUS[1] women and girls from across Turtle Island[2] have been stolen from our communities through a violent social phenomenon now commonly referred to as "missing and murdered Indigenous women and girls" (MMIWG). In every province and territory, in urban centres, small towns, reserves and rural locations, Indigenous females of all ages and from all walks of life have been brutally murdered or have disappeared, fate officially unknown. In its wake, this violence has left families and communities devastated — many of whom have had to fight to have Canadian state institutions, including police forces, the judicial system, and, indeed, federal and provincial/territorial governments, take this violence seriously.

From 2016–19, the Government of Canada, under the leadership of Prime Minister Justin Trudeau, conducted a national public inquiry into this violence. "Not high on our radar" (CBC News 2014) for the previous Conservative government of Stephen Harper, this national inquiry represented a long and hard-fought battle on the part of Indigenous women (many of whom are family and friends of the murdered and missing) and their communities for a formal government investigation of the violence of MMIWG. Mandated to occur between September 1, 2016, and December 31, 2018, the inquiry was led by five commissioners, all but one of whom are Indigenous women, including representation from each of the three major Indigenous groups in Canada (First Nations, Inuit, and Métis). The commissioners were tasked with investigating the "systemic causes of all violence — including sexual violence — against Indigenous women and girls in Canada," as well as the "institutional policies and practices implemented in response [to this violence], including the identification of practices that have been effective in reducing violence and increasing safety" (Government of Canada 2016). The commissioners were also directed to make recommendations on "concrete and effective action that can be taken to remove systemic causes of violence and to increase the safety of Indigenous women and girls in Canada," as well as "ways to honour and commemorate the missing and murdered Indigenous women and girls" (Government of Canada 2016).

In the lead up to this inquiry, which included public consultation on its creation and content, some Indigenous women began organizing and articulating the critical need for inclusion of Indigenous feminist perspectives. In Vancouver, longtime Indigenous feminist activist Fay Blaney (Xwemalhkwu), in her role as co-chair of the February 14 Memorial March Committee, held a press conferencing demanding that in addition to consulting families, the inquiry process needed to "make room for groups that have worked with vulnerable women for years and are uniquely well-placed to address [the] sexism, racism, and violence that shadow so many victims' lives" (Stueck 2016). Blaney was afraid that feminism would be left out of the inquiry: "It needs to proceed from a feminist perspective … this is an issue of Indigenous women's equality … I didn't hear this coming from them" (CBC News 2016).

In the second edition of *Making Space for Indigenous Feminism*, published as the inquiry was ongoing, I argued that if this inquiry was to achieve its goals of understanding the systemic causes of MMIWG it was imperative that the commissioners consider Indigenous feminist perspectives. To demonstrate this, I offered an Indigenous feminist anti-oppression inquiry into MMIWG that drew attention to the Canadian state's role in this violence. As a settler colonial state, Canada has a historical and ongoing investment in violence against Indigenous women and girls — and, indeed, all Indigenous Peoples — in order to secure and retain unfettered access to Indigenous lands. Through its laws, policies, and institutions, the Canadian state has inflicted extreme violence on Indigenous communities in explicitly gendered and sexualized ways that simultaneously secure patriarchy, white supremacy, and colonial domination. At the same time, it has colonized — attempted to silence and subvert — the efforts of Indigenous women and their allies to address this violence. This analysis remains part of this chapter.

Unfortunately, despite the work of the commissioners, the families, and survivors who guided the process, and all of those who participated, colonialism shaped and continues to shape the national inquiry and its aftermath. In this revised chapter, I offer a new analysis of the inquiry accompanied by a significant change in my relationality to the topic. While I come to this discussion as an Indigenous feminist scholar who has researched Canadian state-sponsored anti-violence directed at Indigenous women and girls for almost two decades, I now also come as a participant. In October 2018, I testified at the inquiry as an expert and experiential witness on sexual violence and human trafficking. My reflections, as such, are based on both intellectual and lived experiences.

AN INDIGENOUS FEMINIST ANTI-OPPRESSION FRAMEWORK

My analysis of the violence of MMIWG begins with an articulation of the particular Indigenous feminist framework I employ. As noted in this collection, feminism is not "a homogeneous static monolith" (St. Denis 2007, 43) but, instead, "viewed as multiples: *feminisms* analyze the diversity of women's cultural, political, and in other ways specific experiences" (Green 2007, 21). Given this multiplicity of feminisms, it's imperative to outline the particular feminist framework employed here.

The framework I advance is what I call an Indigenous feminist *anti-oppression* framework, emphasizing its overriding commitment to ending all forms of domination and violence. It draws on Indigenous and non-Indigenous feminist, anti-colonial/decolonizing, critical anti-racism and anti-oppression theories, and is influenced by my anti-violence work with Indigenous women and their communities.

Like my colleagues in this collection, this framework starts from a place of honouring and respecting the knowledges and experiences of Indigenous women and girls. As experts in their own lives, their leadership and perspectives must be included in any discussion, decision, and action with the potential to impact their lives. As the popular political slogan states, "nothing about us without us."

This framework recognizes the simultaneous impact of colonialism, racism, and patriarchy on the lives of Indigenous women and girls and their communities while advocating to dismantle these dominant systems of oppression collectively. The primary theoretical underpinning that provides the "guide map" for this critical project is borrowed from the writing of critical anti-racist feminist scholar Sherene Razack (1998, and with Mary Louise Fellows 1998) on "interlocking systems of oppression." This approach understands dominant systems of oppression, including colonialism, racism, and patriarchy, as operating simultaneously and working in and through each other in mutually sustaining ways to secure hierarchal relations of dominance in our societies. These systems are structured by "dominance through difference" (Fellows and Razack 1998), employing actual and perceived differences (physical, cultural, social, and so forth) to eject some groups of people from humanity and, thus, the fruits, rights, and protections of official human citizenship — including the basic human right to live lives free from violence and exploitation. As Fellows and Razack (1998, 343) explain:

> The containment of the Other is a making of the dominant self. To exclude Others from membership in the human community, that is, to name, classify, and contain the Other through a number of representational and material practices, assures the material basis for domination while enabling the members of the dominant group to define themselves.

In other words, dominant systems of oppression work in interlocking ways to secure an elite on the backs and bodies of other human beings that this elite has deemed less worthy. Critically, because these systems operate by marking subordinate groups as different while leaving dominant groups unmarked (as in not belonging to any racial category, for example), this "leaves these processes of domination obscured, thus intact" (Fellows and Razack 1998, 341).

Efforts to examine and eradicate these dominant systems of oppression, then, must pay close attention to how they operate in and through one another, and address them simultaneously. However, in doing this work, it is critical to avoid what Fellows and Razack (1998) call "the race to innocence." The danger here is that we use our oppression in one system to avoid examining our privilege in another and, thus, our complicity in the oppression of others. Because of the multiple systems of oppression involved, our lives are simultaneously shaped by oppression and privilege. Ignoring our privileges not only secures our complicity in the oppression and violence perpetrated against others, but also, ultimately, against ourselves: "attempts to change one system while leaving the others intact leaves in place the structure of domination that is made of interlocking hierarchies" (Fellows and Razack 1998, 336). Examining our privilege(s), then, is an essential part of the practices to achieve freedom for any of us. In the words of the Aboriginal Women's Action Network (AWAN 2011), an Indigenous feminist women's group based in Vancouver, this requires "a collective definition of freedom" recognizing that "your freedom is tied to ours and ours to yours."

Interlocking systems of oppression are dependent on violence for their success, and in a later section I will detail how this has worked in the case of Indigenous women and girls in Canada. It is for this reason that I have emphasized anti-oppression in my theoretical framework: dismantling dominant systems of oppression is essential to ending violence against Indigenous women and girls, and all other socially marginalized and oppressed people.

MMIWG: THE SCOPE OF A "NATIONAL TRAGEDY"

In a Western society that demands statistical evidence to support claims, it has been challenging to pinpoint exact numbers of missing and murdered Indigenous women and girls across Canada. For example, at the conclusion of the Sisters in Spirit (SIS) initiative — a five year, federally funded ($5 million) research, education, and policy initiative addressing the root causes and trends related to MMIWG — in March 2010, the Native Women's Association of Canada (NWAC) had documented 582 cases since the 1960s, identified through reports from families and consultation of public records (such as newspapers and court documents). Around this same time, Walk4Justice, a grassroots organization led by Indigenous activists Skundaal/Bernie Williams (Haida/Nuchatlaht/Stellat'en) and Gladys Radek (Gitxsan/Wet'suwet'en), claimed to have identified more than three thousand cases of MMIWG (Williams and Radek 2010, 2). While the two organizations might have collaborated to produce an enhanced database of cases, they were never given the chance. In the second round of federal funding for their work on MMIWG, ongoing work on NWAC's database of cases was prohibited (which is discussed in greater detail later in this chapter).

Instead, the federal government funded a national operational overview of Royal Canadian Mounted Police (RCMP) files pertaining to MMIWG, finding 1,181 cases: 1,071 homicides and 164 missing women and girls (RCMP 2014, 3). A significant issue with these numbers (and, indeed, other police force statistics) is the absence of established guidelines for determining how police officers collect information relating to Indigenous Peoples, meaning that the Indigeneity of some victims might not be identified in case files (NWAC 2010, 15). Moreover, concerns have been voiced that the deaths of some women and girls have mistakenly been deemed "accidental" instead of suspicious death or homicide in police investigations (NWAC 2009; Troian 2016).

In terms of a total number of MMIWG, I hold the position of journalist Warren Goulding. In his examination of the murders of Indigenous women in Alberta and Saskatchewan committed by convicted serial killer John Martin Crawford in the 1980s and 1990s, Goulding writes:

> As the investigation moved into November (1994), the RCMP enlisted the help of other agencies to sift through the public records for reports of missing Native women in Western Canada. In the end, the search turned up nearly five hundred women, reported missing in the previous three years, who matched the general criteria of the age and background of the Saskatoon victims. Officials later disputed that number, but the number itself was almost irrelevant. Whether it was one hundred or five hundred, it was clear that something like an epidemic was raging virtually unchecked in Western Canada. Whether by accident or design, choice or foul play, the whereabouts of an enormous number of aboriginal women were officially unknown. (2001, 33)

For families and communities, the death of one Indigenous woman or girl is too much, let alone the thousands suggested by these estimates. An "accurate" count is unnecessary: far too many Indigenous women and girls have gone missing or been murdered over the last few decades.

At the same time, the research surrounding these numbers provides some invaluable insights into this violence. For example, analysis of NWAC's SIS database revealed that over two-thirds of their cases occurred in the western provinces of British Columbia, Alberta, Saskatchewan, and Manitoba. Seventy percent of cases occurred in urban areas; however, NWAC (2010, 27) urged caution in acting on this finding:

> While it is clear that the issue of missing women and girls is overwhelmingly an urban issue, the high rates of mobility of Aboriginal peoples, and particularly Aboriginal women and families, creates a different dynamic for cases of missing and murdered Aboriginal women and girls than would be experienced in the non-Aboriginal urban population. What this means is that even when cases may be linked to an urban area, there are often other circumstances impacting women and families, such as temporary or semi-permanent residence in a city and having close ties to a home community that is also impacted by the disappearance or death of a woman or girl. Cases on reserve and in rural areas, however, must also receive equal attention to identify appropriate recommendations for justice intervention. This issue is reiterated by family members who have expressed frustration over the fact that rural cases do not seem to get as much attention as those in urban areas, a situation one family member described as "racism-plus."

More than half of the NWAC-identified cases involved females under age thirty-one, and many of the women were mothers. "Knowing the number of women who were mothers," the organization contends, "speaks to the intergenerational impact of women who have gone missing or been found murdered, and the need to provide supports and services to the children left behind" (NWAC 2010, 24). This analysis also found that Indigenous women and girls were more likely to be killed by strangers (16.5 percent of cases) than non-Indigenous women (6 percent of cases). Finally, the report contends that nearly half of all cases remain unsolved (2010, 17), with different clearance rates across the provinces and territories (2010, 18).

The final report of the RCMP operational overview also provided important insights into this violence. It confirmed what many have known for decades: Indigenous women have been disproportionately targeted for violence. Despite representing 4.3 percent of the female population, Indigenous women constituted 11.3 percent of missing females and 16 percent of female homicide cases in Canada between 1980 and 2010 (RCMP 2014). Moreover, statistics derived between 1996 and

2011 show that Indigenous women were, on average, five and a half times more likely to be victims of homicide than non-Indigenous women.

This report contends, in contrast with NWAC, that the majority of cases have been solved. The RCMP (2014) claims a female homicide solve rate of nine out of every ten deaths, regardless of ancestry (88 percent for Indigenous women and 89 percent for non-Indigenous women). They did, however, confirm NWAC's finding of variance in clearance rates across the provinces and territories.

It is imperative to understand the phenomenon of MMIWG as representing the proverbial "tip of the iceberg" when it comes to violence against Indigenous women and girls in contemporary Canadian society. Research demonstrates that Indigenous women and girls experience disproportionately high rates of all forms of violence, including intimate partner violence (Bopp, Bopp, and Lane 2003; Brennan 2011), family violence (Government of Canada 2008), and sexual violence (Bopp et al. 2003; Brennan 2011). One study suggests that 75 percent of Indigenous females under the age of eighteen have experienced some form of sexual assault (Bopp, Bopp, and Lane 2003, 27). We also know that Indigenous women and girls are aggressively targeted for sexual exploitation and human trafficking and make up anywhere from 50–80 percent of the violent street-based survival sex trade in major Canadian cities (Sethi 2007; NWAC 2014). The high prevalence of violence in the lives of Indigenous women and girls has resulted in its "normalization" as a brutal fact of life (Shaw 2013, 11, 21; Kuokkanen 2014).

STATE OF PERPETUAL VIOLENCE

How did we get to the point where violence against Indigenous women and girls is a "normal" part of life in Canada? As Indigenous women have been telling the Canadian state for decades through their participation in state-sponsored anti-violence initiatives, including previous investigatory commissions such as the Canadian Panel on Violence Against Women (1991–93) and the Royal Commission on Aboriginal Peoples (1991–96), the extreme forms of violence Indigenous women and girls experience in contemporary Canadian society are a direct consequence of settler colonial domination (Bourgeois 2014).

Understanding the connection between the two requires critical interrogation of the Canadian state. Canada is a settler colonial nation built on the historic and ongoing domination of Indigenous Peoples and the occupation and exploitation of stolen Indigenous lands (Green 2014; Coulthard 2014). This colonial project succeeds through racist and sexist ideologies that portray Indigenous people as inferior, deviant, and inherently dysfunctional.

The effects of colonialism are gendered, and the colonial gaze has a gender-specific derogatory and essentialized frame for Indigenous women. A powerful component of this ideology has been the myth of the "squaw": the dominantly held belief in the inherent sexual availability and, thus, violability of Indigenous women and girls (Acoose 1995; Smith 2005). This ideological dehumanization of Indigenous females justifies both settler domination over Indigenous Peoples and lands and violence perpetrated against Indigenous women and girls. Indeed, within this system, violence against Indigenous women and girls is the most efficient means to securing and maintaining the colonial order in settler society.

The focused destruction of Indigenous women and girls plays a fundamental role in colonial domination: "In order to colonize a people whose society was not hierarchical," argues Andrea Smith (2005, 23), "colonizers must first naturalize hierarchy through instituting patriarchy" and, thus, "patriarchal gender violence is the process by which colonizers inscribe hierarchy and domination on the bodies of the colonized." This isn't to suggest that violence against Indigenous women and girls was absent from pre-colonial Indigenous societies; however, the matriarchal and matrilineal ordering of many of our societies (LaRocque 1994; Anderson 2000; Mann 2000), combined with swift and sometimes severe responses to violence (Anderson 2000; Mann 2000), curtailed its presence in our communities.

Alongside physical violence, colonialism depends on structural forms of violence to marginalize and oppress Indigenous women and girls and, by extension, their communities and nations. Perpetuated through social and political institutions, these structural forms of violence further increase the vulnerability of Indigenous women and girls to physical violence. In the discussion that follows, I explore some of the ways in which the Canadian state has perpetuated and enabled violence against Indigenous women and girls.

THE VIOLENCE OF THE INDIAN ACT

Since its enactment in 1876, the federal Indian Act has defined almost every aspect of being an Indigenous person in Canada, including legally defining which of us "officially" count and don't count as "Indians" and, therefore, who the Canadian state is obligated to provide for under existing and future treaty obligations (Eberts 2014, 148). Critical to the state's settler colonial project, the Indian Act has not only secured the racial binary of "Indian" and "Canadian" (predominantly imagined as white), but also that of "Indian" and "non-Indian" amongst Indigenous communities in Canada. Until a 1939 ruling of the Supreme Court, Inuit were excluded from the legal category of Indian, as were Métis and other non-Status Indians until a 2016 Supreme Court ruling (*Daniels v. Canada*).

However, the core legal definition of an "Indian" has largely been "any male person of Indian blood reputed to belong to a particular band, and any child of such person and any woman who is lawfully married to such a person" (Gibbins and Ponting, cited in Comack 2014, 62). Defined through men, the Indian Act imposed patrilineality and patriarchy on many previously matrilineal and matriarchal societies, therefore severely limiting the safety and social security these orderings of our communities had provided.

Through sexist marriage and lineage provisions that unfairly target Indigenous women and their children only, the Indian Act has eliminated millions of "official" Indians for whom the federal government would carry responsibility through treaty obligations, with the effect of forcibly removing untold numbers of women and children from their nations and communities (an act of human trafficking, as I have argued elsewhere [Bourgeois 2015]). While Bill C-31 eliminated the controversial marry-out clause (wherein a woman lost her status under the Indian Act if she married a man without status; however, a man who did the same not only retained his status, but status under the Act was also extended to his wife and children) in 1985, sex discriminatory lineage and membership components continue to target Indigenous women and children (Cannon 2011); and Indigenous women reinstated under Bill C-31 have experienced challenges and resistance to returning to their home communities (Dick 2006). By excluding Indigenous women from status under the Indian Act, these sex discriminatory provisions, as Mary Eberts (2014, 152–53) argues, promote family fragmentation and community exile that eliminate critical sources of support and heightens the vulnerability of Indigenous women and children.

The Indian Act has contributed to the oppression of Indigenous women and girls in other ways. By imposing democratically elected band council governance on reserve communities, the Indian Act undermined and eliminated many of our traditional matriarchal forms of leadership and governance (Anderson 2000, 2009). To strengthen this blow, Indian women were prohibited from participating in these elections or serving on these band councils between 1876–1951. The cumulative effect was the patriarchal ordering of Indian governance and leadership across Canada, with the interests, perspectives, and needs of Indian men foregrounded in the governance of our communities (Anderson 2009). While this exclusion was repealed, its legacy continues to be felt through underrepresentation of Indian women within band and national (Assembly of First Nations) Indian governance — although their numbers are increasing (Anderson 2009, 100). While it remains to be seen how the 2016 Supreme Court ruling in *Daniels v. Canada* or the ongoing legal efforts of Indigenous women like Sharon McIvor will impact the future of the Indian Act, its past and present have been driven by the entrenchment of patriarchal domination and violence in Indigenous communities, therefore securing continuity with dominant Canadian society and its uses of racist, sexist oppression and violence.

HUMAN TRAFFICKING AND EXTERMINATION

Alongside the legislative assault of the Indian Act, the Canadian state has enabled and perpetuated violence against Indigenous women and girls through its institutions, most notably the Indian residential school and child welfare systems. As the Truth and Reconciliation Commission (TRC) made clear in 2015, gross neglect and all forms of physical and sexual abuse were prevalent and came to define the experiences of Indigenous girls and young women in the state and church-run Indian residential school system, which operated in Canada from the 1820s until 1996. Compulsory attendance legislation backed by legal penalties for non-compliance was secured through state Indian agents (Comack 2014, 63–64). The rationale for residential schools hinged on the dominant settler colonial belief in the inferiority and inadequacy (particularly in terms of the assimilationist goal of these institutions) of Indigenous Peoples as parents, and, according to Eberts (2014, 149–50), "among the many reasons why the Indigenous mother was considered an inappropriate influence on her own children was the alleged hypersexuality of Indigenous women." The intergenerational trauma created through the dehumanizing and violent residential school system continues to reverberate throughout our communities, with the consequence of increased violence within our communities. The research of NWAC (2010) through its SIS initiative identified the violence and intergenerational trauma caused by the Indian residential school system as an underlying factor of the violence experienced by MMIWG.

Canadian child welfare systems have taken over the apprehension and removal of Indigenous children from their families and communities, with statistics suggesting there are currently more Indigenous children in the custody of the state than at the height of the Indian residential school system (Fallon et al. 2021). Since the 1960s, child welfare institutions have forcibly removed Indigenous children from their families and secured their fostering or adoption with primarily non-Indigenous families. Advocates and researchers have revealed high rates of physical and sexual violence, psychological distress, and death experienced by Indigenous children in Canadian child welfare systems. Indeed, many of the MMIWG had involvement with this system, and some, like fifteen-year-old Tina Fontaine, murdered in Winnipeg during the summer of 2014, were involved with this system at the time of their deaths or disappearances. As with residential schools, NWAC's SIS research identified involvement with the child welfare system as an underlying factor contributing to the violence experienced by MMIWG (NWAC 2010).

As I have argued elsewhere (Bourgeois 2015), the forced removals and confinements of Indigenous children by both the Indian residential school and child welfare systems, along with forced relocations of entire Indigenous communities from their land bases and forced relocations required for Indigenous Peoples to access basic health services, constitute historical and ongoing Canadian state engagement in the crime of human trafficking. According to existing Canadian legislation, human trafficking involves the use of deception, coercion, manipulation, and violence to exploit the bodies and labour of others for profit and personal gain; and Canada is the only country to legally demand that trafficking victims prove that they feared for their safety if they failed to comply with the demands of their trafficker (Perrin 2010).

Each of the relocations outlined above have involved explicit deception, coercion, and manipulation on the part of the Canadian state to exploit (primarily through forced movements and confinements) the bodies of Indigenous Peoples for the specific purpose of advancing its settler colonial project of domination over Indigenous Peoples and, by extension, Indigenous lands and resources. For example, the confinement of "Indians" to "Indian reserves" was critical to the colonial project because it secured unfettered access and control of Indigenous lands and resources and, thus, a land base for the Canadian state. As is well documented, this was achieved through fraudulent, coercive, and broken treaties with Indigenous nations and communities, along with violence (Harris 2002; Alfred 2009; Gehl 2015). The theft and confinement of Indigenous children through the Indian residential school and child welfare systems — both of which have been directed at assimilating and, thus, exterminating (legally, culturally, and physically) Indigenous Peoples and eliminating Canada's "Indian" problem — depended on deception, force, and violence. As the settler colonial project has been sustained through rampant violence against Indigenous women and girls and, indeed, all Indigenous Peoples, many of us live in a perpetual state of fear in Canadian society.

THE INJUSTICE SYSTEM

The Canadian legal system (laws, courts, and police) has a long history of failing to protect Indigenous women and girls from violence, while simultaneously exonerating perpetrators and erasing this violence — thanks largely to the sexualized and racialized discourses of inferior and degenerate Indigenous femininity (Razack 2002; Erickson 2011; Eberts 2014). Instead of protecting them, the legal system has tended to criminalize Indigenous women who encounter it, as exhibited by very high rates of incarceration (Hylton 2002; Erickson 2011; Comack 2014).

Prostitution presents a perfect example of this. The dominant colonial discourse of the inherently sexual availability and violability of Indigenous females has, throughout Canadian history, enabled the conflation of Indigenous femaleness with prostitution (Comack 2014; Bourgeois 2014), which is reinforced, in turn, by the high numbers of Indigenous women and girls who, whether by choice, need, or force, have been involved in the sex trade. As I have argued elsewhere (Bourgeois 2014), Canadian colonial history demonstrates that the state has frequently employed prostitution as a means of legally securing control over Indigenous women and, by extension, their nations and communities. Criminalization of Indigenous ceremonies, such as the potlatch, and implementation of the pass system were justified, in part, by concerns about the immorality posed by the prostitution of Indian women. Moreover, an amendment to the Indian Act in 1892 created a distinct legal category for Indian women charged with prostitution, increasing its criminal severity from a "common nuisance" and summary offence to crime against morality and an indictable offence (Erickson 2011, 62–63). While currently being challenged, Canadian criminal code provisions continue to criminalize Indigenous women involved in prostitution.

At the same time, Canada's (in)justice system has long used prostitution as justification for minimizing the violence perpetrated against Indigenous women and girls and for exonerating perpetrators. Lesley Erickson's (2011) study of Prairie courts between the late 1880s and early 1900s shows that perpetrators often employed the stereotype of Indigenous sexual promiscuity, including accusations of prostitution, to their legal advantage. In her analysis of the trial surrounding the 1995 murder of Pamela George (a Saulteaux woman originally from the Sakimay First Nation) in Regina, Razack (2002) demonstrates how, one hundred years later, prostitution continues to over-define Indigenous femininity, with the effect of minimizing the violence of perpetrators through separation from the Canadian colonial project requiring violence against Indigenous women and girls. Razack uses similar analysis on the murder of thirty-six-year-old Cindy Gladue (Cree) in Edmonton in 2011, demonstrating the central role that prostitution played in making both the murder and the courts' response to it a form of colonial terror and extraordinary violence (Razack 2016).

Prostitution is also at the root of Canadian state inaction in response to violence against Indigenous women and girls, perhaps best exemplified in the cases of Vancouver's missing women. Between the late 1970s and early 2000s, at least sixty-eight women disappeared and/or were murdered from Vancouver's Downtown Eastside (DTES) community. While most commonly portrayed in mainstream media as a community of abject poverty, addiction, criminality, and prostitution (Culhane 2009; Hugill 2010), the DTES is also a caring community whose members, along with families and friends of MMIWG, recognized this pattern of violence and sought police and governmental responses. The final report of the British Columbia Missing Women Commission of Inquiry surrounding these cases points to the criminalization of prostitution under Canada's criminal code as producing an adversarial relationship between police and women in the DTES, which contributed to the delay in catching serial killer Robert Pickton, who was preying on this community (Oppal 2012). We also know from this report that police officers and administrative staff made disparaging remarks and refused to take action because of the real or perceived involvement of the missing women in prostitution.

The result of this blatant inaction was sixty-eight missing and murdered women. Despite being formally indicted for the murders of twenty-five of these women and suspected in the deaths of many more, Pickton was only convicted of second-degree murder in six of these cases and sentenced to life in prison. While justified by the Attorney General for British Columbia as a move to curtail additional expenditures of time and energy to pursue charges that couldn't expand on Pickton's existing life sentences, the decision not to pursue those additional charges or prosecute additional cases against Pickton may be interpreted by some as representing this ongoing pattern of minimizing violence against Indigenous and non-Indigenous women associated with prostitution.

COLONIZING INDIGENOUS WOMEN'S RESISTANCE

Another significant way that the Canadian state has perpetrated violence against Indigenous women and girls in Canada is through its repeated and sometimes aggressive attempts at colonizing (silencing and subverting) Indigenous women's anti-violence efforts. The National Inquiry into Missing and Murdered Indigenous Women and Girls has been a long time coming and must be understood as the outcome of decades of arduous, heartbreaking organizing and effort on the part of Indigenous women, their organizations, communities, and allies. For example, in Vancouver, under the leadership of Indigenous women (many of whom are family and friends of missing or murdered women), the DTES community has organized an annual memorial and march for MMIWG since 1991. For thirty-three years, this event has demanded the Canadian state take action to address violence against Indigenous women and girls. Since the 2000s, Indigenous women have organized solidarity events in major cities (including Edmonton, Winnipeg, Toronto, Thunder Bay, and Montreal), as well as many rural and Indigenous communities.

As mentioned throughout this chapter, NWAC has played a critical role in securing Canadian state response to the issue of MMIWG. NWAC's efforts to obtain a Canadian state response to violence against Indigenous women officially began in 2002, when it raised the issue in a report to a United Nations special rapporteur investigating human rights violations in Canada. In 2004, NWAC collaborated with Amnesty International Canada on the report *Stolen Sisters: A Human Rights Response to Discrimination and Violence Against Indigenous Women in Canada*, condemning Canada for failing to protect Indigenous women and girls from violence. Building on the attention created by that report, NWAC pursued federal funding, and after more than a year and a concerted media campaign, succeeded in securing a commitment of $5 million over five years (2005–10) for the SIS initiative.

However, the arrival of the Harper Conservative regime in 2006 contributed to the colonization of these efforts. For the duration of his entire nine-year tenure as prime minister of Canada, Stephen Harper refused to consider holding a national public inquiry into MMIWG. As Indigenous women and girls were disappearing and dying in the hundreds across this country, Harper ignored outcries while he and his government calculatedly sabotaged Indigenous women's efforts to address this violence. Advancing his "tough on crime" political agenda, Harper funnelled millions into policing, including funding the RCMP operational overview and creating a national missing persons centre. As critics have pointed out, this amounts to investment in the ongoing criminalization and incarceration of Indigenous Peoples. His government also refused to address much of the social, political, and economic marginalization and exclusion that makes Indigenous women and girls highly vulnerable to exploitation and violence.

REFLECTIONS ON THE NATIONAL INQUIRY INTO MISSING AND MURDERED INDIGENOUS WOMEN AND GIRLS

While his predecessor refused, the national inquiry was a priority for Prime Minister Justin Trudeau, who self-identifies as a feminist (Kingston 2016), albeit not a colonizer.

Did this feminism make its way into the inquiry? Did the inquiry meet the demands I outlined in the original version of this chapter?

Yes and no.

Before I unpack this answer, it's essential to disclose my relationship with the inquiry. In the immediate aftermath of the 2012 release of the final report of the Province of British Columbia's Missing Women Commission of Inquiry (Oppal 2012), which examined the failings surrounding the investigation and apprehension of serial killer Robert Pickton in the deaths and disappearances of women from Vancouver's Downtown Eastside, demand for a national inquiry into MMIWG increased. At the time, I was completing my doctoral research examining Indigenous women's involvement in Canadian state-sponsored anti-violence efforts, including inquiries, since the 1980s. While my research celebrated the leadership and political savviness of Indigenous women, it also documented the colonizing effects of the strategies, including inaction on the findings and recommendations. Moreover, as a survivor of this violence and someone deeply involved in the activism demanding justice for MMIWG, I couldn't fathom participating in another state-sponsored investigation while Indigenous women and girls continued to disappear and/or die across this country. Consequently, I wrote a blog for the Huffington Post suggesting that a national inquiry wasn't necessarily the best answer (Bourgeois 2012). When the national inquiry was established, I supported the right of other Indigenous Peoples, especially family members and survivors, to participate but kept my distance given my concerns about the process. That was until October 2018, when I was asked to testify as a scholarly expert and experiential witness as a survivor of sexual violence and human trafficking. Despite my misgivings about the process, I decided I would forever regret not accepting this opportunity to speak my truth, especially since so many sex-trafficked women like me didn't survive and weren't present at the inquiry. Consequently, I testified virtually on October 17, 2018. In some ways, the National Inquiry into Missing and Murdered Indigenous Women and Girls exceeded my expectations. After the TRC'S containment of Canada's colonial violence to "cultural genocide" — the implication of which is that it was Indigenous cultures and not peoples who were targeted for elimination through residential school systems — I feared similar minimization of the violence experienced by Indigenous women and girls in this country. Instead, the National Inquiry into Missing and Murdered Indigenous Women and Girls made clear that this was race and gender-based genocide, unqualified, perpetrated by Canada against Indigenous Peoples. This ruling was made in accordance with international and national laws and detailed throughout the more than one thousand pages of findings in the final report and a special supplemental report devoted to a legal analysis of genocide. While the inquiry was careful to note the bias and limitations of such laws given that they were drafted in the absence of Indigenous and gender-based perspectives, it nonetheless demonstrates their applicability to both colonial and gender-based genocide and establishes legal precedence for their future use in these domains.

Given its existence as a Canadian state-sponsored anti-violence response, it is significant that the inquiry took a firm stand and called Canada out for its critical role in perpetrating genocide against Indigenous Peoples. While celebrating this finding, I also recognize its limitations. This finding is rooted in international law, specifically the United Nations Genocide Convention (1948), which lacks the legal and material teeth to force Canada to comply and end its genocidal colonial domination over Indigenous Peoples and their lands. Moreover, given that Canada's existence as a nation-state is predicated on this ongoing genocidal violence, it's unlikely that governments will act on their own accord to end this genocide.

The analyses delivered in the inquiry's final report (National Inquiry into MMIWG 2019) reflects the Indigenous feminist anti-oppression framework I outlined in this chapter. Indeed, this is part of the reason that the final report exceeds one thousand pages: the inquiry took time to unpack the distinct experiences of First Nations, Métis, and Inuit women, girls, and 2SLGBTQIA+ (Two-Spirit, lesbian, gay, bisexual, trans, queer, questioning, intersex, asexual plus) people within dominant interlocking social systems of oppression including white supremacy, heteropatriarchy, colonialism, capitalism, and ableism. The findings are laser focused on demonstrating Canadian state complicity in this violence at every turn. And while documenting the violence experienced by Indigenous women, girls, and 2SLGBTQIA+ people, the report also celebrates their resilience and resistance. This framework is also reflected in the 231 Calls for Justice that demand change on multiple fronts to dismantle these dominant systems of oppression.

While I value these analyses, another limitation that needs to be acknowledged is the lack of representation of Afro-Indigenous people in the inquiry. Shared colonial histories of displacement brought and continue to bring Black and Indigenous Peoples together, resulting in descendants that reflect both groups. White supremacy operates by both targeting people through racism and through our complicity with this racism. While directly experiencing colonial racism, Indigenous Peoples also participate in anti-Black racism, and Afro-Indigenous people report experiencing ostracism and exclusion from Indigenous communities. Including their perspectives would strengthen the inquiry's findings and ensure that recommendations reflect the needs of all Indigenous Peoples.

I appreciate attempts to incorporate Indigenous ways of knowing and being into this process. I am grateful for the Indigenous people who shared their wisdom, experience, and time with the inquiry to ensure that our ways of knowing and being were part of this process. I am grateful that our ways of knowing and being are reflected in the final report. Kinanâskomitino'wo'w.

At the same time, it remained a colonial process that, in many ways, became a source of trauma for me. I wasn't permitted to share my knowledge and truths on my own terms; instead, I was walked through my testimony by a lawyer appointed to serve the commission and was forced to respond to questions from some of the approximately one hundred parties granted standing to participate in the investigatory work of the inquiry. In addition to experiencing lateral violence from another panelist, a series of questions from parties with standing dismissing the lived realities of sex trafficking forced me to disclose details of my own experience that I didn't want to share, at which point I formally withdrew from the process. Despite the circle of support that surrounded me during and after the inquiry, the process traumatized me. I experienced post-traumatic stress disorder (PTSD) symptoms comparable to those immediately following my escape from being sex trafficked. If I'm honest, it took me two years to feel normal again after testifying.

My greatest misgivings about the inquiry remain Canada's response. Research and experiential knowledge, my own included, suggest that despite appearances of committing to change, the Canadian state is innately invested in colonial genocide for its very existence and, as such, is not only unlikely to make meaningful change to protect Indigenous women, girls and 2SLGBTQIA+ people, but also likely to attempt to colonize — appropriate, control, and/or eliminate — Indigenous anti-violence efforts in support of its survival. I have zero faith in the Government of Canada, and this is reinforced by their response to the final report. It took two years for the Government of Canada to formally respond, a delay they blamed on the COVID-19 pandemic. This needn't have been an either/or situation — the needs of all groups should be met by the government. Instead, by its own admission, the Government of Canada privileged COVID. Racism, argues geographer Ruth Wilson Gilmore (2007, 28), "is the state-sanctioned or extra-legal production and exploitation of group-differentiated vulnerability to premature death," and the government's actions reflect this: while both pandemics — MMIWG and COVID — involve premature death, the government chose to ignore the one targeting Indigenous women and girls primarily.

The work of Indigenous women led to the development of the *Missing and Murdered Indigenous Women, Girls and* 2SLGBTQQIA+ *People National Action Plan,* which was released in 2021. Developed with guidance from the National Family and Survivors Circle and other Indigenous organizations including the Assembly of First Nations, Pauktuutit Inuit Women of Canada, and Les Femmes Michif Otipemisiwak, the National Action Plan outlines key actions for stakeholders, including the federal and provincial/territorial governments, to meaningfully address violence against Indigenous women and girls. The National Action Plan's progress report (2022, 26) recognized ongoing efforts, but it also made clear that "more action is needed to address the colonial structures, institutions, agencies, legislation, services, policies, and programs, that continue to cause harm and loss of life."

For its part, the Government of Canada has provided funding for anti-violence initiatives, services, and supports; and has implemented policy in the areas of anti-racism, mental health, gender-based violence, and human trafficking. Unfortunately, these responses are a bandage on a gaping bloody wound created and maintained by the colonial Canadian state that only decolonization can heal. As this chapter makes clear, violence against Indigenous women and girls is a requirement for Canadian colonialism, so anything less than decolonization will fail to end this violence. As a perpetrator, Canada owes Indigenous Peoples reparations for the deaths and disappearances of our women and girls; however, the current funding model paired with policy implementation pretends to acknowledge and support Indigenous self-determination and sovereignty while reinforcing the right of the Government of Canada to dictate the terms of engagement and, thus, control how Indigenous Peoples respond to this violence. Affirming this authority reinforces the existence of the colonial Canadian nation-state and, as such, ensures a future of violence against Indigenous women and girls.

NOTES

1 A note on language: throughout this chapter I privilege use of the term "Indigenous" to refer collectively to First Nations, Inuit and Métis peoples in Canada. While these groups are commonly referred to as "Aboriginal" by the Canadian state, I refrain from using this term out of respect for the many Indigenous groups in Canada who have expressed opposition to its use on the basis of it being a government-imposed term (Marks 2014). I have not eliminated or replaced its use in names (such as Aboriginal Women's Action Network) or quotes. I use "Indian" strategically to trace the divisions perpetuated through the Indian Act. Again, I have not replaced its use in names or quotes. Finally, I have made every effort to name specific Indigenous communities and, whenever possible, have done so in their own language.

2 Turtle Island is how many Indigenous Peoples refer to the territory that constitutes North America, and for the purposes of this chapter, Canada.

REFERENCES

Case Law/Legislation

Daniels v. Canada (Indian Affairs and Northern Development). 2016. Supreme Court of Canada 12 (CanLII)

Other

Acoose, Janice. 1995. *Iskwewak Kah'Ki Yaw Ni Wahkomakanak: Neither Indian Princesses Nor Easy Squaws.* Toronto: Women's Press.

Alfred, Gerald Taiaiake. 2009. "Colonialism and State Dependency." *Journal of Aboriginal Health* 5, 2. jps.library.utoronto.ca/index.php/ijih/article/view/28982.

Amnesty International. 2004. *Stolen Sisters: A Human Rights Response to Discrimination and Violence Against Indigenous Women in Canada.* amnesty.ca/sites/amnesty/files/amr200032004enstolensisters.pdf.

Anderson, Kim. 2000. *A Recognition of Being — Reconstructing Native Womanhood.* Toronto: Sumach Press.

___. 2009. "Leading by Action: Female Chiefs and the Political Landscape." In *Restoring the Balance: First Nations Women, Community and Culture,* edited by Gail Guthrie Valaskakis, Madeleine Dion Stout, and Eric Guimond. Winnipeg: University of Manitoba Press.

AWAN (Aboriginal Women's Action Network). 2011. "Aboriginal Women's Action Network Statement Opposing Legalized Prostitution & Decriminalization of Prostitution." https://wunrn.com/2011/04/canada-aboriginal-womens-statement-against-legalized-prostitution/.

Bopp, Michael, et al. 2003. *Aboriginal Domestic Violence in Canada*: Ottawa: The Aboriginal Healing Foundation. https://www.ahf.ca/files/domestic-violence.pdf.

Bourgeois, Robyn. 2012. "National Inquiry on Missing, Murdered Women Not Best Answer." *HuffPost Canada,* December 21. https://www.huffpost.com/archive/ca/entry/national-inquiry-on-missing-murdered-women-not-best-answer_b_2333262.

___. 2014. "Warrior Women: Indigenous Women's Anti-Violence Engagement with the Canadian State." Unpublished doctoral thesis, Toronto: University of Toronto.

___. 2015. "Colonial Exploitation: The Canadian State and the Trafficking of Indigenous Women and Girls in Canada." UCLA *Law Review* 62.

Brennan, Shannon. 2011. *Violent Victimization of Aboriginal Women in the Canadian Provinces, 2009.* Ottawa: Juristat. statcan.gc.ca/pub/85-002-x/2011001/article/11439-eng.pdf.

Cannon, Martin J. 2011. "Revisiting Histories of Legal Assimilation, Racialized Injustice, and the Future of Indian Status in Canada." In *Racism, Colonialism, and Indigeneity in Canada,* edited by Martin J. Cannon and Lina Sunseri. Toronto: Oxford University Press.

CBC News. 2014. "Full Text of Peter Mansbridge's Interview with Stephen Harper." December 17. cbc.ca/news/politics/full-text-of-peter-mansbridge-s-interview-with-stephen-harper-1.2876934.

___. 2016. "Murdered Women's Inquiry Must Confront Barriers Indigenous Women Face in Canadian Society." January 17. cbc.ca/news/canada/british-columbia/missingwomen-carolyn-bennett-inquiry-feminism-1.3407921.

Comack, Elizabeth. 2014. "Colonialism Past and Present: Indigenous Human Rights and Canadian Policing." In *Indivisible: Indigenous Human Rights,* edited by Joyce Green. Halifax and Winnipeg: Fernwood Publishing.

Coulthard, Glen Sean. 2014. *Red Skin, White Masks: Rejecting the Colonial Politics of Recognition.* Minneapolis: University of Minnesota Press.

Culhane, Dara. 2009. "Their Spirits Live Within Us: Aboriginal Women in Downtown Eastside Vancouver Emerging into Visibility." In *Keeping the Campfires Burning: Native Women's Activism in Urban Communities,* edited by Susan Applegate Krouse and Heather A. Howard. Lincoln and London: University of Nebraska Press.

Dick, Carolyn. 2006. "The Politics of Intragroup Difference: First Nations' Women and the *Sawridge* Dispute." *Canadian Journal of Political Silence* 39, 1.

Eberts, Mary. 2014. "Victoria's Secret: How to Make a Population of Prey." In *Indivisible: Indigenous Human Rights,* edited by Joyce Green. Halifax and Winnipeg: Fernwood Publishing.

Erickson, Lesley. 2011. *Westward Bound: Sex, Violence, the Law, and the Making of a Settler Society.* Vancouver: UBC Press.

Fallon, Barbara, et al. 2021. "Denouncing the Continued Overrepresentation of First Nations Children in Canadian Child Welfare: Findings from the First Nations/Canadian Incidence Study of Reported Child Abuse and Neglect-2019." *Assembly of First Nations.* cwrp.ca/sites/default/files/publications/FNCIS-2019%20-%20Denouncing%20the%20Continued%20Overrepresentation%20of%20First%20Nations%20Children%20in%20Canadian%20Child%20Welfare%20--%20Final.pdf.

Fellows, Mary Louise, and Sherene Razack. 1998. "The Race to Innocence: Confronting Hierarchical Relations among Women." *Journal of Gender, Race & Justice* 335.

Gehl, Lynn. 2015. "Canada's Indian Policy Is a Process of Deception." *Briarpatch*

Magazine, March 2. briarpatchmagazine.com/articles/view/canadas-indian-policy-is-a-process-of-deception.

Gilmore, Ruth Wilson. 2007. *Golden Gulag: Prisons, Surplus, Crisis, and Opposition in Globalizing California.* Berkeley and Los Angeles: University of California Press.

Goulding, Warren. 2001. *Just Another Indian: A Serial Killer and Canada's Indifference.* Calgary: Fifth House.

Government of Canada. 2008. "Aboriginal Women and Family Violence." canada.ca/en/public-health/services/health-promotion/stop-family-violence/prevention-resource-centre/aboriginal-women/aboriginal-women-family-violence.html.

———. 2016. "Terms of Reference for the National Inquiry into Missing and Murdered Indigenous Women and Girls." rcaanc-cirnac.gc.ca/eng/1470141425998/1534527073231.

———. 2019. *Reclaiming Power and Place: The Final Report of the National Inquiry into Missing and Murdered Indigenous Women and Girls.* mmiwg-ffada.ca/final-report/.

Green, Joyce. 2007. "Taking Account of Aboriginal Feminism." In *Making Space for Indigenous Feminism,* edited by Joyce Green. Halifax and Winnipeg: Fernwood Publishing.

———. 2014. "From Colonialism to Reconciliation Through Indigenous Human Rights." In *Indivisible: Indigenous Human Rights,* edited by Joyce Green. Halifax and Winnipeg: Fernwood Publishing.

Harris, R. Cole. 2002. *Making Native Space: Colonialism, Resistance, and Reserves in British Columbia.* Vancouver: UBC Press.

Hugill, David. 2010. *Missing Women, Missing News: Covering Crisis in Vancouver's Downtown Eastside.* Halifax and Winnipeg: Fernwood Publishing.

Hylton, John. 2002. "The Justice System and Canada's Aboriginal Peoples: The Persistence of Racial Discrimination." In *Crimes of Colour: Racialization and the Criminal Justice System in Canada,* edited by Wendy Chan and Kiran Mirchandani. Peterborough: Broadview Press.

Kingston, Anne. 2016. "Is Justin Trudeau a Fake Feminist?" *Maclean's,* September 8. macleans.ca/politics/ottawa/is-justin-trudeau-a-fake-feminist/.

Kuokkanen, Rauna. 2014. "Gendered Violence and Politics in Community." *International Feminist Journal of Politics* 17, 2.

LaRocque, Emma. 1994. *Violence in Aboriginal Communities.* Ottawa: Clearinghouse on Family Violence.

Mann, Barbara Alice. 2000. *Iroquoian Women: The Gantowisas.* New York: Peter Lang.

Marks, Don. 2014. "What's in a Name: Indian, Native, Aboriginal, or Indigenous?" *CBC News Online,* October 2. https://ca.news.yahoo.com/whats-name-indian-native-aboriginal-101500776.html.

National Action Plan. 2021. *The 2021 Missing and Murdered Indigenous Women, Girls, and 2SLGBTQQIA+ People National Action Plan.* mmiwg2plus-nationalactionplan.ca/eng/1670511213459/1670511226843.

———. 2022. *The 2022 Progress Report on the Missing and Murdered Indigenous Women, Girls, and 2SLGBTQQIA+ People National Action Plan.* mmiwg2plus-nationalactionplan.ca/.

NWAC (Native Women's Association of Canada). 2009. *Voices of Our Sisters in Spirit: A Report to Families and Communities, 2nd Edition*. nwac.ca/assets-knowledge-centre/NWAC_Voices-of-Our-Sisters-In-Spirit_2nd-Edition_March-2009.pdf.

———. 2010. *What Their Stories Tell Us: Research Findings from the Sisters in Spirit Initiative*. Ottawa: Native Women's Association of Canada. nwac.ca/assets-knowledge-centre/2010_What_Their_Stories_Tell_Us_Research_Findings_SIS_Initiative-1.pdf.

———. 2014. *Sexual Exploitation and Trafficking of Aboriginal Women and Girls: Literature Review and Key Informant Interviews — Final Report*. nwac.ca/wp-content/uploads/2015/05/2014_NWAC_Human_Trafficking_and_Sexual_Exploitation_Report.pdf.

Oppal, Wally. 2012. *Forsaken: The Report of the Missing Women Commission of Inquiry, Volume I*. Victoria: Province of British Columbia.

Perrin, Benjamin. 2010. *Invisible Chains: Canada's Underground World of Human Trafficking*. Toronto: Viking Canada.

Razack, Sherene H. 1998. *Looking White People in the Eye: Gender, Race, and Culture in Courtrooms and Classrooms*. Toronto: University of Toronto Press.

———. 2002. "Gendered Racial Violence and Spatialized Justice: The Murder of Pamela George." In *Race, Space, and the Law: Unmapping a White Settler Society*, edited by Sherene H Razack. Toronto: Between the Lines.

———. 2016. "Gendering Disposability." *Canadian Journal of Women and the Law* 28, 2.

RCMP (Royal Canadian Mounted Police). 2014. *Missing and Murdered Aboriginal Women: A National Operational Overview*. Ottawa: Government of Canada. rcmp-grc.gc.ca/en/missing-and-murdered-aboriginal-women-national-operational-overview.

Sethi, Anupriya. 2007. "Domestic Sex Trafficking of Aboriginal Girls in Canada: Issues and Implications." *First People Child & Family Review* 3, 3.

Shaw, Candice. 2013. *The Contours of Family Violence in Indigenous Communities: The Prevalence and Effectiveness of Initiatives Implemented to Address Indigenous Family-Based Violence*. Montreal: Institute for the Study of International Development, McGill University. mcgill.ca/isid/files/isid/pb_2013_02_shaw.pdf.

Smith, Andrea. 2005. *Conquest: Sexual Violence and American Indian Genocide*. Cambridge, MA: South End Press.

St. Denis, Verna. 2007. "Feminism Is for Everybody: Aboriginal Women, Feminism, and Diversity." In *Making Space for Indigenous Feminism*, edited by Joyce Green. Black Point and Winnipeg: Fernwood Publishing.

Stueck, Wendy. 2016. "Inquiry into Missing and Murdered Women Needs Funding, Advocates Say." *Globe and Mail*, January 12. theglobeandmail.com/news/british-columbia/inquiry-into-missing-and-murdered-women-needs-funding-advocates-say/article28140337.

Troian, Martha. 2016. "'No Foul Play' Found in Deaths of Dozens of Indigenous Women, But Questions Remain." *CBC News Online*, June 28. cbc.ca/news/canada/manitoba/unresolved-cases-of-missing-and-murdered-Indigenous-women-1.3651516.

Truth and Reconciliation Commission. 2015. *Honouring the Truth, Reconciling for the Future Summary of the Final Report of the Truth and Reconciliation Commission of Canada*. trc.ca/websites/trcinstitution/index.php?p=890.

United Nations. 1948. *The Convention on the Prevention and Punishment of the Crime of Genocide (Genocide Convention)*. un.org/en/genocideprevention/documents/atrocity-crimes/Doc.1_Convention%20on%20the%20Prevention%20and%20Punishment%20of%20the%20Crime%20of%20Genocide.pdf.

Williams, Bernie, and Gladys Radek. 2010. "Walk4Justice Summary; 2010." unbc.ca/sites/default/files/sections/northern-fire/walk4justice_summary2010.pdf.

SEVEN

Gender Reveals That Matter

Cis-Heteropatriarchy, Settler Colonialism, and Child Welfare

Megan Scribe

FORMER CHILDREN IN "CARE" HAVE established clear links between their experiences coming of age in child welfare custody and Canadian settler colonialism. Indigenous-authored creative non-fiction texts highlight the sexist, misogynistic, and transphobic dimensions of the child welfare institution (see Colleen Cardinal 2018 and jaye simpson 2020). Along these lines, the National Inquiry into Missing and Murdered Indigenous Women and Girls (NIMMIWG) maintains that Canada's existing child welfare system, "inflicts violence on Indigenous women, girls, and 2SLGBTQIA+ people and contributes in significant ways to a lack of safety" (Government of Canada 2019, 354). This is not new information. NIMMIWG commissioners point out that between 1994 and 2015, eight reports were released with approximately twenty-eight recommendations on the need to improve child welfare (2019, 349). Despite the prominence of gender within diverse survivor accounts and Indigenous-led research on child welfare, the figure of the Indigenous child circulating in legislation and policy (and even advocacy) presents as ungendered. The problem is that gender-neutral discourse isn't neutral at all. In a cis-heteropatriarchal society, individual life paths are largely determined by sex and gender assignment from the moment of birth. Indigenous girls, Two-Spirit, and trans* Indigenous children are particularly vulnerable to cis-heteropatriarchal laws, policies, and social practices.[1] Gender-neutral discourses elide the material realities of all

Indigenous children in child welfare custody. Attending to gender can expose the entanglement of cis-heteropatriarchy and settler colonialism in child welfare and, more broadly, Canada.

Gender-neutral discourse circulating in child welfare law and policy obfuscates the material realities of Indigenous children in custody and, ultimately, conceals the centrality of cis-heteropatriarchy in the creation and administration of colonial institutions. Indigenous advocates need to seriously consider the role of gender to dismantle these oppressive structures and systems. This chapter begins by making explicit the entanglement of cis-heteropatriarchy and settler colonialism. The next section outlines Canada's history of Indigenous child welfare management to expose socio-political and legal violence and Indigenous interventions. This analysis is grounded in the Manitoba context, but many aspects of it can be usefully applied elsewhere. The final part takes readers through the typical life cycle of colonial care for Indigenous girls from infancy into adolescence. In a cis-heteropatriarchal and settler colonial society, gendering the figure of the Indigenous child circulating in child welfare law, policy, and social discourse matters. Former children in care and Indigenous-led research clearly articulate how gender informs the trajectory of Indigenous Peoples' lives. As this chapter makes plain, some gender reveals can shed light on oppressive systems yet to be dismantled in pursuit of decolonization.

GENDERED AT BIRTH

Once a child is born in Manitoba, medical professionals perform basic health checks and assessments immediately following the birth. It is at this point that the infant receives a sex assignment of either male or female. Most infants are assigned a sex and gender before they receive a name.

In a cis-normative society organized along a sex and gender binary, sex assignment is believed to correspond with gender identity. With respect to both sex and gender assignments, there are only two options in Western society: male/man or female/woman. While these classification systems offer a straightforward either/or proposition, nature is not so neatly delineated. The sex and gender binaries refuse to account for intersex and trans* experiences of gender identity. Nevertheless, gender socialization commences following sex and gender assignment. There are significant socio-legal implications that come with sex and gender assignments. An individual's sex and gender assignment determine access to certain types of health care, education and training, employment and professional advancement, and legal rights and recognition. In short, sex and gender organize every aspect of modern life.

There are colonial dimensions to sex and gender classification. Since inception, the Indian Act has foisted Western gender ideologies onto Status Indians registered under the Act. Initially, Indians registered under the Act were defined as "Any male person of Indian blood reputed to belong to a particular band; Secondly. Any child of such person; Thirdly. Any woman who is or was lawfully married to such person" (1876, 43–44). This androcentrism persists throughout the original document and every iteration that followed. From 1876 to 1951, Status Indian men had the ability to enfranchise if they attended post-secondary or joined the military. If these men were married and/or had children, all members of the family would thus become Canadian citizens and lose access to Treaty Rights. Between 1951 and 1985, Status Indian women could lose their status if they married a non-Status Indian man. The same did not hold true for Status Indian men. Matters relating to land ownership, inheritance, and band leadership also highlight the ways gender has and continues to organize Indigenous life. Indigenous feminists have made significant strides in correcting gender discrimination within the Indian Act (see Eberts et al. in this volume), but there's been little movement to grapple with the ways the gender binary itself organizes the body of law.

MANITOBA'S MILLENNIAL SCOOP

Indigenous children did not initially fall within the purview of provincial child welfare mandates established in the late nineteenth century. The British North America Act established that the federal government was exclusively responsible for all matters relating to "Indians and lands reserved for Indians" (1867). Indian residential and day schools were Canada's answer to Indigenous child and family welfare. By the time child welfare legislation had been established in different parts of Canada, federally funded Indian residential and day schools had been in operation since the late nineteenth century. Amendments to the Indian Act in 1920 implemented mandatory enrolment to these institutions for children aged seven to sixteen. The decline of these schools coincided with the end of compulsory enrolment in 1948, and the 1951 amendments to the Indian Act granted provinces greater reach into the lives of Indigenous children and families. Between the 1960s and 1980s, a period known as the Sixties Scoop, thousands of Indigenous children were adopted to mostly white families across Canada, the United States, and parts of Europe. While the institutional formations and processes have changed, the underlying ideology and objective remains the same: removing Indigenous children from their homes under the guise of care and concern.

Indigenous children, families, and communities resisted in formal and informal ways. Survivor accounts described hiding from authorities, running away from schools and adoptive families, written petitions by parents and leaders, and personal coping strategies. By the 1980s, Indigenous child welfare advocates gained socio-political traction that led to moratoriums on Indigenous adoption and significant legislative reform.

Despite discursive shifts and legislative reform, Indigenous children continued to enter care in high numbers. In fact, it has been observed that there are more children in care today than at the height of the residential school era (Blackstock 2003, 331). This Millennial Scoop occurs on the grounds of over one hundred years of assimilatory and genocidal policy targeting Indigenous children and against the backdrop of the Truth and Reconciliation era. Legislative reform and increased awareness have apparently not addressed the underlying genocidal logics of child welfare in Canada. Legislative reform has yet to challenge the validity of provincial child welfare systems in the lives of Indigenous Peoples. Instead, Indigenous Peoples and communities are invited to operate the machine that is child welfare in Canada. Perhaps one of the most notable and troubling differences between the Sixties Scoop and the Millennial Scoop is that Indigenous officials have become enlisted in apprehending Indigenous children.

Based on sheer numbers, the Millennial Scoop in Manitoba has been devastating. Indigenous children comprise 91 percent of the 9,196 children in Manitoba care (Minister of Families 2022, 103), and the province has become emblematic of Canada's flawed child welfare system. With the establishment of Manitoba's Child Protection Act (1898), provincially mandated "child savers" initially focused on children of European descent. With Lake St. Martin Indian Residential School opening its doors in 1874, the first of nineteen residential schools in Manitoba, Indigenous children were not within the purview of the Act. A mere ten Indigenous children were held in child welfare custody in 1956, including one deaf child from Sioux Valley who attended a specialized school during the weekdays and returned home most weekends (Child & Family Services of Western Manitoba 1999, 21). By 1968, the rates had increased exponentially with Indigenous children making up 40 percent of the overall child welfare population (Child & Family Services of Western Manitoba 1999, 22). Since then, the Province of Manitoba has come under close scrutiny for its participation in the Sixties Scoop.

In 1985, Associate Chief Judge Edwin C. Kimelman authored the *Review Committee on Indian and Metis Adoptions and Placements*, a report more commonly known as *No Quiet Place: Final Report to the Honourable Muriel Smith, Minister of Community Services*. Kimelman put forth 109 recommendations to address the large number of Indigenous children placed for adoption in predominantly non-Indigenous homes throughout Canada and the United States. Kimelman concluded that the high number of out-of-province adoptions was merely a symptom of a larger problem with provincial and federal approaches to Indigenous child welfare management. Despite the crucial findings, the numbers of children entering Manitoba care seems to have increased in lockstep with increasing public awareness and legislative reform.

Some of the most significant changes to Manitoba's child welfare system in the last thirty years have been prompted by the deaths of Indigenous girls in state custody. In 1988, Manitoba commissioned the Public Inquiry into the Administration of Justice and Aboriginal People (known as the Aboriginal Justice Inquiry [AJI]) following the death of Helen Betty Osborne in 1971 and J.J. Harper in 1987. The delayed inquiry into Osborne's death is not altogether surprising given the sluggish police investigation into the abduction, torture, sexual assault, and murder of the nineteen-year-old teenage girl by four white men in The Pas, Manitoba. Osborne was originally from Norway House Cree Nation, Manitoba, but had relocated for high school in 1969. She had been living with a host family at the time of her death and had just started Grade 9 at Margaret Barbour Collegiate Institute. A police investigation immediately commenced following Osborne's death on November 13, 1971, but many believed the officers took the matter less seriously because Osborne was Indigenous and the suspects were white. In 1988, the inquiry commenced with the mandate to investigate whether misogynistic racial prejudice informed the investigation into

Osborne's death and, more broadly, to "investigate, report and make recommendations to the Minister of Justice on the relationship between the administration of justice and aboriginal peoples of Manitoba" (Hamilton and Sinclair 1991). While the commissioners found no evidence that racism delayed the police investigation, they concluded that racism played a significant role in Osborne's death. Besides individual racism, the commissioners investigated structural racism embedded within all aspects of Canadian society, including the criminal justice system for youth and adults, policing, jails and prisons, child welfare, and education. The commissioners noted the longstanding pattern of removing Indigenous children from their families from Osborne's death up to the inquiry proceedings (1991, 92).

The inquiry into Osborne's death initiated significant child welfare legislative changes for the new millennium. Following the AJI final report, the Aboriginal Justice Implementation Commission formed in 1999 to carry through on the AJI recommendations. This led to the formation of the Aboriginal Justice Inquiry-Child Welfare Initiative in 2000. The objective of this joint initiative between the Province of Manitoba, Manitoba Métis Federation, the Assembly of Manitoba Chiefs, and the Manitoba Keewatinook Ininew Okimowin was to develop First Nations and Métis child welfare services. Over the next several years, the parties collaborated on design principles, conceptual mapping, and public consultation with First Nations and Métis stakeholders, which ultimately led to the proclamation of The Child and Family Services Authorities Act on November 24, 2003. The Act outlined Manitoba's Child and Family Services (CFS) devolution of power from the Director of Child Welfare to four new authorities organized by geographic zones across the province. While the new system granted authorities province-wide jurisdiction and greater power to First Nations and Métis peoples, authorities were ultimately accountable to the provincial and federal governments (Commission of Inquiry into the Circumstances Surrounding the Death of Phoenix Sinclair 2012).

The death of five-year-old Phoenix Victoria Hope Sinclair on June 11, 2005, further revealed fundamental flaws within Manitoba's child welfare system. For many, the discovery of Sinclair's death came months after it occurred. It was because of the persistence of Sinclair's loved ones that the young girl's remains were eventually recovered nine months following her death. Indigenous communities from across Manitoba gathered around the bereaved to collectively mourn and demand justice. Given Sinclair's lifelong involvement with Manitoba's child welfare system, family and community advocates demanded to know how the system could allow this young girl to disappear unnoticed under its watchful gaze. Many had pointed out the carceral nature of child welfare and further established links between foster care and the carceral system. It was widely understood that Sinclair's disappearance and death were not isolated incidents, but reflective of systemic problems affecting all Indigenous children in Manitoba. As part of this call for justice by Manitoba's child welfare system, demands for truth and change were made.

A number of changes to Manitoba's child welfare system followed the discovery of Sinclair's death, including the implementation of a new triage system called Differential Response, the injection of new funds to bring the system online, and the redistribution of case worker loads. On March 2011, the Lieutenant Governor in Council ordered the Inquiry into the Circumstances Surrounding the Death of Phoenix Sinclair. Commissioner Ted Hughes was tasked with inquiring into the child welfare services that Sinclair and her family received, any circumstances besides those related to child welfare related to Sinclair's death, and why Sinclair's death remained undiscovered for nine months. The inquiry was organized into three phases to first examine Sinclair's immediate circumstances, followed by changes to the child welfare system since her death, and finally the broader matter of Indigenous Peoples' relationship to the child welfare system in Canada. By the time Hughes released the three-volume report (2013) with sixty-two recommendations, the inquiry was already one of the most expensive inquiries in Manitoba at an estimated $10 million (Canadian Press 2014). This landmark inquiry, as the AJI before it, initiated significant changes to Manitoba's child welfare system.

These official responses into the deaths of Indigenous girls in state care have initiated the province's most significant inquiries, led to structural reform in the child welfare system, and directed attention to the matter. And yet, gender remains a peripheral concern to provincial legislative reform. The Manitoba Advocate for Children and Youth released a special report in 2021 focused on nineteen Manitoba children who were maltreated and died while in care between 2008 and 2020. The advocate stated, "Despite the massive public inquiry into Phoenix Sinclair's death and the 62 recommendations that were made from that evidence, children are still dying of maltreatment similar to what Phoenix experienced" (2021, 6). Attending to gender can expose the entanglement of anti-Indigenous racism and cis-heteropatriarchy leading large numbers of Indigenous children into child welfare custody where many experience harm while in care.

BIRTH ALERTS

In delivery rooms across Canada, a birth alert announces the arrival of an Indigenous baby. This longstanding practice authorizes hospital staff to contact child welfare with any suspicion that a newborn may be vulnerable to abuse or neglect. With statistics showing Indigenous children comprising 53.8 percent of the total number of children in foster care (Statistics Canada 2022) and 496 Manitoban newborns apprehended in 2021 (Malone 2022), birth alerts are particularly devastating for Indigenous families. Safety assessments are hastily formed by hospital staff, who may have just met expectant parents. Staff may note the expectant parents' lack of prenatal care or scant personal belongings as evidence of parental neglect as opposed to systemic inequities. Once sounded, the birth alert initiates a lifelong entanglement between Indigenous families and the child welfare system. The Legislative Review Committee into Manitoba's child welfare legislation called for an end to the birth alert process in 2018 (Legislative Review Committee 2018, 34). This call was later echoed in *Reclaiming Power and Place: The Final Report of the National Inquiry into Missing and Murdered Indigenous Women and Girls* (Government of Canada 2019). Despite the province announcing the end of birth alerts as of July 2020, Manitoba CFS continues to apprehend Indigenous newborns.

Birth alerts attest to the persistent colonial logic constructing Indigenous children as vulnerable to their dysfunctional parents with child welfare officials poised to intervene. In a settler society, "vulnerability" and "dysfunction" are projected onto Indigenous Peoples as tactics for advancing Canadian settler colonialism. This formulation renders children "salvageable" and adults as "too far gone." This logic extends to Indigenous Peoples as a whole who are largely portrayed as a doomed race without settler intervention (Razack 2015). Settler logic maintains that "saving" Indigenous Peoples involves stripping the youngest of culture and kin. The problem with this logic is that Indigenous children grow up and become Indigenous adults.

Constructing Indigenous parents as unable to care for their children parallels the broader logic that Indigenous Peoples cannot self-govern. For Indigenous Peoples, reaching the age of majority has not historically conferred the same legal rights and responsibilities as Canadian adults. Indigenous Peoples, like children, are socially and legally defined as vulnerable and in need of state protection. The federal government has readily assumed this paternalistic role over Indigenous Peoples; first with section 91(24) of the British North America Act (1867) conferring legislative authority over "Indians, and lands reserved for the Indians." Following the British North America Act, the Indian Act (1876) further entrenched legislative paternalism by assuming authority over nearly every aspect of Indian life including "reserves, lands, moneys and property of Indians in Canada" (Indian Act 1876). The parent-child dynamic established through colonial legislation facilitates Canadian assimilatory polices meant to absorb the Indigenous population into the body politic. While the language of "wardship" has largely fallen out of favour, Canada's paternalistic management of Indigenous Peoples persists.

Any newborn for whom a birth alert has been issued also becomes the subject of a child welfare record documenting the encounter. For those newborns assigned female at birth (AFAB), this record-keeping poses uniquely gendered consequences. In addition to being marked as vulnerable, AFAB newborns receive a deferred mark of criminality bound up with heterosexist reproductive presumptions. First Nations Family Advocate Cora Morgan reveals, "I had a woman who had her first baby at 38 years old, and because she aged out of the system, they had flagged her baby. She had been out of care for 18 years" (Government of Canada 2019, 365). Those assigned female at birth subject to birth alerts reveal seemingly contradictory colonial logics: Indigenous newborns are perceived as vulnerable; yet, the reproductive potential of AFAB newborns triggers settler suspicions of criminality. Karen Stote (2015, 8) reminds, "Aboriginal women, in their ability to reproduce future generations of Indigenous peoples, represented and continue to represent an impediment to the colonial project." Indeed, cis-heteropatriarchal and colonial logics mark AFAB newborns as future threats to Canada.

Section 9(4) of Manitoba's Child and Family Services Act requires hospital staff to notify the Director of Birth when "a hospital or other institution has received care during pregnancy or accouchement an unmarried child or a child with respect to whose marriage there exists reasonable doubt." While birth alerts officially ended in July 2020, Manitoba continues to track teenage pregnancies. This section disproportionately targets Indigenous expectant parents, and expectant mothers in particular. The expectation that expectant parents should be married is born from Western ideologies surrounding families and relationships that have been imposed and reinforced through Canada's socio-political efforts to establish its national identity. Canada has historically relied on marriage and divorce laws to assert its status as a respectable white settler society while at the same time constraining Indigenous women's political authority (Carter 2008).

Section 9(4) is not focused on marriage alone, but the unwed child (i.e., teenage parents). Teenage parents are constructed as social deviants and burdens to society in general; this is compounded by racism and colonialism for Indigenous teenage parents. The ward relationship between the federal government and Indigenous Peoples has generated an unfair and pernicious assumption that Indigenous people are a burden to Canada. Once the Director of Birth is notified about an unmarried child seeking healthcare services, the deferred mark of criminality becomes permanently affixed to the child and they are no longer considered vulnerable in the view of child welfare authorities.

"BEYOND CONTROL": TRANSITIONING INTO ADOLESCENCE

Foster Care

Most Indigenous children taken in care will spend the entirety of their childhood and adolescence in precarious custody. According to Raven Sinclair (2007), one feature distinguishing the Millennial Scoop is the greater reliance on long-term temporary placements as opposed to adoptions. Adoptions are less frequent, so many of the children live in foster care placements. Foster care was never meant to be a framework for raising children. The placements procured for children in care by Manitoba's CFS can best be described as a state of exception, what Giorgio Agamben has described as the realm of bare life. In his words (1998, 11), "At once excluding bare life from and capturing it within the political order, the state of exception actually constituted, in its very separateness, the hidden foundation on which the entire political system rested." Thinking about temporary placements as zones of exception and the consignment of children to bare life offers a way of understanding how minimum standards of care, bereft of comfort and affection, are considered acceptable. Thinking about foster care as bare life denaturalizes these custodial arrangements and establishes connections between Canada's conceptualization of "care" and its colonial regime.

CFS is one matter of concern, but CFS placements are a different kind of beast. Foster placements are defined and regulated by the provincial Child and Family Services Act and Child and Family Services Authorities Act. Both acts state that it is the shared responsibility of the director and authorities to "ensure the development of appropriate placement resources for children" (The Child and Family Services Act 2003, clause 4(1)(j); Child and Family Services Authorities Act 2003, clause 19(l)). It is the CFS *Standards Manual* that provides instruction on how best to interpret the two legislative bodies. Chapter 5 of the manual outlines resource management, licensing and licensing appeals, foster home placements, care responsibilities, support and respite, and removing foster children. Volume 2 of the standards manual, Facility Standards, deals more closely with the licensing and operation of group homes, treatment centres, and other childcare facilities. While volumes one and two of the CFS *Standards Manual* provide extensive guidance on appropriate child placements into foster homes and group homes, both legislation and policy fail to provide insight into children's experiences with CFS placements. What this means is that child welfare law and policy documents provide an account of placements told exclusively from the perspectives of officials with little to no inclusion of the primary rights holders.

CFS claims to place greater emphasis on family reunification. As such, temporary placements such as foster homes, group care facilities, and treatment centres tend to be the most common placements. CFS has relied on both public and private non- and for-profit agencies for placement services and facilities for years. As recent as August 2020 did CFS give 120 days' notice to one of its major contractors (Annable 2020). According to the Child and Family Services Act, a foster home is defined as "a home other than the home of the parent or guardian of a child, where no more than four children who are not siblings are placed by an agency for care and supervision but not for the purposes of adoption" (The Child and Family Services Act 2023). A group home, on the other hand, is defined as "a home where ordinarily not fewer than five or more than eight children are placed by an agency for full time care and supervision" (The Child and Family Services Act 2023). And finally, another long-term placement arrangement is the treatment centre, which is defined by the Act as "any place established or designated by the minister primarily for the care and treatment of more than 8 children and includes facilities operated by any government department for those purposes but does not include facilities for the reception and temporary detention of a child" (The Child and Family Services Act 2023). While these facilities are considered temporary in nature, it is often the case that once taken into CFS custody, a child in care will spend the remainder of their childhood in one or more of these types of arrangements.

The caregivers in each type of arrangement vary significantly. For the most part, foster homes are led by those designated as foster parents. This can include a wide range of individuals who are not necessarily trained in child welfare but have the minimum skillset and living arrangements to provide this service. Group homes and treatment centres call on individuals with specific skillsets and can best be described as staff who work in rotating shifts. The qualities sought in a foster parent differ significantly than those qualities sought in group home and treatment staff. Foster parent eligibility is extended to both individuals and couples, with or without children, who live in an apartment or house in rural or urban settings. According to the CFS website, some "special qualities" that social workers look out for in prospective foster parents include: "the warmth to care for a foster child and make him or her feel wanted and loved; the tolerance to accept a child from an unstable family background, who may or may not want to be with a foster family; the patience to work with a child who may be withdrawn or hyperactive" (Department of Families 2022b). While these qualities are valued, they are not required.

The standards for care provided by group home and treatment staff are outlined in volume two of the standards manual. This document outlines the minimum criteria for all staff, including caregivers. Staff must

> demonstrate language, writing and comprehension skills at a level high enough to effectively communicate with residents and to prepare written records; be medically, physically and emotional able to do the required work; possess knowledge of licensing legislation, regulations and standards …; possess current certification in First Aid and CPR for the age of

children being cared for ...; be at least 18 years of age; provide a satisfactory criminal record check dated within three months before starting work with the organization; and provide a satisfactory child abuse registry check dated within three months of starting work with the organization. (Department of Families 2022a, 15)

Note that in the foster parent interview, which at least considers "special qualities," the question of a staff member's ability to provide children with care or comfort is not raised at all.

Absconding

The CFS *Standards Manual* for unplanned absconding from placements describes a damaged and out-of-control child. In Chapter 4, Section 7, the CFS *Standards Manual* outlines the policies and procedures in place in the event of both planned and unplanned absences. Planned absences might include overnight stays for medical treatment, educational field trips, and family visits. This is relatively short segment of the section. The bulk of this section of the manual instructs guardians and staff on official protocols and procedures in the event of an unplanned absence.

This section of the *Standards Manual* is bolstered by several sections within CFS legislation. In Section 17, the Act offers several examples defining a child in need of protection. This includes subsection (2): a child who is beyond the control of a person who has the care, custody, control, or charge of the child. Some of the behavioural patterns that guardians and staff are trained to observe include evidence of chronic missing person reports and/or absconding from home or placement within the last six months, a pattern or history of assaultive or violent behaviour, gang involvement or association, and involvement in criminal activity. This chart depicts a deviant child who refuses care and, instead, chooses criminality. Both the legislation and the manual describe this child as "beyond control," meaning that the guardians and staff have little power or ability to prevent absences.

The section focused on high-risk victimization indicators suggests an inevitability in a child's unplanned absence. Indicators like histories of severe and/or chronic abuse, sexual exploitation, exposure to domestic violence, and exposure to violence in the community again indicate that this child will run away as a fact. Unlike the section outlining behavioural indicators, the section on victimization does not paint a picture of a deviant child, but rather one who is damaged beyond repair. There is little consideration of systemic changes that could meaningfully address child concerns.

This manual fails to examine the conditions motivating Indigenous children to run away: CFS's failure to provide children with adequate care and stable placements. The CFS infrastructure simply cannot accommodate the large numbers of children taken into custody. As such, CFS outsources care to for-profit companies and has relied on temporary placements like hotels. The group homes and foster homes cannot provide for Indigenous children's needs, leading children in state care to bounce from placement to placement. With few resources and support, running away is one of the only options that exists for Indigenous children in care. Yet, official narratives frame the matter as deviant and damaged children who cannot be controlled. This narrative offers no insight into the dangerous placements these children are running away from and the friends and family they run toward.

Indigenous girls confront uniquely gendered risks when running away. For Indigenous girls, there is a distinct and specific history of gender-based and racialized targeted killing. This is not to say that Indigenous boys do not experience targeted abductions and murder, but the underlying logics have a separate but related history. Trans* girls too face violence that bears similarities and characteristics, but because we live in a transphobic and cis-heteronormative society, there is an amplified risk that does not exist in the same way as for Indigenous cis girls.

The manual instructs guardians and staff to report missing children to local law enforcement. In Winnipeg, this would include contacting the Missing Person Unit of the Winnipeg Police Service. This guidance fails to account for police surveillance, criminalization, and abuse directed at Indigenous women, girls, and trans* people. In the Inquiry into the Death of Helen Betty Osborne, commissioners Sinclair and Hamilton detailed several instances of police brutality against Indigenous girls held in educational custodial arrangements. In several instances, police apprehended and questioned Indigenous teens without the permission of the guardians. And in one instance, a witness testified that a police officer became frustrated with the then teen girl's responses and slammed her into the police cruiser (Hamilton and Sinclair 1991, 41). Human Rights Watch has conducted an extensive investigation into the links between violence against Indigenous women and girls and Canadian law enforcement, and found that not only are Indigenous women and girls under protected, they are subject to police abuse (2013, 7–8). Guidance instructing guardians and staff to report missing children in care to police is informed by colonial fantasies and not Indigenous girls' and trans* teenagers' realities.

ABANDONED IN ADULTHOOD

By framing adolescent Indigenous teen girls as beyond control, child welfare officials can more readily abdicate responsibility for these so-called deviant teens. There are two official methods that facilitate this abandonment. First, there is the Independent Living Program that is available to children in care between the ages fifteen and eighteen. The second and final stage of abandonment is applied to all children in care. It is commonly referred to as "aging out of care." In the past, little more than a birthday marked this transition; however, aging out has come under public scrutiny in the last several decades and today in Manitoba, Agreements with Young Adults (AYA) exists to provide former children in care with transitional support as they exit the child welfare system. While CFS provides minimal support with this transition, former children in care rarely have true independence from this system. Until more recently, former children in care who become pregnant have been flagged for birth alerts for no other reason than the fact that they have a child welfare history. These transitional mechanisms bring the official narrative full circle: Indigenous girls are born vulnerable and in need of protection, but ultimately these girls inevitably grow into a threat.

Independent Living Program

Manitoba CFS offers a wide range of independent living arrangements for older children in care. While often referred to as the Independent Living Program, no such standardized model for this type of service delivery exists within the province. Rather, CFS independent living arrangements are delivered through individual initiatives by CFS agencies/authorities. For the most part, the services and supports that are made available through these programs depend on the agency through which it is offered. That said, there are some common eligibility criteria many of these programs have in common. In general, independent living programs are only available to children in care who are aged fifteen to eighteen. Many of these programs require that youth participate in skills development training that is intended to help youth transition into adulthood. These skills programs usually emphasize cooking, cleaning, employment and educational training, and budgeting. In 2006, a comprehensive review was conducted that found that former and current youth in these living arrangements struggled significantly and were provided little support.

Winnipeg CFS has been running an Independent Living Program since 1991. It offers independent living arrangements through the agency and it also relies on externally operated independent living programs. There is no standardized living budget set through this program, but most agencies provide provincial per diem rates. When transitioning into independent living arrangements, youth in care are eligible for a one-time start-up payment that is intended to assist with securing shelter and purchasing furniture.

The emphasis placed on practical skill-building is reflective of child welfare approaches to managing Indigenous children in care in general. There is a significant rift between what youth describe as crucial life skills and necessities and what is provided by child welfare. While child welfare provides the minimum payment to get an apartment, youth point out that the amount provided can only get them an apartment in poorly managed buildings (Schibler 2006, 60). Youth acknowledge that by the time they enter these arrangements they are familiar with basic budgeting, cooking, and cleaning skills; however, they describe feeling completely unprepared for the emotional and psychological demands of independent living (Schibler 2006, 64). Oftentimes, Indigenous girls who grew up in care have experienced multiple, overlapping traumas and yet, the transition into independent living provides no supports for these experiences. It is at this stage in care that youth are being prepared to transition into adulthood. CFS *Standards Manual* establishes the policy and protocol around this transition planning. This preparation policy is revealing. While family and community might vision with youth expansive futures that could include careers and educational training, CFS transition planning reflects bare life. This is a foreclosed futurity that is mapped out by CFS for children in care.

Agreements with Young Adults

Aging out of the child welfare system is abrupt and leaves youth unprepared for the realities of adulthood as an Indigenous person in Canada. In Manitoba, support services are available to those aged eighteen to twenty-one under the AYA program. This is a voluntary program that provides youth with transitional supports as they exit child welfare and enter adulthood. Some of these include supports for education goals, transitioning into adult services and independent living, entering a treatment program, and training. Through this agreement, youth exiting care can access basic maintenance funding and possibly apply for additional funding depending on the circumstances. Some of the eligible expenses this fund can cover include: household supplies, food, rent, health and personal care, transportation, and health care. Significantly, the *Standards Manual* makes clear that if a former child in care continues to reside in their foster home, the eligible expense coverage outlined above would not be provided, and no respite is paid to the foster family under this agreement.

The AYA monthly budget tells a story about individuals who must choose between life necessities like shelter, food, transportation, education, and health care. In this story, "extras" like entertainment are not an option. In this story, responsible adults budget the meagre funds to meet their basic needs. If they are unable to do so, these individuals are portrayed as irresponsible or unable to cope with the demands of adulthood. Upon exiting care, many Indigenous girls experience financial instability and poverty. According to the *Standards Manual*, all individuals entering AYA are provided a baseline monthly allowance. Former children in care and advocates have made clear that the amount provided barely covers the cost of living and forecloses many possibilities (Greenslade 2023). In order to secure housing using the baseline monthly allowance, it is reported that young adults must rent in poorly run apartment buildings in neighbourhoods where they feel unsafe. The little remaining funds are meant to cover transportation, food, personal hygiene products, and health care not covered through the Non-Insured Health Benefits program.

The AYA budget necessarily compels young adults to live month to month. With no ability to save and no inherited nest egg, dreaming and visioning for the long term simply is a luxury that is not available to Indigenous girls exiting care. In the last ten to fifteen years, public pressure has led to the creation of post-secondary funding for former permanent wards of CFS.

The official narrative presumes that individuals have been adequately prepared to creatively make these limited funds meet every life need. This narrative does not, however, account for the complex trauma and ongoing violence former children in care have endured as a result of their time in CFS custody. Further, this narrative does not account for the inadequate preparations. Life skills and transitional planning are written into CFS policy; however, youth testimony reveals that often this does not happen or the workshops they are mandated to attend do not prepare youth for budgeting for systemic poverty (Schibler 2006, 64–68).

For those Indigenous girls who have aged out of care and eventually become pregnant, until as recently as 2020 the birth alert policy meant that a note was placed in this girl's medical records to register that she was a former child in care and that a birth alert should be issued for this reason alone. As outlined earlier in this chapter, birth alerts continue to be issued in the event that a "child" delivers a child. In the Child and Family Services Act, it is stated that if a legal minor in care is admitted into a hospital to deliver an expectant child, hospital staff are required to notify child welfare officials. Given the fact the average age an Indigenous person becomes a parent is younger than the national average, it is safe to say that birth alerts disproportionately impact Indigenous people and continue to configure the Indigenous mothering experience. Apparently moving through the child welfare system is enough to signal that an expectant mother requires child welfare intervention. This signals a significant problem with the system. However, the system itself positions child welfare involvement as a problem with the individual.

FORECLOSED FUTURES

The official narrative presents a story about vulnerable Indigenous children who require the intervention of the state. In each rendering, children and their circumstances are portrayed as gender neutral. Missing from these accounts are considerations of the ways anti-Indigenous racism and cis-heteropatriarchy organizes Canadian law, policy, and social life. As Indigenous girls transition into adolescence, there is a significant pivot in how they are portrayed in official documentation. No longer seen as helpless and vulnerable, Indigenous teenage girls are reconstructed as deviant and dysfunctional. Portrayed as "beyond control," CFS literature explains why Indigenous girls run away and are disappeared. This account does not provide insight into inadequate CFS infrastructure or the bare life interpretation of care made available to children and youth in care. The framing tends to emphasize Indigenous girls' high-risk lifestyles as the central factor that ultimately place them at risk. Then, an abrupt transition into adult preparation commences during the final years in care. From approximately the ages of fifteen or sixteen, Indigenous youth in care begin life skills development and transitional planning. It appears that CFS is preparing these youth for foreclosed futures. These foreclosed futures do not account for or support Indigenous youth's hopes and dreams. For Indigenous girls, Two-Spirit, and trans* Indigenous children, these foreclosed futures are constricted by pervasive cis-heteropatriarchy.

Without a critical anti-colonial, Indigenous feminist analysis, readers are left with a story about troubled girls who cannot be salvaged despite the best efforts of the child savers. This is a story that establishes the need for child welfare systems. What this story leaves out are the gendered and colonial dimensions of child welfare systems in Canada. Attending to the experiences of Indigenous girls, Two-Spirit, and trans* Indigenous children can draw out the mutually constitutive nature of cis-heteropatriarchy and settler colonialism in Canada.

NOTE

1   My use of the term trans* throughout this chapter is informed by Jack Halberstam's usage in *Trans*: A Quick and Quirky Account of Gender Variability*. He deploys trans*, "to open the term up to unfolding categories of being organized around but not confined to forms of gender variance ... the asterisk modifies the meaning of transitivity by refusing to situate transition in relation to a destination" (2017, 4).

REFERENCES

Case Law/Legislation

An Act for the Better Protection of Neglected and Dependent Children, S.M. 1898, c. 6.
British North America Act, 1867.
Indian Act, S.C. 1876, c. 18.
Indian Act, S.C. 1951, c. 29.
The Child and Family Services Act (Manitoba), 2003, C.C.S.M. c. C80.
The Child and Family Services Act (Manitoba), 2023, C.C.S.M. c. C80.
The Child and Family Services Authorities Act (Manitoba), 2003, C.C.S.M. c. C90.

Other

Agamben, Giorgio. 1998. *Homo Sacer: Sovereign Power and Bare Life*. Redwood City: Stanford University Press.

Annable, Kristin. 2020. "Manitoba Government Cutting Ties with Private Foster Care Agency B & L Following Review." *CBC News*, August 21. cbc.ca/news/canada/manitoba/foster-care-private-manitoba-1.5695413.

Blackstock, Cindy. 2003. "First Nations Child and Family Services: Restoring Peace and Harmony in First Nations Communities." In *Child Welfare: Connecting Research, Policy, and Practice,* edited by K. Kufeldt and B. McKenzie. Waterloo, ON: Wilfred Laurier University Press.

Canadian Press. 2014. "Manitoba Sits on Phoenix Sinclair Report Until After Byelections." *CBC News*, January 9. cbc.ca/news/canada/manitoba/manitoba-sits-on-phoenix-sinclair-report-until-after-byelections-1.2490267.

Cardinal, Colleen. 2018. *Ohpikiihaakan-ohpihmeh (Raised Somewhere Else)*. Halifax: Fernwood Publishing.

Carter, Sarah. 2008. *The Importance of Being Monogamous: Marriage and Nation Building in Canada to 1915*. Edmonton: University of Alberta Press.

Child & Family Services of Western Manitoba. 1999. *The History of Our First 100 Years 1899–1999*. Brandon: Child & Family Services of Western Manitoba.

Commission of Inquiry into the Circumstances Surrounding the Death of Phoenix Sinclair. 2012. *Exhibit #10: Aboriginal Justice Inquiry—Child Welfare Initiative (AJI-CWI)*. July 21. phoenixsinclairinquiry.ca/.

Department of Families. 2022a. *Child and Family Services Standards Manual*. Winnipeg: Province of Manitoba.

___. 2022b. "Foster Care." Winnipeg: Province of Manitoba.

___. 2022c. "List of Services and Supports." Winnipeg: Province of Manitoba.

Government of Canada. 2019. *Reclaiming Power and Place: The Final Report of the National Inquiry into Missing and Murdered Indigenous Women and Girls*. mmiwg-ffada.ca/final-report/.

Greenslade, Brittany. 2023. "Changes Needed to Cutoff Age for Child and Family Services Support, Manitoba Youth Advocacy Network Says." *CBC News*, March 15. cbc.ca/news/canada/manitoba/child-family-services-cutoff-age-youth-homelessness-1.6778269.

Halberstam, Jack. 2017. *Trans*: A Quick and Quirky Account of Gender Variability*. Berkeley: University of California Press.

Hamilton, Alvin C., and C. Murray Sinclair. 1991. *Report of the Aboriginal Justice Inquiry of Manitoba*. Winnipeg: Public Inquiry into the Administration of Justice and Aboriginal People.

Hughes, Edward (Ted) N. 2013. *Commission of Inquiry into the Circumstances Surrounding the Death of Phoenix Sinclair*. Winnipeg: Manitoba Community Services.

Human Rights Watch. 2013. *Those Who Take Us Away: Abusive Policing and Failures in Protection of Indigenous Women and Girls in Northern British Columbia, Canada*.

Kimelman, Edwin C. 1985. *No Quiet Place: Final Report to the Honourable Muriel Smith, Minister of Community Services. Review Committee on Indian and Métis Adoptions and Placements*. Winnipeg: Manitoba Community Services.

Legislative Review Committee. 2018. *Transforming Child Welfare Legislation in Manitoba: Opportunities to Improve Outcomes for Children and Youth.* Winnipeg: Province of Manitoba.

Manitoba Advocate for Children and Youth. 2021. *Still Waiting: Investigating Child Maltreatment after the Phoenix Sinclair Inquiry.* Winnipeg: Manitoba Advocate for Children and Youth

Malone, Kelly Geraldine. 2022. "Ending Birth Alerts a 'Red Herring' that Doesn't Address Root Causes of Child Apprehension, Experts Say." *CBC News*, September 19. cbc.ca/news/canada/manitoba/birth-alerts-child-welfare-agencies-indigenous-children-1.6587623.

Minister of Families. 2022. *Manitoba Families: Annual Report.* Winnipeg: Province of Manitoba.

Razack, Sherene H. 2015. *Dying from Improvement: Inquests and Inquiries into Indigenous Deaths in Custody.* Toronto: University of Toronto Press.

Schibler, Billie. 2006. *"Strengthening Our Youth": Their Journey to Competence and Independence.* Winnipeg: Office of the Children's Advocate.

simpson, jaye. 2020. *it was never going to be okay.* Madeira Park: Harbour Publishing.

Sinclair, Raven. 2007. "Identity Lost and Found: Lessons from the Sixties Scoop." *First Peoples Child & Family Review* 3, 1.

Statistics Canada. 2022. "Indigenous Population Continues to Grow and Is Much Younger Than the Non-Indigenous Population, Although the Pace of Growth Has Slowed." www150.statcan.gc.ca/n1/daily-quotidien/220921/dq220921a-eng.htm.

Stote, Karen. 2015. *An Act of Genocide: Colonialism and the Sterilization of Aboriginal Women.* Halifax: Fernwood Publishing.

SECTION III

LAND | RELATIONALITY | LOVE

EIGHT

Towards an Anti-Colonial Feminist Care Ethic

Eva Jewell

IN *THE TROUBLE WITH WHITE WOMEN,* Kyla Schuller (2021, 83) recalls the story of Alice Fletcher, the first woman appointed to a Harvard institution research position in 1882 — several decades before female undergraduate students were even admitted to the institution. Fletcher was from an affluent white family in New York and was well educated as a result. Her scholarly and political pursuits led her to anthropology, a burgeoning field rife with plenty of subjects to study (read: Indigenous Peoples in North America) and a proclaimed urgency to study them before they "vanished" under the disastrous and unapologetic violence of settler colonialism. Fletcher's prolific work in the field was motivated by her unending urge to "save" Indigenous Peoples in the prairies and plains of what is currently the United States, among them Lakota, Omaha, Ho-Chunk, and Pawnee nations. "Yet she positioned Native peoples as her charges and herself as the benevolent and powerful white mother," writes Schuller. In Fletcher's own words, "The Indians cling to me like children, and I must and will protect them" (2021, 83).

In the footnote of an article celebrating her life and contributions to archiving "the vanishing Indian," Joy Rohde, Alice Fletcher, and Matilda Stevenson (2000, 9) write that Fletcher's work reflected "attitudes common in the late nineteenth century." A true product of her time, the feminist colonizer was keen to usher the "childlike Indians" into modernity with the kind but firm disposition a white mother might provide. Indeed, she was instrumental to the development of the United States'

1887 Dawes Act, which systematically dispossessed millions of acres of land from dozens of Indigenous nations, and today is considered one of the most devastating federal policies to impact tribal sovereignty. The Dawes Act managed to enforce blood quantum, private land ownership, and heteronormative patriarchy in one fell swoop, since only singular male heads of house on the tribal rolls were provided with acreage (north of the border, the Canadian government achieved the same effect with the reserve system and Indian Register, both instruments of the 1876 Indian Act).

Reflecting on Fletcher, it might not come as a surprise (to Indigenous and racialized non-white people) that white women who purport to care *for* us are trouble *to* us. There is a deep-felt recognition that "care" for Indigenous Peoples is not actually care at all. Care is harm, care is violence, care is misery, care is death, care is genocide. In her scholarly examination of Indigenous girlhood, Megan Scribe (2020) identifies colonial care as a discrete mechanism that works in tandem with settler bureaucracy to enact violence in the lives of Indigenous Peoples, specifically girls. In *Life Beside Itself*, Lisa Stevenson (2014, 7) writes of anonymous care, another form of colonial care: "a regime of care that requires life to become an indifferent value — that is, a regime in which it doesn't matter who you are, just that you stay alive." Colonial care regimes insist that "care should be administered indifferently, without it mattering for whom" (2014, 5). Under this regime, care is the site where we as Indigenous Peoples experience the violent denial to our intergenerational kin responsibilities. In care, we are bereft of the embodiments our ancestors ensured for us. Billy-Ray Belcourt's (2018b) elucidation on the biosocial conditions of the reserve can demonstrate how anonymous, colonial care works to render our worlds abandoned. Settler colonialism, after all, seeks not only to clear out our lands, but also our bodies (Altamirano-Jiménez 2022). In colonial logic, our *selves* — when cleared of our ability to care for, receive and transmit our distinct knowledges, orders, languages, systems, sciences, technologies, and kinships — become empty vessels to be malleated. Rehabilitated from the Indian: that deviant, irrational, primitive politically homologous child (Rollo 2016), into the healed, aligned, biopolitical citizen (Million 2013). As Belcourt (2018a, n.p.) writes, "If we are to adequately tell a story about the care of the self in a settler state like Canada, we must begin with the invention of the so-called New World, that brutalizing project of globalization that eroded, with vicious precision, the social worlds of Indigenous peoples from coast to coast to coast." This for us, is the legacy of care. Care, as an English word, in the geopolitical context of settler colonialism, tumbles around, resonant in my mind, and I can't seem to separate the harm and violence from the concept.

This is a reading and reflection of white feminist care ethics from an Anishinaabekwe (Anishinaabe femme) perspective. More specifically, it is an honest story about the killjoy experience of critiquing white feminist care ethics from an Anishinaabe embodiment and *felt* experience (Million 2013), and about the settler colonial reality in which early and ongoing feminist care theory is ensconced. In her 2010 article "Killing Joy: Feminism and the History of Happiness," Sara Ahmed describes the feminist killjoy as an intervening, disruptive figure who — upon gaining consciousness of harm and suffering as caused by structural inequities — questions the state of public happiness. The feminist killjoy is a "spoilsport" who refuses to accept expectations of docile affect in the face of oppression, and thus their presence interrupts so-called shared atmospheres: "To be oppressed requires that you show signs of happiness, signs of being or having been adjusted" (2010, 582). As I will elaborate, feminist care ethics was a space of empowerment for those early care scholars — many of them white — to illuminate the value of care, its moral dimensions, as well as to grapple with its denigration as a gendered and often feminized sphere. In this way, the field is no doubt rife with insights. Yet amidst much of the strength-based theory that white feminist care ethics conceptualizes, it's difficult not to be a killjoy when reading the settler colonial subtext of this feminist project. While feminist care scholars posit that care makes this world possible, I argue that unless it's actively and attentively anti-colonial, it is at the expense of the worlds that pre-exist and exceed this one. I hope to also invite broader, more robust discussions on concepts of care in Anishinaabe'aadziwin (Anishinaabe ways of life) and other Indigenous worldviews and ways of life.

In my work with Andrea Doucet, a prolific scholar in the field of feminist care ethics and a generous mentor, I've thought about the uncomfortable nuance of how care theory is produced in settler colonial contexts; particularly how this is articulated in care for "worlds" that reproduce a violent settler colonial society. Though I often do read feminist care ethics with curiosity to its application in the work I'm involved in on gendered work and care experiences in Indigenous communities (Jewell et al. 2020; Jewell et al. 2022), my Anishinaabe femme embodiment cannot deny the complex feelings of bitterness and resentment that I sense when I am reading in this field. Part of me wonders if feminist care ethics scholarship can never resonate for me because it emerged in a world that erased the one my community had rights to.

I was introduced to the field of care ethics in 2018 when I took up a postdoctoral fellowship with Andrea Doucet (Canada Research Chair in Gender, Work, and Care) at Brock University in the Niagara Region of Southern Ontario. A local urban Indigenous community organization requested the assistance of researchers at Brock University to investigate how employment engagement challenges were impacting members of the urban Indigenous community. Doucet, herself a white settler scholar, agreed to guide the project on the condition that she could hire and mentor an emerging Indigenous scholar in a postdoctoral fellow position to lead the research. That year I was finishing the completion of my dissertation and heeding the advice of my doctoral supervisor Dian Million, who wisely suggested I consider taking a postdoctoral research position before diving into the high demands of a tenure track job. My path converged with Doucet's when I applied to the postdoctoral position at Brock University. While I was not familiar with the field of feminist care ethics and its impact on gendered work experiences, I did bring with me the skills of how to navigate inquiry in Indigenous communities.

Andrea Doucet's guidance through our work together enabled me to develop a voice — if even emerging — of my own on the topic of care experiences in Indigenous communities. Her mentorship helped me to further develop and apply my community-oriented social research skills in that urban environment where Anishinaabe and Haudenosaunee families gathered. The urban community composition in the Niagara Region is one that I also embody (my mother is Anishinaabe and my father is Oneida — one of the nations in the Haudenosaunee Confederacy), and the culture of two distinct nations living side by side and together is one I've grown up in (my First Nations community of Chippewas of the Thames is neighbour to Oneida Nation of the Thames). It was a meaningful space that I was well positioned to work within — being familiar with the distinctions of each worldview and identity, as well as the nuances and tensions of relationality in this dynamic. This familiar landscape fostered my deepening understanding of care as a relative of the community; as a junior Indigenous scholar, I was able to maintain and move with a sense of responsibility to a community not unlike my own to secure that pathway of accountability that Doucet was looking to establish when she agreed to the project. This learning and working relationship, which brings Doucet's depth of knowledge in critical care scholarship and feminist care ethics into conversation with my interest and experience in reclamation work in Anishinaabe communities, has been an important site of mutual learning for our team. With this collaborative relationship as the foundation, I began to articulate my perspective on feminist care ethics informed by critical Indigenous feminist scholarship and my own community-oriented research praxis.

I encountered feminist care ethics in my postdoc at a time when I was seeking a space to fine-tune my community-facing research skills. In our work in the Niagara Region urban Indigenous community, we applied The Listening Guide and its layered readings to the unique experiences of Indigenous worker-carers (a term used for people who work full time and provide care to an adult full time) (Jewell et al. 2022). After all those long conversations on the care we witnessed in the urban Indigenous community with whom we were working, I wondered why there was a lingering feeling of resentment when I encountered feminist care ethics? As much as the literature resonated with me — particularly with the Anishinaabe concepts I had been brought up with like interrelatedness as a fact of life or relational autonomy — why did I sense a deep indignation to the story of care as told by celebrated feminists whom I paradoxically respected and appreciated?

FEMINIST CARE ETHICS: THEORIZING THE PRIVILEGE OF CARE

Feminist care ethics emerged as a field in the late 1970s during a widely cited debate between Harvard psychologist Carol Gilligan and her mentor-turned-colleague Lawrence Kohlberg. A fundamental figure in the field of moral development theory and a leading psychologist of his time, Kohlberg's interest in human moral development was informed by his experience as a Jewish American man in World War II. His imprisonment by British troops for his involvement in a Zionist paramilitary mission to illicitly transport Eastern-European Jewish refugees into Mandatory Palestine (Garz 2009, 13) prompted deep reflections on the moral and political conditions of his imprisonment. He would then pursue a prolific career studying moral reasoning and the psychology of moral development. Kohlberg, rooted firmly in the positivist tradition and patriarchal norms of academia, launched longitudinal studies measuring cognitive reasoning and their links to moral judgment — studies in which Gilligan was a research assistant. Kohlberg supposed his research could inform a universal moral development scale that would measure the spectrum along which humans understand, rationalize, and perform morality (Mauthner 2019). But in some of the studies that informed this universal moral development scale, Kohlberg selected research participants consisting entirely of American boys from white middle-class backgrounds. Consequently, as Gilligan would point out, the increasingly powerful field of psychology was universally defining and measuring human morality by the particular (and very much not universal) experience of arguably the most privileged population in the world.

Gilligan challenged Kohlberg's studies on moral development, and particularly his conclusion that women tended to have "lower moral reasoning levels" in comparison to men (Reiter 1996, 33). Kohlberg observed that women were reluctant to take universal stances in his studies and often demanded "greater contextual detail" to inform their moral judgments — and concluded that they must be underdeveloped (Gary 2022, 2). The scale not only failed to include an equal number of women's voices, but it also failed to contextualize their experiences based on their gendered socialization (Gilligan 1982 [1993], 67). Furthermore, it did not account for the oppressive conditions of living in tension with patriarchal expectations. Gilligan argued instead that women used a different, more socially responsive and complex process to determine their moral stances, and that their cognitive sense of morality is developed and informed by an ethic of care, whereas Kohlberg's assumption was that men's morality is informed by an objective ethic of justice. Gilligan (1982 [1993], xviii) would dispute this positivist assumption that Kohlberg and other psychologists were touting:

> The so-called objective position which Kohlberg and others espoused within the canon of traditional social science research was blind to the particularities of voice and the inevitable constructions that constitute point of view. However

well-intentioned and provisionally useful it may have been, it was based on an inerrant neutrality which concealed power and falsified knowledge.

In her formative 1982 text, *In a Different Voice,* Gilligan theorized the beginnings of the ethic of care, a branch of feminist philosophy that considered humans as relational subjects and explored how voice, identity, and point of view were constructed in social conditions. Gilligan disputed that universal assumptions could be made about human moral development. She pointed to several issues, among them a) the lack of female subjects in the research studies that created the scale (and where they were involved, their perspectives were wildly misunderstood and misrepresented), b) the lack of attention to the role patriarchy had in the socialization of girls and women, and c) how girls and women constructed identity and voice under conditions of that patriarchy (Gilligan 1982 [1993]). Gilligan (2015) would later build on these findings into The Listening Guide, a feminist relational framework of inquiry that she co-developed with a working group of graduate students in the 1980s.

Considered a "pioneer in the field," Gilligan ultimately faced critiques that much of her scholarship and study focused on white, middle-class perspectives (Mauthner 2019). Feminist care ethics has grown significantly since Gilligan's work, and while the field was "once labeled a 'feminine ethic,'" it was later "redefined as an explicitly feminist project focusing not simply on the gendered distribution of care labour but on the injustice of the patriarchal domination that configured it" (Gary 2022, 3). Virginia Held (2006, 9) notes that care ethics "developed as a moral theory relevant not only to the so-called private realms of family and friendship but to medical practice, law, political life, the organization of society, war and international relations." Feminist scholars articulated and defined the value and moral dimensions of care, its ontological and epistemological value, and "the extent to which certain people are commonly directed to spheres and norms of feminine caretaking and compulsory service for others" (Whyte and Cuomo 2016, 235). But like Gilligan's work, the first feminist care ethicists centred white, American, upper middle-class and privileged feminist perspectives and experiences — many citing their own experiences as mothers or caregivers as a basis for foundational theory in the field (Gary 2022, 5).

INTERLOCUTORS AND KILLJOYS: CRITIQUES OF FEMINIST CARE ETHICS

Mignon Duffy (2005) found that the field's theoretical emphasis on "elevating" care to a nurturing activity tended to overlook the marginalized, exploited, and socially reproductive labour of racialized non-white women. In other words, the emphasis of care as an affective activity — removed from the physical nature of domestic care labour that many racialized non-white women occupy informally and/or in the care sector workforce — served to emphasize, theorize, and *moralize* elements of care that only white women largely experienced. For Black, Indigenous, migrant, and racialized non-white women with histories of colonial genocide and oppression, care (and its moralized dimensions) is a loaded matter. In the context of histories where Black, racialized, non-white, and Indigenous women are forced to provide care to the colonizer (or to the colonizer's interests), and where this care occurs at the expense of caring and reproducing our own worlds, care as an "ethic" takes on sore layers not felt or experienced by white women. In a 2023 teach-in titled "Black Women Care Ethics," Breya Johnson (35:47) states: "Gilligan ... argued that women's moral development can be characterized by responsibility and care. Our moral development! What does that say about our relationship to extractive labour when our morality and our sense of identity is all pent up in this idea that we are responsible — and we must care for things?" Johnson's problematization of Gilligan's ostensibly empowering theory certainly provides a different context for moral dimensions of care when we consider that Black women have historically had no choice but to provide care for the white colonizer. More, Joy James's (2016, 256) Captive Maternal describes this ongoing exploitation by pointing to the caring, productive, and reproductive labour that feminized (and all genders of) Black people employ, only to reify the state that then enacts terror upon them.

Regarding the whiteness of feminist care ethics, Audrey Thompson (1998, 524) details how early scholars in the field of feminist care ethics had a tendency toward "colourblind theorizing," a politely racist disposition: "It is only in a racist society that pretending not to notice colour could be construed as a particularly virtuous act." In effect, colourblind theorizing presumes white experiences to be universal. By neglecting to attend to the impact of racial privilege on white women's experiences of care, foundational concepts in feminist care ethics omitted Black, Indigenous, racialized, non-white, and migrant women's experiences of care (1998, 529).

Indian feminist scholar Uma Narayan intervened in the feminist ethic of care discourse when she pointed to the notable absence of post-colonial analysis in the field's concepts of care. The "white man's burden" — a double-duty colonial axiom that presumes moral responsibility over the Other while justifying stealing their land — is, after all, a claim to care. Narayan (1995, 136) argued that while feminist care scholars theorized interrelatedness and interdependence as the essence of their care, they did not go far enough in considering the impacts their presence was having in colonial contexts: "White women had their own brand of paternalistic roles towards the colonized, and often shared in roles that constructed the 'natives' as children." The realm of colonial care from morally obligated white saviours is surely a gendered project — white men positioned as knowing what's best for us politically, and white women knowing what's best for us socially.

Since colonial invasion of Turtle Island, Indigenous Peoples have been subjected to the colonizer's presumption of care — itself a *(mal) interpretation* as Hayden King (2020) styles it — of relational kinship orders that were common in Indigenous diplomatic practices. The "Indian problem" as it were, was the "white man's burden" to bring feral savages into the light and grace of God (Rollo 2016). Political theorist Toby Rollo writes that Europeans understood Indigenous Peoples as homologous to children, lacking political agency and subjecthood, as well as possessing deficient reason and speech. Moreover, childhood is understood as an undeveloped — feral even — naturally subservient state of the human condition. In Western philosophical logic, children do not voluntarily progress out of their bestial state of worldly sin and must therefore be coerced through violence. The logic of this coercive process informed faith-based education pedagogies (2016, 62). Here, we see the classic Western logic of domination postured as care, transfigured into the colonial practice of mandatory faith-based education, and widely enforced through the various state-sponsored residential school and boarding school systems Indigenous Peoples around the globe would endure for centuries. Serving to ensure "the heterosexualization of family and of morality so as to eclipse any apprehension of the immorality of empire" (Alexander 2005, 3), the entire settler colonial project, genocide against Indigenous Peoples, the white man's burden, the abandonment of Indigenous worlds for violent assimilation into the misery of social death (Belcourt 2018b) — all takes place under the guise of care. Care for the empire, care for the settler, the reproductive world making of a dominant and "more deserving society" rooted firmly in white Christian ethos.

Joan Tronto and Berenice Fisher (1990, 40) took up early definitive work in feminist care ethics, writing that care is "a species activity that includes everything that we do to maintain, continue and repair our 'world' so that we can live in it as well as possible. That world includes our bodies, our selves and our environment, all of which we seek to interweave in a complex, life-sustaining web." In their definition, "the world" occurs in the North American geopolitical context. Environments for which they theorize to care have distinct political and social histories. Ironically, their ability to theorize care for worlds and environments is made possible by the violent project of settler colonialism and Indigenous erasure. Tronto (1998, 17) wrote that in the phases of care, caregiving "requires knowledge, and there's a moral dimension to caregiving in that it requires competence, since incompetent caregiving is not only a technical problem, but a moral one." In the post-contact treaty era in some parts of the geopolitical context of what is currently Canada, relational practices between settlers and Indigenous Peoples were wrought from worldviews where kin making was a foundational legal order. The primary logic of these political diplomatic orders from various Indigenous perspectives a) obliged settlers to participate in the care and responsibility of newly forged relatedness with the land and its natural law and b) permitted settlers to reside and live in lands under which the natural law of balance and interdependence were honoured. To apply Tronto's concept of competence in caregiving — care being the matter that activates and maintains relationality — settlers proved to be an incompetent participant in abiding by the natural legal orders required of them in these early treaty agreements.

Retroactively applying contemporary care ethics to past practices may seem unfair, but I argue that claiming benevolence for the early white feminist normalizes a dimension of innocence and incompetence that is central to white-first liberation. As aforementioned, early care feminists spoke of their own care experiences and the worlds they were reproducing in motherhood, those which they inherited from the labour of their foremothers and whose care practices included reifying a world that normalized settler colonialism. Natasha Mauthner (2019) notes this as a central critique of the field due to its beginnings in the second-wave feminist movement. Supposing that surely Indigenous Peoples and their experiences were erased and not widely understood at the time contradicts that Indigenous relational practices with early settlers made settler presence in this world possible. Those sophisticated ethics of care bound through complex diplomatic orders of kin creation (Borsk 2023) were very much present in the legal and social contexts of early settlement. Moreover, it is widely regarded that Indigenous women, notably Haudenosaunee women, inspired the first rumblings of feminist thought amongst white women (Anderson 2020).

This history is curiously absent from much of North American mainstream feminist care scholarship, which purports to care for lands and environments without attention to its history or pre-existing legal frameworks, not to mention the political responsibilities of being a settler in these lands. I note this with a mind to Gary's (2022, 6) caution about comparative work with feminist care ethics — there is a "colonial extractivist dynamic potentially at play where Women of Color feminisms or non-Western philosophies are mined for resources and brought in to save care theory from white feminism." White feminism's self-preserving tendency at least partially explains why early, exclusionary feminist movements could draw upon Indigenous social norms as inspiration for their own liberation, without regard to honouring the social and kin contracts that allowed for their enduring (and ultimately violent) presence.

CARE AS SOCIAL REPRODUCTION

Though I and many others offer critiques of the field, feminist care ethics has transformative potential as a site for reflection on the matter and stakes of relationality in a settler colonial context. It can offer a framework for settlers to engage in anti-colonial praxis and is a useful analytic for critical analysis of how settler colonialism is reproduced. These dimensions, if expanded upon, could do more than simply "progress the field" toward what Gary (2022) describes as a pluralist project. There are practical applications for the coalition building that feminist care ethics aspires to engage. Part of me has little desire to be concerned with the matters of a scholarly field that seems far from the focus of culturally reproducing my own Anishinaabe'aadziwin, and I am conflicted with proposing care ethics as a possible site of "settler harm reduction" (Tuck and Yang 2019, xiv; Franks 2020). After all, Gary (2022, 4) offers a caution to the field's transitional era toward pluralism: "If it neglects the multiplicity of forms of domination while portraying itself as a liberatory endeavour, care theory will fail as a pluralist feminist project." Still, feminist care ethics offers literature for understanding the instruments of settler colonialism and how they function to reproduce its cultural, social, and political conditions. Further, early care scholars, many of them white feminists, unwittingly provided analysis of historically private practices of care and illuminated how everyday households reproduce the very public experience of settler colonialism. Congruently, it can be a useful tool to reflect on how settler spheres of care impacted Indigenous realities — particularly Two-Spirit, queer, femme, and child embodiments — which were dispossessed of their powerful care rights and responsibilities through patriarchal and genocidal policies.

Care is the site wherein culture is produced and reproduced in new generations, informing and reinforcing social norms. Drawing from Émile Durkheim, who laid the foundations for the field of sociology, French sociologist Pierre Bourdieu (1977) described the link between cultural and social reproduction, specifically the role that educational institutions have in reproducing how cultural capital is distributed. As an example, it is a widely known fact that the elite send their children to prestigious private educational institutes, and that Ivy League universities preserve a portion of their admissions to legacy families. Conversely, schools on the reserve are chronically underfunded, and public education in poorer areas may be burdened with higher social needs as a result of the marginalization of communities. Bourdieu argued that cultural capital is relative to material capital and is a symbol for communicating implicit inequities between stratified classes and lower classes: "Any capital, whatever the form it assumes, exerts a symbolic violence as soon as it is recognized, that is, misrecognized in its truth as capital and imposes itself as an authority calling for recognition" (Bourdieu and Wacquant 2013, 298). The recognition of these symbols might be conveyed and taught in the "private sphere" of the settler colonial home, itself a part of a broader class system, as it contains within it a set of norms and behaviours that are relative to the class of the family. Feminist care scholars expanded on social reproduction, arguing that the feminized labour of care has played a critical role in preparing, nurturing, and reproducing the cultural norms that are expected in the society outside of the home. Kate Bezanson (2006, 22) writes that "the concept of social reproduction captures the varied processes involved in maintaining and reproducing people, specifically the labouring population, and their labour power on a daily and generational basis." Further, it is the "formation and transfer of skills, knowledge, social and moral values, identities and cultures." Social reproduction occurs in the home and serves to repopulate the economy and citizenry of the state.

Indeed, philosopher Joy James gestures to settler imperial reproductive world making as Womb Theory. James (2016, 256) specifically traces the United States' trajectory of colonization — a seminal implantation of settler worlds into and onto stolen, fertile lands — to the socially reproductive womb that American exceptionalism serves for "Western Democracy": "in transitioning a colony through a republic into a representative democracy with imperial might, the emergent United States grew a womb." Womb Theory summons imagery of female reproductive organs and environments to reveal the "generative properties of the maternals it held captive" (2016, 256). Captive Maternals "stabilize with their labour the very social and state structures which prey upon them" (James 2021, 244). Pointing to the anti-Black racism of celebrated Western thinkers from Aristotle to Foucault, Joy James (2016, 257) refuses to conflate Western theory — and white feminist theory in particular — with intellectual sophistication, instead using the term Womb Theory in a direct confrontation to the "trauma and theft that produced Western democracy dependent upon slavery." Womb Theory is thus derived from "the freedom to theorize that comes directly from the exploitation of Black captive females" (Baraitser and Spigel 2020) and deliberately undertheorizes "violence against Captive Maternals' reproductive labor, commodified emotional affect, sexual consumption, connectivity, and longevity for the enrichment of the lives of others" (James 2016, 257). In sum, Joy James's Womb Theory is a cutting analysis of the commodification of Black care (specifically Black maternal exploitation) and "the ways in which the womb has been a primary site of racialized control, dispossession and violence at the heart of national reproduction of white settler states such as the United States" (Ihmoud 2021, 299).

If care is socially reproductive, care is political. In considering the dimensions and power that matter of relationality has, what Indigenous social worlds and realities are made (im)possible through care? Critical Indigenous, Black, and decolonial feminisms provide an analytic that allow us to ask these questions and envision their responses. Reproducing Indigenous worlds through care is a necessary act for Indigenous futures, land back, language reclamation, and decolonization. Yet, Indigenous Peoples have been systematically prohibited from socially and culturally reproducing our norms, behaviours and embodiments. This is not, as Tuck (2009) might say, to "centre damage," but to acknowledge that despite structural attempts to erase our worlds, we are still here. While we are still here *culturally* reproducing our worlds as Indigenous Peoples — a culture that is both informed by respective Indigenous worldviews and felt experiences of surviving the various conditions of violence under settler colonialism — the mainstream *social* world that so many of us live and interact within is still a settler colonial world that does not reflect our values and ways of life. Where our worlds were once systematically prohibited by the state, they are now politically underfunded, unsupported, and under-resourced through deliberate policy choices in what Pasternak (2016, 318) describes as "fiscal warfare," which defines "the terms by which Indigenous bodies may live, within a narrow band of compliance with liberal forms of self-management." First Nations must live in compliance with the Indian Act, maintained by what Pasternak describes as a public-facing "discourse of accountability." This was the subject of national attention in the winter of 2012 when Attawapiskat Chief Theresa Spence conducted a fast in the public eye to protest the unlivable housing conditions people in her First Nation were experiencing — despite being so close to the site of a diamond mine that quite literally extracts commodities of luxury from the land (2016, 318). In this arrangement, the mainstream settler public's attention into uniquely Indigenous experiences of settler colonialism is weaponized as support or disapproval of the expenditures on reserves where they will never have to live. Settler colonial states, and arguably, the body politic (with very real interest in maintaining the structure of the state), are simply not invested in the enrichment and reproduction of our distinct worlds as Indigenous Peoples, let alone the cost of anything above survival. Morally ambiguous anonymous care paired with fiscal warfare discourses of accountability form a convenient release from liability to better align with the interests of maintaining the state.

Like Marxism, care ethics scholarship can have utility in that it can articulate and critique the technical terms of competent care, care experiences, phases of care, and the moral dimensions of care. All of these concepts exist for themselves, in their own rights, in Indigenous knowledges. Like much of the Marxist tradition, care ethicists often fail to apply a settler colonial geopolitical analysis in their works and tend to focus instead on class, gender, and race (in a multinational context). Examining the morality of socially reproducing a settler colonial world — one that can only exist because of the erasure and elimination of Indigenous worlds that pre-exist it — fails to account for a critical component of the broader geopolitical structures that inform care.

CARE IN RECONCILIATION

I will now explore the relevance of care ethics in the context of colonialism and reconciliation rhetoric in Canada. In late May of 2021, Tk̓emlúps te Secwépemc announced the discovery of 215 unmarked graves outside of the former Kamloops Indian Residential School (Dickson and Watson 2021), prompting a media storm in the summer of 2021 that thrust Canada's Indian residential school system into the international spotlight. As Canada's genocidal history was exposed, Canadians began searching for answers. Established in 2008, Canada's Truth and Reconciliation Commission (TRC) heard testimony from thousands of survivors of Canada's Indian residential school system across the country, culminating in a six-volume final report released in 2015. Accompanying the report were 94 Calls to Action meant to redress the ongoing structural legacies that Indigenous Peoples experience in Canada and advance reconciliation (TRC 2015). These Calls, as Gitxsan scholar and child rights advocate Cindy Blackstock (2022, 17) aptly put it, are the "Survivor's work plan" for Canada. In their 2015 federal campaign platform, the Liberal Party (led by Justin Trudeau) promised to fully implement all 94 of the Calls to Action. As of 2022, only thirteen of the 94 Calls to Action have been completed (Jewell and Mosby 2022). Since 2019, I have co-authored an annual check-in on the progress toward completing the TRC's 94 Calls to Action with Ian Mosby for Yellowhead Institute. In the first two years that we published our reports (prior to the Kamloops revelations), there was little public uptake or interest on whether or not the Calls to Action were being implemented. But after Kamloops, the issue of child graves outside of Indian residential schools brought an urgency to what action Canada had committed toward reconciliation. Galvanized by the announcement of more than 750 possible unmarked graves outside of the former Marieval Indian Residential School (Eneas 2021), the now mounting physical evidence of child death continues to horrify Canadians. There has been a significant increase in attention to the Calls to Action as media outlets and Canadians searched for evidence that there was justice for these children, that this was an issue that was being taken care of. Unfortunately, our reports provided little solace to an aching Canadian public whose identity built on delusions of caring benevolence were now entirely upended. Interestingly, we found that in the three weeks following the Kamloops revelations, three Calls to Action were completed — more movement on the Calls to Action than in the previous three years combined — and that each were hardly among the transformative, urgent Calls to Action that would materially change conditions for Indigenous Peoples (Jewell and Mosby 2021). Canada was working hard to appear that it cared. In its hasty implementation, Canada invoked the appearance of a caring response, indeed, a *moral* response — and, in so doing, attending to the grief of Canadians with the balm of "making good on a promise" — to divert from the reality of its own incredible, ongoing violence.

If anything has compelled settlers to reflect on the meaning of their presence in these lands, it is the post-Kamloops era of reconciliation. Having studied Canada's performance of reconciliation over the years from a critical Anishinaabe perspective, I am often asked by Canadians, "What can *I* do?" Individual Canadians feel compelled to engage in acts of reconciliation where their country has failed, but there is the problem of the neoliberal condition where "change" is individualized and paired with consumptive behaviours; whatever small gesture becomes a temporal, symbolic act that, in the end, still upholds settler colonial systems. By way of example, Phyllis Webstad (2021), a Secwépemc woman and survivor of St. Joseph's Mission Residential School, began telling her story to children in 2013. Her story of her grandmother's loving care being represented by an orange shirt (which would later be taken from her upon arrival at the institution) began as a powerful pedagogical tool that conveyed to a new generation of children the gravity of what it meant for Indigenous children to be taken away from the care of their families. Since then, "Orange Shirt Day," observed on September 30, evolved into an event typically seen in Canadian public schools across the country until it rhetorically merged with the National Day for Truth and Reconciliation in 2021. The ensuing National Day for Truth and Reconciliation is now symbolized by wearing an orange shirt in an homage to Phyllis's grandmother's care. Orange T-shirts have since become an important commodity, and the annual observance of this day is accompanied by the availability of orange products for purchase in the month of September, not least of which is a special orange sprinkle donut by Canadian coffee chain Tim Hortons. Webstad's felt experience of being dispossessed of her grandmother's care demonstrates that in a neoliberal context, these avenues of "solidarity" are commodifications that reify settler colonial capitalist practices and a Canadian culture of symbolized benevolence. Such is the nature of individualizing change in a neoliberal context. As Tuscarora author Alicia Elliott tweeted on September 30, 2022, "The government and politicians, who have power to make real change, have encouraged everyday Canadians to think reconciliation is achieved through individual capitalist consumption."

There is utility of feminist care analysis in contemporary Indigenous worlds, as it can inform our critiques and engagements with matters such as reconciliation. If inclusive of a settler colonial analysis and if aiming toward anti-colonial praxis, I propose that feminist care ethics can assist settlers to reflect on their daily practice of how they embody, normalize, and contribute to the perpetuation of settler colonial conditions, with space for considering how care can transform rather than reproduce settler colonial structures. Having analyzed the instruments of reconciliation rhetoric over the years, I've come to understand that reconciliation is an aspirational project with necessary precursors to its actualization. There are, in my mind, two discrete forms of reconciliation, about which other scholars like Rachel Flowers (2015), Tracey Lindberg (CBC Radio 2017), David MacDonald (2019), and Ginger Gosnell-Myers (2022) have also written. The first discrete form of reconciliation is for Indigenous Peoples: it is a commitment to repairing the relationship, understanding, and connection we have to our worldviews, languages, care practices, governance structures, and ways of life that residential schools and the Sixties and Millennium Scoops violently disrupted. Canada's policy of genocide stole hundreds of thousands of Indigenous children from their nations. Children who ought to have been populating distinct, unique, rights-bearing Indigenous nations and societies with renewed generations of knowers and members. If 150,000 children attended Indian residential schools, and congruently with the schools, many more were adopted into white homes during the Sixties and Millennium Scoops, then it follows that millions of people — parents, grandparents, aunts, uncles, cousins, clans, houses, and any variation of kin structures unique to Indigenous governance systems — were violently dispossessed of their inherent right to care for their children. This speaks to the power that our nations pose if they are socially and culturally reproduced. To reconcile for Indigenous Peoples is not to reconcile with the state and normalize the hellscape that is settler colonialism. It is not to educate settlers or inform their curiosities of our differences. I am of the mind that for Indigenous Peoples, reconciliation is a spiritual, cultural, and ontological reparative project with deep political implications like land back, cash back, and worlds back so that we can reproduce our futurities as peoples with distinct, longstanding, and pre-existing relationality with our lands. We did not choose for white "care" to disrupt our worlds. But our acts of repairing the care we extend to ourselves, our land, and our relatives is the work of "reconciliation before reconciliation," as Lindberg (CBC Radio 2017) has described it.

It is no secret that reconciliation is the contemporary, popular, discursive means by which Canadians understand Indigenous issues. The concept of reconciliation is critiqued for its malleable qualities that allow it to be twisted and co-opted by the Canadian state as a feel-good, moderate, harm-reduction approach (Franks 2020) that fails to transform the structures that violate Indigenous Peoples and our lands, waters, and non-human kin. And yet, I've found utility in the concept if only to serve as a topical segue to impressing the importance of anti-colonial, restorative, resurgent practice in our own communities. It is a useful springboard for considering how we "reconcile" or confront the colonial legacies that continue in our communities.

There is, indeed, a need for much deeper consideration of this care, or of this reconciliation, that we extend to ourselves as Indigenous Peoples. As the early feminist care ethics scholars found, care is a feminized activity despite it being necessary for all, and it is an aspect of human life that has been denigrated under patriarchy, capitalism, and colonialism. An honest and truthful look at care in our own communities might reveal the same patriarchal, colonial power issues at play. Like other populations, Indigenous women, queer, and feminized people bear much of the care labour in our communities and continue to be targets of violence: "The disturbing frequency of domestic and sexual violence among Native people is nothing other than a result of centuries of settler colonial violence and dispossession" (The Red Nation 2021, 99). Considering that "reconciling with ourselves" is a labour of care and an act of social and cultural reproduction, it must then be rooted in an Indigenous feminist tradition of critical intervention, as Gina Starblanket (2017) explains in her chapter "Being Indigenous Feminists: Resurgences Against Contemporary Patriarchy" in the second edition of the *Making Space for Indigenous Feminism* volume. Resurgent practices necessarily invoke cultural memory, the formation of which is never neutral since it involves deliberate choices about which knowledge is "relevant," and which knowledge can be "forgotten" (2017, 25). Starblanket (2015, 27) asserts then, that maintaining a critical mind to how cultural memory is constructed — with particular focus on which practices are remembered for their alignment with political narratives like cis-heteropatriarchy — is a vital and necessary component to the action of resurgent endeavours; else these movements reproduce the same structures that harm our communities. Concepts of care in any one of our Indigenous worlds is a broad practice, a way of life, a profound attunement to the relational matter of kin with transformative possibility. To remember and reclaim this modality is powerful, if done so with a mind to Starblanket's cautions about unwittingly reifying the very structures of oppression we are attempting to dismantle.

For settlers, reconciliation is a reckoning with and commitment to changing behaviours, practices, beliefs, and structures that normalize settler colonial violence and white supremacy. It is a radical re-membering of the responsibilities that come with the right to be on this land, and the original laws, relationships, kinships, and treaties that permit them to be here. It is an acknowledgement of the limits of settler rights in these lands, and the long, ongoing history of violence against the land and her original inhabitants that amounts to the crime of genocide. The majority of Canadian activity, occupation, industry, and infrastructure has been built without the consent of the nations on whose lands these exist. For settlers, reconciliation means acknowledging the role of change in the home, by deeply reflecting on what worlds are created in everyday moments — the construction of situations, as French sociologist Lefebvre

(2014) theorized — and how to leverage this into community organizing and action. Feminist care ethics, if attentive to how care contributes to the social and cultural reproduction of settler colonialism, can provide us with insights into everyday transformative actions that can propel settlers toward meaningful reckoning with their colonial reality. Brannelly and Boulton (2017, 5) note in their assertion that feminist care ethics can provide guidance in Indigenous–non-Indigenous research relationships, enabling "explicit consideration of issues of politics, privilege and ethics, calling for recognition of inequality and responsibility for action in solidarity with the people affected."

While feminist care ethics can provide settlers with relational guidance (particularly when it comes to reconciliation), vigilance is required to remain attentive to the liberatory goal of relationality. This is not always a feel-good exercise. To return to my killjoy sentiment, I summon Rachel Flowers's (2015) experience intervening in settler feminist solidarity, which she details in her piece "Refusal to Forgive: Indigenous Women's Love and Rage." Flowers resists settler scholar Stephanie Irlbacher-Fox's characterization of Indigenous women's direct action as evidence of growth from "frustrated anger" to "powerful loving action." Irlbacher-Fox effectively implied in her 2012 essay "#IdleNoMore: Settler Responsibility for Relationship" that anger for Indigenous women is an ineffectual sentiment and that loving action is a more purposeful, positive affect with greater potential for change. The implication here is that settlers are more likely to support Indigenous causes if they are couched in heartwarming displays of love that are more comfortable to view for settler onlookers. The work of reclaiming care for Indigenous Peoples, even if it is couched in heartwarming sentiments that are comfortable for settler onlookers, is still very much an act of undoing colonial worlds and power. My critique of feminist care ethics and my killjoy approach is very much a project of Jean Améry's *ressentiment*, to which Flowers (2015, 44–45) refers in her work as "the intolerance for the way in which descendants of the perpetrators are allowed to facilitate a forgetting of the past." Early feminist care scholars, in their endeavour to empower feminized, moral dimensions of care, neglected to attend to the geopolitical context of their presence and claims to care. While a powerful concept for the movements of Indigenous reclamation, settler reckoning, and perhaps Indigenous-settler relations, care's political dimensions and its role in social/cultural reproduction cannot be overstated.

While feminist care ethics literature is "diversifying" from its traditions in white feminist scholarship (Gary 2022) to include powerful perspectives of care from Black and Indigenous care experiences (among many others not mentioned in this chapter), there is much work to be done to adopt an analysis of the specificity that is the settler colonial geopolitical context of care ethics. Learning from a rich Indigenous feminist literature from the likes of Dian Million (2013, 2020), Kim Anderson (2011), Cutcha Risling Baldy (2018), Laura Harjo (2019), and Mishuana Goeman (2013) (to name but very, very few) can offer insight into how care and social reproduction of Indigenous worlds is anti-colonial labour taken on by femme embodiments — labour that is subversive to the very care labour white women engage in to uphold their settler colonial worlds. Contemporary feminist care ethics can be helpful in that it identifies how instruments of settler colonialism are reproduced through care in social and cultural reproduction. As an Anishinaabe interlocutor engaging with feminist care ethics, I don't think the role of white women's care in the broader scheme of violence against Indigenous Peoples, specifically women, queer/Two-Spirit people and children, can be overstated. White women were culpable in the genocidal project of settler colonialism, which eroded Indigenous worldviews in the name of white dominance, guised as the very care and responsibility that is theorized as dignified labour.

It is also important to expand on how we as Indigenous Peoples socially and culturally reproduce our worlds and, while not the sole focus of this chapter, more attention to how care has been gendered under colonial patriarchy and disproportionately placed on the shoulders of Indigenous femme embodiments is necessary. This is the work that I am committed to continuing as an Anishinaabe interlocutor with feminist care ethics. In an age where political projects such as reconciliation are commonly framed through notions of interrelatedness and care, where care is then increasingly taken up as a relational claim between settler Canadians and Indigenous Peoples, it is imperative that we focus on our respective responsibilities in the work toward creating the conditions for reconciliation. It's possible that reconciliation is a space we will come to in the future, but the conditions in which cultural and social worlds are reproduced must change for that to be a possibility. There must be meaningful reflection on the conditions of settler colonial violence that continue to be reproduced on stolen Indigenous lands and a commitment toward centring Indigenous lives, worldviews, and legal orders as the framework for reconciliation. I think that feminist care ethics is a potential site for a more mainstream analysis of how the logics, structures, and behaviours that uphold settler colonialism are reproduced, and white women's role in that reproduction — if even in commentary on the utility of our affect in resisting colonial violence — cannot be overstated. For this to be a possibility, mainstream feminist care ethics scholars need to be taking up more analysis and critique of how care and social reproduction in the geopolitical context of settler colonial states necessarily means upholding a power dynamic within which Indigenous Peoples, among others, face violence. Until then, as Gary (2022) notes, feminist care ethics as a liberatory project will fail. Not only will it fail to resonate with Indigenous feminist scholarship, it will fail to recognize its complicity and contributions to ongoing violence, ironically, in the name of care.

REFERENCES

Ahmed, Sara. 2010. "Killing Joy: Feminism and the History of Happiness." *Signs: Journal of Women in Culture and Society* 35, 3. doi.org/10.1086/648513.

Alexander, M. Jacqui. 2005. *Pedagogies of Crossing: Meditations on Feminism, Sexual Politics, Memory, and the Sacred.* Durham: Duke University Press.

Altamirano-Jiménez, Isabel. 2022. "Our Movements Need Some Love as Well: Indigenous Women Activism and Relationality." Panel presentation, Indigenous Feminisms Symposium, April 22, 2022. Victoria: University of Victoria.

Anderson, Kim. 2011. *Life Stages and Native Women: Memory, Teachings, and Story Medicine.* Winnipeg: University of Manitoba Press.

___. 2020. "On Seasons of an Indigenous Feminism, Kinship, and the Program of Home Management." *Hypatia* 35, 1. doi.org/10.1017/hyp.2019.10.

Baraitser, Lisa, and Sigal Spigel. 2020. "Editorial." *Studies in the Maternal* 13, 1: 1. doi.org/10.16995/sim.313.

Belcourt, Billy-Ray. 2018a. "Settler Structures of Bad Feeling." *Canadian Art Magazine,* January 8. canadianart.ca/essays/settler-structures-bad-feeling/.

___. 2018b. "Meditations on Reserve Life, Biosociality, and the Taste of Non-sovereignty." *Settler Colonial Studies* 8, 1.

Bezanson, Kate. 2006. *Gender, The State, and Social Reproduction: Household Insecurity in Neo-liberal Times.* Toronto: University of Toronto Press.

Blackstock, Cindy. 2022. "Ending Racial Discrimination in Child Welfare." In *Calls to Action Accountability: A 2022 Status Update on Reconciliation,* edited by Eva Jewell and Ian Mosby. Toronto: Yellowhead Institute.

Borsk, Michael. 2023. "Conveyance to Kin: Property, Preemption, and Indigenous Nations in North America, 1763–1822." *The William and Mary Quarterly* 80, 1. muse.jhu.edu/article/881410.

Bourdieu, Pierre. 1977. "Cultural Reproduction and Social Reproduction." In *Power and Ideology in Education,* edited by Jerome Karabel and A.H. Halsey. Oxford University Press.

Bourdieu, Pierre, and Loïc Wacquant. 2013. "Symbolic Capital and Social Classes." *Journal of Classical Sociology* 13, 2.

Brannelly, T., and A. Boulton. 2017. "The Ethics of Care and Transformational Research Practices in Aotearoa New Zealand." *Qualitative Research* 17, 3.

CBC Radio. 2017. "Cree Academic and Novelist Tracey Lindberg on Reconciliation Before Reconciliation." January 23. cbc.ca/radio/ideas/cree-academic-and-novelist-tracey-lindberg-on-reconciliation-before-reconciliation-1.3945719.

Dickson, Courtney, and Bridgette Watson. 2021. "Remains of 215 Children Found Buried at Former B.C. Residential School, First Nation Says." *CBC News,* May 29. cbc.ca/news/canada/british-columbia/tk-emlúps-te-secwépemc-215-children-former-kamloops-indian-residential-school-1.6043778.

Duffy, Mignon. 2005. "Reproducing Labor Inequalities: Challenges for Feminists Conceptualizing Care at the Intersections of Gender, Race, and Class." *Gender & Society,* 19, 1.

Elliott, Alicia (@wordsandguitar). 2022. "What I Hate About Truth & Reconciliation Day." Twitter, September 30. twitter.com/wordsandguitar/status/1575874161402032129.

Eneas, Bryan. 2021. "Sask. First Nation Announces Discovery of 751 Unmarked Graves Near Former Residential School." *CBC News,* June 24. cbc.ca/news/canada/saskatchewan/cowessess-marieval-indian-residential-school-news-1.6078375.

Flowers, Rachel. 2015. "Refusal to Forgive: Indigenous Women's Love and Rage." *Decolonization: Indigeneity, Education & Society* 4, 2.

Franks, Scott James. 2020. "Towards Implementing the Truth and Reconciliation Commission's Calls to Action in Law Schools: A Settler Harm Reduction Approach to Racial Stereotyping and Prejudice Against Indigenous Peoples and Indigenous Legal Orders in Canadian Legal Education." Unpublished master's thesis, York University.

Gary, M.E. 2022. "From Care Ethics to Pluralist Care Theory: The State of the field." *Philosophy Compass* 17, 4.

Garz, Detlef. 2009. *Lawrence Kohlberg — An Introduction.* Verlag Barbara Budrich.

Gilligan, Carol. 1982 [1993]. *In a Different Voice: Psychological Theory and Women's Development.* Cambridge: Harvard University Press.

___. 2015. "The Listening Guide Method of Psychological Inquiry." *Qualitative Psychology* 2, 1.

Goeman, Mishuana. 2013. *Mark My Words: Native Women Mapping Our Nations.* Minneapolis: University of Minnesota Press.

Gosnell-Myers, Ginger. 2022. "A Proposal for National Day for Truth & Reconciliation, Two Ways." In *Calls to Action Accountability: A 2022 Status Update on Reconciliation,* edited by Eva Jewell and Ian Mosby. Toronto: Yellowhead Institute.

Harjo, Laura. 2019. *Spiral to the Stars: Mvskoke Tools of Futurity.* Tucson: University of Arizona Press.

Held, Virginia. 2006. *The Ethics of Care: Personal, Political, and Global.* Oxford University Press.

Ihmoud, Sarah. 2021. "Born Palestinian, Born Black: Antiblackness and the Womb of Zionist Settler Colonialism." In *Antiblackness,* edited by Moon-Kie Jung and João H. Costa Vargas. Durham: Duke University Press. doi.org/10.2307/j.ctv-1grbbwr.17

Irlbacher-Fox, S. 2012. "#IdleNoMore: Settler Responsibility for Relationship." *Decolonization: Indigeneity, Education & Society,* December 27. decolonization.wordpress.com/2012/12/27/idlenomore-settler-responsibility-for-relationship/.

James, Joy. 2016. "The Womb of Western Theory: Trauma, Time Theft, and the Captive Maternal." *Carceral Notebooks* 12, 1.

___. 2021. "Presidential Powers in the Captive Maternal Lives of Sally, Michelle, and Deborah." In *Antiblackness,* edited by Moon-Kie Jung and João H. Costa Vargas. Duke University Press. doi.org/10.2307/j.ctv1grbbwr.17.

Jewell, Eva, et al. 2020. "Social Knowing, Mental Health, and the Importance of Indigenous Resources." *Canadian Review of Social Policy* 80.

Jewell, Eva, et al. 2022. "'Looking After Our Own Is What We Do': Urban Ontario Indigenous Perspectives on Juggling Paid Work and Unpaid Care Work for Adult Family Members." *Wellbeing, Space and Society* 3, 100102.

Jewell, Eva, and Ian Mosby. 2021. *Calls to Action Accountability: A 2021 Status Update on Reconciliation.* Toronto: Yellowhead Institute.

___. 2022. *Calls to Action Accountability: A 2022 Status Update on Reconciliation.* Toronto: Yellowhead Institute.

Johnson, Breya. 2023. "Black Women Care Ethics: Radical Love and the Anti-Black World." Black Women Radicals. March 27, 2023. YouTube video, 1:26:40. youtube.com/watch?v=-KJFHOAFaVA&ab_channel=BlackWomenRadicals.

King, Hayden. 2020. *An Annotated Guide to the (Mal)interpretation of Confederation Era Treaties in Canada.* Toronto: Yellowhead Institute.

Lefebvre, Henri. 2014. *Critique of Everyday Life: The One-Volume Edition.* Verso Books.

Liberal Party of Canada. 2015. "Liberals Call for Full Implementation of Truth and Reconciliation Commission Recommendations." June 2. liberal.ca/liberals-call-for-full-implementation-of-truth-and-reconciliation-commission-recommendations/.

MacDonald, David B. 2019. *The Sleeping Giant Awakens: Genocide, Indian Residential Schools, and the Challenge of Conciliation.* University of Toronto Press.

Mauthner, Natasha S. 2019. "Gilligan, Carol." In SAGE *Research Methods Foundations,* edited by Paul Atkinson, Sara Delamont, Alexandru Cernat, Joseph W. Sakshaug, and Richard A. Williams. Thousand Oakes, CA: Sage Publications.

Million, Dian. 2013. *Therapeutic Nations: Healing in an Age of Indigenous Human Rights.* Tucson: University of Arizona Press.

___. 2020. "Resurgent Kinships: Indigenous Relations of Well-Being vs. Humanitarian Health Economies." In *Routledge Handbook of Critical Indigenous Studies,* edited by Brendan Hokowhitu, Aileen Moreton-Robinson, Linda Tuhiwai-Smith, Chris Andersen, Steve Larkin. London: Routledge.

Narayan, Uma. 1995. "Colonialism and Its Others: Considerations on Rights and Care Discourses." *Hypatia* 10, 2.

Pasternak, Shiri. 2016. "The Fiscal Body of Sovereignty: To 'Make Live' in Indian Country." *Settler Colonial Studies* 6, 4. doi.org/10.1080/2201473x.2015.1090525.

Pasternak, Shiri, and Naiomi Metallic. 2021. *Cash Back: A Yellowhead Institute Red Paper.* Toronto: Yellowhead Institute.

The Red Nation. 2021. *The Red Deal: Indigenous Action to Save Our Earth.* Brooklyn: Common Notions.

Reiter, Sara Ann. 1996. "The Kohlberg–Gilligan Controversy: Lessons for Accounting Ethics Education." *Critical Perspectives on Accounting* 7, 1.

Risling Baldy, Cutcha. 2018. *We Are Dancing for You: Native Feminisms and the Revitalization of Women's Coming-of-age Ceremonies.* Seattle: University of Washington Press.

Rohde, Joy, Alice Cunningham Fletcher, and Matilda Coxe Stevenson. 2000. "'From the Sense of Justice and Human Sympathy:' Alice Fletcher, Native Americans, and the Gendering of Victorian Anthropology." *History of Anthropology Newsletter* 27, 1.

Rollo, Toby. 2016. "Feral Children: Settler Colonialism, Progress, and the Figure of the Child." *Settler Colonial Studies* 8, 1.

Schuller, Kyla. 2021. *The Trouble with White Women: A Counterhistory of Feminism.* New York: Bold Type Books.

Scribe, Megan. 2020. "Indigenous Girlhood: Narratives of Colonial Care in Law and Literature." Unpublished doctoral dissertation, University of Toronto.

Starblanket, Gina. 2017. "Being Indigenous Feminists: Resurgences Against Contemporary Patriarchy." In *Making Space for Indigenous Feminism, second edition,* edited by Joyce Green. Halifax: Fernwood Publishing.

Stevenson, Lisa. 2014. *Life Beside Itself: Imagining Care in the Canadian Arctic.* Berkeley: University of California Press.

Thompson, Audrey. 1998. "Not the Color Purple: Black Feminist Lessons for Educational Caring." *Harvard Educational Review* 68, 4.

TRC (Truth and Reconciliation Commission of Canada). 2015. *Truth and Reconciliation Commission of Canada: Calls to Action.* ehprnh2mwo3.exactdn.com/wp-content/uploads/2021/01/Calls_to_Action_English2.pdf.

Tronto, Joan C. 1998. "An Ethic of Care." *Generations: Journal of the American Society on Aging* 22, 3.

Tronto, Joan C., and Berenice Fisher. 1990. "Toward a Feminist Theory of Caring." In *Circles of Care: Work and Identity in Women's Lives,* edited by E.K. Abel and M.K. Nelson. SUNY Press.

Tuck, Eve. 2009. "Suspending Damage: A Letter to Communities." *Harvard Educational Review* 79, 3.

Tuck, Eve, and K. Wayne Yang. 2019. "Series Editors' Introduction." In *Indigenous and Decolonizing Studies in Education: Mapping the Long View,* edited by Linda Tuhiwai-Smith, Eve Tuck, and K. Wayne Yang. London: Routledge.

Webstad, Phyllis. 2021. *Beyond the Orange Shirt Story.* Victoria: Medicine Wheel Education Press.

Whyte, Kyle, and Chris J. Cuomo. 2016. "Ethics of Caring in Environmental Ethics: Indigenous and Feminist Philosophies." In *The Oxford Handbook of Environmental Ethics,* edited by Stephen M. Gardiner, and Allen Thompson. Oxford University Press.

NINE

Our Movements Need Some Love as Well
Indigenous Land Defence and Relationality

Isabel Altamirano-Jiménez

THE ISTHMUS OF TEHUANTEPEC IS LOCATED in Mexico's southern narrowest stretch of land. This region, specifically the community of Juchitán, is known for being a home to strong matriarchs who dominate the economy. The Isthmus is also known for being a paradise for Muxes, often referred to as a third gender. Travellers, artists, and academics have all contributed to the circulation of narratives about the prominence of Zapotec women and the role they play in local markets and their families. These women are also known for their participation in land defence movements, most recently against the Interoceanic Corridor, a multimodal megaproject aimed at accelerating the circulation of goods through the Atlantic Ocean and the Gulf of Mexico. Women land defenders have claimed the right to say no to resource extraction and gender violence within their communities. Although a growing body of literature has focused on Indigenous women's experiences of gender violence as a result of the expansion of the extractivist frontier, less attention has been paid to how limiting conceptions of gender violence erase the experiences of Two-Spirit and gender non-conforming individuals.

This chapter aims at filling this gap.[1] I have three interconnected goals. First, I use body-land as an analytic to explore how relationships to other living beings such as wind and sea prefigure our relationships to land, thus moving us beyond framing land as the only entity that enables Indigenous existence. I have written elsewhere that body-land can be understood as the ontological relationships between people and territory, which combine with collective histories to shape Indigenous Peoples' present-day social practices (Altamirano-Jiménez 2020, 2021). Body-land requires us to think of bodies with capital B and land with capital L. That is, not just in terms of human bodies but rather the multiplicity of non-human bodies that constitute our specific territories and waterscapes and the generative capacities that emerge when these bodies come together. Second and relatedly, I demonstrate that going beyond essentialized understandings of relationality in land and water defence and resurgence movements implies that we must consider how people's distinctive and overlapping social locations and experiences produce tensions and contestations over how shared cultural meanings are lived and embodied. Third, by focusing on the Isthmus of Tehuantepec, I engage Indigenous feminist scholarship produced both in Anglo and Spanish North America, seeking to establish a dialogue between two bodies of literature that have remained separated to date. Specifically, I am interested in how the concept of body-land may enable us to resituate discussions of gender violence against Indigenous women, Two-Spirit, and trans individuals.

RELATIONS OF LAND, WIND, AND WATER

The Isthmus of Tehuantepec is located between the Gulf of Mexico and the Pacific Ocean. It is a plateau covered by rivers, sea coast, and marine lagoons, 220 kilometres wide in its narrowest part. The northern slopes are home to tropical forests rich in biodiversity; this is a zone where the flora and fauna of North and South America connect. The southern slopes are hot and dry and contain some of the largest lagoon systems in Mexico. The Isthmus manifests itself as a complex world composed of different entities and relations. Wind is considered a dual entity. The north wind, or Tehuano, is considered male and it is characterized by a continental, cold, dry wind that comes from the Arctic and is unpredictable. The south wind, in contrast, is gentle, warm, and damp, comes from the oceans, and is always welcomed. Wind, like water, is fluid and in constant motion. Wind and water shape the conditions of the Isthmus, producing different moments and movements while transforming the perceived fixity of the land.

Zapotec, Ikoot, and Zoque peoples inhabiting the Isthmus have established particular relationships with these entities and the world around them. When wind, land, and water enter into a relationship with each other, they determine sea salt levels, fish stock, and the transition from a dry to a wet season. When wind and water come in contact with each other, their relationship can be either beneficial or destructive. Too much water, too much wind, or too much friction among these entities can affect the land, the ocean, and communities. Humans' obligation is not to judge how these entities manifest at different times. Rather, as Elizabeth Povinelli (2016, 58) argues when writing about the experiences of Indigenous Peoples in the Northern Territory of Australia, the fundamental task of human thought is to discern what these manifestations may indicate about the current arrangement of existence. This implies that relationships are not static but becoming and evolving over time.

While body-land refers to the ontological relations that connect people and territory and the entities that manifest in it, I have argued elsewhere that these interbeing and interelemental relationships are not given. Relationships and interactions can involve consent, affect, friction, and refusal. Making relatives, landing relationships in place requires conscious actions and practices that bring multiple human and non-human bodies together to make something happen. I have called these "body-landing" practices (Altamirano-Jiménez 2023). Through actions such as ceremonies, invoking the non-human world, thanking it, dreaming it, and communicating with it, human and non-human bodies can be brought together into generative interdependence, affective responsibility, and reciprocal relationships. In contrast, the absence of these conditions can create relations of domination, friction, contestation, and refusal, affecting the co-constitution of the world we live in. By paying attention to these practices, I am interested in making an inclusive view of relationality visible and showing that being in a relationship with diverse bodies is an action, a verb, not just a declaration. I will return to this point later in the chapter.

THE ISTHMUS AS A GEOPOLITICAL HOT SPOT

There are other stories to tell about the Isthmus. The Indigenous communities that inhabit the region are mostly organized through communal land and the ejido system, which is a form of collective land tenure granted by the state after the Mexican Revolution from

1910 to 1917. Ejidos used to be protected by Article 27 of the Mexican Constitution of 1917 until 1992. Although the creation of the ejido system protected the integrity of lands, it granted only usufruct rights to Indigenous Peoples and peasant communities (Altamirano-Jiménez 2013, 40). Many of the Isthmian communities still rely on subsistence fishing and agriculture. Throughout history, these peoples have developed a strong political stand, which has served to contain external attempts to re-organize their territories (Rubin 1994). The Isthmus of Tehuantepec is also the site of a development project, the Interoceanic Corridor, an expansive multimodal infrastructure and development project, connecting different natural resource extraction nodes.

The Isthmus is a strategic location for capital accumulation due to its geopolitical setting and abundance of natural resources (Altamirano-Jiménez 2017). This culturally and biodiverse region has been the target of state intervention, foreign interests, and private investments since Spanish colonization to this day. As a geopolitical hotspot, the Isthmus shortens the distance between the Pacific Ocean and the Gulf of Mexico, accelerating the circulation of goods. After Mexico became a new country, the United States invaded it. The Mexican American War followed the annexation of Texas, which Mexico considered part of its territory. Later, during the Mexican Civil War of the Reform, the Mexican government negotiated the McLane–Ocampo Treaty with the United States, seeking to finance its activities in 1859. This treaty would have granted perpetual transit, military, and extraterritorial rights across the Isthmus to the United States. Although the United States Senate never ratified the treaty due to the internal political tensions between northern and southern states, it was a controversial treaty (Sexton 2011, 135). In Mexico people saw this treaty as a government betrayal because it was ceding its sovereignty to the United States.

To the Mexican government, on the other hand, the region was too important to be left to Isthmian Indigenous Peoples (Altamirano-Jiménez 2013, 187). After the failure of the McLane–Ocampo Treaty, the Isthmus became central to statecrafting. The Trans-Isthmus Railway infrastructure, built to accelerate the movement of goods, became a symbol of nineteenth-century modernization of Mexico (Garner 1995, 339). This railway was emblematic of the export-oriented development implemented by Porfirio Díaz but became obsolete after the opening of the Panama Canal in 1914, which monopolized the cargo that passed through the Isthmus (McClure 2022, 3). Indigenous communities consistently opposed the imposition of these development projects. Indigenous revolts eventually merged with the Mexican Revolution of 1910. Thanks to Indigenous land defence movements, the Mexican government was forced to protect Indigenous land rights in the Constitution of 1917 even if with limitations. Article 27 created the ejido system and also recognized Indigenous communal land titles. Communal ownership of land and resources has been central to the social reproduction of Indigenous communities and resistance movements. However, despite the constitutional recognition, Indigenous territories were under constant threat throughout the twentieth century.

Indigenous communities and organizations have long been concerned about these threats. In Oaxaca, organizations such as the Organización para la Defensa de los Recursos Naturales y Desarrollo Social de la Sierra Juaréz (ORDENASIJ) (Organization for the Defence of Natural Resources and Social Development of Sierra Juaréz), Comité de Defensa de los Recursos Naturales y Humanos Mixes (CODREMI) (Committee for the Defence of the Mixes Natural and Human Resources), Comité Organizador y de Consulta para la Unión de los Pueblos de la Sierra Norte de Oaxaca (CODECO) (Organizing and Consultation Committee for the Union of the Peoples of the Sierra Norte de Oaxaca), and Indigenous intellectuals including Floriberto Díaz Gómez (a Mixe from Tlahuitoltepec) and Jaime Martínez Luna (a Zapotec from Guelatao), initiated a process of revitalization of Indigenous legal traditions in the early 1980s. Comunalidad, or the ethos of living in community, became a central political strategy for land defence (Altamirano-Jiménez 2013; Rendón Monzón 2003).

The renewed interest of external actors in the Isthmus began right after the ratification of the North American Free Trade Agreement (NAFTA). In what was now a neoliberal context, law and economic rationalism were used to represent Mexico as a backward, pre-modern country in need of transformation. Anglo North American property regimes and natural resource management practices were envisioned as solutions to improve the country's economy. As Chickasaw theorist Jodi Byrd (2011, xxiii) notes, racialization and deficiency discourses are concomitant to the global expansion of the capitalist system, which secures white dominance and property relations. In anticipation of the implementation of NAFTA, the World Bank granted Mexico a conditional loan to implement extensive structural adjustments required to welcome Canadian and American investment. From the bank's perspective, Indigenous Peoples' communal land ownership was clearly an obstacle to building a modern economy and solving poverty. This financial institution viewed Indigenous subsistence agricultural lands as wastelands that had no place in a modern economy (World Bank 1990, 65). As a result, the Mexican government modified the Constitution of 1917. Article 27 changed to liberalize Indigenous control over their lands and to attract investment. Although it has been argued that efforts to privatize Indigenous land have been a present element across different moments of Mexican history (McClure 2022, 10), NAFTA was significant in that it accelerated capitalist accumulation and new forms of land dispossession. Changes to the Electricity Public Service Law also made it possible for private investors to develop wind power generation under the framework of a self-supply model. Similarly, the Mining Law was rewritten to legally establish free market mining (Altamirano-Jiménez 2017).

Development plans for the Isthmus were formalized in 1994. The government of Ernesto Zedillo proposed the Comprehensive Development Plan, which aimed at integrating the region to the global market through the development of eleven different sectors, including wind power generation parks and interoceanic infrastructure. His successor, Vicente Fox, attempted to expand the project by creating joint development ventures with Central American countries (Servicio Internacional Para la Paz 2020). While most of these projects were not fully developed, wind power industrial parks were built in different communities. Because in Oaxaca Indigenous communities still control their lands, corporations' attempts to access the land needed to build wind generation parks resorted to illegal practices, including false promises, coercion, and intimidation (Altamirano-Jiménez 2021; Dunlap 2017).

In his efforts to accelerate the transformation of the region into a multimodal development hub, in 2006 Mexican then-president Felipe Calderón organized a series of public colloquiums to promote the wind power riches of the region to foreign investors. Embracing energy transitions, president Calderón gave investors the opportunity to stake a claim to specific areas on an atlas (Altamirano-Jiménez 2017, 31). While wind is an invisible, fluid natural force, it requires access to land to capture it. The performance of the event fostered the fantasy of staking claims on terra nullius in order to possess wind (Altamirano-Jiménez 2021). Staking claims on the land emptied the land of Indigenous bodies, histories, and relations to land. Moreover, while discourses of sustainable development and energy transitions promote the idea of a world where our future binds us together, they are shaped by power relations and asymmetries between the Global North and South. Just as colonialism has benefited countries of the Global North, energy transitions constitute a new colonial mode of resource extraction that continues to dispossess Indigenous Peoples (Howe and Boyer 2016, 218).

This is the context of the Isthmus Interoceanic Corridor, which was officially announced in 2019 after current president Andrés Manuel López Obrador took office. President López Obrador came to power promising a new, fairer relationship with Indigenous Peoples. He claimed that this corridor would promote development, reduce the stagnation caused by lack of investment, generate jobs, and restore natural resources and biodiversity through public-private investment (Secretaría de Gobernación 2020). The corridor is envisioned as a "Hassle Free Zone," which guarantees the coordinated support from the state, different levels of government, diligent approval for concessions, and legal certainty for investors. Free zones create an environment of certainty for corporations with lower taxes and fuel prices (Secretaría de Gobernación 2020). López Obrador announced that ten industrial parks of between five hundred and one thousand hectares would be built. Ironically called "Development Poles for Wellbeing," these industrial parks would be added to the twenty-eight existing industrial wind parks and the 47,000 hectares already granted in concessions to mining companies (Duhalt 2021).

Using a populist discourse and charging opponents for being conservatives and neoliberals, López Obrador has aggressively expanded the scope of neoliberal policies in Indigenous regions. Through narratives of sustainable development and promises of prosperity for all, land dispossession is operationalized through everyday violence. Transforming Indigenous land into zones of extraction not only enables the destruction of entire ecosystems but also the bodies and the worldviews of Indigenous Peoples who inhabit them (Altamirano-Jiménez 2021, 7).

The expansion of extractive activities has brought corporations into conflicts with Indigenous communities who have mobilized to defend their water, land, sea, and wind (see Dunlap 2019; Avila-Calero 2017; Altamirano-Jiménez 2017; and others). From colonialism to the present, the extraction of natural resources has been characterized by a pattern of ecological destruction and a structure of violence. As a fundamental historical-structural dimension of colonial extractivism, violence is a central element of the global economic system. Land dispossession is not only about the unjust taking of lands but also a relation of violence that defines new subjectivities and relationships between bodies and territory and among people. As such, the dispossession of Indigenous lands and the violent extractive processes that affect the land, wind, and sea cannot be analytically separated from the everyday racialized and gendered violence that is inflicted on human bodies.

MATRIARCHS, MUXES, AND NGUIUS

As noted earlier, the Isthmus, specifically the community of Juchitán, is often represented as being home to strong Zapotec matriarchs who have a strong presence in the local economy. The earlier references to the prominent roles of Zapotec women are found in the sixteenth century in the writings of colonial chroniclers. These references reveal the wide range of daily activities, which were vital to the social, spiritual, and political life of their communities (Sousa 2017). These narratives later inspired intellectuals and artists such as Frida Kahlo, Tina Modotti, and Diego Rivera, who contributed to disseminate representations of Zapotec women as symbol of empowerment (Gómez Suárez and Miano Borusso 2008, 168). This place is also known for being a paradise for Muxes, which rests upon the institutionalization of a third gender. References to Muxes can also be found in colonial chronicles of the sixteenth century (Gómez Suárez and Miano Borusso 2008, 166). Although recent research has represented Zapotec women's activism against resource extraction as somehow natural or expected from matriarchs, my research problematizes the absence of Muxes and Nguius (lesbians, queers, trans, Two-Spirit individuals) in these accounts of land defence. I argue that centring the gendered body in our conceptions of relationality is key to providing a more complex understanding of land and water defence and resurgence struggles.

Although Zapotec women play central roles in the economic, social, and cultural life of our communities in the Isthmus of Tehuantepec, explanations for this difference in relation to other Indigenous women differ. For some scholars, Juchitán is described as a matriarchal or matri-focal society that revolves around the idea of the "strong mother" and an economy based on relationships of reciprocity or mutual aid (Bennholdt-Thomsen 1997, 1, 27; Chiñas 1992). From this perspective, Juchitán is understood as an egalitarian place where the roles of women are socially and economically important. For others, in contrast, Juchitán cannot be described as a "matriarchy" (Miano Borusso 2002; Stephen 2002). While Zapotec women make important economic contributions and have some authority, it is often confined to the household (Kellogg 2005, 110). Compared to other Indigenous women in Mexico, Zapotec women have historically had and continue to have a strong presence in the local and regional economy. This presence is reinforced by the communal social organization, which is characterized by extensive and dense networks of relationships sustained primarily by women. Mothers or the women of a family are the "individual nodes" sustaining such networks in matrifocal communities (Miano Borusso 2002, 166). These networks are maintained by a system of social prestige that enables the distribution of wealth through community fiestas and celebrations.

Muxes, on the other hand, are a unique group of Zapotec biological males, who upend conventional conceptions of binary notions of gender and sexuality. Many openly dress as women and assume traditional feminine roles and are accepted into the larger communities. However, they are neither strictly trans nor do they identify as women; Muxes defy gender binaries and instead express fluid sexualities. They often identify as a third gender. The term Muxe comes from the sixteenth century and derives from the term "muyer," or mujer (woman) in old Spanish. Muyer was the term Spaniards used to designate those individuals who crossed over boundaries of gender (Lacey 2008; Williams 1992). Muxes' roles and desires were, under the constrains of Spanish colonial gender binary, misunderstood and misrecognized as simply "women."

While it is widely known that in the Isthmus of Tehuantepec, specifically in Juchitán, both women and Muxes are highly visible, Nguius are not. Nguius (literally meaning "man") are lesbian, bisexual, trans, and queer individuals that play a masculine role and engage in masculine activities. Like Muxes, they do not conform to binary conceptions of gender and sexuality and remain highly invisible in our communities. According to Muxe activist Amaranta Gómez Regalado (2016), Nguius can be considered a fourth gender that, nonetheless, does not enjoy the same recognition Muxes do. Practices of social control of people's sexuality are often more permissive for men and Muxes than for women and Nguius. Bodies perceived to be female but that identify otherwise and refuse to expand the networks of kinship that are so valued in Zapotec communities are disciplined (Aguilar Flores and Barrera Bassols 2020, 41). These differences in how sexuality is currently understood in the region are shaped by the heteropatriarchal system, which devalues some bodies more than others.

Nevertheless, romanticized narratives about strong matriarchs and the acceptance of Muxes (Chisholm 2018) fail to seriously examine how colonialism and patriarchy have shaped contemporary embodied experiences of being Zapotec. The colonization of gender and sexuality imposed foreign configurations of family and intimacy that were embodied unevenly. The discipline of the church and adopted community values were and continue to be stricter for women than for men and Muxes, who have generally been freer to express their personhood (Picq and Tikuna 2019). This legacy together with contemporary processes of migration, adopted ideas of hegemonic masculinity and femininity, and the phenomenon of normalcy and ideal bodies have impacted Zapotec communities (Sartini 2020).

Although these communities' dynamics are not new, they have been exacerbated by economic disinvestment in Indigenous communities, policies that have made Indigenous livelihoods precarious, and external forces aimed at fragmenting people's relationships to land, sea, and wind. Moreover, the impunity with which misogyny, homophobia, and transphobia unfolds obscures the severity of gendered violence in Mexico. Despite narratives of strong matriarchs and sexual inclusion, in the Isthmus gendered and sexualized violence is on the rise (La Prensa Latina 2023). The Mesoamerican Initiative of Land and Human Rights Defenders has shown that Oaxaca has the highest rates of gendered violence in the country (Manzo 2017). During the 2021 International Women's Day, activists denounced that despite supposedly promoting well-being of Isthmian peoples, the Interoceanic Corridor Master Plan is silent about gender violence (Manzo 2017). The plan, like the current government's rhetoric, is not only blind to gender violence but through its silence, it sanctions it.

THE CONTESTED TERRITORY OF PLURAL BODIES

Debates regarding the impact of resource extraction often deploy a masculinist understanding of territory (Altamirano-Jiménez 2021; Zaragocin and Carreta 2020). However, as Moreton-Robinson argues, relations to territory are gendered and multi-layered. Human embodiment is mediated by social relations and relationships to the non-human world (Moreton-Robinson 2013, 339). Indigenous women, Muxes, and Nguius' experiences are shaped by their livelihoods, shared experiences of racism, discrimination, colonialism, and gender roles. These intersecting systems of oppression and the subsequent power relations that flow from them into the social, political, historical, and material conditions of our lives are embodied. As Mishuana Goeman (2013, 15) has noted, these conditions and relations shape how we see and inhabit the world and how the ontological relationship between land and bodies has been disrupted over time.

The territorial restructuring that has unfolded in Mexico and Latin America in the last three decades has made visible the connection between the expansion of capitalist accumulation and gendered violence. This expansion is constituted by new processes to control, exploit, and extract new and old resources; dispossess Indigenous lands; disarticulate Indigenous local economies; and discipline bodies that cannot be absorbed into the economy through violence (Navarro Trujillo 2019, 14–15). To resist these processes, hundreds of resistance movements have appeared in the Mexican geography. Indigenous women and femme individuals have been at the forefront of such struggles. In the Isthmus of Tehuantepec, Indigenous women have organized demonstrations and engaged local, national, and international movements and women's organizations. In interviews conducted in December 2019 and January 2020, and between May and June 2022, Indigenous women expressed a visceral concern that industrial wind power development, mining, and the Interoceanic Corridor are putting their bodies and children and grandchildren's futures at risk. They spoke of how the commodification of resources is limiting their food sovereignty and changing the social fabric of their communities. The slogan that organizations and activists use — "wind, land and sea are not for sale, they are loved and defended" — conveys how these activists understand their relations to territory.[2] At different gatherings and events, Binnizá land defenders have insisted that Indigenous Peoples are not against development *per se*, but against land grabbing. They have explained that extractivism effects are already felt in biodiversity loss, soil and water contamination, and privatization of the region's lagoon system, and that the Interoceanic Corridor will only mean the destruction of Indigenous territories (Altamirano-Jiménez 2021; Avila-Calero 2017; Chávez 2014). Through their stories, women centre a form of embodied knowledge to name the violence that they experienced in their bodies, which are connected to the geographic spaces in which they are located.

Indigenous women activists claim that the fight to defend territory is intergenerational and is about our present and future relationships to the sea, land, and wind. Although this way of understanding relationships prefigures a future in which these entities may enable our very own communal existence, not everyone has the same interpretations of culture and what is the best way to defend territory. For example, although Indigenous men land defenders claim they are supportive of women participating in activism and even taking prominent roles, they continue to dominate political spaces. Women engage in emotional labour to uplift their organizations and manage the emotions that emerge in highly repressive contexts. Moreover, gendered dynamics shaping these movements reproduce heteronormative ideals of proper womanhood, concealing the challenges women land defenders face. Women activists are often the targets of attacks, acts of intimidation, and gender violence. Indigenous women are often arrested on fabricated charges and their reputation destroyed in their communities. In small, close-knit Indigenous communities, spreading rumours about women's morality has been a common way to disrepute their political work (Altamirano-Jiménez 2021, 329). While the atypical matrifocal culture of this region serves as a backdrop to speak about Indigenous women's activism, ideas about their reproductive capability frequently equate Mother Earth's generation of life with women's responsibility to simultaneously care for the environment, their families, and communities. These ideas are also reproduced by some older women activists, who claim that as life givers, it is their responsibility to defend life.

In contrast, younger women activists are more critical of gender relations. They often work with different organizations and collectives involved in a variety of initiatives to work towards the resurgence of the Zapotec language, culture, music, health, and so forth. They expose and trouble the gender discrimination, sexual harassment, and violence they undergo in their everyday lives in different spaces. In interviews, younger research participants observed that reproducing narratives of strong matriarchs only obscures class and gender differentiation. They illustrate that there is a social hierarchy that privileges men and Muxes and conceals women's political and economic contributions to their communities and families. These young activists hold that while land defence is key to our survival as Zapotec people, it cannot be separated from gender discrimination and violence. As one Indigenous research participant noted in an interview, "Men like to say they love and respect Mother Earth, how about extending that love to women … also Muxes, and Nguius? I am telling you, our movements need some love as well" (Personal communication, Oaxaca City, January 6, 2020). Similarly, the Colectivo de Mujeres Istmeñas en Defensa del Territorio (Collective of Isthmus Women in Defence of Territory) manifested, "We firmly believe that we need to construct stronger organizations that don't repeat or reproduce the patriarchal violence of the capitalist system … this system in its multiple manifestations is the enemy" (Vargas 2016). Thus, while younger Zapotec activists agree with the importance of revitalizing and resurging cultural identity, they also warn that it is important to be careful with which practices and customs we want to strengthen. As Starblanket and Stark (2018, 177) have observed, how relationships are embodied may enable or constrain political resurgence movements.

Women activists, academics, and feminist organizations have noted that the struggle to defend territory needs to be simultaneously anti-capitalist, anti-colonial, and anti-patriarchal. Some activists have articulated the notion of cuerpo-territorio, or body as a territory, to connect what happens to their bodies to what happens to their territory. In this way, land dispossession, resource extraction, and the violence inflicted on the land are connected to the domination logics that affect their gendered bodies (Navarro Trujillo 2019, 26; Cruz 2017; Cabnal 2010). However, how body as territory is taken up varies from context to context and from body to body. For example, the Latin American campaign El Machismo Mata, No Más Feminicidios (Machismo Kills, No More Feminicide) is a campaign that seeks to empower women so they can live free of violence and conceives of gendered violence as a phenomenon that only affects women as a universal category. Indigenous women, Muxes, Nguius, trans, and Two-Spirit individuals' experiences of violence end up subsumed within statistics of feminicide (Chaca 2021; Martínez 2022). Moreover, the multidimensional character of gender violence against Indigenous women, Nguius, Muxes, and Two-Spirit individuals is obscured. Living in an Indigenous woman, trans, or Two-Spirit body heightens the risk that one's body will not be valued or protected, and in the case of demise, accounted for. Colonialism, racism, misogyny, homophobia, and transphobia structure the conditions under which Indigenous people live and struggle. Universal accounts of gender violence and resource extraction can, in my view, neglect that the making of the extractive frontier has historically targeted Indigenous women and Two-Spirit bodies most persistently, albeit differently (Altamirano-Jiménez 2021). These bodies have, since colonization, been rendered less valuable for what they represent: social reproduction, Indigenous kinships, non-binary gender relations, governance traditions, and different ways of being in the world (Wilson 2015; Simpson 2016).

In Mexico as in Latin America, the contemporary expansion of natural resource extraction is usually marked by the absence of the rule of law. In this context, different actors operate to pursue their own interests. The state not only redirects once communal and public patrimonies into the hands of foreign corporations; its authority co-exists alongside additional actors including corporations, old oligarchies, paramilitary groups, and organized crime, which mobilize their power to deconstruct existing Indigenous territorialities for their own benefit (Altamirano-Jiménez 2021, 2). Exacerbated domestic, sexual, gender, and political violence can be understood as expressions of processes of removing Indigenous bodies from the land and the upsurge of patriarchal forms of domination. Thus, in theorizing gender violence and colonial extractivism, the relationships that are part of the intimate, domestic, interpersonal, and community life are as important as the relationships Indigenous Peoples have with their territory and the non-human world.

In problematizing binary thinking, this chapter calls for a more expansive, fluid, and contextualized understanding of gender and sexuality in order to properly resituate discussions of gender violence. The idea of the body as territory (cuerpo-territorio), the first home (la primera casita) that needs to be defended and reclaimed is useful. The body is the first entity where we experience joy, sadness, and pain, and is central to the practices of landing relations I referred to earlier. Similar to Cherokee scholar Qwo-Li Driskill (2004), who equates the body with home in order to develop the notion of "sovereign erotics," Indigenous feminists in Latin America have articulated body as territory as a journey to reclaim one's first home in order to reconstitute it in transformative ways (Cabnal 2010; Paredes 2011). The idea of body as territory prompts recognition that what surrounds us, including our communities, families, intimate relations, and our territories, must be part of the conversations about gender violence and decolonization and resurgence efforts.

However, an analysis of newspapers and social media of the campaign My Body, My Territory illustrates the uneven ways in which Indigenous and non-Indigenous activists have mobilized the idea in the Latin American context. For some, it is a political declaration that involves new forms of individual self-care, relationship with the body, health, sexuality, and so forth. For others, body as territory has also become a banner for broader feminist alliances against gender violence (Leinius 2021). According to Mayan Q'eqchi'-xinka feminist Lorena Cabnal (2010), for Indigenous women, body as territory is grounded on a communitarian ethos that simultaneously supports individual and collective life and action. Body as territory has certainly fostered dialogue between Indigenous and non-Indigenous feminist movements. However, such conversations show the tensions that arise from not taking the relationship between body and land seriously (Leinius 2021, 206). Often these processes reduce relationality to ideas of the "sensuous" and "embodiment," dismissing the political, cultural, and ontological meaning of territory for Indigenous Peoples. As a young Indigenous research participant put it, "Non-Indigenous feminists often co-opt our ideas and processes and attempt to speak for us" (Personal communication, Isthmus of Tehuantepec, June 2022). Importantly, these tensions conceal that not all bodies relate to territory in the same way and that universal conceptions of bodies can erase trans, queer, Two-Spirit, Muxes, Nguius, and femme experiences as well as different ways of embodying humanity.

In the Isthmus, Muxes and Nguius have mobilized to defend their autonomy to love and live in their own terms. Like Driskill's discussion of the erotic that extends beyond the personal, they have articulated a discourse in which gender violence is conceived of as violence against the Zapotec culture (Diehl et al. 2017, 392). In doing so, they explicitly connect gender and sexuality to peoplehood. This epistemological connection allows this community to validate their identities, aspirations, and experiences within their communal contexts without need to refer to Western frameworks. As Driskill (2004, 50, 53) notes, colonizing regimes have sought to control notions of sexuality and have used sexual and gender violence as tools to gain power over Indigenous people's bodies and, consequently, their communities. Unlike limited, non-Indigenous notions of the body as territory, Indigenous feminist articulations presuppose that any discussion about sovereignty, autonomy, decolonization and land and water defence starts with the freedom to choose how to be in our body/home/territory. In this way, the relationships that are part of the self — the erotic, domestic, and communal life — become as important as relationships to territory and non-human beings. Making visible the gratuitous violence that is inflicted on Indigenous bodies, bodies of land, bodies of water, and bodies of Indigenous knowledge, involves a responsibility to actively refuse and trouble the underpinning logics of colonial, patriarchal, transphobic, and homophobic violence. From this perspective, relationality or the very act of being in relationships across spaces and time evokes motion, actions, multi-directions, multi-temporal frameworks, multiple species, and plural bodies.

FLUIDITY AND TRANSFORMATION

Using a body-land analytic, this chapter has problematized how romanticized ideas of relationality obscure gendered experiences of land and water defence movements. Focusing on the Isthmus of Tehuantepec and the fight against the expansion of the extractive frontier, it documented that land defence struggles are gendered processes simultaneously mediated by social relations, relationships to the non-human world, notions of culture, and conceptions of territory. People's embodied experiences of territory are shaped by their livelihoods, shared experiences of racism, discrimination, colonialism, and gender roles. However, romanticized, binary accounts of land and water defence obscure the challenges faced by plural bodies.

These experiences inform not only how we see and inhabit the world but also the visions we have for defending territory and the non-human world. In thinking through these issues, I am reminded of Zapotec stories, encounters among diverse bodies, the fluidity of water and wind, the perceived fixity of land, and how their relationships manifest. I wonder, how might multiple bodies (bodies of water, bodies of land, Indigenous women, Muxes and Nguius) build transformative relationships? When water and wind come into relationship, they produce different encounters, including contact and frictions. When wind and water interact, they not only shape the climatic conditions of the

Isthmus, they also open the space for transforming the land through these encounters and frictions. Like encounters, frictions have the potential to be productive if we are attentive and willing to think through them with depth and nuance. They can entail engaging in difficult, uncomfortable conversations and acknowledging that building relationships happens at many scales — in our intimate relationships, our homes, communities, and struggles — and it requires consent. Relationships involve refusal: the refusal of colonial violence and hierarchical, gendered, racial, anthropocentric thinking. Theoretically, I showed that body-land allows us to deepen our analysis of the overlapping ways in which both power and resistance manifest in our bodies, intimate and social relations, communities, Indigenous struggles, and relationships with other feminisms. Relations of power and domination must be re-examined to come to understand our current circumstances. It is not merely the repetition of cultural practices and relational stories that make us Zapotec people or enable transformation. Giving our movements some love starts with the difficult task of learning how our relational practices are enacted in our everyday lives and what they may indicate about the current arrangement of our existence as Zapotec people.

NOTES

1   This research was funded by the Insight Grant Land, Body and Consent and Canada Research Chair in Comparative Indigenous Feminist Studies. An iteration of this work was published in Kress and Horn-Miller 2023.
2   Translations are those of the author.

REFERENCES

Aguilar Flores, Adriana, and Dalia Barrera Bassols. 2020. "Las otras 'Nguiu' del Istmo de Tehuantepec. Experiencias de campo" [The Other 'Nguiu' from the Isthmus of Tehuantepec]. *Revista Debates Insubmissos* 3, 9. researchgate.net/publication/343273527_LAS_OTRAS_NGUIU_DEL_ISTMO_DE_TEHUANTEPEC_-_EXPERIENCIAS_DE_CAMPO/fulltext/5f20d4c4299bf1720d6dae7a/LAS-OTRAS-NGUIU-DEL-ISTMO-DE-TEHUANTEPEC-EXPERIENCIAS-DE-CAMPO.pdf

Altamirano-Jiménez, Isabel. 2013. *Indigenous Encounters with Neoliberalism: Place, Women, and the Environment in Canada and Mexico*. Vancouver: UBC Press.

———. 2017. "The Sea Is Our Bread: Interrupting Green Neo-Liberalism in Mexico." *Marine Policy* 80.

———. 2020. "Free Mining, Body Land and the Social Reproduction of Indigenous Life." In *Turbulent Times, Transformational Possibilities? Gender and Politics,*

Today and Tomorrow, edited by A. Dobrowolsky and F. Macdonald. Toronto: University of Toronto Press.

———. 2021. "Possessing Land, Wind and Water in the Isthmus of Tehuantepec, Oaxaca." *Australian Feminist Studies* 35, 106.

———. 2023. "Body Land, Water and Resurgence in Oaxaca." In *Indigenous Resurgence in the Age of Reconciliation,* edited by H. Kiiwetinepinesiik Stark, A. Craft, and H.K. Aikau. Toronto: University of Toronto Press.

Avila-Calero, Sofia. 2017. "Contesting Energy Transitions: Wind Power and Conflicts in the Isthmus of Tehuantepec." *Journal of Political Ecology* 24, 1.

Bennholdt-Thomsen, Veronica. 1997. *Juchitán la ciudad de las mujeres* [Juchitán the City of Women]. Oaxaca: Fondo para la Cultura y las Artes.

Byrd, Jodi. 2011. *The Transit of Empire*. Minneapolis: University of Minnesota Press.

Cabnal, Lorena. 2010. *Feminismos diversos: el feminismo comunitario* [Diverse Feminisms: Communitarian Feminism]. ACSUR-Las Segovias.

Chaca, Roselia. 2021. "Presentan muxes trans del Istmo de Oaxaca carteles para prevenir la discriminación" [Muxes and Trans against Discrimination]. *El Universal*, October 7. oaxaca.eluniversal.com.mx/sociedad/presentan-muxes-trans-del-istmo-de-oaxaca-carteles-para-prevenir-la-discriminacion.

Chávez, Adazahira. 2014. "Resistencia a las Eólicas en Oaxaca. Donde el viento vale oro." Entrevista con Bettina Cruz Velázquez [Resistance Against Wind Power in Oaxaca. Where Wind Is Gold. Interview with Betina Cruz]. *La Jornada Ojarasca*, October 11. jornada.com.mx/2014/10/11/oja-viento.html.

Chiñas, Beverly. 1992. *The Isthmus Zapotecs: A Matrifocal Culture of Mexico*. Wadsworth/Thomson Learning.

Chisholm, Jennifer. 2018. "Muxe, Two-Spirits, and the Myth of Indigenous Transgender Acceptance." *International Journal of Critical Indigenous Studies* 111.

Cruz, Delmy Tania. 2017. "Una mirada muy otra a los territorios-cuerpos femeninos" [A Different Gaze to Feminine Body-Territories]. *Solar* 12, 1. researchgate.net/publication/326446571_UNA_MIRADA_MUY_OTRA_A_LOS_TERRITORIOS-CUERPOS_FEMENINOS_1_A_very_other_gaze_at_the_territories-female_bodies.

Diehl, Alessandra, et al. 2017. "Social Stigma, Legal and Public Health Barriers Faced by the Third Gender Phenomena in Brazil, India and Mexico: Travestis, Hijras and Muxes." *International Journal Social Psychiatry* 63, 5.

Driskill, Qwo-Li. 2004. "Stolen from Our Bodies: First Nations Two-Spirits/Queers and the Journey to a Sovereign Erotic." *Studies in American Indian Literatures* 16, 2.

Duhalt, Adrian. 2021. "The Interoceanic Corridor of Mexico's Isthmus of Tehuantepec and the North-South Development Gap." *Rice University's Baker Institute for Public Policy*. June 12. bakerinstitute.org/research/interoceanic-corridor-mexicos-isthmus-tehuantepec-and-north-south-development-gap.

Dunlap, Alexander. 2017. "Wind Energy: Toward a 'Sustainable Violence' in Oaxaca, Mexico." NACLA 49. tandfonline.com/doi/epdf/10.1080/10714839.2017.1409378?needAccess=true.

———. 2019. "Wind, Coal, and Copper: The Politics of Land Grabbing, Counterinsurgency, and the Social Engineering of Extraction." *Globalizations*. DOI:10.1080/14747731.2019.1682789.

Garner, Paul. 1995. "The Politics of National Development in Late Porfirian Mexico: The Reconstruction of the Tehuantepec National Railway 1896–1907." *Bulletin of Latin American Research* 14, 3.

Goeman, Mishuana. 2013. *Mark My Words: Native Women Mapping Our Nations*. Minneapolis: University of Minnesota Press.

Gómez Regalado, Amaranta. 2016. *Guendaranadxii: la comuninada muxhe del isthmo de Tehuantepec y su relación erotica afectiva* [The Muxhe community of the Isthmus of Tehuantepec and Erotic-Affective Relationships]. Honours thesis, Universidad Veracruzana.

Gómez Suárez, Águeda, and Marinella Miano Borusso. 2008. "Dimensiones discursivas del sistema de sexo y género entre los indígenas zapotecas del Istmo de Tehuantepec (México)" [Discursive Dimensions of Systems of Gender and Sex among the Zapotecs from the Isthmus of Tehuantepec]. *Papers* 88. ddd.uab.cat/pub/papers/02102862n88/02102862n88p165.pdf.

Howe, Cymene, and Dominique Boyer. 2016. "Aeolian Extractivism and Community Wind in Southern Mexico." *Public Culture* 28, 2.

Kellogg, Susan. 2005. *Weaving the Past: A History of Latin America's Indigenous Women from the Pre-Hispanic Period to the Present*. Oxford University Press.

Kress, Margaret and Kahente Horn-Miller (eds.). 2023. *Land as Relation. Teaching and Learning through Place, People and Practices*. Toronto: Canadian Scholars Press.

La Prensa Latina News Editor. 2023. "Wave of Violence Against Women Spurs Alarm in Mexican Border City." *La Prensa Latina Bilingual Media*, August 11. laprensalatina.com/wave-of-violence-against-women-spurs-alarm-in-mexican-border-city/.

Lacey, Marc. 2008. "A Lifestyle Distinct: The Muxe of Mexico." *New York Times*, December 7. nytimes.com/2008/12/07/weekinreview/07lacey.html.

Leinius, Johanna. 2021. "Articulating Body, Territory, and the Defence of Life: The Politics of Strategic Equivalencing between Women in Anti-Mining Movements and the Feminist Movement in Peru." *Bulletin of Latin American Research* 40, 2. doi.org/10.1111/blar.13112.

Manzo, Diana. 2017. "Crece la violencia contra mujeres defensoras de la tierra y el territorio en Istmo de Tehuantepec" [Violence Against Land Defenders Increases in the Tehuantepec Isthmus of Tehuatepec]. *Desinformémonos*, March 13. desinformemonos.org/crece-la-violencia-mujeres-defensoras-la-tierra-territorio-istmo-tehuantepec/.

Martínez, Verónica. 2022. "Avanzan derechos para la comunidad LGBT+, pero siguen los pendientes" [LGTBT+ advance, but there is still much to do]. *Cuestione*, June 24. cuestione.com/nacional/avanzan-derechos-comunidad-lgbt-hay-pendientes-agenda-legislativa/.

McClure, Julia. 2022. "Conquest by Contract: Property Rights and the Commercial Logic of Imperialism in the Isthmus of Tehuantepec (Southern Mexico)." *Bulletin of Latin American Research* 41, 4. onlinelibrary.wiley.com/doi/epdf/10.1111/blar.13356.

Miano Borruso, Marinella. 2002. *Hombre, mujer y muxe'en el Istmo de Tehuantepec* [Man, Woman, and Muxe in the Isthmus of Tehuantepec]. Mexico City: Instituto Nacional de Anthropolgia, Plaza y Valdés.

Moreton-Robinson, Aileen. 2013. "Towards an Australian Indigenous Women's Standpoint Theory. A Methodological Tool." *Australian Feminist Studies* 28, 78.

Navarro Trujillo, Mina Lorena. 2019. "Mujeres en defensa de la vida contra la violencia extractivista en México" [Woman Defending Life against Extractivist Violence in Mexico]. *Política y Cultura* 51. polcul.xoc.uam.mx/index.php/polcul/article/view/1373/1342.

Paredes, Julieta. 2011. *Hilando Fino, desde el feminismo comunitario* [Threading from Communitarian Feminism]. La Paz: Comunidad Mujeres Creando Comunidad.

Picq, Manuela L., and Josi Tikuna. 2019. "Indigenous Sexualities: Resisting Conquest and Translation." *E-International Relations,* August 20. e-ir.info/pdf/79088.

Povinelli, Elizabeth. 2016. *Geontologies: A Requiem to Late Liberalism*. Duke University Press.

Rendón Monzón, Juan José. 2003. *La Comunalidad, modo de vida en los pueblos indios* [Communality, a Way of Life among Indigenous Peoples of Mexico]. Mexico City: Dirección General de Culturas Populares e Indígenas.

Rubin, Jeffrey. W. 1994. "COCEI in Juchitán: Grassroots Radicalism and Regional History." *Journal of Latin American Studies* 26, 1.

Sartini, Ilaria. 2020. "Muxes: Between Globalization and Identity Impacts of New Female Models on Gender Performance." Paper presented at the *International Conference on New Findings on Humanities and Social Science*. dpublication.com/wp-content/uploads/2020/11/16-7016.pdf.

Secretaría de Gobernación. 2020. "Programa para el Desarrollo del Istmo de Tehauntepec 2020–2024" [Development Program for the Isthmus of Tehuantepec 2019–2024]. www.gob.mx/ciit/documentos/programa-para-el-desarrollo-del-istmo-de-tehuantepec-2020-2024.

Servicio Internacional Para la Paz. 2020. "FOCUS: The Trans-Isthmus Corridor, A Not-So-New Project of the New Government." June 3. sipaz.org/focus-the-trans-isthmus-corridor-a-not-so-new-project-of-the-new-government/?lang=en.

Sexton, Jax. 2011. *The Monroe Doctrine: Empire and Nation in Nineteenth Century America*. New York: Hill and Wang.

Simpson, Audra. 2016. "The State Is a Man: Theresa Spence, Loretta Saunders and the Gender of Settler Sovereignty." *Theory and Event* 19, 4. muse.jhu.edu/article/633280.

Sousa, Lisa. 2017. *The Woman Who Turned into a Jaguar, and Other Narratives of Native Women in Archives of Colonial Mexico*. Stanford University Press.

Starblanket, Gina, and Heidi Kiiwetinepinesiik Stark. 2018. "Towards a Relational Paradigm—Four Points for Consideration: Knowledge, Gender, Land and Modernity." In *Resurgence and Reconciliation: Indigenous-Settler Relations and Earth Teachings*, edited by Michael Ash, John Borrows, and James Tully. Toronto: University of Toronto Press.

Stephen, Lynn. 2002. *Zapata lives! Histories and Cultural Politics in Southern Mexico*. Berkeley: University of California Press.

Vargas, Martín. 2016. "Colectivo de mujeres istmeñas se manifiesta contra la violencia" [Ithsmian Women Collectively Manifest against Violence]. *Istmo Press,* December 14. istmopress.com.mx/uncategorized/colectivo-de-mujeres-istmenas-se-manifiesta-contra-la-violencia/.

Williams, Walter. L. 1992. *The Spirit and the Flesh: Sexual Diversity in American Indian Culture*. New York: Beacon Press.

Wilson, Alex. 2015. "Our Coming In Stories. Cree Identity, Body Sovereignty and Gender Self-Determination." *Journal of Global Indigeneity* 1, 1. ro.uow.edu.au/cgi/viewcontent.cgi?article=1011&context=jgi.

World Bank. 1990. *World Development Report*. Washington: World Bank

Zaragocin, Sofia, and Martina Angela Carreta. 2020. "Cuerpo-Territorio: A Decolonial Feminist Geographical Method for the Study of Embodiment." *Annals of the American Association of Geographers* 111, 5.

TEN

Mana Wahine and Mothering at the Loʻi
A Two-Spirit/Queer Analysis

Hōkūlani K. Aikau

IN THIS CHAPTER I GRAPPLE WITH a puzzle I struggled with for the many years I worked with ʻĀina Momona (AM), a Native Hawaiian non-profit organization working to restore the loʻi kalo (wetland taro farming) system in the island of Oʻahu.[1] This puzzle centres on two very distinct experiences of my time working at the loʻi. On the one hand, my experience of the loʻi is that it is a place filled with mana wahine (female generative power and authority) and on the other, it is a place that is normatively heterosexist where a gendered division of labour and the traditionalization of heteropatriarchy are enacted. In this chapter, I critique the way heteropatriarchal traditionalism is used to silence Native feminisms and our critique of sexism, homophobia, and transphobia in our own communities. It was difficult to write this piece because I love the people who I worked with at this site, I love the land, and yet I struggled to understand why I would remain silent in the presence of sexist and homophobic behaviours and attitudes when in other aspects of my life I would speak up. Queer Indigenous feminist theory and critical Indigenous masculinity studies helped me make sense of how the loʻi could be both a place imbued with mana wahine and a site where heteropatriarchal traditionalism is sedimented. These theoretical tools provide me with frameworks with which to disrupt traditionalized heteropatriarchy so that the (queer) mana wahine ever present at the loʻi can be seen, expressed, and cultivated.

I use two ethnographic moʻolelo (stories) to illustrate these two distinct ways of experiencing the loʻi. They take place at a Native Hawaiian wetland restoration project on the island of Oʻahu. ʻĀina Momona has been working to restore these lands since 2008. The first story is one of many I could share about my daughter. It is intended as an illustration of how the mana (spiritual power) of ʻāina (land, that which feeds) can empower us. The second story is also one of many that I could tell about how heteronormative gender binaries are learned impositions that have become sedimented in various ways at this site, specifically in the form of gendered divisions of labour. Together the stories are intended to juxtapose at least two very different approaches and sets of values operating simultaneously in this place.

Drawing upon my experiences as a volunteer and fieldnotes from participant observer research, I make the case that the loʻi is a site teeming with a gender-non-conforming mana wahine. In bringing a Two-Spirit/queer (2SQ) analysis to re-read mana wahine at the loʻi, I intend to expand the meaning of wahine beyond its typical translation as woman/female to include feminine energy or spirit that can be, but is not necessarily, associated with the female body or the gender identity approximating "woman/women" in the settler colonial context. Rather, I argue that mana wahine is a powerful energy that is embodied and can be harnessed by bodies not assigned female at birth. A Two-Spirit/queer lens allows me to consider the metaphorical, material, and political orders operating simultaneously at the loʻi, drawing inspiration from Simpson's 2SQ reading of tradition (Simpson 2017).

When I read mana wahine and the generative powers at the loʻi using this lens, I was able to consider what a non-cis, non-heteronormative conception of this land-based work could look like and could in fact be. In doing so, I centre a relational approach to Indigenous resurgence and Native feminist theory that attends to how bodies are differentially impacted by colonialism, heteropatriarchy, and white supremacy and decolonization and the restoration of ea (sovereignty, breath, life) (Goodyear-Kaʻōpua et al. 2014). My analysis and personal reflections contribute to visioning ʻŌiwi feminist futures that bring about material and metaphorical decolonization, liberation, and justice.[2]

My motivations for thinking and writing about this topic *now* is personal and political. At a personal level, as a mother of three cis kids, I am committed to challenging heteronormativity and heteropatriarchy in order to give my children alterNative models for living and expressing gender and sexuality. For my daughter, this is particularly pressing as I watch a beautifully strong, capable, self-confident kaikamahine (girl/daughter) doubt her power and authority — her mana. We moved away from Hawaiʻi when she was six years old to Turtle Island where we lived in a Conservative state in the United States. It has been some time since she was with ʻāina. On a daily basis, she is fully immersed in settler colonial logics of white supremacy, capitalism, and heteropartriachy, the stuff that structures and animates public schooling in the Conservative US city where we live. I see her become increasingly less confident and in need of constant reassurance of her mana as a wahine. Thus, my first objective is to look to our — hers and my — ʻŌiwi ancestors for models of mana wahine that can help my daughter (and sons) express their genders in empowering ways that do not reproduce or rely upon heteronormative patriarchy or a toxic Indigenous heteropatriarchal masculinity. In the words of Stó:lō poet and activist Lee Maracle (2002, 17) in *I Am Woman: A Native Perspective on Sociology and Feminism*,

> I want to look across the table in my own kitchen and see, in the brown eyes of the [men] who [share] my life, the beauty of my own reflection. More. I want to look across my kitchen table at the women of colour who share my life and see the genius of their minds, uncluttered by white opinion. I want to sit with my [almost] grown [daughter] and experience the wonderment of our mutual affection. I want us to set the standard for judging our brilliance, our beauty, and our passions.

I want my daughter and sisters and sons and students to know "not the woman on the billboard for whom physical work is damning, for whom nothingness, physical oblivion is idyllic. But a woman for whom mobility, muscular movement, physical prowess are equal to the sensuous pleasure of being alive." When I watched my daughter working and playing in the mud at the loʻi, I saw her mana expanded through muscular movement as she became fully absorbed in the experience of being with ʻāina. I use a Two-Spirit/queer lens to illuminate how the loʻi holds the potential for an otherwise to settler colonial heteronormativity. Indeed, I argue that a 2SQ mana wahine is ever present and open to us in the loʻi.

My second motivation is to contribute my intellectual labour to those thinkers/doers working to dismantle and decolonize heteropatriarchy and white supremacy in Indigenous communities. I am thinking with Nishnaabekwe scholar, poet, activist, and musician Leanne Betasamosake Simpson (2017) and her book *As We Have Always Done: Indigenous Freedom Through Radical Resistance*. Indigenous feminists have documented the micro and macro ways heteropatriarchy and heteronormativity were imposed on and have become sedimented in Indigenous nations (Hall 2009; Chang Hall and Kauanui 1994; Silva 2004; Goeman and Denetdale 2009; Gunn Allen 1992; Barker 2008, 2017; Simpson 2009, 2016; Merry 2000; Kauanui 2018).

Simpson and others have argued that settler colonialism targeted women, children, and 2SQ people because they pose an ever-present threat to settler legitimacy and futurity. Simpson writes, "Indigenous bodies, particularly the bodies of 2SQ people, children, and women, represented the lived alternative to heteronormative constructions of gender, political systems, and rules of descent. They are political orders" (2017, 41).

Along with Simpson, I look to my ancestors for original instructions for how to understand a 2SQ mana wahine that has the power and authority to refuse to replicate capitalism, heteropatriarchy, and whiteness in a place that I experience as always already holding this power and authority. The stories featured in this chapter focus on my family's experiences at the lo'i. In 2011, I began working at the lo'i as a volunteer at the monthly community workdays. From 2012–14, with funding from a grant, my relationship shifted from community volunteer to researcher. After the grant ended, I maintained my relationship with 'Āina Momona as my family and I continued to volunteer there.³ The lo'i has opened many opportunities to reconnect with the land- and water-based practices of my ancestors and has radically transformed my understandings of gender, sexuality, menstruation, and reproduction. This chapter is intended to share what I have learned at the lo'i working alongside Hāloa/kalo (taro) and mahi 'ai kalo (taro farmers) about how to be more expansive in our understandings of gender so that we can confront the way homophobia and sexism have become normalized in many Native communities.

MO'OLELO

March 24, 2015: The students and faculty participating in an international academic exchange are working at the lo'i. Most of the group is clearing the stream of overgrown weeds in order to restore water flow to the

ʻauwai (channels that move water from stream to ponds and back to the stream). I am working with a small group pulling weeds in the loʻi. My daughter is with us. She has been coming here since she was two years old; she is now five. She steps up and shows the students from Canada how to carefully slide from the kuāuna (banks) into the knee-deep mud. Leading them down the narrow rows, she shows them how to walk carefully making sure not to step on the small kalo plants, pointing out, as they make their way down the row to where they will begin their work, which plants to pull and which plants to leave. I am working a few rows away and overhear her conversations with these graduate students visiting from the University of Victoria. I laugh at the authority in her voice. She says to the two First Nations women with whom she is working, "In the olden days, Hawaiians didn't get poi from plastic bags, they got it from kalo." She keeps working and talking for the rest of the morning. At the end of the work session, she helps the students get out of the pond and takes them to the stream to wash off and play in the cold spring-fed waters. She approaches washing and play with the same authority as she did pulling weeds and caring for kalo. At five years old, she knows the loʻi in a fully embodied and empowered way. I am proud and a little sad wishing that I had opportunities such as these when I was her age. I'm glad I can give her this now.

January 2017: My daughter and I attend another community workday. We are happy to be at the loʻi but on the whole the workday is not remarkable: there is a small group of volunteers and we spend most of the morning pulling weeds. Towards the end of the morning, the executive director invites the volunteers to join them on Monday (Martin Luther King Jr. Day) for another workday because they will be hosting the Day of Service for a major healthcare company in Hawaiʻi. After we are done working, I asked him if they need help on Monday. He says they expected more than a hundred volunteers, and an extra set of hands will be appreciated. He says to be back on Monday around 7:30 a.m.

Monday: I arrive at 7:30 and join the staff who are gathered at the picnic tables under the tents drinking coffee and talking story. Kaʻiulani, a newer staff member and the only woman working for AM at the time, arrived much earlier and was busily setting up for the day — staging wheelbarrows with all the tools each work crew will need. She takes a break and sits with us at the table and asks the executive director if we could start the orientation with oli (chant) and share some moʻolelo (stories). Kamaliʻi, the community outreach and education specialist, answers, "Nah, no need. Why waste that kine stuff on these guys." I am not surprised by his statement and shrug it off because this was not the first time he has said things like this. I finish my coffee and leave the table with Kaʻiulani to help her finish setting up for the volunteers. The others, mostly men, stay at the table and keep talking.

When volunteers arrive, they file off the bus and gather under the tents. A brief introduction is offered with no moʻolelo or oli. In fact, the introduction is so brief it does not include the usual history of the site and a summary of their goals. This is odd. I would later learn that Kamaliʻi was annoyed by "these kinds of volunteers" who only show up once a year at best. The executive director was frustrated because the number of volunteers who choose to work at the loʻi has dwindled: they expected approximately 175 people but only about seventy-five showed up. This is a stark contrast to prior years when they had as many as 300 volunteers. They were frustrated that so few people were attending their site.

At the end of the morning of work, the crews rinse off in the stream and start walking back to the educational area for lunch. Most of the staff do not join the volunteers but eat their lunch under the tents in their area. Kaʻiulani stays with the volunteers, answering questions and talking story. I want to get the muddy gloves clean before I leave knowing that they will not get cleaned. As I clean the gloves, I overhear a couple men telling homophobic jokes. I shake my head in frustration and finish rinsing the gloves laying them out to dry in the sun. With my task finished and not wanting to hang out with the "guys," I pick up my lunch and go looking for Kaʻiulani. I find her under the tents with the volunteers. I give her a kiss and hug and mahalo her for everything she does for the volunteers, for the staff, and for the ʻāina before getting in my car to drive home. This is not my best day at the loʻi.

GENDERED LABOUR AT THE LOʻI

The second story is one of many that I could tell about the gendered division of labour at this site and how heteronormativity has become sedimented in the everyday practices of maintaining the farm. The gender division of labour opperating at the loʻi is not the one Lilikalā Kameʻeleihiwa (1999, 7) describes as a part of the ʻAikapu religion that established "the separation of male and female in labor, in cooking, in food, and in sacrifice." The ʻAikapu restricted women from eating four foods associated with the four pre-eminent male gods but in turn men would be responsible for growing, preparing, and feeding the community according to the new custom. Additionally, only men would be reserved for human sacrifice; women would be spared from that aspect of the religion. Hawaiian scholars describe the ʻAikapu system as being founded upon gender complementarity rather than the hierarchical binary system that emerged along with the enlightenment in Europe (Tengan 2008) and that came to Hawaiʻi with Christian missionaries (Kauanui 2018; Cook 2019).

As Kameʻeleihiwa stresses, male akua (deities/gods) did not make decisions without first getting approval from female akua. ʻAikapu was established only after Papahānaumoku (Earth mother who births islands) gave Wākea (sky father) and his religious leaders her approval to proceed with the new laws. ʻAikapu would end when female aliʻi (chiefs/rulers) decided to end it. Rather, the gender division of labour I saw at work at the loʻi was based on Western gendered hierarchical binaries where certain tasks associated with men/masculinity are valued as more important than those associated with women/femininity. Within this kind of structure, it is much more acceptable for women to engage in "men's work" because of their subordinate position in the hierarchy but men, because of their superordinate position, are far less likely to engage in "women's work."

The second story is also about how homophobic attitudes and sexist langauge are often allowed because no one wants to question the authority of a Native Hawaiian man — and it's usually the same man who makes these comments while the rest of us either remain silent (as I have done) or join in the "fun." This story, then, is also about what Māori scholar Brendan Hokowhitu (2015, 88) describes as one of the symptoms of Indigenous masculinity's mimicry of invader masculinity,... the divestment of the feminine out of the masculine.... The foundation of post-contact Indigenous masculinity, thus, was based upon what Indigenous masculinity was not. Such foundational insecurity has led to ritual displays of physical manliness and hypermasculinity, along with the traditionalization of heterosexuality, homophobia, and patriarchy.

Hokowhitu goes on to describe how this version of Indigenous masculinity is reproduced through the "inculcation" of the heteropatriarchal Indigenous family. While he describes how this process operates in Aotearoa/New Zealand, it has explanatory power for this story taking place in Hawai'i as well. He writes,

> The governance of Indigenous men into patriarchal roles was ratified through the organization of European bourgeois domestic life; the ideology and practice of "separate spheres." So-called traditional Indigenous culture came to reflect gender-role separation where a domestic sphere of action was defined for women, whereas men (but not all men) controlled the finances and, importantly, the political and public spheres. (2015, 89)

What he describes is how European gender norms were imposed on and then adopted by Indigenous Peoples, who replicated those same gendered division of spheres and labour but now in the guise of "tradition." This separation of spheres when combined with heteropatriarchy established the subject position of heteropatriarchal Indigenous man as the arbiter of "traditional" Indigenous culture. He explains, "The assimilation of invader masculinity into Indigenous masculinity led to the public face of power at least to be exclusively male" (2015, 89).

Hokowhitu's thinking helps me explain why all of us (and I am complicit in this as well) at the lo'i appear to be deferential to this one Hawaiian man — why we do not challenge him when he says homophobic things and why he decides who is worthy of "oli" and who is not. His Indigeneity is authorized by his ability to speak the language, his familiarity with various cultural practices, and his experience as an educator. When we hold him up against a heteropatriarchal Indigenous masculinity, he is not found wanting; indeed, his homophobic and sexist sentiments actually measure up perfectly to what is expected of this subject position.

At that time, Ka'iulani was the only woman on staff and she only worked part time at the farm. When I first started volunteering at the lo'i in 2011 there was more gender balance among the staff. And even then, there was a stark gendered division of labour. While everyone helped with preparing, planting, and cultivating kalo, the men did most of the intensive farming duties, such as using the weedwacker and tractors, while the women were responsible for support roles including the emotional labor of managing volunteers and choreographing their experiences.[4] The women oversaw the introductions, conducted the orientations, and got everyone organized into work groups for the day. The stories told during the introduction were the things they wanted visitors to remember — the important stuff that made the work meaningful. They were also responsible for preparing lunch for the volunteers. This meant that they had to decide what to serve, shop for all the ingredients, and start preparing lunch at least one hour to thirty minutes before volunteers ended work for the day. Once lunch was nearly ready, they would return to the work crews and give volunteers instructions for how to get cleaned up before lunch. During lunch they fielded questions and learned more about the volunteers. They saw this part of the day as critical for making connections with volunteers so that they would return the following month for the next community workday.

Towards the end of the grant period, there was significant turnover in staff and almost all the Native Hawaiian men and women who had been working there left or were let go. This was a tumultuous time at the lo'i. Over the next few years, new staff were hired — all of them men, except Ka'iulani. During the transition period, AM did not provide lunch for volunteers, they stopped doing culturally grounded orientations at community workdays, and the numbers of volunteers declined.[5] As the story above illustrates, AM saw a precipitous decline in volunteers. From my years as a participant observer, it appeared to me that none of the men were willing to take up the responsibility of doing the emotional labour necessary for choreographing a meaningful experience for volunteers. Rather, they were much more invested in maximizing volunteer labour. Even when I had conversations with the farm manager and executive director about how to improve volunteer experiences, they did not take up the kuleana (responsibility) of doing the emotional labour of helping volunteers make connections with the place and the work. Indeed, at the Day of Service described in the moʻolelo, the staff did not feel compelled to interact with volunteers beyond what was necessary to get tasks on the to-do list ticked off.

When I was at the loʻi more recently I met a new employee, a person who presented as wahine, working as the agricultural technician. I was there on a regular workday and when we finished working, I had an opportunity to talk story with her about her experiences at the loʻi. I came away from that conversation with two clear messages. First, she too saw the loʻi as a valuable place where families can come and share a cultural experience with their keiki (child/children). Second, it is a place where she feels rather alienated. At the time of our conversation, she had been there for a little over a year. When she first started, she was the only woman working there; Kaʻiulani had left to take a position elsewhere. For her, being the only woman surrounded by men was unfamiliar to her experience growing up on Maui where she was "around women 24/7. Men are just completely outnumbered." Being from a place surrounded by women to a place surrounded by men she said, "it's a completely different vibe, obviously, that I'm not used to … I was kinda out of it for a little bit." She went on to explain that it is not that she dislikes working with the men, but they bring a different energy and cultural expertise. More recently, AM has hired a new community engagement coordinator who also presents as a wahine. This new staff member is much more present at the farm, "pretty much every day working with us and if she doesn't have a group she is working on the farm with us cutting grass, harvesting whatever." With a second woman on staff, this young wahine felt like things were better but there was still something missing, something cultural. She wanted more of a Hawaiian presence at the farm.

What I am offering is more than a feminist sociological critique of the gendered division of labour at the loʻi — although this too is important. A critique of capitalist modes of production and how gender binaries are foundational to this system is necessary if we are going to dismantle the system. When I heard the new staff member talk about that thing that is missing, what she was not talking about are the gendered divisions of labour at this site. I propose that what is missing is the presence of a queer mana wahine that I believe exists at the loʻi but is difficult to feel because of the dominance of traditionalized heteropatriarchy in the form of a gendered division of labour and homophobic jokes. The first story of the joy and sense of authority my daughter expresses while working at the lo'i exemplifies what I mean by a queer mana wahine.

THEORIZING A QUEER MANA WAHINE

In theorizing a queer mana wahine, I am inspired by the work of Simpson (2017, 129) who writes, in the context of Nishnaabeg intelligence, "my sense is that my Ancestors lived in a society where what I know as 'queer,' particularly in terms of social organization, was so normal it didn't have a name." I share a similar sense with regard to how my ancestors understood gender and sexuality. In this section I make three moves to make the case that this is a place always already queer. First, I draw out a notion of mana wahine that is not limited to the gender identity approximating "woman/women" in the settler colonial context. Rather, I think about mana wahine as an expression of a pono (balanced, proper) duality of spirit that includes both female and male spirit. Here I am thinking with Dian Million's (2023) theorizing of spirit as ethos. It is a duality that is fully embodied in all human and other-than-human beings. If we understand mana wahine as a spiritual, generative feminine power/force that emerges from Papahānaumoku (the foundation who births islands in the Hawaiian context) and is embodied in all beings, then my second move turns me to consider Hāloa/kalo as a gender-non-conforming being who cannot be contained by cis and heteronormative binary imaginaries. This reality has grown over time as I have been in relationship with them for the past decade. Finally, my last move brings the duality of spirit together with a non-cis, 2SQ analysis to contend that mana wahine is ever present at the lo'i given the relationship between Hāloa and the Hawaiian akua (deity, gods, elemental forces) Haumea and Hina.

In Hawai'i, a dual masculine and feminine spirit is considered pono — balanced, correct, complementary, and co-present. This duality is not about equality and it is not a binary. Duality as pono could also be exemplified in 'ōlelo Hawai'i (the Hawaiian language) where we have no gender pronouns. We do, however, have terms for female (wahine) and male (kāne), so there was clearly an understanding of differences in bodily presentation, but these differences were not gendered along binary or heteronormative lines where femininity is tethered to and follows femaleness and masculinity is tethered to and follows maleness. Rather, gender might not have lined up in these ways at all.

If we think about mana wahine in this context, as a key aspect of a pono duality of spirit that is fully embodied in all human and other-than-human beings when we celebrate mana wahine, what I am calling forward is a wahine spirit that exists in all beings and not limited to those bodies designated female at birth. Again, it is a duality that is fully embodied in all human and other-than-human beings. When I speak of mana wahine, what I am calling forward is a wahine spirit that exists in all beings, albeit in differential ways. My thinking aligns with how Renae Maihi describes mana wahine in a Māori context:

> [Mana wahine is] an understanding that Mana in its original source comes from the Atua & lives within us all. That is the spirit, power, ihi, wehi & mana of Papatuanuku & her descendants. As we know her descendants include Atua Taane therefore to me Mana wahine is the balancing & nurturing of the MANA of nga Atua Wahine ME nga Atua Tane that exists in us all. *Renae Maihi.* (Pihama 2018, para. 26, emphasis added)

Mana lives within us all and derives from the mana of Papatuanuku or Papahānaumoku and her descendants. As Maihi describes, mana wahine, as spirit, is not limited to those beings assigned wahine at birth. Rather, mana wahine is genealogical — it is embodied within us because we all are descendants of Papatuanuku/Papahānaumoku/Earth Mother — her generative, procreative power lives within us alongside the mana from our other ancestors.[6]

When I first started volunteering at the loʻi, not only did I start learning about how to cultivate kalo, I also learned the moʻolelo that explains how kalo, the plant form of the human baby Hāloanākalaukapalili (Hāloa), is the kaikuaʻana, elder sibling, of Kanaka (human persons). Every version of the story of Hāloa that I have heard describes Hāloa as a kāne, a male child, who was stillborn and buried in the land. At the place where their lifeless body was buried, the first kalo plant grew. In these (re)tellings of the story, kalo is unambiguously male. As such, I interacted with kalo as male, as a male older sibling. But over time as I grew to be more familiar with kalo and got to know them in more intimate ways, I started to think about kalo in much more 2SQ ways. My relationship with Hāloa/kalo directly shaped my expanding of gender and my expanding notions of gender reshaped my relationship with

Hāloa. Indeed, I experienced their queerness through their reproductive and generative expression.

Botanically, kalo has no gender or sex *per se*. Indeed, they have the capacity to reproduce in at least three ways.[7] At the loʻi, the most common way that kalo reproduce is with the assistance of humans through transplantation. We cultivate the kalo, removing its leaves (lau) and corm (kalo) while preserving the stalk (hā) and about a half inch to one inch of the corm called the kōhina — kōhi-ʻana (the practice of breaking or cutting the huli from the corm). The huli — the hā and the kōhina — are replanted. The same huli can be replanted many times.

As the huli grows new leaves and matures, they develop strong corm and ʻohā (buds on new corm) begin to protrude from the corm. The buds grow and new shoots appear, and we call them keiki (child, children). If left in the ground, the kalo plant will continue to produce keiki, and those keiki will mature and if left alone will produce more keiki. Plants that are left in the ground and allowed to continue their life cycle will produce a flower (pua). I have only seen pua on a handful occasions because kalo are usually harvested before they get to this stage in development.

If, as moʻolelo tell us, Hāloa is kāne and, thus, kalo is also kāne, then what does it mean about our ancestors' understanding of the world and gender, reproduction, and procreation that this male elder sibling could birth new keiki? What can we learn from our ancestors and our elder sibling about how to express and honour gender in expansive and pono ways?

My experience of being with and caring for Hāloa through all aspects of their life cycle has radically shifted everything I knew about them. Increasingly, I experienced and related to Hāloa as a gender-nonconforming being who embodies a queer mana wahine. Even as I shifted my gendered understandings of Hāloa and expanded by sense of mana wahine, I continued to ask what generative forces make it possible for Hāloa to produce keiki. What elemental akua are also present at the loʻi that create the conditions for Hāloa to birth keiki? As I continued my personal journey of reconnecting with my culture and language, I came to learn that Haumea and Hina are two of many akua and elemental forces whose presence play a key role in the igniting the generative and procreative potential at the loʻi.

Haumea is a very powerful being in Hawaiian cosmology. According to Kanaka literary scholar kuʻualoha hoʻomanawanui, "Haumea [is] the red earth woman who reincarnated herself over and over, with gods and goddesses born from different parts of her body" (hoʻomanawanui 2010, 28).

Papahānaumoku was also known as and called Haumea. For a time, Haumea and Wākea lived on the mountain range that divides the districts of Koʻolaupoko, Ewa, and Kona. Moʻolelo tell us that Haumea named her grandson Heʻeia in order to commemorate important events that took place there. It is also a place where Haumea loved to fish in the bay and she and Wākea made sweet tasting sticky poi from the kalo that grew in the area (Sterling and Summers 1978). Hina is also a powerful akua with feminine spirit that guides the rhythmic cycles of the moon and whose lunar abilities control the rhythm of the sea. Hina embodies growth and reproduction. In the ocean, she is the coral reef; the pūkoʻa (the coral heads) are Hina's genitalia where she gives birth to sea urchins, seaweed, reef creatures, and their cousins of the land —freshwater shrimp, mosses, and small ferns (Kameʻeleihiwa 1999). As described above, the etymology of the word kōhina refers to the process of preparing huli for transplantation. However, the sounds the word makes when spoken evokes Hina. Sonically, it sounds like kō – hina — of or belonging to Hina. I am excited by the idea that my ancestors, in their love for word play, gave that portion of the corm a name that was instructive *and* playful. I want to believe that they saw the regenerative possibilities of naming that portion of the corm of Hāloa, the kōhina, as belonging to Hina. And when the kōhina is planted in ʻāina, the physical manifestation of Papa-Haumea, Hāloa becomes lovingly surrounded and procreatively empowered by the mana wahine of both Hina and Haumea, which allow them to give birth to future generations. When we expand our understandings of gender, sexuality, and reproduction, we open up new conditions of gender possibility that very well may align with how my ʻŌiwi ancestors understood Hāloa's procreative power as being in intimate relationship with Haumea and the embodiment of Hina.

My return to the Hāloa story is intended to meditate on how to reconnect with our ancestors by reattaching our "minds, bodies, and spirits to the network of relationships and ethical practices that generates grounded normativity" (Simpson 2017, 44).

As Simpson (2017, 23) explains, "grounded normativity isn't a thing; it is generated structure born and maintained from deep engagement with Indigenous processes that are inherently emotional, intellectual, and spiritual." Through a pono plurality of wahine/kāne we see the generative possibilities of 2SQ grounded normativity enlivened in Hāloa. With this alternative reading of "tradition" we have an opportunity to break out of the trappings of heteronormativity, patriarchy, and homophobia. With this insight we recognize that cultivating kalo is no more a man's job as blue is a boy's colour. These are social constructs intended to reproduce gender binaries that support heteronormativity and heteropatriarchy under the guise of tradition.

What I am putting forward is an invitation to return to the original instructions of our Indigenous ancestors in order to un-learn settler colonial trappings of sexism, homophobia, and transphobia.[8] And if we read the story of the division of labour at the loʻi and the new staff member's desire for more women to work at the loʻi through the lens of an expansive view of mana wahine, we might also hear her calling for a greater recognition of the mana wahine (feminine power/eros) that is present throughout the loʻi.[9]

Indeed, Hokowhitu's observations of traditionalization of heterosexuality, homophobia, and patriarchy can be extended to explain how mana wahine is obscured at the loʻi. Another example of heteropatriarchal traditionalization is the notion of wāhine as haumia (defiled, unclean) when we are on our menstrual cycles.[10] When I first started attending community workdays at this loʻi and others, we, the female volunteers, were instructed that if we were on our maʻi (menstruation, sick/ill) we were not allowed to work in the loʻi with kalo.[11] The volunteer coordinators, sometimes men and sometimes women, explained that it was because wāhine were haumia (often translated as defiled) during this time and should not be in the loʻi for fear of contaminating kalo. While I recall feeling uncomfortable hearing this, I accepted the information as a "traditional" practice and complied with the instructions. And as I became more comfortable with my role at the loʻi and the staff allowed me to help with volunteers, I too carried on the "tradition." But rather than stress wahine as haumia, I stressed our sacredness as the reason for our separation. In my own way I was trying to respect the tradition of separation while also providing a more generous/feminist explanation that during our maʻi wāhine are especially powerful and that is why we needed to be separated from kāne, of which Hāloa/kalo was one.

Makana Kāne Kuahiwinui's research on Native Hawaiian menstruation practices and understandings also pushes back against the negative connotations of haumia and maʻi. She writes,

> When my period arrived, I didn't have a name for it, but Hawaiians called it, amongst many other things, "ka wā haumia," loosely translating to, "the time of haumia." Haumia being defined as: "Uncleanliness, filth, defilement, abomination; defiled, indecent, obscene, vile, lewd, unclean … contaminated, sordid." (Pukui and Elbert 1986, 61)
>
> The translation of haumia has left me puzzled, confused and curious, did Hawaiians really think that menstruation was "defiling" and "vile?" (2018, 1–2)

This confusion and curiosity becomes the guiding inspiration for her research and resonates with my concerns about how gender operates at the loʻi. What she found is that while the definition of haumia in the Pukui and Elbert Hawaiian langauge dictionary does indeed associate the term with notions of filth, defilement, and uncleanliness, she also argues that this definition is incomplete.[12] Rather, her research of the etymology of the term, its constituent parts, and its references in moʻolelo provides evidence that the negative connotations that link menstruating women to uncleanliness and defilement, were the product of malicious mistranslations of the original story.[13] In contrast, she argues that haumia, a term comprised of the root "hau" that has two meanings — dirty, unpleasant *and* ruler — and the suffix "mia," a passive participle, suggests a much more powerful meaning. Kāne Kuahiwinui (2018) also traces our contemporary understandings of "traditional" menstruation practices to the story of Luʻukia, a high-ranking wahine living in Waipiʻo valley on Hawaiʻi Island, who goes to Puʻukawaiwai when she is menstruating in order to maintain maluhia (peace, quiet, security, tranquility, serenity) in the community. Kāne Kuahiwinui found that current understandings are in part shaped by competing translations of the story. The dominant translation attributes Luʻukia being separated from the community to being haumia — in a state of uncleanliness. When Kāne Kuahiwinui read the original moʻolelo, she gleaned a very different lesson from the story. She argues that if we bring both definitions of hau into our translation and account for the passive participle, mia, what we get is a term that positions the subject, Luʻukia/menstrating wahine, like rulers much like the akua (female deities) "Haunuʻu, Hauwahine, Haulani, Haumakapuʻu and Haumea" (2018, 48).

Kāne Kuahiwinui contends that when we read the Luʻukia story from this vantage point, then, the separation of women from the rest of the community is not about her defilement or filth but about her heightened state of sacredness — her akua-like status — and separation is about maluhia, peace and tranquility.[14]

Over the years, my thinking about the practice of separating menstruating women from Hāloa has shifted based on my continued interaction with them and new scholarship by ʻŌiwi researchers such as Kāne Kuahiwinui. Kāne Kuahiwinui not only radically revises our understanding of the story and notions of separation, she also pushes back against the negative connotations of the term maʻi that link menstruation to sickness/illness. Instead, she offers the term ka waimaka lehua, lehua's tears, as an alternative.[15] Even as I appreciate this intervention, the question of whether women with waimaka lehua should be allowed to work in the loʻi or not remains open for debate and discussion. If kalo is already encircled in Haumea's embrace and if Kāne Kuahiwinui is correct that during ka waimaka lehua menstruating women are most like Haumea, why would she be separated from Hāloa? It seems to me that we would not.

AN EXPANSIVE NOTION OF ʻOHANA (FAMILY)

I fully and unequivocally support the need for more women to work at the loʻi. Indeed, until we fully dislodge and dismantle the gender binaries that have rooted themselves in Indigenous places and practices, we need people who are willing to do the emotional labour that assists volunteers in becoming hoa (friends, caretakers) to ʻāina. Unfortunately, for now, the people more willing to do this kind of work are folx who identify as women. At the same time, I also am putting forward an alternative way of thinking about this work as more than about gendered labour. I am also writing this chapter because our moʻolelo and our hānau mua (elder sibling), Hāloa, provide us with a 2SQ grounded normativity that is an alternative to toxic Indigenous heteropatriarchy. What I want to say but didn't say when we sat down that Tuesday afternoon in March because I didn't fully understand these things then, is that mana wahine is all around us. When we step into the mud we are hau-mia — immersed in, embraced by, in a state of being with Haumea. When we plant huli, we immerse Hāloa's "kōhina" in Haumea's body and the co-power of Hina and Haumea impregnate Hāloa who will birth new keiki. This is 'ohana, a non-heteropatriarchal, non-heteronormative family. A family where kāne is surrounded by the mana of nā wahine. A family where kāne are supported to fulfill their destiny to birth new life and feed the Lāhui (nation). When we open ourselves to a 2SQ grounded normativity that lives in this place we can become empowered by their spirit. When we submerge ourselves in the mud, allow it to cover our skin, seep into our pores, get under our nails, stain everything, we too become empowered by mana wahine — the power of Hāloa, Hina, and Haumea — that is alive in this place. And all of this brings me back to my first story and my daughter.

As I said, I have been bringing my daughter to the lo'i since she was little. The first story is about how confident and comfortable she feels there. As I have also said, this is only one story among many that I could tell about what it might be like for her to grow up cultivating a relationship with Hāloa, Hina, and Haumea. It is also a story about how I still struggle to cultivate the kind of relationship she had at age five with this place and our ancestors. It is a story about how this place is a kind of piko — an umbilical cord to a place of convergence and empowerment where she has been feed physically, spiritually, and emotionally since she could walk.[16] It is a story of how she had, at that time, never known life without the lo'i and kalo, without Hāloa, Hina, and Haumea. It is also a commitment made by a mother to her daughter to teach her that menstruation is not defilement, uncleanliness, a sickness or illness, or a time when we must be separated. Rather, she will know menstruation to be a time when she embodies the mana wahine of our Hau wāhine — ruling women.

The story is about what it means for me to mother at the lo'i and the material effects of mālama 'āina (caring for the land) for my daughter, who feels empowered there. It is about how she joyfully and confidently immerses herself in the mud among the weeds and the algae and the kalo and the i'a (fish) and the crawfish and the frogs. How she is her most confident, self-sufficient, self-determining self when we are there working. This story is about me, as a mother, wanting to give my daughter a different experience of what it means to be a wahine (woman). It is about giving my daughter opportunities to connect to her great-grandmother and great-great-great-grandmother, who also cultivated kalo.

In their absence, it is also about my boys. My sons do not like the mud and the muck. They prefer the māla, dry-land gardening. The loʻi is too wet, too teeming with life. As cis kāne, perhaps being surrounded by that much mana wahine is overwhelming. Perhaps the work I need to do as a mother is to continue to nurture the mana wahine in them so they can embrace the 2SQ that surrounds us and that is within them. Perhaps I should also take comfort in knowing that while the boys do not like to cultivate kalo, they enjoy tranforming kalo into paʻi ʻai (steamed and pounded kalo) and poi (paʻi ʻai with water added) so they can feed our ʻohana. Perhaps this story is also metaphorical. For my sons, it is a lesson about how important it is to honour the mana wahine in them. What is their kō-hina? How do I surround them with the procreative powers of Haumea so they can hānau (give birth) to new life and hānai (feed, nourish) the Lāhui just as their kaikuaʻana (elder sibling of the same gender) has done and continues to do? With Hāloa as their role model, my sons can grow up knowing they too have the mana wahine to birth new life and feed the nation. With Hāloa as their role model, they do not have to rely on toxic Indigenous heteropatriarchy. They can embrace their mana wahine rather than reject it.

While I am incredibly sad to have taken my daughter away from this place that she loved, we can cultivate mana wahine when we are not at the loʻi. I can remind her of our ancestors so that when she is confronted with the toxic heteronormativity and white supremacy that fills the air and burns our nose and lungs when we breath, she is able to turn inward and remember that Hāloa, Hina, and Haumea are part of us. They are our ancestors. When we are in the loʻi they act on us from the outside in. As our ancestors they can act on us from the inside out — in our bones, in our blood, in our cells, in our spirit. While these stories focus on one particular land-based restoration project and on my own family, they address larger concerns about heteronormativity and heteropartriarchy as external and internal forces expressed through a toxic Indigenous heteropatriarchy that go beyond these examples.[17] Indeed, issues of gender and sexuality are essential for enacting a larger political project of decolonization and Indigenous resurgence. As we attend to the process of how to reconstitute our Indigenous nations we must do so without reproducing the oppressive structures imposed by colonialism and then adopted and called culture/tradition/authenticity. This chapter is offered as one example of the lessons our ancestors left for us so that we can learn to co-create futures that celebrate the spirit in all its multiplicity. In doing so, we honour our 2SQ children, siblings, cousins, partners, and parents while also providing non-gender-conforming queer role models for cis, heterosexual beings.

NOTES

1. A version of this chapter was published in *Australian Feminist Studies* in 2021. It has been revised and reprinted here with permission.
2. Throughout the chapter I use Kanaka ʻŌiwi and Native Hawaiian interchangeably to refer to the Indigenous Peoples of Hawaiʻi. I also use the term ʻŌiwi and Native interchangeably as an adjective to describe Indigenous practices, values, etc., distinct to the peoples and places of Hawaiʻi. I do not italicize Hawaiian terms. I provide a brief translation upon first usage and, where necessary for my argument, expand the meaning in the body of the text.
3. All names used in the chapter are pseudonyms.
4. In 2012, one staff member, a person who approximates the Western category woman, was openly queer and she/they moved back and forth between men's and women's duties. For example, her/their ability to bridge the gender division of labour was most evident when it came to making poi. She/they was responsible for cooking the kalo over propane stoves and helped the men with grinding the cooked kalo using an industrial meat grinder. She/they also helped the other staff who presented as women with cleaning the kalo and packaging the poi for distribution. While we could optimistically interpret her position as an example of how gender fluidity can operate at the loʻi, my observations only reinforce how entrenched gender divisions of labour are at this site. See (Aikau and Camvel 2016) for an in-depth analysis of poi production at this site.
5. I want to be clear that the dynamics I am describing took place at a community workday. Community workdays are open to the general public; all are welcome. The protocol and practices are different when, for example, the staff host students from Hawaiian language immersion schools or Hawaiian culture-based charter schools. I did not attend any of those workdays, but the staff described the differences during our informal conversations and during formal interviews.
6. For Kanaka ʻŌiwi scholar kuʻualoha hoʻomanawanui (2010, 28), "mana wahine describes an indigenous, culturally-based understanding of female em/power/ment that is rooted in traditional concepts such as moʻokūʻauhau [genealogy], aloha ʻāina [love of land/nation] and kuleana (responsibility). It is the physical, intellectual and spiritual (or intuitive) power of women." My analysis builds upon these insights by expanding the category women/woman beyond the Western binary framework.
7. I use reproduction as only one of many indicators for Western sex-gender alignments.

8   For a more in depth discussion of Indigenous queer theory, see Driskill et al. 2011.
9   My thinking about feminine eros and power is informed by Haunani-Kay Trask's first book, based on her dissertation, "Eros and Power," and by adrienne maree brown's reading of Audre Lorde, specifically her 1978 speech "Uses of the Erotic: The Erotic as Power." See Trask 1986; brown 2019.
10 Wāhine, when spelled with the kahakō over the "a", is the plural form of the term. Without the kahakō marks both the singular noun and the category/subject position "woman."
11 It is also possible the ancestors did not link ma'i as menstruation with illness or sickness. See wehewehe wikiwiki: hilo.hawaii.edu/wehe/?q=ma%CA%BBi.
12 In my cross reference of the term in other dictionaries, I too found the definition of haumia to be consistent across all texts.
13 In chapter three of her master's thesis, Makana Kāne Kuahiwinui provides a thorough methodological explanation of how Thrum intentionally mistranslates the Lu'ukia mo'olelo, where negative connotations of the separation of women during menstruation is derived and inserts Western patriarchal ideas into the text. And importantly, she explains how these negative connotations of haumia are connected to misunderstandings of notions of kapu and noa, arguing that many of our taken-for-granted understandings of these three terms perpetuate Western heteropatriarchal values masquerading as tradition.
14 See Kame'eleihiwa (1999) for another example of the relationship between haumia and the female akua, Haumea.
15 Kame'eleihiwa uses the phrase ke kulu waimaka lehua (the flowering of the red lehua blossom tears) to describe menstruation (Kame'eleihiwa 1999, 6).
16 I was introduced to the concept of piko as convergence of people, places, and practices by No'eau Peralto, a student in a graduate seminar co-taught with the faculty at the University of Hawai'i at Mānoa and the University of Victoria (Corntassel et al. 2018).
17 For another example of how to practise decolonization at the interpersonal level see Hunt and Holmes (2015).

REFERENCES

Aikau, Hōkūlani K., and Donna Kameha'ikū Camvel. 2016. "Cultural Traditions and Food: Kānaka Maoli and the Production of Poi." *Food, Culture, & Society* 19, 3.

Barker, Joanne (ed.). 2008. "Gender, Sovereignty, Rights: Native Women's Activism against Social Inequality and Violence in Canada." *American Quarterly* 60, 2.

___. 2017. *Critically Sovereign: Indigenous Gender, Sexuality, and Feminist Studies.* Durham: Duke University Press.

brown, adrienne maree. 2019. *Pleasure Activism: The Politics of Feeling Good.* Chico: AK Press.

Chang Hall, L.K., and J.K Kauanui. 1994. "Same-Sex Sexuality in Pacific Literature." *Amerasia Journal* 20, 1.

Cook, Kealani. 2019. *Return to Kahiki: Native Hawaiians in Oceania.* Cambridge, United Kingdom; New York: Cambridge University Press.

Corntassel, Jeff, et al. 2018. *Everyday Acts of Resurgence*. Olympia, Washington: Daykeeper Press.
Driskill, Qwo-Li, et al. (eds.). 2011. *Sovereign Erotics: A Collection of Two-Spirit Literature*. Tucson: University of Arizona Press.
Goeman, Mishuana R., and Jennifer Nez Denetdale. 2009. "Native Feminisms: Legacies, Interventions, and Indigenous Sovereignties." *Wicazo Sa Review* 24, 2.
Goodyear-Kaʻōpua, Noelani, et al. (eds.). 2014. *A Nation Rising: Hawaiian Movements for Life, Land, and Sovereignty*. Durham: Duke University Press Books.
Gunn Allen, Paula. 1992. *The Sacred Hoop: Recovering the Feminine in American Indian Traditions*. Boston: Beacon Press.
Hall, Lisa Kahaleole. 2009. "Navigating Our Own 'Sea of Islands': Remapping a Theoretical Space for Hawaiian Women and Indigenous Feminism." *Wicazo Sa Review* 24, 2.
Hokowhitu, Brendan. 2015. "Taxonomies of Indigeneity: Indigenous Heterosexual Patriarchal Masculinity." In *Indigenous Men and Masculinities: Legacies, Identities, Regeneration,* edited by Robert Alexander Innes and Kim Anderson. Winnipeg: University of Manitoba Press.
hoʻomanawanui, kuʻualoha. 2010. "Mana Wahine: Feminism and Nationalism in Hawaiian Literature." *Anglistica* 14, 2.
Hunt, Sarah, and Cindy Holmes. 2015. "Everyday Decolonization: Living a Decolonizing Queer Politics." *Journal of Lesbian Studies* 19, 2.
Kameʻeleihiwa, Lilikalā. 1999. *Nā Wahine Kapu: Divine Hawaiian Women*. Honolulu: ʻAi Pōhaku Press.
Kāne Kuahiwinui, Makanaalohamaikalani. 2018. "Ka Waimaka Lehua: Menstruation Through a Hawaiian Epistemology." MA thesis, Honolulu: University of Hawaiʻi at Mānoa.
Kauanui, J. Kēhaulani. 2018. *Paradoxes of Hawaiian Sovereignty: Land, Sex, and the Colonial Politics of State Nationalism*. Durham: Duke University Press.
Maracle, Lee. 2002. *I Am Woman: A Native Perspective on Sociology and Feminism*, Rep Sub edition. Vancouver: Raincoast Books, Press Gang Publishers.
Merry, Sally Engle. 2000. *Colonizing Hawaiʻi: The Cultural Power of Law*. Princeton: Princeton University Press.
Million, Dian. 2023. "Spirit and Matter: Resurgence as Rising and (Re)creation as Ethos." In *Indigenous Resurgence in an Age of Reconciliation,* edited by Heidi Kiiwentinepinesiik Stark, Aimée Craft, and Hōkūlani K. Aikau. Toronto: University of Toronto Press.
Pihama, Leonie. 2018. "Mana Wahine Is ..." Wordpress. *Leonie Pihama: Kaupapa Māori as Transformative Indigenous Analysis* (blog). leoniepihama.wordpress.com/2018/10/10/mana-wahine-is/.
Pukui, Mary Kawena, and Samuel H. Elbert. 1986. *Hawaiian Dictionary: Revised and Enlarged Edition*. Honolulu: University of Hawaiʻi Press.
Silva, Noenoe K. 2004. *Aloha Betrayed: Native Hawaiian Resistance to American Colonialism*. Durham: Duke University Press Books.
Simpson, Audra. 2009. "Captivating Eunice: Membership, Colonialism, and Gendered Citizenships of Grief." *Wicazo Sa Review* 24, 2.

___. 2016. "The State Is a Man: Theresa Spence, Loretta Saunders and the Gender of Settler Sovereignty." *Theory & Event* 19, 4.

Simpson, Leanne Betasamosake. 2017. *As We Have Always Done: Indigenous Freedom through Radical Resistance*. Minneapolis: University of Minnesota Press.

Sterling, Elspeth P., and Catherine C. Summers (eds.). 1978. *Sites of Oahu*. Honolulu: Bishop Museum Press.

Tengan, Ty Kāwika. 2008. *Native Men Remade: Gender and Nation in Contemporary Hawaiʻi*. Durham: Duke University Press.

Trask, Haunani-Kay. 1986. *Eros and Power: The Promise of Feminist Theory*. Philadelphia: University of Pennsylvania Press.

SECTION IV

DECOLONIALITY | MOVEMENT | FUTURITIES

ELEVEN

Decolonization Is a Queer Desire
Poetics, Politics, Negativity

Billy-Ray Belcourt

A POEM IS A WAY TO BEGIN. Here is queer Diné poet Jake Skeets' "Virginity":

> Clouds in his throat, / six months' worth. / He bodies into me / half cosmos, half coyote. / We become night / on Bread Springs / road. Shirts off, / jeans halfway / down, parked / by an abandoned / trailer. "No one / lives here," / he whispers. / We become porch / light curtained / by moth wings, / powdered into ash. (2018, 27)

In this paper, I will offer up some thinking about the force of negativity and negative affect in depictions of queer Indigenous sex and sexuality. I will pursue the argument that the queer Indigenous imagination bears a more ambivalent relation to self-sovereignty than normative theories of Indigenous political life typically take as one of their constitutive facets. Decolonization is about desire after all (Tuck 2009), and desire can be as much a matter of becoming the night outside an abandoned trailer as it can be about some scene of self-actualization or emotional repair. It isn't that self-actualization and emotional repair are silly pursuits (I'm relying on them for explanatory purposes), but rather that becoming night, becoming a porch light "curtained / by moth wings, / powdered into ash" all indicate a form of being where the fragilities of the self and the messiness of queer longing aren't sites of political failure. I want a new grammar of decolonial possibility and gesture in which to want to be undone doesn't mean that one has been destroyed or erred from a revolutionary struggle. One can be undone without being ruined.

TWO THEORETICAL PRELUDES

The first prelude is Audre Lorde's "Uses of the Erotic: The Erotic as Power," which rescues the erotic from patriarchal devaluation and treats it as the freedom-making "resource" that it is. Lorde (2020, 30) writes: "The erotic is a measure between the beginnings of our sense of self and the chaos of our strongest feelings. It is an internal sense of satisfaction to which, once we have experienced it, we know we can aspire." While there are aspects of Lorde's essay with which I have to disidentify (the positing of the erotic as a distinctly "female" plane), I find this connection between selfhood and chaos at the core of the erotic that doesn't require a total flattening out of chaos productive. Lorde rails against the "European-American male tradition" that has made use of the erotic as a drama of marginalization, which severs women from other women and ultimately all of us from one another. Lorde's erotic, on the other hand, is about making connection and about attuning to a "mode of living and sensation" that is grounded in the body and, because of this, world-changing (2020, 36).

The second prelude: I both draw from and rework queer theories of negativity; the most infamous of which, Lee Edelman's *No Future* (2004), calls for a complete embargo on futurity due to its enmeshment with what José Esteban Muñoz (2009) calls "straight time," a modality of time in which all living bends toward the project of biosocial reproduction in the interest of heteropatriarchal domination. A less bleak form of negativity is outlined by Jack Halberstam (2011, 173) in "Unbecoming: Queer Negativity/Radical Passivity"; there, Halberstam is interested in "a feminism grounded in negation, refusal, passivity, absence and silence," one that "offers spaces and modes of unknowing, failing and forgetting." In contradistinction to a psychoanalytic tradition that presumes the generationality of the category of woman, Halberstam zeros in on "the terms of the negation of the subject rather than her formation, the disruption of lineage rather than its continuation, the undoing of self rather than its activation" (2011, 175). Halberstam conceptualizes passivity as a way of disrupting "the organizing logic of agency and subjectivity" that is ultimately a colonial logic (2011, 180). Different forms of femininity open up in the wake of this disruption, ones that are unproductive and outside the gender binary, ones that are conducive of difference rather than bound to the reification of whiteness. Halberstam's thinking is in the direction of illegibility and unknowability and in the conclusion, in reference to Yoko Ono's legendary durational performance work Cut Piece, asks: "Can we think about this refusal of self as an anti-liberal act, an anarchist statement of pure opposition that does not rely upon the liberal gesture of defiance but addresses power and refusal in different ways?" (2011, 192) Throughout the essay what's evident is Halberstam's general aversion to (and if not aversion then suspicion of) form, whether familial or social, and thus to repetition and reproduction as lived experiences of politics. If there is an interest in form, it's in those forms that are still unimaginable. This openness to the unimaginable is about revolution and freedom, which, they remark in a later essay, "will come in a form we cannot yet imagine" (2013, 11).

The thinking of Edelman and even (though less scathingly) those in the more identitarian camp like Muñoz and Halberstam has been classified as a "subjectless queer critique." Jodi Byrd (2020, 107) argues that this mode of queer theorizing aims to decentre identity, the self, and place as a way of thwarting the sabotaging tendency to posit some people as subjects of social transformation and not others. To use an older feminist language, some people — namely white queers — are made into the makers of meaning, while the doubly and triply marginalized remain the bearers of meaning, those whose ongoing subjugation bestows meaning and purpose onto the more privileged (Mulvey 2014, 360). However compelling this turn to indefiniteness might be, however righteous it might feel to envisage political life in contradistinction to the individual and the nation, Byrd (2020, 107) reminds us that this "lack of fixity is ... still and importantly grounded through the ongoing dispossession of Indigenous lands." The subjectlessness and placelessness of queer critique requires a disavowal of Indigenous territorial and identitarian claims that precede the violence of the nation-state. Ironically, a subjectless queer critique might actually amount to a universal politics that once again consigns Indigeneity into the zone of political impossibility, eliding deeply felt and philosophically attuned relations to land and ecosystem. In a 2018 roundtable with *The New Inquiry* (Belcourt et al. 2018), I gave the following as an example of the failure of queer publics to manifest a way of life that was un-institutional and contra a "neat image of homosexuality" (Foucault 2020, 136): the use of "tribes" to organize sexual desire on the dating app Grindr. Tribe coheres as a collectivizing category only if we organize queer time as post-Indigenous genocide — that is, only if "tribe" is emptied of all material specificity and Indigeneity figures, if at all, as an immaterial figment of the past, a social non-entity.[1] Sexual desire becomes part of the corpus of texts and discursive tactics that comprise the colonial context. In mundane fashion, Grindr users contribute to the ongoing symbolic destruction of Indigeneity as a matter of cruising, of fucking and being fucked. While I don't think those who perform a subjectless queer critique would endorse Grindr's tribal fetish, there is in mind a similar metaphysical gesture involved in both that fortifies colonial permanence. A subjectless queer critique, then, might not actually be available to queer Indigenous Peoples as anything other than yet another self-colonizing option.

Because knowledge is embodied and because I'm both queer and Indigenous, some of queer theory's interventions into subjectivity and place cohere and others don't. I'm Cree, which is to say that I belong to a people, a nation, and lands and waters. Like the Indigenous poets I think with, it isn't that I'm opposed to nationhood in and of itself but instead to forms of nationhood that reinscribe the violence of property and heteropatriarchy. A queer notion of decolonization isn't about self-sacrifice or masochism (though I'm sure it could be thought in relation to these); my point is that sometimes our desires and our erotic impulses entail a dissolution of the self and the subject that disturbs neoliberal fantasies of the subject of politics as a self-sustained, sacrosanct entity, which have to varying degrees shaped contemporary understandings of Indigenous sovereignty. The kind of theoretical intervention I'm envisioning is neither the normalizing desires of some strains of what Byrd (2020, 118) calls "Indigenous liberalism" that seek to rid queerness of its non-normativity by turning to the pre-contact past, nor is it an Indigenizing of queer theories of subjectlessness. Rather, my contention is that if decolonization is a desire to unmake the world and build it anew, then queer sex and queer sexual life are spheres and practices through which that desire is felt and enacted. Decolonization is a mode of queer desiring; it might even be erotic. That is, there is something queer about decolonization that has to do with the coloniality of normative conceptions of the self and gender and the cis-heteropatriarchy of social form. A world unmoored from these is in the end a queer and decolonial world.

THE POETICS OF QUEER INDIGENOUS NEGATIVITY

The negativity of intimacy is everywhere in Natalie Diaz's *Postcolonial Love Poem* (2020). The "post" in the title isn't a slippage; it's evidence of what I think of as the anti-presentism of decolonial thought and action. In love we feel and are pulled by the presence of the world-to-come, what Muñoz (2009, 25) calls a moment of "queer relational bliss," the bliss of exceeding the afterlife of the past and the confines of the immediate now. To be anti-presentist is a negative stance; it is to occupy the knowledge that the present isn't all there is and thus that one's subjecthood is indeterminate. Diaz's "post" isn't about deferring to a future time when recognition and inclusion are made available to us but instead, like Muñoz, in performing the utopian in the space of the everyday. She writes:

> If I try running off into the deep-purpling scrub brush,
>
> you will remind me,
> *There is nowhere to go if you are already here*,
>
> and pat your hand on your lap lighted
> by the topazion lux of the moon through the window,
>
> say, *Here, Love sit here* — when I do,
> I will say, *And here I still am*. (2020, 81)

The "already here" is a geopolitical coordinate; it anchors the poem in a spatial and temporal structure that is at odds with the zones of unfreedom that constitute the colonial present. The love in Diaz's love poems feels to me like antidotes to the cruel "American arithmetic" in which we are "less than one, less than / whole" (2020, 18). In said poem, Diaz sketches an ontological condition in which Indigenous Peoples are vacated of ethical import, and at its close she writes: "Only a fraction / of a body, let's say, *I am only a hand*— / and when I slip it beneath the shirt of my lover / I disappear completely" (2020, 18). This negativity is evoked to both signify the fact of Indigenous erasure as well as the world-shattering quality of love, of how much is at stake when, as Layli Long Soldier (2017, 61) puts it, we don't always begin in the body. Love in colonial times is an ethical imperative unto itself. We need to love so as to build a new world. I for one can only love if it is transformative. The language of love isn't the language of the state, its grammar isn't that of an "American arithmetic"; it is post-colonial. At the end of the book's final poem, "Grief work," we see this thesis sharply rendered:

> I do my grief work
>
> with her body—:
>
> labor to make the emerald tigers
>
> in her throat leap,
>
> lead them burning green to drink
>
> from the deep-violet jetting her breast.
>
> We go where there is love,
>
> to the river, on our knees beneath the sweet
>
> water. I pull her under four times,
>
> until we are rivered.
>
> We are rearranged.
>
> I wash the silk and the silt of her from my hands—:
>
> now who I come to, I come clean to,
>
> I come good to." (Diaz 2020, 94)

Notable here is the entanglement of grief and love, that Diaz doesn't make them oppositional but shows how we are co-constituted by them. Love is what comes with "grief work," is how we don't "perform / what they say about our sadness" (2020, 30), how we "are rearranged" and shown to be more than non-beings outside the frame of life and the ethical. As I said in my second book *NDN Coping Mechanisms* (Belcourt 2019), what I want from love I want from revolution. The textuality of our grief is a minor fortune. Grief isn't always a foreclosure of relationality and interconnection; in our shared suffering a new kind of sociality emerges. To borrow Ann Cvetkovich's (2012, 3) phrase, bad feelings might actually "be the ground for transformation."

Becoming night, disappearing completely when a lover's hand reaches beneath a shirt — these are the images of a queer Indigenous negativity. In the queer Indigenous imagination, wounds aren't simply what we're left with after we've been destroyed or heartbroken; they are also worlds. I want to return to Skeets' *Eyes Bottle Dark with a Mouthful of Flowers*. In it, there are a series of poems that share the same name, "In the Fields," and so I want to read them together. "Field" here indicates both a grassy or desert expanse in which life does and doesn't happen and, in my mind, it also indicates the way we are fielded by others and come into being in the throes of sex and art and language. In one poem, Skeets writes:

> My tongue runs across his shoulders, stone bells affixed to bone. Cathedral noise in the socket, a rotten lisp. Pipelines entrench behind his teeth. I hear a crack in his lung like burning coal. I hear his lips kissing mine as a sermon. My pelvis daises as he chants my body back to weeds. One day he'll forget about wounds and lower himself too into bellflower. (2018, 46)

Skeets' landscape of desire is replete with violence; both the violence of the border town and of the deterioration of the body — a rotten lisp, cracked lungs like burning coal. But there's also the image of a body being reshaped and brought "back to weeds" by way of a man's chants. In a sense, one man brings another man back to life. Skeet thus radically remakes the category of man and situates it in a queerer and more feminist frame. The queer Indigenous body isn't an anthropological given; it doesn't exist in a static frame prior to decolonizing gestures. The subject of decolonization isn't necessarily a predetermined one. A queer notion of decolonization regards the body not in utter comprehension but with a sense of fluidity and fluctuation that makes queer and trans Indigenous lives more possible and our modes of desiring into political undertakings unto themselves.

In another of the "Fields" poems, Skeets (2018, 58) turns his analytical eye to the politics of poetic composition. In a visual poem in which the words "crow" and "letters" are disaggregated and dispersed across the page, he writes: "crows / scavenge / remains / like / letters / on white space." The poem itself is narrowed to a column in the middle of the page; its affect is one of crampedness. "Letters" appears as if it is about to be devoured. The point is to bring into focus the always-already brutal encroaching of white space, which perhaps mimics the always-already brutal enclosure of history as well as the movements of those empowered by the fantasy of terra nullius. These are invasions that the Indigenous poet contends with all the time. Still, some kind of poetic work can be done in the margins in the name of beauty. In the last of the "Fields" poems, Skeets writes: "We can be beautiful again beneath / the sumac, yarrow, and bitter water" (2018, 76). There is a field of subjectivity that is full of sumac, yarrow, and bitter water. The "we" is instructive here; it indexes the collectivity of the erotic as well as the way we collectively transform irrespective of and in opposition to the trauma that infringed upon our queer beauty to begin with.

Poetic language is important in decolonial struggle because of its queer relation to the material and the literal. Its metaphorical heft makes the "post-" of Diaz's post-colonial thinkable, the "we" of Skeets' field inhabitable. I suppose what I'm after is a poetic sense of the decolonial that takes seriously what Jodi Byrd (2020, 113) calls "the immateriality of Indigenous queer love." Due to our fundamental estrangement from the categories of both normative gender and normative Indigeneity, queer Indigenous Peoples live in the world but aren't entirely of it. As Skeets' and Diaz's poems suggest, the sexual is a place where we can enact our worldliness and inhabit our bodies even if that inhabiting involves an experience of undoing or is carried out in the shadow of violence. Sometimes we need to be undone in order to be made anew. This doesn't mean we have failed to bring about another world. In fact, I think it is precisely how we cleave ourselves from the strictures of the present and practice social forms in which Indigeneity and queerness are simultaneously livable and not at metaphysical odds.

AN ODE TO QUEER INDIGENOUS THEORY

Beginning with a 2016 essay in *Decolonization* called "Can the Other of Native Studies Speak?" I've spent much of my intellectual life so far thinking about what I described as "the unthinkability between queer and Indigenous" where many of us stage our lives. At the time, I was concerned with how the nascent subfield of Indigenous masculinities positioned masculinity as a normative subject and agent of decolonial struggle, a positioning that elided earlier Indigenous feminist critiques of the masculinist bent of mainstream Indigenous activism (e.g., Million 2009). I was additionally troubled by the subfield's biologically essential view of masculinity that further entrenched queerness in unthinkability or made it out to be an anomaly. Any queer reading in this framework would be self-marginalizing and/or conducted in the margins. It seemed symptomatic of a larger trend in Indigenous studies to both deliberately and unconsciously heterosexualize its objects of study.

While I still agree with these assessments, it occurs to me now that an institutional formation like Indigenous studies or any other discipline for that matter might be the wrong place to go looking for queer refuge. In other words, the un-institutional is what imbues our thinking and modes of desiring with radical power. The sexual is where Indigeneity and queerness are co-constituting categories, as is evidenced in the queer Indigenous poetry analyzed above. I contend that this poetic work amounts to a kind of queer Indigenous theory. Rather than institutionalize queer Indigenous theory and locate it in the university, I want to propose a notion of queer Indigenous theory as a lived and embodied one that is continuously given expression in poetry and the creative arts more broadly. Leanne Betasamosake Simpson's egalitarian view of theory is instrumental in this regard. She writes:

> A "theory" in its simplest form is an explanation of a phenomenon, and Nishnaabeg stories in this way form the theoretical basis of our intelligence. But theory also works a little differently within Nishnaabeg thought. "Theory" is generated and regenerated continually through embodied practice and within each family, community, and generation of people. "Theory" isn't just an intellectual pursuit — it is woven within kinetics, spiritual presence, and emotion, it is contextual and relational. It is intimate and personal, with individuals themselves holding the responsibilities for finding and generating meaning within their own lives. (2014, 7)

The bedroom and other sex scenes can thus be understood to be sites of theoretical production and sometimes even decolonial activity. Poetry is how queer Indigenous writers translate this theoretical production into an affective field that we can inhabit in the act of reading.

Skeets' "My pelvis daises as he chants my body back to weeds" is a theoretical statement, one that relies on the power of metaphor to make the abstract visible. The poet Anne Carson (2000, 31) argues that metaphor describes the mind's experience of error and that it is a pleasurable experience. Metaphor is how poets destabilize the world's hegemonic hold on our imaginations (see Aguirre's chapter in this volume). Chanting a body "back to weeds" is not simply figurative; Skeets describes a moment in which the queer Indigenous body is brought into being through the sex act. This suggests that sex is bound up in the process of Indigenous becoming or subjectification and that this process is both material and immaterial — in the space of the prefigurative or the anticipatory, of "forward-dawning futurity," as Muñoz (2009, 1) put it. The meaning we generate in our lives and work as queer Indigenous writers is the utopian belief in our lovability and therefore in our indomitability.

Joshua Whitehead's novel *Jonny Appleseed* (2018) is instructive as well as an example of a text that functions according to a queer Indigenous theoretics. Throughout the novel Whitehead attests to the ways in which colonialism has eroded older understandings of gender and sexuality and supplanted them with homophobia and transphobia. Whitehead shows what Alex Wilson (2015) teaches us, that queer Indigenous and Two-Spirit youth experience some of the most violent forms of subjugation in the present moment. But glimmers of queer futurity also permeate Whitehead's novel; in one scene, for example, when the protagonist comes out to his kokum over the phone, she tells him that in Cree there's a word for who he is and that she has stories to tell him, teachings to impart; Wilson calls this process of returning to Cree philosophies of gender and sexuality "coming in," a counter to the individualist and neoliberal notion of coming out that dominates mainstream depictions of queer life (2015, 3). Whitehead's Indigiqueer protagonist isn't merely an extension of some preordained agenda but rather a representation of "complex personhood," which is Avery Gordon's (2008, 4–5) phrase for the fact that we are all, though in specific ways, constituted by contradiction and emotions that are sometimes at odds with one another, but most importantly we are "simultaneously straightforward and full of enormously subtle meaning" that isn't wholly determined by dominant institutions. Whitehead's Jonny bears in his body the terrible knowledge of homophobia but he also desires a reserve, an Indigenous community, in excess of that violence, in excess of the colonial history that limits affective possibility for queer Indigenous people. The Indigenous novel is thus where a subjugated knowledge can surface and pressurize received notions of ethics and historical and present truth in a state where both ethics and truth are highly mediated. Like poetry, the Indigenous novel is how we sculpt new discursive territory from which to insist that another world is possible.

In Gordon's conception of complex personhood, the stories we tell about ourselves matter; Gordon remarks that we "weave between what is immediately available as a story and what [our] imaginations are reaching toward" (2008, 4). This emphasis on the imaginative reminds me of Muñoz's image of queerness as an ideality that pulls at us from the future (2009, 1). What's common in both of these formulations is the anti-presentism of decolonial thought, even if neither necessarily or always viewed what they were doing as decolonial. In reaching toward what isn't available to us, in being enticed by queerness's futurity, we are jolted out of a romance of the present. The present isn't a dead end after all. Queer Indigenous writing, infused with poetic insight, can be a method by which we enact the imaginative power to destabilize the ontological stability of the present. How and to what end is of course up to the work of individual writers, but it seems to me that in the work of Skeets, Diaz, and Whitehead queer Indigenous people are already in the future. We are not mired in trauma, nor do we always know with certainty what our desires will bring about. That we desire in contradiction to the brutality of history, ongoing loss, and theoretical blind spots from all directions is evidence of our refusal to succumb to the symbolic death imposed upon us. Our desire, literary and actual, is a political and theoretical force that allows us to make claim to the decolonial future, which will always-already be queer.

NOTE

1. I don't mean to set up a binary between the material and immaterial that suggests the former is an inherent political necessity and the latter its opposite. Rather, I'm flagging the ways Indigenous Peoples' material presences in what is now called North America are under siege as an effect of colonialism. We are made immaterial in the settler imagination in order to be exploited, disappeared. Not all forms of immateriality are terrible, though. Queerness maintains a capacious relation with the immaterial due to how elastic and shape-shifting queer forms of life are.

REFERENCES

Belcourt, Billy-Ray. 2019. *NDN Coping Mechanisms: Notes from the Field*. Toronto: House of Anansi Press.

Belcourt, Billy-Ray, et al. 2018. "Top or Bottom: How Do We Desire?" *The New Inquiry*, October 10. thenewinquiry.com/top-or-bottom-how-do-we-desire/.

Byrd, Jodi. 2020. "What's Normative Got to Do With It?" *Social Text* 38, 4.

Carson, Anne. 2000. *Men in the Off Hours*. Toronto: Vintage Books.

Cvetkovich, Ann. 2012. *Depression: A Public Feeling*. Durham: Duke University Press.

Diaz, Natalie. 2020. *Postcolonial Love Poem*. Minneapolis: Graywolf Press.

Edelman, Lee. 2004. *No Future: Queer Theory and the Death Drive*. Durham: Duke University Press.

Foucault, Michel. 2020. "Friendship as a Way of Life." In *Ethics*, edited by Paul Rabinow. London: Penguin Books.

Gordon, Avery. 2008. *Ghostly Matters: Haunting and the Sociological Imagination*. Minneapolis: University of Minnesota Press.

Halberstam, Jack. 2011. "Unbecoming: Queer Negativity/Radical Passivity." In *Sex, Gender and Time in Fiction and Culture*, edited by Ben Davies and Jana Funke. New York: Palgrave Macmillan.

———. 2013. "The Wild Beyond: With and For the Undercommons." In *The Undercommons: Fugitive Planning and Black Study*, written by Fred Moten and Stefano Harney. New York: Minor Compositions. s3.amazonaws.com/arena-attachments/1460896/a899a5ebf2ec18e9468f6c29cbef1911.pdf?1511808313.

Long Soldier, Layli. 2017. *Whereas*. Minneapolis: Graywolf Press.

Lorde, Audre. 2020. "Uses of the Erotic: The Erotic as Power." In *The Selected Works of Audre Lorde*, edited by Roxane Gay. New York: W.W. Norton.

Million, Dian. 2009. "Felt Theory: An Indigenous Feminist Approach to Affect and History." *Wicazo Sa Review* 24, 2.

Mulvey, Laura. 2014. "Visual Pleasure and Narrative Cinema." In *Film Manifestos and Global Cinema Cultures: A Critical Anthology*, edited by Scott MacKenzie. Berkeley: University of California Press.

Muñoz, José Esteban. 2009. *Cruising Utopia: The Then and There of Queer Futurity*. New York: New York University Press.

Simpson, Leanne Betasamosake. 2014. "Land as Pedagogy: Nishnaabeg Intelligence and Rebellious Transformation." *Decolonization* 3, 3.

Skeets, Jake. 2018. *Eyes Bottle Dark with a Mouthful of Flowers*. Minneapolis: Milkweed Press.

Tuck, Eve. 2009. "Suspending Damage: A Letter to Communities." *Harvard Educational Review* 79, 3.

Whitehead, Joshua. 2018. *Jonny Appleseed*. Vancouver: Arsenal Pulp Press.

Wilson, Alex. 2015. "Our Coming In Stories: Cree Identity, Body Sovereignty, and Gender Self-Determination." *Journal of Global Indigeneity* 1, 1.

TWELVE

Mad Indigenous Womanhood
The Psycho-Politics of Settler Colonialism

Cara Peacock

GROWING UP I HEARD THE REFRAIN that "Native women are crazy" frequently expressed by people, Indigenous and non-Indigenous. This comment, made as a joke or not, supposes that Indigenous women are in some way poorly adjusted mentally and can serve as a caution and warning of their potentially volatile nature. While Indigenous Peoples face higher rates of mental illness, emotional distress, and suicide, historically the prevailing treatment and research into the mental health of Indigenous populations has been undertaken by settlers using colonial and non-Indigenous concepts and epistemologies (Nelson and Wilson 2017). My grandma Katherine Peacock (née Goulais), an Anishinaabekwe from Nipissing First Nation, spent most of her adult life in and out of mental institutions in Sudbury and North Bay, Ontario. I have asked my dad a number of times if he knew what exactly his mom had been diagnosed with — was it schizophrenia? Bipolar disorder? However, my dad insists that he does not know. Instead, my grandma simply occupies the blurred category of "madness."

This chapter examines how the colonial gendered constructions of madness naturalize the oppression of Indigenous women and how the psychiatric discipline can function to facilitate settler colonial statecraft and sovereignty. It is also a prompt to interrogate the prevailing conceptions of mental health and illness that animate the treatment of madness and to consider what epistemic justice for those marked as mad Indigenous women might require. By epistemic justice, I mean the capacity for Indigenous women to participate in the creation of the concepts and categories by which they might come to understand themselves and the world.

My analysis reveals the constitutive features, problems, and historical formations of psychiatry's colonial heteropatriarchal character and its broader social and political effects for Indigenous women through an intersectional historical examination. I utilize personal narrative and experiential knowledge in the form of a three-part story, detailing my own experiences of mental illness and psychiatric treatment and my knowledge of Grandma's experience with psychiatry. My personal narrative serves several functions: 1) to validate the lived experiences of Indigenous women as knowledge and theory; 2) to further apprehend the nature of colonial heteropatriarchal sanism; and 3) to rematriate mad Indigenous women's ways of being and knowing.

Throughout, I draw on the term "mad" or "madness," referencing the antipsychiatry, mental patient liberation movements, and critical mad studies, which invoke madness as a category of analysis where structures and relations of power mediate the individual's encounters with organized psychiatry. These movements have sought to name psychiatric violence, to resist pathologizing, and to create counter-knowledge and subjugated knowledge as a means of contesting hegemonic, epistemic formations. Importantly, the epistemic and physical violence of psychiatry is intimately tied to the socio-political processes of colonialism, which play an important role in the development and application of the field.

COLONIAL EPISTEMIC VIOLENCE

Rajeev Bhargava explains that colonialism involves a unique form of epistemic injustice that "occurs when the concepts and categories by which a people understand themselves and their world [are] replaced or adversely affected by the concepts and categories of colonizers" (2013, 415). Effectively, knowledge and its production come to be structured under colonial hegemony through the veneration of the colonizer's ways of knowing and through the erasure and elision of Indigenous ways of knowing. Heteropatriarchy likewise shapes colonial relations of power, meaning that Indigenous women's knowledges become further marginalized by the intersecting forms of racialized and gendered oppression, both in and outside of their communities (Altamirano-Jiménez and

Kermoal 2016). Colonial binaries are order-instituting mechanisms and are fundamental to the social and political logics of settler colonialism (Moreton-Robinson 2015; Wolfe 2006). Indigenous women are rendered irrational through external constructions of Indigeneity and womanhood, wherein their oppression operates through these various colonial binaries: civilized/savage, settler/Native, man/woman, and rational/irrational. Audra Simpson (2016) further explains that the settler colonial state is an ongoing project that requires the deaths of Indigenous women as they embody the inverse of white womanhood, having held social and political power before colonization and thus representing an alternative political order that threatens the white heteropatriarchal character of settler sovereignty. Indigenous women's lives mark a failure to perish, or as Simpson puts it: the "stubborn, resolute, and sovereign refusal to die" (2016, 14). Indigenous women's exposure to violence and premature death is thus integral to settler colonial dispossession, statecraft, and sovereignty, and these various binaries and logics work to ensure the containment of our subjectivities and knowledges.

While those who call Indigenous women "crazy" are not offering a clinical diagnosis, this phrase nevertheless supposes that Indigenous women are in some way irrational or nonsensical, having somehow aberrated from the norm and the definitive model of rationality or sanity. But what is normal, rational, or sane? Michel Foucault, in *Madness and Civilization*, contends that madness is not a fixed or objective category but rather shifts to include certain people as an exercise of power and has historically enabled psychiatry to exert control over those with behaviours or dispositions considered deviant (1965). Madness is further understood as the distorted reflection of reason, engrained in cultural belief as one-half of a static binary structure, and treated as something dangerous while evoking feelings of sympathy, fear, and disgust; this conception solidifies the mad as abnormal and needing to be contained from a normal population (Kafai 2013). Psychiatric constructions of racialized peoples further create rationales and justifications for both historical and ongoing colonialism, partially achieved through the assumption that psychiatry is objective, scientific, and thus legitimate knowledge (Kanani 2011). Even when there is an acknowledgement that mental injuries are incurred from colonial projects such as residential schools, it nevertheless comes with the imposition of the colonizer's methods for healing, which continues the project of white supremacy and deculturation (Tam 2013). The preceding literature explains how the label of "crazy" or "madness" comes with its own set of social and material realities that both obfuscate the origins and cause of the psychosis, as well as the particular forms of violence it is deemed to warrant.

PART I: DEVIANCE

I'm sitting and talking with my psychiatrist. We are changing my medication again. My brain feels like an impossible puzzle that refuses to be solved.

My psychiatrist asks me if I ever get angry while driving.

I mull over his question, visibly awkward, and answer "Yes, I actually had to stop driving for a bit because I felt like I was getting too angry, like an unhealthy amount of anger."

He asks if I have problems managing my anger.

I pretend to mull over the question, as though I do not readily know the answer. "Yeah, sometimes I wonder if I have anger issues and that always surprises people because I am usually so quiet."

My diagnosis is changing, and it comes as a relief. I realized long ago that my brain did not let me function well in this world. However, there remains this niggling fear that maybe it's something else. That maybe I'll end up crazy, that I already am.

I feel on edge and tell a friend, "You know, my grandma was institutionalized in the '60s and '70s, she was a Native woman and they treated her so horribly."

I continue, "I feel like I'm going to end up just like her." With fear I add, "They'll lock me up and mistreat me." My grandma occupied my mind as a fear of some inevitable future that awaited me. Not because she was mad, but because of what it would mean for me.

Sometimes my friend would ask, "What happened to her — what did they do?"

I wouldn't reply.

I'm in high school, sitting in class, and completely absorbed in our lesson on the life of Martin Luther. Luther had taken up a monastic vow with the Order of Hermits of St. Augustine where he would be bound to a strict, demanding, and isolating modus operandi. Monasteries were self-sufficient communities and intended to be removed from the deleterious influences of the outside society by shutting off from the world.

I was very quiet and shy my entire childhood. Kids frequently told me, "I've never heard you speak; I don't even know what your voice sounds like." I was the one that the rowdy kid got sat next to after disrupting class, and try hard as they might, they could not cajole me into talking. Naturally teachers loved me, but other kids would occasionally remark that they thought I was rude, assuming that I didn't like them because I didn't talk to them. But when I did try to put myself out there, I often came across poorly to others. I was told by friends that others were surprised to find, after finally talking with me, that I was so *weird*. Being socially inept, it took an embarrassingly long time to understand that they didn't mean "weird" in a quirky and harmless way, they meant weird in a bad and off-putting way. I felt like I was in a lose-lose situation and that life was like a play where everyone had the script and knew all their lines except me.

Learning about Luther had ignited a fervent interest in me towards the medieval monastic life. I was devastated to learn that only men could be monks, barring me from hypothetically taking up a monastic vow. Amazingly enough the fact that I didn't live in medieval Europe hadn't solidified the monastic life as impossible for me — no, patriarchy was to blame! My interest in the hermitic monk life stemmed from my desire to be a part of a community where my quiet and solitary nature might be celebrated as a strength and a virtue instead of condemned as a personal character failure to be overcome. Socializing had too many hidden risks; I didn't want to overcome being quiet, and it seemed the only way to win was not to play.

MADNESS, INDIGENEITY, AND GENDER IN NORTH AMERICA

There is a lack of literature exploring the dynamics of race and psychiatry and a further lack of historical record concerning the lived experiences of racialized peoples in North America. Notably, there is even less literature that examines Indigenous people's particular experiences within psychiatry, let alone Indigenous women's. To understand how psychiatry can facilitate violence against Indigenous women requires a historical analysis that locates the experiences of Indigenous people and women within the history of psychiatry in the settler colonial context of North America, with a primary focus on Canada. I examine the psychiatric discipline through both Indigenous and settler histories, applying what historian Keith Carlson calls an "Indigenous historical consciousness," which places Indigenous perspectives at the forefront and examines the history of American and Canadian society from Indigenous histories (2010, 112). To organize my analysis, this section primarily focuses on the historical formation of the asylum/mental hospital and its role in facilitating colonial gendered violence.

Mental institutions initially began to crop up in North America in the 1800s as a reformist move intended to help those with mental illness who required care but would have otherwise been placed in jails, almshouses, or left to care for themselves. The Asylum for Insane Indians in South Dakota was the first and only mental hospital for Indigenous people and ran from 1903–34, the same period known for forcing Indigenous children into boarding schools. Many Indigenous people were committed for their acts of transgression against colonial authorities, for arguing with a reservation attendant, for refusing to give up ceremonial or traditional ways, or for reasons that were entirely unrelated to mental illness but simply as punishment (Kanani 2011). The asylum committed almost four hundred people, both men and women, and at least 121 people died at the facility during its short operation (Richards 2018). Leda Williamson described the violent mistreatment she experienced in the asylum, recounting how she had been kicked repeatedly and shoved against a bench, breaking it upon impact; the attendants responsible were Ada and Benjamin DeCory, both former employees of the Rapid City Indian School. This asylum functioned as a site of violence and premature death for Indigenous people who failed to adhere to settler assimilation, much like the functioning of Indian boarding schools.

Erika Dyck and Alex Deighton (2017) note that unruly settlers and Indigenous people were both excluded from mainstream narratives of progress in Canada, but the former might find themselves segregated in a psychiatric or penal institution while the latter was expected to live on segregated reserves, further stating that there is limited evidence to suggest that the involuntary commitment of persons was systematically selected based on race. While the number of Indigenous people in mental hospitals was relatively small, they were nevertheless still subjected to both psychiatric and penal institutionalization in the nineteenth and twentieth centuries. Clinical files of Indigenous people at British Columbia's public mental hospitals between 1879 and 1950 show that most were labelled as mentally ill for having breached social and racial conventions (Kanani 2011). Dr. Jilek-Aall, a psychiatrist who worked with Indigenous people in the Fraser Valley of British Columbia through the 1960s to '70s, contended that Indigenous people had "little, if any, notion of the function of [psychiatry]," dismissing the validity of their fear and apprehension towards psychiatric treatment and the following advice given to an Indigenous youth by his grandfather:

> The white man has two ways of getting rid of Indians who make trouble for him: he puts them in prison or in the mental hospital. Stay away from the mental hospital! If you go to prison you always know how much time you have to do; but you never know when they will let you out of the mental hospital! (quoted in Jilek-Aall, 1976, 354)

The Indigenous community members rightfully understood the colonial realities that underpinned psychiatric practices and institutions, recognizing mental hospitals and prisons as violent mechanisms that could be weaponized by settler authorities to control and contain them, and thus understood the function of psychiatry and exercised a rational and necessary apprehension. The experiential and historical knowledge of Indigenous people, as well as the historical documentation, demonstrate that race, and specifically divergence from socially constructed racialized norms, was in fact a constituting factor for their involuntary commitment and mistreatment within asylums.

Ingrid Waldron explains that relationships were drawn between pathology, race, and human sexuality within North America, leading racialized peoples to become cast as hypersexual and thus constituted as deviant and pathological (2016). The interrelatedness of sexual deviance and madness also has roots in a gendered logic. Jane Kromm explains that in the nineteenth century, madness would come to be understood as a feminine disorder with representations of madness largely figuring women, negatively portraying them as aggressive, sexually provocative, primarily self-abusing, and a site for sexual display (1994, 508). Effectively, these depictions functioned to further social control over women's sexuality and ambitions by pathologizing their deviation from patriarchal models of womanhood. Phyllis Chesler, in *Women and Madness* (2005), explains that in 1972 psychiatric patients were primarily women and were more likely to be involuntarily committed, while also being treated and diagnosed by doctors who were primarily men. The overall structure of the psychiatric institution was also patriarchal, with doctors possessing a Father-Judge authority and women being constituted as childlike and infantilized, considered cured once she is able to act as a submissive mother and wife. While Chesler was writing from experiences and statistics largely situated in the 1960s, she nevertheless demonstrates the highly heteropatriarchal bias that shaped historical psychiatric practices and institutions. Race and gendered logics importantly structure how mental asylums and the psychiatric discipline are conceived of and come to operate.

Importantly, women still outnumber men in diagnoses of madness and are also more likely to be subjected to psychiatric treatment, hospitalization in an asylum, physical restraint, electro-convulsive therapy (ECT), psychosurgery, psychological therapy, and psychotropic drug treatments (Ussher 2011). According to Don Weitz (2013, 161–62), as of decade ago electroshock therapy (ECT) was still widely used in Ontario and two to three times more likely to be performed on women than men, with young mothers and elderly women being most at risk. There are also no mandatory ECT reporting laws or regulations in Canada that require hospitals to report all shock procedures, medical complications, and ECT-related deaths, and there are numerous recorded instances of women being pressured or forced to receive ECT against their wishes by psychiatrists. In effect, heteropatriarchal bias continues to structure the psychiatric discipline and enable violent containment and management of women who defy colonial gender norms.

It is telling that the creation of Indian residential/boarding schools and penal systems coalesces alongside the establishment of the psychiatric asylum, illustrating the settler colonial drive to expand colonial institutions and ways of being to further social and political control. Asylums were often employed for the transformation of degenerates into productive citizens, much like prisons and residential schools, which mirrors the settler colonial Indian policy that sought to make subjects out of sovereign peoples. These mechanisms are a part of the broader process of settler colonial statecraft, functioning to erode Indigenous sovereignty by denying Indigenous Peoples the authority and capacity to govern themselves socially and politically. The forcible removal of Indigenous Peoples from their communities and the estrangement from their families further functions to disrupt their traditional kinship systems and the propagation of Indigenous ways of life by containing them within assimilative and violent institutions. Asylums exhibit the settler colonial eliminatory logic that seeks to destroy Indigenous life and ways of being and were employed as a technology of control and containment to maintain and legitimate settler colonial rule.

Over time, asylums would suffer from underfunding, overcrowding, and poor management, and the 1960s would see a demand for reforms that would culminate in a widespread deinstitutionalization and the closure of many psychiatric hospitals. The closure of psychiatric hospitals was not accompanied by an increase in community care and resources; instead, many of those released would face a life of danger, neglect, and vulnerability to poverty, homelessness, and incarceration. Importantly, while these forms of long-term asylums and Indian residential schools have formally closed, prisons nevertheless continue to operate as an important technology of colonial gendered violence. Indigenous women in Canada bear a disproportionate burden of poverty, homelessness, and incarceration, are overrepresented in carceral systems, and are the fastest growing prison population, constituting half of the federal prison population despite making up only 5 percent the women's population (Bingham et al. 2019; Shefman 2022). Psychiatric practices continue to rely on allegedly expert opinions that portray racialized peoples as violent, aggressive, and unpredictable, while excluding the patient's voices and effectively silencing them; this creates a system impermeable to criticism that enables the violent and disproportionate criminalization of the mentally ill and the false associations of mental illness and violence to continue unchecked (Joseph 2014). The mental health system continues to engage and treat Indigenous women as violent, aggressive, uncontrollable, and unpredictable, subjecting them to containment, coercive treatment, and physical and chemical restraint within both prisons and mental health institutions. Psychiatry is still employed as a technology of colonial gendered violence and while it has undergone numerous reforms over the twentieth century, the assimilatory and violent containment of treatment continues unabated in many forms.

While little literature and historical documentation exists about the experiences of Indigenous women, the overall historical analysis demonstrates how colonial heteropatriarchy shapes psychiatric practices and the discourse of what is considered sane and deviant. Defying colonial and patriarchal norms has resulted in marginalized and racialized peoples being diagnosed as mad, enabling violence against them and their containment within asylums and prisons. By being perceived as deviant and degenerate, through their hyper-sexualization and failure to live up to colonial heteropatriarchal models of white womanhood, Indigenous women are labelled as mad. When deemed ill or disordered, Indigenous women then need to be changed, controlled, repaired, or altered. Indigenous women are already rendered disposable and a threat to settler colonial statecraft and sovereignty, but the label of madness further marks them as dangerous and deviant, thus naturalizing mechanisms of control and containment, and further masks the layers of violence brought against them. The category of madness comes to coalesce and operate with other colonial binaries of difference — civilized/savage, settler/Native, man/woman, rational/irrational, and sane/mad.

PART II: MAD, INDIGENOUS WOMANHOOD

I'm sitting with my dad when I ask him about his mom, my grandma. I never met her, and she passed when I was young. My dad rarely speaks of her. He tells me that in his earliest memories she was in and out of the hospital and the absences got longer and longer, "until I didn't get to see her again," he says.

There's a staid pause; he comments that she was treated in the '60s and '70s and that psychiatry was rather crude and cruel during that time, "even if you were white" he adds. My grandma existed as this nebulous entity during my childhood — all I had were fragmented stories of her, a foggy picture of who she was or even what she looked like. There are no pictures of her in my dad's house, nor pictures of my grandpa — I just see pictures of his grandkids and his own children. My dad had often said he had grown up without a mom and without a dad really. My grandpa had spent most of his time working, while my dad and his siblings were left to take care of themselves. My uncle's wife remarked that it was rather incredible that these kids raised themselves; my dad shrugs, as though it simply is what it is.

I go back to visit my reserve as an adult. My dad asks his cousin if their moms, who are sisters, went to residential school — he does not know. Our cousin tells us that my grandma and her siblings didn't go to residential school, that her granny scooped up the kids and ran into the bush before the RCMP arrived. However, they did spend time at a Catholic day school where they were hit and chastised each time they spoke Anishinaabemowin. This story reminds me of my mom's great granny, known to my family as "big granny" — she only spoke Cree and could not (or perhaps did not want to) speak English. When my big granny was a kid her parents also packed up their things in the middle of night and ran into the bush to avoid the RCMP as they came to take the kids away. I think of her little house, without heating or plumbing, with a few light bulbs strung up on the ceiling — she had a little wood stove and an outhouse, nestled in the bush on the outskirts of Slave Lake. Her and my mom would talk and laugh in Cree. I would pretend to understand and laugh too.

My dad said my grandpa had taken him a couple times to visit her at the asylum when he was a kid, but he remarks to me as an adult that "it's definitely not a place for children."

We visited my dad's family once in Ontario when I was a kid. He drove from Grande Prairie, Alberta, to Kagawong, Ontario, with his five daughters in a six-seater truck.[1] He went to visit his mom during that trip, and I asked to come, and he simply said no, that I didn't need to see her. I didn't understand then, I just wanted to meet my grandma. I had never seen her — in pictures or in person. But I realize now, it's not a place for children.

My grandma must exist somewhere in these absences — as an outline, a spectre, a haunting — never fully there but always felt somehow. She leaves traces of her world behind, and I am trying to follow its trail. Still, I do not know where she is.

My dad rarely spoke of his mom. The stories I heard were from hushed conversations with my sisters as a kid.

My older sister tells me how she and our dad talked about our grandma — dad says she was in mental institutions and gone for most of his childhood. Her voice is lower now than before. She received electroshock therapy. Apparently, the doctor who treated her would be later found out for malpractice. He was known to use a higher voltage in electroshock therapy than was needed — purposely using too much, hurting his patients. She looks away and tells me she has never seen my dad sad like that.

And sometimes, for a moment, I think about how terrifying, how horrible that would be.

And then I quickly stop myself.

I walk through our reserve as an adult, for the first time, observing the lake hugging the shore and the jagged cliffside topped with trees and bush. I wish the bush could have offered refuge and reprieve then, that once again she could have escaped into the protection of the trees. Then, maybe I could have found her residing and speaking Anishinaabemowin and laughing in the bush. But she couldn't. And though the bush could not hide her as it once had, I still could not find her.

MAD INDIGENOUS WOMANHOOD AND BEYOND

While many Indigenous women have been subjected to mistreatment and violence at the hands of psychiatry for a failure to adhere to colonial and gendered norms, many experience genuine mental suffering that requires care and support. But they have no hope of finding it within oppressive and violent systems. However, I draw on both instances, weaving them together in my account consciously, as a means of obfuscating the borders of sane/insane. Madness represents a restructured reality, reconstructed when people's experiences intersect with psychiatry and are reinterpreted and re-storied by the discipline (Liegghio 2013). This process renders the individual and their personal experiences into a kind of nothingness that will be replaced with a professionalized interpretation and construction, effectively emptied of subjectivity. I hope to problematize the understanding of madness and how it overwrites Indigenous women's knowledges and being, because whether Indigenous women experience neurodivergence or mental distress, a label of madness functions to strip them of agency and humanity and renders them vulnerable to mistreatment, violence, and premature death. This section examines the broader implications of colonial heteropatriarchal sanism and draws on Indigenous women's understandings of mental health to theorize beyond its oppression. In doing so they affirm the legitimacy of their knowledges and solutions and as an act of rematriating of our ways of being and knowing.

Colonial heteropatriarchal sanism obscures the fullness of existence to those deemed mad, but there are ways to move beyond and celebrate mad women's identities, to reclaim those aspects of being a woman that heteropatriarchy labels crazy, and to create practices that bring back into existence their ways of knowing and being (Burstow 2005). Erin Soros (2018, 84) explains that Indigenous literature problematizes the settler-model for understanding mental illness and madness; in Lee Maracle's novel, *Celia's Song* (2014), the experience of hearing voices is not understood as a symptom but rather is considered part of the healing process, and in "A Mind Spread Out on the Ground," Alicia Elliott's answers lead not to a medical interpretation of Indigenous suffering but rather serves as a devastating critique of what her people's minds and bodies have had to survive and continue to resist (Elliott 2017, as cited in Soros 2018, 74). Stó:lō writer Terese Marie Mailhot, in *Heart Berries: A Memoir* (2018), shares stories from her life, such as her experience with bipolar II disorder and her stay within a psychiatric ward. Mailhot notes,

> In white culture, forgiveness is synonymous with letting go. In my culture, I believe we carry pain until we can reconcile it through ceremony. Pain is not framed like a problem with a solution. I don't even know if white people see transcendence the way we do. (2018, 28)

She goes on to mention, "A Native writer read my work and said, 'It's no wonder that this narrator is crazy. She's an Indian, and she's smart. Who could survive that?'" (2018, 120). Mailhot's commentary demonstrates how settler models of mental health are circumscribed by a narrow cultural perspective, but these stories told by Indigenous women resist this conception of their mental health and refuse settler psychiatry as authoritative, effectively affirming their knowledge and reimagining their suffering, healing, and well-being on their own terms. Mailhot also demonstrates how colonization can be maddening for Indigenous women, highlighting how colonial heteropatriarchal sanism operates beyond domains immediately linked to the psychiatric discipline, in more diffuse and ancillary ways.

I am reminded again of my big granny; she was apprehensive of the white man's medicine (e.g., doctors, hospitals, and their prescribed medical treatments) and refused the colonial biomedical system throughout her life, living to be ninety-four. I love telling this story about her because it is a point of pride for me. However, on one occasion when I shared this story with a friend, a white man, I was met with his incredulous scoff and criticism of her as superstitiously rejecting life-saving modern medicine. He was quick to malign her as foolishly unable to understand the obvious benefits and dismissed her as backwards, assuming that there could be no legitimate reasons for her apprehension, much like Dr. Jilek-Aall. The 2020 death of Atikamekw woman, Joyce Echaquan, was caused by the racist and misogynistic neglect of staff in a Quebec hospital while she clearly required care. My big granny was also a midwife to Indigenous women in her community, many of whom were also wary of treatment by white doctors. The historical and ongoing mistreatment of Indigenous women like Joyce Echaquan, as well as the long history of practices like forced sterilization and separation of children at birth, demonstrates the necessity of my big granny's apprehension and practices. I draw on these stories to demonstrate how Indigenous women's concerns are readily dismissed as irrational, outlandish, or crazy across different domains and multiple scales, while further highlighting how settler colonialism is sustained through the willingness of individuals to carry out the operation and reproduction of its logics, from interpersonal relationships to their place of work. In extension, the mechanisms that demean Indigenous women as crazy are also stripping them of credibility, meaning its operation can also legitimize and mask other forms of violence, such as the violence carried out in the healthcare system, or domestic and sexual violence, or their characterization as unfit for political office or public life, to name just a few examples. To genuinely transform these patterns of violence further requires honest self-reflection about how these logics are reproduced across various sites and scales, as Indigenous and non-Indigenous individuals and communities.

Living within a system that readily strips one of credibility can be maddening, but re-storying mad Indigenous womanhood allows us to begin making the world anew by creating new words and stories to understand our mental health and by cultivating communities that can respond with care, support, or even celebrate our differences. Soros explains that the word "bushed" comes to refer to someone who has been in the woods too long, who has become crazy with and through the wilderness, wherein the bush marks out where "madness lies" and infects one's sense (2018, 75). There is a helplessness in watching the pain and suffering of colonial heteropatriarchal sanism, but there is space to create and heal beyond it. Within the story of my grandma, the bush is a place where she and other family members had found safety and as a place of refuge from the dehumanization and violence of colonization. I want to reclaim the bush from being understood as a place where madness lies, waiting to infect. Instead, I offer the bush as a theoretical site where the mad Indigenous woman might be able to recover herself. Where witnesses might also participate in this recovery of humanity, knowledge, and ways of being. I draw on the story of my grandma and other Indigenous women like myself, who must bear the force of colonial heteropatriarchal sanism and its labels of "mad," "crazy," and "irrational," to reply to this colonial technology. By drawing on her story I hope to mark out her humanity and to appreciate her as a person deserving of dignity and respect in the face of colonization's attempt to snuff her out.

PART III: THROUGH THE HAZE

I am trying to recover my grandma as a person, as an Anishinaabekwe. While psychiatry strips mad people of possessing legitimate knowledge, it also obscures their being known by others. The outline of madness obscures the person, leaving a haze and blurring in its place. This haze poses an unknowability that I continue to try and make sense of even now, always feeling the spectre of it, but never able to locate its edges or boundaries. She wasn't always mad, there was a time when she seemed *normal*. What happened? She was still a young mother when she became institutionalized; was it postpartum depression that was never properly attended to? Was the ugliness of colonialism, of forced assimilation, too much? Were there some other abuses I do not know of? Was it simply a genetic issue, a chemical imbalance? I honestly do not know.

My dad left Ontario when he a teenager since work was hard to find in the province and all the jobs were out west. After moving to Alberta at nineteen, my dad would later get married to my mom and they would have six kids together. My dad has often said that he wanted to give us opportunities and experiences that Native kids do not often get — to make our childhoods and lives unlike his own. The story of my grandma is not just her own, it continues to speak into my family's lives. I think of how my dad always identified with his Native heritage, as specifically Anishinaabe. His dad was non-Indigenous, and though his mom was unfortunately absent from much of his life, her world continues to define his. Continues to define my own.

I am sitting at my aunt's house looking at old photos. There's a newspaper clipping of my grandma. The clipping says that she swam across the n'biising.[2] My dad says, "She was always a really strong swimmer."

My dad tells me that when he was a kid he would spend all day swimming in the n'biising, the lake which the reserve rests against. For the first time, I go swimming in that lake too, the one my dad and my grandma know very well. The lake knows them too and I wonder if it knows me. I swim out as far as I can and admittedly it's not very far; I always get scared of deep water. The coldness of the deep water makes me nervous — what's down there? I am in awe that my family and ancestors have navigated these deep, cold waters so easily since time immemorial. I hope one day I can as well.

As I swim out as far as my confidence and stamina will allow, I am amazed and in awe that she could swim across the entire length, the shore on the other side seems unreachable to me. But the depths and coldness of the n'biising were familiar to her, a close relative she and my family had always known.

I think, maybe, I have found a part of her. I want to remember her this way.

I want to remember her swimming across the n'biising with ease, emerging on the other side into the folds of the bush once again.

NOTES

1   It took us three days to get there. I was eight years old, and my oldest sister was sixteen. After our trip my dad, unsurprisingly, said he would never, ever make that long of a trip with us again.
2   Anishinaabek for "little lake," named because of its size compared to the great lakes, though certainly not small. It has a surface area of approximately 873 square kilometres.

REFERENCES

Altamirano-Jiménez, Isabel, and Nathalie Kermoal. 2016. "Introduction: Indigenous Women and Knowledge." In *Living on the Land: Indigenous Women's Understanding of Place*, edited by I. Altamirano-Jiménez and N. Kermoal. Athabasca: AU Press.

Bhargava, Rajeev. 2013. "Overcoming the Epistemic Injustice of Colonialism." *Global Policy* 4, 4.

Bingham, Brittany, et al. 2019. "Gender Differences Among Indigenous Canadians Experiencing Homelessness and Mental Illness." BMC *Psychology* 7, 57. doi.org/10.1186/s40359-019-0331-y.

Burstow, Bonnie. 2005. "Feminist Antipsychiatry Praxis – Women and the Movement(s): A Canadian Perspective." In *Women, Madness, and the Law: A Feminist Reader,* edited by W. Chan, D. Chunn, and R. Menzies. London: The Glass House Press.

Carlson, Keith. 2010. *The Power of Place, the Problem of Time: Aboriginal Identity and Historical Consciousness in the Cauldron of Colonialism.* Toronto: University of Toronto Press.

Chesler, Phyllis. 2005. *Women and Madness.* Chicago Review Press.

Dyck, Erika, and Alex Deighton. 2017. *Managing Madness: Weyburn Mental Hospital and the Transformation of Psychiatric Care in Canada.* Winnipeg: University of Manitoba Press.

Elliott, Alicia. 2017. "A Mind Spread Out on the Ground." *Malahat Review* 197.

Foucault, Michel. 1965. *Madness and Civilization: A History of Insanity in the Age of Reason.* New York: Pantheon.

Jilek-Aall, Louise. 1976. "The Western Psychiatrist and His Non-Western Clientele: Transcultural Experiences of Relevance to Psychotherapy with Canadian Indian Patients." *Canadian Psychiatric Association Journal* 21, 6. doi.org/10.1177/070674377602100601.

Joseph, Ameil. 2014. "A Prescription for Violence: The Legacy of Colonization in Contemporary Forensic Mental Health and the Production of Difference." *Critical Criminology* 22. doi.org/10.1007/s10612-013-9208-1.

Kafai, Shayda. 2013. "The Mad Border Body: A Political In-Betweeness." *Disability Studies Quarterly* 33, 1.

Kanani, Nadia. 2011. "Race and Madness: Locating the Experiences of Racialized People with Psychiatric Histories in Canada and the United States." *Critical Disability Discourse* 3. cdd.journals.yorku.ca/index.php/cdd/article/view/31564.

Kromm, Jane. 1994. "The Feminization of Madness in Visual Representation." *Feminist Studies* 20, 3. doi.org/10.2307/3178184.

Liegghio, Maria. 2013. "A Denial of Being: Psychiatrization as Epistemic Violence." In *Mad Matters: A Critical Reader in Canadian Mad Studies,* edited by B. Lefrançois, R. Menzies, and G. Reaume. Toronto: Canadian Scholars Press.

Mailhot, Terese. 2018. *Heart Berries: A Memoir.* Doubleday Canada.

Maracle, Lee. 2014. *Celia's Song.* Toronto: Cormorant Books.

Moreton-Robinson, Aileen. 2015. *The White Possessive: Property, Power, and Indigenous Sovereignty.* Minneapolis: University of Minnesota Press.

Nelson, Sarah, and Kathi Wilson. 2017. "The Mental Health of Indigenous Peoples in Canada: A Critical Review of Research." *Social Science and Medicine (1982)* 176. doi.org/10.1016/j.socscimed.2017.01.021.

Richards, Richie. 2018. "The Nation's Only Insane Asylum for Indians Was in South Dakota." *Indianz,* September 28. indianz.com/News/2018/09/28/the-nations-only-insane-asylum-for-india.asp.

Shefman, Corey. 2022. "The Indigenous Incarceration Crisis Demands a Bolder Response: Decarceration." *Globe and Mail,* May 11. theglobeandmail.com/opinion/article-the-indigenous-incarceration-crisis-demands-a-bolder-response/.

Simpson, Audra. 2016. "The State Is a Man: Theresa Spence, Loretta Saunders and the Gender of Settler Sovereignty." *Theory & Event,* 19, 4. muse.jhu.edu/article/633280.

Soros, Erin. 2018. "Writing Madness in Indigenous Literature: A Hesitation." In *Literature of Madness: Disability Studies and Mental Health,* edited by E. Donaldson. Toronto: Palgrave Macmillan.

Tam, Louise. 2013. "Whither Indigenizing the Mad Movement? Theorizing the Social Relations of Race and Madness through Conviviality." In *Mad Matters: A Critical Reader in Canadian Mad Studies,* edited by B. Lefrançois, R. Menzies, and G. Reaume. Toronto: Canadian Scholars Press.

Ussher, Jane. 2011. *The Madness of Women: Myth and Experience.* Routledge/Taylor and Francis Group. doi.org/10.4324/9780203806579.

Waldron, Ingrid. 2016. *African Canadian Women Storming the Barricades! Challenging Psychiatric Imperialism Through Indigenous Conceptualizations of 'Mental Illness' and Self-healing.* Ann Arbor: UMI Dissertation Services. psycnet.apa.org/record/2002-95023-087.

Weitz, Don. 2013. "Electroshock: Torture as 'Treatment.'" In *Mad Matters: A Critical Reader in Canadian Mad Studies,* edited by B. Lefrançois, R. Menzies, and G. Reaume. Toronto: Canadian Scholars Press.

Wolfe, Patrick. 2006. "Setter Colonialism and the Elimination of the Native." *Journal of Genocide Research* 8, 4.

THIRTEEN

On Black and Indigenous Relationality
A Conversation

*Robyn Maynard, Leanne Betasamosake Simpson
and Gina Starblanket*

GINA STARBLANKET: Thank you for joining me, Robyn and Leanne. I was hoping to start out by talking about movements within and across traditions of feminist thought — movements that have been both contested and embraced in Indigenous worlds. As I've been working on this edition, I've been spending a great deal of time thinking through the interaction and interrelation of various currents of feminism. Several works in the first and second editions of *Making Space* either implicitly or explicitly draw on Black feminist traditions, women of colour feminisms, and intersectional theories, and recognize their profound influence on Indigenous feminism. I thought in this edition it would be important to reflect deeper on these relationships.

What does it mean for currents of thought and practice to encounter one another; how might they converge, collide, or swell to produce something new? The book you wrote together, *Rehearsals for Living*, takes up crucial questions surrounding the interplay of liberatory politics across diverse political locations, histories and forms of oppression, and subject positions, in terms of what that looks like theoretically but also in on-the-ground social and political organizing. I'm deeply grateful to visit with you and talk about your important work.

Let's start by talking about the title of the book, *Rehearsals for Living*. The plural seems to gesture towards more than one possible rehearsal — can you talk about that choice or intention?

ROBYN MAYNARD: The title was one of the very last things we gave to the book, and only at the end did we finally realize, in coming to this title, that this had been what the project was all about. The book emerged organically, from thinking together, to writing letters to each other, to the decision to transform them into something that could be published. As we were writing to each other, Ruth Wilson Gilmore's words, "abolition is life in rehearsal," were always running through my mind. We were living through a moment of incredible political momentum and mobilization, not only in Toronto where I live but historic protests across Canada and the world that really were political experiments about what it could mean to demand a life otherwise. Rehearsals for living on terms other than the genocidal status quo.

As much as the project's goal was to think about what liberation might mean, we didn't anticipate that we would actually be living through this huge outpouring of rebellion and movement work, that we would be trying to think this through on the ground in the urgencies of real time. So, the plurality of the word rehearsals allows for a sense of ongoingness, a kind of unfinishedness of a thinking about movements as heterogeneous locations through which freedom work is taking place. The title unfolding in that very last moment seems fitting.

We can get bound if we look to one particular movement, whether it succeeded or failed. If we have that kind of metric, we can look to the way that a particular social movement has failed to alter the conditions of dispossession, exploitation, brutality, or to overthrow colonialism or carceral violence. This kind of vision is only partial, because it misses what happens in the making, in the doing. We're in the middle of a major struggle, we've not yet "won" — if that is to be the measure — a deep, embodied liberation. But I would never say, for example, that the Black power movement failed because Black people are still dying. If we think about movements as a dress rehearsal for trying to create the lives that we believe that we deserve — believing, for example, that Black children deserve to be fed and insisting that into the public — those kinds of transformations end up having an afterlife well beyond a particular movement's success or failure. We inherit a multitude of "timelines of otherwise" from past generations, some of which I invoke in the book. Western states and multinationals have systematically assassinated most freedom movements the world over. So one could never say, for example, that the African and Caribbean independence movements — which were partial, unfinished projects — "failed" as a result of internal factors alone. But there is a dualness here because movements are also flawed, and this has been true historically. We continue to be let down in some ways by contemporary movements. Again, thinking about freedom-making as a process, or a plurality of processes, really helps us to still stay committed to the movements we're grounded in while keeping our eyes on the larger horizon.

In the book *Abolition. Feminism. Now.* by Erica Meiners, Beth Richie, Angela Y. Davis, and Gina Dent, they articulate beautifully how grassroots groupings that most of us might not remember — small feminist and anti-racist collectives throughout the 1980s and 1990s in Chicago and elsewhere that did good work but came and went without impacting legislation or making headlines — nonetheless were not failed at all. They seeded these possible future timelines that made possible the moment now, where suddenly we have huge amounts of the population in Chicago and across North America saying maybe we could defund the police. I have written about similar ways that previous generations of Black feminists in Canada seeded much of what is now taken as "common sense" in contemporary movement circles. So "rehearsals" is a way of thinking about the ways that movements and freedom practices live outside of the temporal or spatial boundaries in which we might locate them.

LEANNE BETASAMOSAKE SIMPSON: That line from Ruth Wilson Gilmore was so foundational to this book because in my work I see Indigenous practices, whether those are land-based practices or ceremonial practices or ethical practices — practices of care for the water, the land, and each other — are really generative sites of knowledge production. Any time Indigenous Peoples or people are coming together on the land or in urban settings or on the reserve or in remote settings and are making something otherwise, we are aligning ourselves with our origin stories and generating the world-making knowledge that we would need to imagine beyond this present moment. This is foundational to my work and to *Rehearsals for Living*. I see that the struggle of radical Black feminist abolitionists working and generating Black feminist epistemologies and ontologies as the theoretical work of that movement is distinctive from my struggle and it is entirely as related to my struggle. It is related to imagining and making alternatives outside of the box of capitalism.

We never get it quite right because it is work that is beyond us. It involves visioning; it involves dreaming; it involves this hardcore amount of organizing, conflict resolution, administrative work, care work, mutual aid, all those types of things. These are practical ways of meeting the needs of our communities and they are also knowledge-generating practices. I think of these things as rehearsals. In rehearsal, we don't have to be perfect and if we are momentarily perfect, we *practise* again. We become the practices. It makes a lot of sense to me as a musician because I spend a lot of time in rehearsal, and rehearsals are a durational practice. Many, many Indigenous land- and water-based practices and ceremonies are durational, processes we do together over and over again, in different seasons, in collaboration with living things and our ancestors, across geographies and through time.

In rehearsals, there is more room for imagination, there's more room for a creative sovereignty where you're bringing different artists together to make something, and then you're taking that on the road and doing it over and over in front of different audiences. Being on the road with Robyn, different parts of the book speak to me in different moments with different audiences. I like that movement and I like that thinking. I love it when I read something to an audience and think to myself, "Wow, I no longer think exactly like that, that was a moment in time." It means I've transformed and grown. And I think the epistolary nature of the book emphasizes the quotidian and contextualizes our thinking in the present. I am grateful to those foundational practices of letter writing, of Indigenous feminisms, of Black feminisms.

GINA: That's such a crucial insight, the notion that political theorizing and activism are never perfect; there's going to be mistakes. How could it be perfect unless there was a mould or model, which would restrict and betray the notion of movement. Process is such a contentious thing in feminist organizing and it takes up a lot of time and energy, so I love how you're thinking about the need to be generous with each other and the importance of carving out that space of non-judgment that allows creative energy to flow. You're modelling the ethic you're talking about in your writing.

You're also modelling a particular form of freedom work that is significant in and of itself — you're conceiving of these notions of liberation and freedom that are deeply relational. Women tend to get associated across cultures with creation in terms of bodily and biological capacity to give life, but if we think about the act of "giving life" in a capacious and generative way, you're creating a series of alternatives to more masculinist visions of freedom grounded upon the notion of an autonomous individual or collective. Your vision of freedom — it's relational but it's also very hopeful and future-oriented. Could you talk a bit more about this?

LEANNE: I go back to Anishinaabe thought. We never do anything in isolation. Life and world making — mino-bimaadiziwin, this practice of continually bringing forth more life — it's never done alone. Our origin stories are always different collaborations, different forces of life, different species, different forms of life coming together to figure out a way of living together and bringing forth more life and that happens over and over again.

Relationship building, then, is very important. Often in Nishnaabe thought, you have political practices that move across scales, ethical practices that move across scales, so you have practices of care within families, within clans, within communities, within nations, that relate to the different nations of plants and animals and peoples we're sharing time and space with.

When I think of movement building within Nishnaabe thought, it always starts with visiting, sharing food, sharing songs and ceremonies sometimes, doing something together, getting to know people. It starts with relationships, and that takes a lot of time. It wasn't the first time I met Robyn, but I think the book started with a solidarity gathering in Yellowknives Dene Territory that Robyn and I were a part of. It was part of my work at the Dechinta Centre for Research and Learning, and we spent time together on the land — outside the institution, outside the Internet, outside crises, outside organizing in the moment — to relate and get to know each other. We went fishing, we shared food, we rode snowmobiles, we chatted, and that was it. It wasn't magic, but there was also magic there. Letter writing was an extension of that initial land-based gathering.

The colonial gender binary relegates intimacy and relationship building to the sphere of women. Within Nishnaabeg thought though, doing care work, being kind, developing healthy bonds with all the life you're sharing time and space with is the responsibility of everyone of all genders and orientations.

I was drawn to Robyn because of her work in *Policing Black Lives*. This is an incredibly important book in Canada because it destroys Canadian exceptionalism in terms of the Transatlantic Slave Trade and, as Saidiya Hartman says, its afterlives. It speaks in a meticulous and thorough way to Canada's anti-Black present. I was drawn to Robyn because she's uncompromising in terms of anti-capitalism. Her practice refuses borders and enclosures and the ideas of property, prisons, and the state, because her practice is about building coalitions. Robyn's well practised in movement politics and well read in radical Black feminist thought. And the first letter Robyn wrote me had an intimacy to it; there was a friendship to it. That's part of Indigenous practice; that's part of Indigenous life. There's often an intimacy built into our stories, our ceremonies, our gatherings, our humour, the way that we are in the world. I saw that in Robyn's work, and that made the connection really easy.

We didn't set out to write a book. We set out to write letters to each other, not thinking that the letters would ever be read by anyone else other than the two of us. We were thinking through together. This practice was taking place for the most part during the pandemic; we didn't have a grant, we didn't have research objectives, we didn't have a prospectus, we didn't have any of that. It was an emergent project without supervisors or academic presses telling us how to construct our arguments or the voice we had to write in. We weren't writing in an authoritarian voice or as experts. We didn't have to follow those conventions I find so white and so masculinist. We could relate to each other in the way that felt most natural to us. This was a personal, political project between the two of us that for the creation phase was only about expanding ourselves and our own thinking.

ROBYN: I really love the way you answered that, Leanne. This project began as a care work, as relationship building, as thinking together about the possibilities of liberatory futures. Leanne's work drew me, especially in *As We Have Always Done*. I started thinking about this notion of constellations of co-resistance as a concept I wanted to follow.

I remember being on the land with Dechinta — you bringing me coffee in the mornings, for example, or just watching the way Elders were caring for some of the younger Freedom School kids who had come. It was relation-centric at its core. We were sitting around talking about freedom movements that had inspired us in the past, present, and future, but even less romantically you, as our hosts, were also just making sure everyone was warm enough and had food to eat. Those basic building blocks of relationships of trust are very different than meeting the deliverables of a grant. It allows for tenderness and nurtures possibilities for vulnerability that ended up really being an anchor of the text in a lot of ways.

I think the letter format allowed for that as well; knowledge production in academia is patriarchal in that it trains us to assert a stance of all-knowingness, of telling rather than asking, of responding to critiques with defensive counter critiques. It is a kind of staking out of a territory: you are meant to identify the gaps in literature, and *fill them*. Vulnerability, ongoing reflexivity, and the notion that we may yet be missing something that we hope to find along the way — this is often seen as a weakness. Yet continually asking questions of yourself, learning from others along the way, seeing where you erred or were less clear and keeping up that work to *fix it* — this is a practice I see Leanne modelling that I hold dear, and that I hope to forever maintain both in writing but also in my life and movement work. We need to continue revisiting ourselves, questioning ourselves. As Ruthie writes in the foreword of our book, "practice makes different." The best parts of feminist work have been practising this for a long time.

Vulnerability is scary. But Audre Lorde has so importantly instructed us not to pretend that we're not afraid, not to push fear away and to overcome it totally, but to learn how to live with it. In *The Cancer Journals* she says, "We can learn to work and speak when we are afraid in the same way we have learned to work and speak when we are tired. For we have been socialized to respect fear more than our own needs for language and definition, and while we wait in silence for that final luxury of fearlessness, the weight of that silence will choke us." We can live with it and through it and hold it close but we don't need to let it overcome us. We don't have to divorce ourselves from fears of *getting it wrong*; it can be part of who we are, part of our thinking. I think that's crucial to organizing — you know, work that ended up going horribly wrong, but holds a lesson for us. There are moments where we do have to just continue to reassess if we want to be useful. This is necessarily done with others, necessarily relational. Of course, there is a responsibility to be taken in these moments. There is a responsibility to undertake political education such that we are not senselessly repeating past errors. It is a *thinking through,* and it is never-ending.

To speak to another part of your question, Gina: without straying into gender essentialism, I do think the way women and femmes and folks identifying on the feminine end of the gender spectrum have been pushed into the reproductive labour of our society has meant learning particular skills and playing that role in social movements. We often talk about the violence of forcing that labour upon so many of us, and rightfully so: the racialized and gendered division of reproductive labour and care work is a crucial site of local and global injustice and an ongoing site of transnational feminist struggle! But lately I've also been thinking about how at a smaller scale, so much of care work is also joy even as it's "labour." We know that patriarchy functions to try to strip men of the capacity to care; it does not nurture the capacity for relationality. Cis-heteropatriarchy has gendered our society's divisions of skills and capacities. What it could mean to push back against those normative systems in ways that would allow us all to access both the labour and the joy of that tender care work, to push off its devaluation and allow us all to participate more expansively?

GINA: I really appreciate what you're saying; when we move beyond identity-related differences or the particularity of our political locations, the possibilities for coalition and bridge building become so much more capacious.

At a certain level, it becomes a question of unity versus contextuality. What are the stakes or risks in this question? When you're trying to build those bridges and shift ideas of who you're in solidarity with, do you ever worry that if a movement attempts to attend to too much, then it might lose its focus and specificity? Do movements towards unity and solidarity pose a risk to precision and depth in our critiques and to our diverse political locations/experience of oppression?

LEANNE: Nishnaabe life is all about relationship building and coalition. I'm thinking of those old Elders who talk to the strawberries before they pick them, how they pray to the water in the morning, how they're in constant dialogue and constant conversation, nurturing the relationships all around them all the time. I see my survival and the survival of Indigenous movements as dependent upon coalition building. I see that there are tremendous things to be learned from other anti-colonial movements organizing in our own homelands and in other parts of the world. I see sharing and learning as very rich and generative, and I would push back against this idea that it dilutes or takes away from the gains.

When I was an undergrad, my politics were very much influenced by radical Black feminists because there were books written by radical Black feminists and there wasn't a lot of writing in the '80s and '90s about Indigenous feminisms yet. The Combahee River Collective in 1974 were talking about how their critique comes from this radical Black feminist place because that is where they live their lives — but they did not stop there. They made links and coalitions with other organizations and movements. That was really foundational for me politically and ethically, and it resonated for me with Nishnaabe practice of ethics. So, I say build a very strong movement to address missing and murdered Indigenous women, Two-Spirit and queer people, *and* be aware of and aligned with radical Black feminist abolitionist movements. Go to the February 14th protest at Toronto Police Headquarters *and* then get out to support the Month of Action for a city without police. Be a good relative. Redistribute resources. Study.

That to me is the practice; that is the ethics. That is how we are going to make new worlds. It's not ethical to build a new world for me in my Michi Saagiig Nishnaabeg Territory and be just like, I don't care what you guys do on the Prairies, I don't care what you do in the North, I don't care what is happening in the Niger Delta or in Palestine. That's not an ethical practice. From an Nishnaabe perspective, it is our responsibility to figure out how to fit into this beautiful, chaotic, complex, planetary system of ecology in a way that brings forth more life. We have to refuse racial capitalism, white supremacy, and heteropatriarchy in order to do that. I've learned a lot about colonialism from radical Black feminists, and that has made me a better Nishnaabe. I think it's created more knowledge for all of us to figure out how to refuse and build otherwise.

ROBYN: Even the phrase identity politics we need to rescue from the way it was appropriated by the right — Taiwo calls it "elite capture." If we think about it back to the way the Combahee River Collective had meant it, it was meant to be expansive. The place we are coming from in our own positions — for them, this was their particular experience as Black poor lesbian women — our lived experience is meant to be expansive, a place of departure that can lead us into coalition work, toward freedom. It's meant to be the entry point from which we can understand that all of our liberations are interdependent. The right has made identity politics a sort of "us versus other historically oppressed groups." But at the root, it was about intervening in the notion that, for example, if Black lesbian women are organizing as Black lesbian women, then somehow that means they're not deeply involved in organizing against police killings of Black men or US imperialism. These things are intrinsically linked.

I think this is one of the gifts of this concept and perhaps why it was considered so threatening they tried to destroy it. Because it helps inform both lasting forms of collective struggle based on shared oppression, as well as short-term, strategic coalitions. Having strategic goals at certain political moments has been really helpful in allowing us to make important gains, even when they are necessarily incomplete when weighed against the larger scale of liberation.

So, for example, I can believe that we should end capitalism if the earth is going to survive, *and* it's not necessary for everyone to agree with me about that if we are oriented toward a short-term goal. In 2016–17, all kinds of people in Toronto worked together to get police out of schools in the Toronto District School Board — BLM-TO, LAEN, Education Not Incarceration, and Jane and Finch Action Against Poverty, but also large numbers of teachers, community services, trustees, Black parents, youth — in short, people who were not necessarily aligned on every political idea and coming from different backgrounds but saw, from their own perspective, that Black kids were being imperilled in schools by the presence of School Resource Officers. They won, and while systemic oppression is not gone, we are no longer hearing stories about seven-year-old Black girls being handcuffed in Toronto schools. Given the awfulness of the status quo, that is a win. It was a specific goal that mattered for children, period. That's more than okay; it's fundamentally necessary that sometimes coalitions come and go, as driven by necessity, in a particular moment. They're rarely permanent, and that doesn't mean it's a defeat.

There's a kind of strength in unity so long as that unity is not random, and so long as it is not overly compromised. Some alliances are impossible if you have a conscience: when so-called feminists are aligning with the right to eliminate trans women's access to public and political life, this is a ghoulish form of unity. But there is strength in a strategic and principled unity, when we see our lives as interdependent and understand that we're sharing a common antagonist.

When I think about both changing everything and maintaining specificity in our goals, I think about the last few years of organizing towards defunding/abolishing the police. In Toronto and across Canada, we see these incredible movements born of the earlier movements in defence of Black life, to end police murders, and the broader program of surveillance and terror inflicted on Black folks by policing. But at this time, there's a lot of organizing that's very coalition based. A few months back, I helped to organize a Month of Action against policing that came together under the mantle "Another Toronto Is Possible," and it involved a number of groups and collectives who were coming at policing and police violence from different perspectives. No Pride in Policing, for example, is coming at it from the histories of queer and Black and Indigenous folks being harmed by police. There are people involved who are part of migrant justice struggles. Some of the issues coming up are around the lack of decent housing and the relentless police attacks on folks living in encampments. As co-organizers No More Silence continue to say, the police are actively criminalizing poor Indigenous folks while never taking up their ostensible "job" when it comes to locating missing and murdered Indigenous women. Law enforcement, as the enforcement wing of racial capitalism, is the antagonist in so many people's lives: Black folks, Indigenous, trans, disabled, migrant, and of course these are not mutually exclusive categories. So many groups can organize in short-term coalitions towards a larger aim, which at this point in Toronto is reallocating 50 percent of the police budget to community supports. I don't think that dilutes any of the message because it allows everyone to bring a specific analysis into an interlinked goal, working against one of the drivers of unfreedom in so many of our communities.

We're not in a particularly revolutionary moment right now, three years after the historic protests of 2020. There are moments when one of our communities is particularly active. We saw that with Black radical struggle in recent years; we've seen that with Indigenous land defence. But often in the between times — with no central, widely supported uprising — we see these temporary but important coalitions come together that bring back the ways all our liberatory struggles are tied to one another. That's something really powerful that doesn't take away from what are often more specifically oriented moments of mass unrest.

Solidarities matter as long as we are not asked to push specificity to the side. We know, for example, that in anti-colonial struggles and in some elements of North American Black liberation movements, women were literally told, "Put gender to the side, race first. Let's fight colonialism, we got you after." We saw the horrific outcomes historically when people were forced to subordinate really important kinds of marginalization for another struggle. This teaches us that even in a larger movement, we cannot afford to ask anybody to suppress or efface the very real challenges and specificities of their oppression.

Living as a Black woman in Canada, a country where Black people are 4.3 percent of the population, I don't know that we could, just us, successfully organize toward the abolition of police even if 100 percent of Black people were actively organizing every day toward that goal. So, if we want to imagine what it might mean to build non-carceral futures, I think we need to think both specifically and expansively.

I'm thinking back to Reconstruction in the United States right after the abolition of slavery. There is a reason why Angela Y. Davis is always pushing us to think about abolition democracy in that period, particularly as articulated by the work of W.E.B. Du Bois. It matters because formerly enslaved Black people were not content with the absence of formal enslavement; they were trying to build public schools, access to health, housing — creating the kinds of conditions for people of all races to thrive in the absence of racial violence was the project. In the end, the white ruling class won out, and many poor, working-class white people chose their own exploitation so they could have a position just slightly higher than that of Black folks. Decades of segregation and racial terror against Black people followed but while poor white folks may have had more status, nobody, not even most white folks, could be truly described as free. Even if that unfreedom was mediated crucially through race, gender, class. But the choice to abandon the possibility of a multi-racial, egalitarian democracy was not predestined, and the more people are capable of seeing their liberation as bound up with one another's the better our chances of a more emancipatory outcome next time around. We have something to learn from all of this.

GINA: I really appreciate how you situate the absence of racial violence as the project. Because it's often our own frames that can get us into trouble and limit our vision. For instance, the presumption that feminists are only arguing for their own individual rights is partial and incomplete. In actuality, when you look at the political claims being advanced our work is much more expansive. We're arguing for decolonization, anti-violence, racial equality, anti-capitalism, and so on. I like how you put that at the fore again, because if you interpreted the project as Black acts of radical activism or Black feminism, a lot of people would think "that's not for me" or they would wonder about their role in it. My non-Indigenous students often ask about the relevance of Indigenous feminism and Black feminism in my classes, and I encourage them to think beyond an identity frame and about the feminist commitments and principles they can apply from their positionality. The movements don't have to map onto each other entirely; we can do our own work alongside *and* in relation to one another where there are areas of convergence. I'm thinking of a Venn diagram that has specifics, but then there's also these areas of overlap.

ROBYN: I think that's very correct. For example, Black people are disproportionately killed by the police. But we're not fighting to die at the same proportion as white people. Justice wouldn't be just having more measured stats; it's the end of policing for all people. It's primarily or disproportionately our communities and Indigenous communities being harmed, yes, but there's also a lot of poor white people, a lot of unhoused white people in mental health crises, and though they may not want to recognize it, a middle-class white person is only a few layoffs away from finding themselves in that same position. Right? So, it's about, again, people really understanding that racial capitalism was only meant to profit very few people.

   White folks have a lot to gain from joining in liberatory movements, and though I don't make my primary activism goal educating or convincing, I do think that's fundamentally true. It's what usually brings people into this struggle, not only sympathy, and it shouldn't really only be that. Sometimes you just have to act to support people in a moment. But to understand that your own reality is bound up in the liberation of others — that's what Combahee River Collective was trying to tell us.

GINA: We're all in relation to these matters, right? Just differently situated in relation to them and I love how you each give that perspective to provide a fuller picture on structural forms of oppression. Indigenous feminists have grappled with this question in many forms. I'm thinking, for example, about the call to not defer a critique of gendered violence until liberation. It's a huge question, but process wise: how do we make space for those internal conversations and questions in the face of a range of political priorities?

ROBYN: I think a lot of my own political education was seeing, for example, Ellen Gabriel at the forefront of struggles to defend land and life in Kanehsatà:ke. Hers is not a community I am a part of, but it shaped my understanding of solidarity. It was instructive in my formative years as a baby organizer to witness the way Indigenous women across Turtle Island have been at the forefront of taking on the state around land defence and gendered violence. It's an incredible model and rubric for what anti-colonial struggle has looked like in the place I live. This is something I'm trying to teach my students right now: colonialism was always a gendered project, everywhere. I've learned so much about the history of the Indian Act just looking to the legislative understanding of how colonialism happened here.

Looking to the history of the scramble for Africa, colonialism dismantled communal and other forms of kinship mechanisms such that African woman had to be, as in many European colonies, subjugated politically, socially, economically not only by the colonial state but also by their husbands. If you weren't married, then you literally couldn't move through public space without being policed. Colonialism was a violent insertion of a patriarchal order, a heteropatriarchal order, too, which criminalized most forms of not-heterosexual sex. This is the history of colonialism, slavery, and those who lived this knew it better than anyone. They warned anybody who would listen. Gender can never just be an afterthought, because then we're actually missing something central to the co-constitutive structuring logics of racism, slavery, colonialism, ecological violence, and capitalism.

Even after nominal independence, the ostensibly post-colonial state remained both a carceral state and — in most cases — a patriarchal state. M. Jacqui Alexander writes crucially about post-colonial Trinidad and Tobago: after independence, women, people who were considered to be sex workers, people who were considered to be cross-dressers, they were all criminalized. We saw similar realities in Zimbabwe shortly after independence, and across much of the global Black world in the post-colonial moment. We can see the real, lived, material realities of what happens when we ask — or force, often by violence — women to subordinate their own liberation to the broader project of freedom. People are still living and dying in the aftermath of choices forced upon them by heteropatriarchal forces. Heteropatriarchy was imported through colonialism, sure, but has taken a powerful hold: if we're not careful we will not successfully eradicate it within our own communities. Any meaningful anti-colonial movement anywhere needs to address these things to be successful, so as not to recreate the kind of disposability that emerged in the wake of previous anti-colonial struggles.

LEANNE: This question is hitting me personally because gender violence has been an unwelcomed companion of mine for my entire life. In some ways the answer is in the question: we must be continually attentive and avoid the deferral around gender. Full stop. It is never okay to see an organization or a movement or a political negotiation as more important than addressing gender violence and transforming ourselves and our communities. Gender violence is a tool of colonialism, and it can cause a cluster bomb of damage in individuals and collectives very quickly. I've learned a lot from Black abolitionists around creative and community interventions into violence that are transformative rather than punitive and disciplinary. Our current legal systems, human resources departments, and harassment policies in many ways are designed to perpetuate harm, and so I'm grateful to the labour and brilliance of Black women and Black abolitionists for teaching me ways of addressing harm that centre those that were harmed but also work to transform those causing harm.

Another answer to this question is in *As We Have Always Done*. That book was the response to gender and heteronormative power in the resurgence movement in Indigenous movements at the time. Another answer is in, well, how that book gets positioned in terms of resurgence theory. My work is often positioned as an Indigenous feminist afterthought rather than theory, rather than as significant as some of the other male Indigenous academics. This has been my experience throughout most of my career.

An Indigenous man will say something or write a book and be quite famous, and a queer Indigenous person or an Indigenous woman will have said the same thing and it's ignored. I think that's true for all of us, right? So, I think there's lots and lots of work to be done there and there is a lot to be learned from the citational practices of Black women.

In a different context — I've spent a lot of time with hunters and with trappers, most of whom are cis men, and that's been a great joy of my life. I've had those difficult conversations, particularly with Doug Williams in my own territory. We've talked about all the taboos around menstruation, around skirt wearing, around how we're going to handle all of this in ceremony. I had a longstanding friendship, an intimate relationship of trust over such a long period of time where I had those conversations. And the same thing happens with those Dene Elders around homophobia, around transphobia.

GINA: What I'm hearing is you're making space for those critical conversations and you're doing it in a way that's not alienating but potentially actually transformative. I really appreciate that.

ROBYN: What you're speaking to, Leanne, is so powerful in terms of the direct relational work of building those changes. The politics of the movement for Black lives in 2020, and in the years preceding too, in some ways offered us a movement where we're actually seeing — I'm speaking to my own communities here — Black queer women involved in a movement that's very much grounded and understood as a movement against police killings of Black men, Black boys. But this time we have worked hard, all of us, not to allow the actual labour, the leadership, the real intellectual and political work that Black women do and have done for these movements, to be pushed to the side as it has in the past.

The movement is really writing its own history, and also people are writing their own histories. If we look to books like *No More Police* (Kaba and Ritchie 2022) or *Abolition. Feminism. Now.* (Davis et al. 2022) and in Canada *Defund, Dismantle, Abolish* (Pasternak et al. 2022), we see more clearly the feminist histories of these movements. And we see a telling of the *ongoing* movements being articulated in real time. The media's still going to do what the media's going to do, as will some academics, in terms of obfuscation. Black women's grassroots labours are still disregarded, devalued, and appropriated. But I think this has been *less* possible now than at other moments in history. Movements have still done incredible, powerful work and built infrastructure drawing out the longer histories of abolitionist thinking; some comes from incarcerated people, elders in the Black Panther Party and the Black Liberation Army, all of this. Survivors have really paved the way: survivor-led struggles against domestic violence, survivor-led struggles against all kinds of intimate partner violence are also ways that we can think about safety, a world beyond policing.

Movements today are creating much more expansive visions for what safety could be like for everyone, what abolitionist futures could be like for everyone. It's shown us the power of what can actually change when we centre a wider array of experiences. When we centre the experiences of queer and trans people, it doesn't take anything away from a powerful movement that had people in the street for months in defence of Black life; it enriches it and makes it more powerful and more dangerous to the status quo. It does not shrink but expands liberatory possibilities. Whether or not those possibilities will transform our future, we don't know — because our futures are being written and struggled over as we speak.

REFERENCES

Alexander, M. Jacqui. 2006. *Pedagogies of Crossing: Meditations on Feminism, Sexual Politics, Memory, and the Sacred.* Durham: Duke University Press.

Combahee River Collective. N.D. "The Combahee River Collective Statement." americanstudies.yale.edu/sites/default/files/files/Keyword%20Coalition_Readings.pdf.

Davis, Angela Y., et al. 2022. *Abolition. Feminism. Now.* Chicago: Haymarket Books.

Kaba, Mariame, and Andrea Ritchie. 2022. *No More Police.* New York: New Press.

Lorde, Audre. 1980. *The Cancer Journals.* Spinsters/Aunt Lute Books. monoskop.org/images/1/16/Lorde_Audre_The_Cancer_Journals_2nd_ed_1980.pdf.

Maynard, Robyn. 2017. *Policing Black Lives.* Halifax: Fernwood Publishing.

Maynard, Robyn, and Leanne Betasamosake Simpson. 2022. *Rehearsals for Living.* Chicago: Haymarket Books.

Pasternak, Shiri, et al. (eds.). 2022. *Disarm, Defund, Dismantle: Police Abolition in Canada.* Toronto: Between the Lines.

Simpson, Leanne Betasamosake. 2017. *As We Have Always Done.* Minneapolis: University of Minnesota Press.

FOURTEEN

Decolonization Is Also Metaphorical

Indigenous Feminist and Queer–Two-Spirit Storywork Matters

Kelly Aguirre

IN THIS CHAPTER I TAKE UP the phrase "decolonization is not a metaphor" from the 2012 article by Eve Tuck and K. Wayne Yang — writing in its tenth year of discursive travelling — as a kind of rhetorical prism. Like a prism, the phrase *refracts*. In Zoe Todd's (2017, 142) deployment of a prism metaphor, she describes refraction as "the bending of light through a glass material and its related phenomenon, dispersion — which is the scattering of the wavelengths that make up white light." I can add that this scattering reveals a rainbow of colours both satisfyingly camp and redolent with meaning for a queer person like myself. Though this rhetorical prism refracts in many directions, I'll speak to a complex problem it reveals that provides opportunity for a reaffirmation. This is an opportunity to reaffirm the generative necessity of Indigenous feminist and what I (imperfectly) term *queer–Two-Spirit* storywork to our decolonial movements, which is the aim of this chapter. Hopefully, I'll speak to this without further scattering the light this prism throws on other critical issues too much.[1] Todd suggests Indigenous Peoples' constant and sometimes contradictory negotiations of "sameness and difference" interrupts "colonial thinking" to "reveal its constituent components" (2017, 142). Refraction can therefore evoke a subversive disruption of intentions: white light in, rainbow out. To recall and take up such phrases as Tuck and Yang's in this chapter title and subsequent sections,[2] is to acknowledge our citational and intellectual precedents and the power in these phrases' (re)iteration, particularly when they become received maxims or even slogans. To consider how such phrases refract through repetition indicates how we might also bend the light with them to illuminate the obscured, as the recently departed si'yam Lee Maracle described of critical inquiry.[3] Particularly, problems they may implicate without intention, and which may not be readily apparent when only attending to a phrase's most immediate efficacy for political mobilization.

The problem Tuck and Yang's phrase prismatically helps illuminate for me are recursions — or reinforcing repetitions — of what I'll call *colonial-straight thinking* in a presently normative grammar of decolonization. By normative grammar here I mean both a lexicon and rules of comportment that make up a language and repertoire of practices, aspirations, or ideals that have become broadly standardized and regulative.[4] With colonial-straight thinking I mean both a straightening and colonizing response to difference or dualities in the establishment of norms by ordering them into oppositional and hierarchical categories or binaries, and then attempting to exclude, minimize, or assimilate that which is decided as irreconcilably divergent, to the dominant. This disallows fluidity, porousness, entanglement, and other modes of relation between poles or positions that are considered mutually exclusive. It also disallows conceiving some apparent dualities as positively reciprocal, co-constitutive, or complementary rather than in competition. In conception and application of colonial-straight thinking, I'm here mostly following the late Maria Lugones (2010) and Jodi Byrd (2020). Byrd describes *normative* in queer theory as a shorthand for structural power relations that draw "lines of distinction between what is deemed normal and natural from what is aberrant and deviant," at the sites of bodies and their ruling "ethics, politics, and morality." They quote Jack Halberstram that straight-thinking can then be "characterized by a matrix of rhetorical operations that support the common sense of the moment, commit to foreclosing on critiques of the status quo and reinvest in the ordinary, the good and the true" (Byrd 2020, 114–15). Colonial-straight thinking can in my framing also involve dismissing immanent critiques of "good" rhetorical strategies from within movements. Critiques that respond to any potentially repressive internal ordering of difference.

This includes when such strategies are framed as politically necessary albeit transitional. For example, deference to national liberation as an anti-colonial argument for postponing redress of internalized misogyny and gendered discrimination, which has continuously been intervened on by Indigenous feminists. However, "decolonization is not a metaphor" for me prompts reflection on more oblique issues of colonial-straight thinking in prevailing currents and circles of activism and scholarship I move within and have been profoundly influenced by, specifically associated with the discourse of Indigenous resurgence.

In their 2020 article "What's Normative Got to Do With It?" Byrd discusses resurgence discourse's emphasis on the return of and to land through conceptions of "*grounded normativity*" and "*embodied-materiality*" and touches on how their prevalent significations might provide examples of "straight-thinking." I will unpack and extend this observation to consider how Tuck and Yang's phrase encapsulates a common sentiment regarding what decolonization is and must be and not merely isn't. This raises concerns for me about recursions of colonial-straight thinking, though their work isn't self-situated within and so by no means stands in for the scope of resurgence discourse. These concerns on recursion are, I contend, relevant to both Indigenous feminist and queer–Two-Spirit storywork, while providing an opportunity to reaffirm this storywork *matters* in multivalent senses, not despite but *as* metaphorical. To assert that the use of the word *metaphor* matters, particularly when used to signal and disparage an absence or lack of materiality and (so) value, is to assert storywork is *consequential* in several valences: *Matters* as in issues of relevance to us, as in valuation as important, as having effects and affects, and as processes of manifesting, making, or materializing. Donna Haraway's use of *mattering* can be evoked here to "implode metaphor and materiality" by upholding "projects of description, narration, intervention, inhabiting, conversing, exchanging and building" that do not only critically read but seek to *refigure* "what counts as knowledge in the interests of reconstituting the generative forces of embodiment." Here "the point is to get at how worlds are made and unmade, in order to participate in the processes, in order to foster some forms of life and not others" (Haraway 1994, 59–62).[5]

The rest of this chapter will outline how Indigenous feminist and queer–Two-Spirit storyworking against and outside colonial-straight thinking is refigurative and crucial to interrogate and nuance deployments of a language of normativity, groundedness, embodiment, and materiality in our rhetorical strategies as scholars and activists. Examples can be found in feminist and queer–Two-Spirit engagements with metaphor-laden expressions of traditionalism in relation to gendered subjectivities and relationships with land and water. These examples can also indicate a complementary and non-assimilative confluence of Indigenous feminist and queer–Two-Spirit storywork that disrupts cis-heteropatriarchy in the common-sense grammar of decolonial movements. This is a prismatic rainbow disruption that occurs not only in our political imaginaries but at fundamental levels of onto-epistemology, a concept linking theories or understandings of being and those of knowing (such as Vanessa Watts's [2013] description of Indigenous "place-thought"). It's a setting out of some further terms I'll turn to first.

FOR WHOM METAPHOR MATTERS

Like many I once disidentified with a feminist label as fixed to the whitestream, not feeling principally oppressed by my assignment as a woman. Then I met the work of Indigenous women scholars, poets, orators, writers, artists, and public intellectuals, part of if not a unilinear genealogy, then kin network, woven with all the threads of beautiful tension that can bind an extended family, and which the first editions of *Making Space* and others like Dian Million and Kim Anderson have traced (Million 2009; Anderson 2021). I now consider Indigenous feminist as a *posture* — an analytic and politics that we assume through *what* and *how* we *do* and *why*, rather than as a defensive identarian category, strictly determined by or determining *who* we *are*.[6] I use the term queer–Two-Spirit (Q2S hereafter) to signal a specifically marked as Indigenous yet non-determinative queer analytic and politics similarly.[7] Though this may raise questions of their appropriation or dissolution as postures distinctive to Indigenous women or trans and Q2S people, for example in relation to decolonial feminism, this is presently how I assume these terms.[8] I'm interested in the conversation between Indigenous feminist and Q2S storywork, in which their differences while generatively frictional are also "inter-referential amid the persistent and transforming power of settler colonialism" (Morgensen 2011, 22).[9]

Indigenous storywork is a phrase most associated with Stó:lō methodologist Jo-Ann Archibald (2008; Archibald et al. 2019), though it appears widely in Indigenous studies. To engage in storywork is for some about animating ancestral stories and story forms, in substance and method, within or to give shape to, our scholarship and literatures, or the myriad of other expressive mediums we move through.[10] In academic contexts, this may include a weaving with personal experiential stories to "craft an analysis" (Wesley 2014, 339). This storywork comes with a range of permissions and levels of access to meanings made with them. As a critical theorist, I consider storywork in my context as an intentioned and principled (or self-conscious and conscientious) political praxis of *storying* and *restorying* experiences, events, and phenomena. Not to ascribe right meaning as an authorial imposition on (especially others') stories, but *to tell of, as* in effort to "foster some forms of life and not others" (Haraway 1994, 62). This is how I take *storying* up in this chapter. I follow Lee Maracle and others that storying can involve drawing distinctions as well as patterns and linkages between experiences, events, and phenomena, or to trace movement and pathways taken and potential through time and place. This tracking may be to recount or *re-member* after fragmentation as per Maracle, or may be entirely speculative, to not only give accounts of what *was* and *is*, but what *could* or *might* be, what Beth Brant (1994, 74) characterized as "knowing what has transpired and dreaming of what will come. Listening to the stories brought to us by other beings. Renewing ourselves in the midst of chaos." This is a form of bearing witness toward imbuing affirmational meanings in or transforming our present realities, the sometimes "unbearable circumstances of our lives" (Brant 1994, 70).[11] Storywork as a way of conceiving our theorizing rejects as Maracle put it, the "alienated notion that maintains that theory is separate from story" (2015) and that neither is without worlding force. Story is theory is practice, and in fact it's *work*, in Archibald's (2008, 4) sense of its gravity as labour.[12] It is of the world and it also worlds or re-worlds.

My sense of storywork as an Indigenous feminist and Q2S mode of theorizing or strategy of inquiry specifically,[13] is in its challenge to disparagements of storytelling in the face of physical violence and realities of structural-material oppression as naïve, irrational, escapist, or fantastic — precisely because it has been coded as Native *and* feminine, or *queer* to Euro-Modernity's Man and his ways of being-knowing-doing. In other words, as Native women's work. Storytelling is part of the pre-Modern cultural and so apolitical or infra-political repertoire of the constitutive Others to what Aileen Moreton-Robinson (2011, 414) calls a patriarchal whiteness that operates as a "raced and gendered epistemological a priori."[14] To tell stories against violence in belief of their mattering is a form of magical thinking, a brown effeminate "coping strategy that involves making words stand in for the world" (Jackson 2002, 17–18, 35).[15] This is evoked for me when Tuck and Yang (2012, 2) open their article with a quote from Frantz Fanon's great manifesto *Les Damnés de la Terre* that decolonization "cannot come as a result of magical practices." For Fanon the colonized eventually relinquishes a "ritualized pantomime" of liberation through futile performances of agency like dance and storytelling, "discovers reality and transforms it through his praxis." Invariably "with his back to the wall, the knife at his throat, or to be more exact the electrode on his genitals, the colonized subject is bound to stop telling stories" (Fanon 2004, 20–21). In the assault on his body and being, *he* will be made to *act*. The literal destroys the figurative. Reality destroys the imaginative. Materiality destroys metaphor.[16] I've grappled a long time with this passage in *Les Damnés* in its implications for Indigenous politics when Fanon is invoked, and this leads me to the concept of grounded normativity in resurgence discourse, part of a lineage of activist scholarship influenced by the esteemed Martinican doctor's anti-colonial theory and rhetorics.

BODIES ON THE GROUND TO STAND ON: GROUNDED NORMATIVITY

> "Colonialism is as much about the symbolic diminishment of Indigenous peoples as the displacement of our physical presence …" — Justice (2018, xviii)

A 2020 critical engagement with "Decolonization Is Not a Metaphor" by Black studies scholars Tapji Garba and Sara-Maria Sorentino (2020, 766) describes how beyond the article's importance to the "socio-historic context" in which it emerged and in which it's been deployed by academics and activists to centre land back/back to land in conceptions of decolonization, it also articulates (somewhat ironically) "metaphysical commitments that divide the material from the symbolic":

> When metaphor "invades decolonization" (Tuck and Yang 2012: 3) the very possibility of decolonization is destroyed, as it is stolen from its literal referent and transported to the realm

of semantic superabundance. Recovering and reviving what metaphor has stolen is meant to reorient the proper scope and scale of decolonial struggle. (Garba and Sorentino 2020, 765)

What was stolen is land. But land in its materiality divided from and prioritized over the symbolic then becomes reduced to an object of loss and so, an object for recovery. This recovery is made prerequisite to the regeneration of damaged Indigenous lifeworlds in which land is not a thing, but place, kin, episteme — "dense, reciprocal, life-affirming relations that peoples form and have formed over millennia" (Million 2021, 394). Garba and Sorentino also trace how anti-Blackness and slavery are reified, engulfed, and made derivative in the model of settler colonial violence and then decolonization forwarded by Tuck and Yang. Like them I'm concerned about the "collaps[e] [of] difference under a presumptive totality" but in what is agreed to as "proper" to decolonial struggle tacitly objectifying and delimiting the meaning of land and the bodies on or of "it."

In Glen Coulthard and Leanne Betasamosake Simpson's (2016, 254) definition, resurgence involves "measures and tactics designed to protect Indigenous territories and to reconnect Indigenous bodies to land through the practices and forms of knowledge that these practices continuously regenerate," with grounded normativity being "the ethical frameworks provided by these."[17] Coulthard has elsewhere described how "Indigenous resurgence is at its core a *pre*figurative politics," that is, anticipatory to bringing forth another world (2014, 159 emphasis mine). Story is often gestured to in resurgence discourse as integral to these Indigenous ethical frameworks and knowledge practices through which peoples might "reclaim epistemic ground" toward "the reclamation of *material* ground" (Sium and Ritskes 2013, 3 emphasis mine). These are frameworks and practices that certainly reflect a refusal of bifurcations in Indigenous relational onto-epistemologies like land/knowledge, place/thought, human/non-human, and body/mind.[18] Indeed, Simpson (2011, 33) has forwarded storytelling's prefigurative role as "a lens through which we can envision our way out of cognitive imperialism, where we can create models and mirrors where none existed, and where we can experience the spaces of freedom and justice." Return of and to land as context for the array of storied practices that reproduce a people's distinct and emplaced "perceptual orientation" is inarguably crucial (Mack 2011). Land is, in Mishuana Goeman's (2015, 73–74) terms, a vibrant nexus of materializing and meaning-making processes rather than "claimed object," "literally and figuratively the placeholder that moves through time and situates Indigenous knowledges."

Yet a prioritization of certain storied practices of reclaiming integral Indigenous relationships with land does emerge in resurgence discourse that conveys a proscriptive range of activities "on it." That is, practices which are not only *normatively grounded* in a conception of land's fundamental materiality and fixedness like a claimed, lost, and so recoverable object but are also articulated as active or actualized in particular ways deemed tangible, productive, pragmatic, and useful. Those that most matter as proper and indeed *real* work for decolonization are those engaged *first from* and *on* the literal ground. The *figurative* in prefigurative is diminished. Simpson's widely circulated 2014 article "Land as Pedagogy" exemplifies the assertion that "putting your body on the land" at the frontlines of dispossession is the only fundamentally valuable way to regenerate and sustain Indigenous knowledge systems like Nishnaabewin (Simpson 2014, 8):

> The people that are actively protecting Nishnaabewin are not those at academic conferences advocating for its use in research and course work but those that are currently putting their bodies on the land. In many ways, the fight for Nishnaabewin is not taking place in Parliament, on social media, or on the streets in urban centres; rather, it lies with communities like Grassy Narrows, and those on the ground who are active practitioners of Nishnaabewin or who are actively protecting their lands from destruction. (Simpson 2014, 21, see also 13)

The above characterization of an active life's innate physicality and necessary locations dismisses a certain academic intellectualism also linked to the perceived limitations of urban Indigenous emplacements as valued sites of dwelling and forms of mediation. Including expansive online/virtual and other extra-material territories and conceptual spaces like the sonic, which Simpson elsewhere engages through her music, poetry, and short stories. We might then consider further ironies and dangers of replicating a kind of theory of value tied to a certain form of Indigenous labour mixed with land. Presumptions of who and how we might be grounded and bodied on the land narrowly proscribed through certain activities and practices can evoke essentializing and ableist notions of Indigeneity, in which those deemed ungrounded or unbodied are impaired and exiled.[19] This suggests a recursion of colonial-straight thinking despite, and even through, internal recognition of diversity as traditional to Indigenous socialities in resurgence discourse. Byrd points this out regarding Simpson's articulation of a seemingly contradictory return to "queer normativity" in her 2017 *As We Have Always Done*, and I'd extend to her inclusive gestures to disability.[20]

On the straightening and so disappearing inclusion of queerness into any *normativity*, Byrd suggests that simply "affirming a liberatory intent and fore*grounding* the anticolonial imperative" to resolve tensions in this word may be to silence "that which has always been erased from and abjected in the deadly onslaught of colonialism" (Byrd 2020, 118 emphasis mine). Here they recall Billy-Ray Belcourt's question "Can the Other of Native Studies Speak?" He posed that question on silences regarding the mattering — that is, the very possibility of *being* — Indigenous *and* queer, in the pasts, presents, and futures imaginable by the field. To be, in a more recent braiding term, *Indigiqueer*.[21] Native studies' territory, like resurgence discourse, is traced around the giveness of Indigeneity from a need to reclaim ground on which to stand for its subject and our collective subjecthood, ground that as Byrd put it "colonization stripped from beneath our feet" (2020, 111 also 107). Land is then the literal *and* figurative ground of "Indigenous normativity," set against the ungrounded settler who desires to possess it. This is an Indigenous *common sense*. Yet what of the divergent or queer work and life that evades normalization or always recedes on the horizons of embodiment, groundedness, or at least recognition as such? What of unbodied storywork, or certain bodies on the ground, the Turtle's back, whose own backs we may stand on with unknowing of what they do, might or cannot bear?[22]

The catastrophic reifying force of colonial worlding through story can't be overstated, including the deadly discursive invention and narrative violence deployed to mark and make us matter differentially along raced and gendered lines, that we might then be killed with impunity (Wynter 1995; Starblanket and Hunt 2020) and our lands laid waste (Voyles 2015). As Shiri Pasternak (2016, 319) has suggested, "this death is not metaphorical." Yet, decolonial transformation requires unmaking these narratives as well as a re-storying re-*figuration* of otherwise forms of *life* both existing and possible. The word *metaphor* evokes the poetic worlding from woundedness that Indigenous women and Q2S people have long been made to signify, located as we are in the interstices of apprehension by colonial-straight terms of sensibility, intelligibility, and legibility *as mattering*. Even if, as Billy-Ray Belcourt (2016) suggests, this may be an "elsewhere so *otherworldly* it's hard to think about how life might be lived there." Belcourt's work reminds that we can't discount life that hasn't always, may not, or *not yet* matter — except metaphorically.[23] Yet queer utopianism is often read as "failure in the face of a stultifying regime of pragmatism and normativity" (Chambers-Letson et al. 2019, X). This is where we can move to consider and uphold the *pre-* and *re*figurative force of both Indigenous feminist and Q2S storywork with the example of water metaphors. Processes of mattering and embodied-materiality's equivalence to land as solid ground are disrupted when considering *bodies of and like water*.[24]

BODIES THAT FLOW, BODIES THAT CARRY WATER: EMBODIED-MATERIALITY

> "and i am like the water / that comes before new life."
> — Belcourt, from "The Cree Word for a Body Like Mine is Weesgageechak" (2017a, 9)

Water as life and metaphor demonstrates how embodied-materiality is evoked in Indigenous feminist storywork to honour or affirmatively reclaim women's roles and responsibilities in our communities. Specifically, evoking an incarnate potential for natality, the capacity to birth the new, or reproduce and nurture Indigenous life and lifeways as their carriers and transmitters. As Jo-Anne Fiske articulated in her 1996 article "The Womb is to the Nation," metaphoric figurations of nationhood in Indigenous political discourse have often accorded with a notion of traditionalism naturalizing social roles determined by dimorphic sex-gender differentiation.[25] The article came on the heels of constitutional clash between malestream nationalist and feminist associations in Canada such as the Assembly of First Nations (AFN) and Native Women's Association (NWAC) during the 1980s and early 1990s. Yet Fiske (1996, 71) identified a discursive alignment between these *representative bodies* in this regard. In her terms, this generation's decolonial imaginary involved a concept of "neotraditional community for which essentialist womanhood stands as a metaphor." But women's nascent motherhood as a kind of collective responsibility became a ground to argue for the deferral of equality rights, and masculinist sovereignty as the politics of precedence. Scholars including Audra Simpson (2016) have more recently unpacked how Indigenous women's bodies as "more than flesh" are made to symbolize land and otherwise (e.g., matriarchal or "gynocratic") socialities, political and legal orders, and so both the desire and threat that *engenders* colonial-capitalist violence. Women can then be storied in scholarly and activist discourse as leaders of survivance against externally wrought environmental destruction, genocide, epistemicide, and political annihilation.[26] Articulations of women as water protectors against extractivism in its many forms (Klein 2013) but particularly industries like oil and gas because they are "traditionally water-carriers" also reflect this. Yet the corporeality of the marked-as-feminine body — its particular configurations of flesh and feeling, presumed as those of a womb-having body (or akin to one) — remains a metaphoric "floating signifier" to reckon with in the words of Stuart Hall. It's one repeated within ongoing grammars of decolonization that we continue to organize through. This prompts consideration of Q2S storywork evoking relations with water in ways that extend their cis feminine significations to masculine, femme, or non-cis persons with diverse fleshy and felt embodiments, which I will touch on here.

As Kim Anderson (2000, 186) discusses in her influential *Recognition of Being*, the sacred force of water as creative, regulative, and transformative in Indigenous feminist storywork dignifies "female body image" and "feminine cycles." Particularly, associations of the marked-as-feminine body with the cyclical and reproductive processes of pregnancy and menstruation. She cites reflections on these associations by Sylvia Maracle, Edna Manitowabi, and others. Regarding the importance of renewing coming-of-age ceremonies for girls entering puberty for example, Manitowabi relates that this can affirm how "we all flow. We all bleed, and that's how we bring forth life. That's how we mould and shape life" (Anderson 2000, 186). Maracle describes how water can "take the shape of any vessels we put it in" and for water to also remake the shape of things over time, as women have both maintained continuity and influenced change in their societies: "We recognize that we don't have the kind of power where you bang your fist on the table, but we have the power of the water — that sort of everyday going against something that ultimately changes the shape of the thing" (Anderson 2000, 184–185). Joanne Barker (2019, 14) recently suggested that water's association with a power of mutability is a "life-giving that is held, cared for and embodied by women and women-identified individuals." Barker doesn't directly address the significance of the latter as an ambiguous move to non-binary or trans inclusion to this embodiment as vessels of/for water. Including how this may imply Q2S as "supplement to the category of Indigenous woman," who are then seen to already be "queered" as deviant to the settler order of white cis-heteronorms (Byrd 2020, 113). Appending Q2S people to the category of woman, associated with a certain life-giving embodiment regardless of self-identity (e.g., trans masculine people and trans men) while also obscuring or assimilating trans women to Q2S (Pyle 2019) raises the problem of recursive colonial-straight thinking.

Embodiment is itself often deployed as a figurative term for *exemplifying*, yet its use in resurgence discourse and Indigenous feminist storywork references a more literal incarnation of women's feeling knowledges and "theory from life" (Million 2009, 2014). What of the difference of Q2S intimacies with water and its significations felt by those whose bodies may not birth or bleed from a womb?[27] Or one whose body is experienced as a vessel overflowing, flooding with uncontainable excess, or bearing others' shame, or ebbing and flowing as the water itself, which Belcourt's poem excerpted above pours out? His body's fluidness also describes forms of reproduction and transmutability, (re) creative forces of a different kind, akin if not assimilable. To be "unbodied" by love and sex, to experience a body "spilling outside itself," he wonders elsewhere, is perhaps a "failing to live up to the promise of self-sovereignty" (Belcourt 2017b). Q2S love and sex, like any deemed excessive, as in its sometimes imperative to joy or pleasure, disrupts metrics of utility or productivity; and its failures to contain or multiply in cis-het terms disrupts a politics tethered to notions of autonomous bodies and subjectivity couched in them. This is not the atomizing or individuated "focus on anti-reproductive futures" of "white queer theory" however (Vimalassery, Hu Pegues and Goldstein in Byrd 2020, 113). Q2S storywork also emerges from interstitial and "unbecoming" experiences of embodied-materiality certainly but is absolutely concerned with our space and roles in political-cultural reproduction and Indigenous futurities.

In a 2016 article "My pronouns are Kiy/Kin," Jas Morgan reflects on their experiences with gendered roles in spaces of ceremony as an aabitagiizhig or Two-Spirit person receiving teachings on both water's femininity and mutability. They ask what would happen if

> I tried to move in a fluid nature through and within them, like the fluidity I feel about the space my own embodied gender takes up within community? ... if I were honest about the ways that felt right for me to flow through those spaces like the very water we prayed over? (Morgan 2016)

Kai Pyle (2020, 119) suggests Morgan's reflections on their non-binary kinship with water "offer alternative ways of looking at gendered teachings" that complement those "about men and women."[28] Such engagements with traditionalism indicate how Q2S storywork doesn't displace feminist storywork's efforts at decolonial refiguration of gendered roles and relations to dignify women. Though they *do* disrupt *straight*-forward conceptions of a narrowly cis embodied-materiality associated with land or water as feminine. This includes giving accounts of felt experiences that exceed totalization by the body as a solid or static container, like those assumed to reflect the capacities of certain bodies to materialize or matter in particular ways to certain reproductive ends. For instance, Byrd (2020, 110) notes per Gayle Salamon how transgender studies makes "legible the disjunction between corporeality and the felt sense of the body" which then "amplifies how we might, after Judith Butler, make bodies that matter." Indeed, Q2S storywork expands potentialities for how the perpetuation of nations and traditions may be *conceived* (dual meaning intended).

Here trans-specific reflections are important and we might gesture to the impact of Saylesh Wesley's (2014) self-described storywork with her grandmother who "conjured" a Halq'eméylem title to honour and situate her trans womanhood within a dynamic Stó:lō language continuum. Such naming is absolutely a decolonial "magical practice" of refiguring trans and Q2S space and roles, in sometimes fraught but loving familial relation with that of cis women. In Wesley's (2014, 345) reflection on respect for her grandmother and all Stó:lō Siseles' authority as law makers, she also notes that transformative knowledge flows both ways: "I have truly become not only her granddaughter, but also her friend and teacher who helps to reshape her worldview, which includes my queer identity." Regarding this reciprocity, Wesley asserts that to re-establish trans and Q2S space and roles, matriarchal systems of governance must be restored (2014, 345–46). Returning to Barker's ambiguous non-binary and trans inclusion as its life-giving vessels, the course of her reflections runs to describe water (2019, 2) as an Indigenous feminist analytic of "interlocution" or the "confluence of knowledge within and between (partial, implicated, contradictory)"; a concept with which we can consider "the movement and form of when and how and with whom we know."[29] Such a sense of confluence might be considered in the flow between Wesley and her grandmother and also between Indigenous feminist and Q2S storywork in this new edition of *Making Space*.

MEETING ON A SHORELINE

In their article, Tuck and Yang aimed to intervene against equivocations, abstractions, and diversions in the way *decolonization* might be made entirely figurative and detached from land, what Strakosch and Macoun (2020) called the "violence of analogizing." But to metaphorize isn't necessarily to analogize between the incommensurable or engage in abstracting substitution of the literal as Tuck and Yang assert. In my call to consider how and why the word *metaphor* matters to upholding storywork, I don't mean to myself equivocate by drawing attention to a semantic distinction that should then negate the intended meaning of Tuck and Yang's intervention. As Tuck and Yang's own impetus for their article and Garba and Sorentino's critique of their analogizing with work on anti-Blackness attests, self-reflexivity in our language matters especially when drawing correspondences or seeking to re-member. However, the disjuncture between intention and effect or affect in the inability to control how our words are received is a risk of telling. Accepting the risks of telling involves relinquishing a play to authorial control, but not accountability. As many eminent thinkers on this remind us, words and stories, once released cannot be called back and they may act as medicine for good or ill in the ways they're subsequently taken up (King 2003, 10; Armstrong quoted in Archibald 2008, 27 and 19).[30] Simply deferring to intention also does not invite an ethic, for instance around taking care with or having reverence for words, which Archibald offers is a principle of Indigenous storywork and Maracle also enjoined (Maracle 2015, 161, also 37–38).

This leads me back to my chapter title's words, grammar, and a close. The conjunctions *and* as well as *also* aren't incidental but a choice on my part. To say that decolonization *is also* metaphorical, asks to consider decoloniality as processes of continual re-*figuration* of otherwise forms of life which can't be distilled to the structural conditions (and absolute necessity) of *land back* alone. Though as Audra Simpson reminds and as Tuck and Yang (2012) assert, when we speak of dispossession "we are speaking of the materiality of land," land is not "just the ground" (Longman et al. 2020). And to say that Indigenous feminist *and* Q2S storywork both matter in these processes is to suggest these are not analogous, but nor are they mutually exclusive or in competition for metaphoric space. Space need not be made into territory with an indivisible sovereign and isn't finite or depletable, though land and water may be. As Dian Million (2015) has put it regarding the notion of recovering emplaced Indigenous onto-epistemologies constituted with/in the complex nexus of meaning in "land," we should attend to the objectification of both in our decolonial grammar regardless of intent. We should then also attend to the implications of framing decolonization as a finite project in response to loss from a perspective of scarcity and deficit rather than unfolding processes of (re)worlding from a perspective of plentitude and expansiveness.[31]

Q2S engagements on fluid traditionalism and refigurations of embodied and felt relationships with water expressed in a fixed gender binary gesture to confluences with Indigenous feminist storywork. Specifically, where both address cis-heteropatriarchy's imbrications with concepts of "normative" Indigeneity that may reiterate limiting conceptions of the bodies on and of land, and land as ground and object of Indigenous political and cultural life. Confluence in this storywork doesn't require absolute fluency of understanding between the experiences they express. To flow back to the prismatic through these watery reflections, what has my exercise in reaffirmation of the multivalent mattering of metaphor for both Indigenous feminist and Q2S storywork illuminated for me? Perhaps as poet Christine Sy evoked so resonantly at our Indigenous Feminisms symposium in April 2022, rather than about finding a common sense as a common ground between us, this confluence is a meeting on a shoreline — where ground meets water, where water might be bodied and ground fluid. Or as Kwaguilth queer and feminist geographer Sarah Hunt (2014, 208) describes, a "space where water meets land and light, where the tides turn all the elements together in an ever-present yet ever-changing jumble."³² For Indigenous feminist and Q2S storyworkers, perhaps this is an intergenerational as *inter-generative* shore where we might matter together, and on our own terms.

NOTES

1. However, the footnote is a rhetorical and stylistic strategy of digression and aside that I deploy intentionally. This includes to disrupt a linear, closed, and expository narrative reading, evoking orality, and the sort of nodal quality of a written text in relationship with an expansive kinship web of meaning-making. It also reflects my thinking's tendency to lateral diversion in many directions.
2. Aileen Moreton-Robinson (2007) and Joanne Barker (2005) are also evoked with "matters," and others' deployment of this term including Daniel Heath Justice on Indigenous literatures and story (2018).
3. For Maracle "bending the light" reveals "hidden being" and "invisible threads" (2015, 242).
4. Colonial straight-thinking is related to what I've elsewhere referred to as "colonial apprehension" — the capture of elusive or evasive Indigenous decolonial practices through efforts at identifying or "making sense" of them, even in well-meaning critical theory. Here Nichols' discussion of recursion has been helpful (Aguirre 2018, 2021, 194). I've particularly been interested in how apprehension operates through mediation by what Belcourt describes as the "genre and form of political speak" that "stomps some of us into the rut of social death" (Belcourt 2017c, 182). Here I'd add mediation by "cultural speak" as its opposite and domain of the "anthropological Native," but that's another story. While my concern with apprehension has previously been directed to rhetorical imperialism and colonialism (Kelly and Black 2018; Ellasante 2021) and external recognition or scrutiny of our movements, like Belcourt, it's replications of colonial straight-thinking inside them I'm concerned with here.
5. Vanessa Watts has mounted a critique of Haraway's anti-essentialism regarding the "earth as mother" and "literal embodiment of the feminine" and her perceived extractive relations with Indigenous "place-thought" where "the material (body/land) becomes abstracted into epistemological spaces as a resource for non-Indigenous scholars to implode their hegemonic borders" (Watts 2013, 31).
6. I've recently found Rinaldo Walcott's discussion of Black Diaspora, as both an analytic and a politics that can be organized through and around, to be helpful (Walcott 2020).
7. I recognize queer–Two-Spirit (Q2S) is an inadequate shorthand for the diverse sexualities and/or gender identities and expressions encompassing the spectrum of Indigenous Two-Spirit and LGBTQIA+ identifications while recognizing the diversity of affiliation and disidentifications this may obscure. I particularly wish to note this regarding trans inclusion within "Q2S," as generous draft reader Jamey Jespersen also invited me to consider. Pyle's (2019) reflections on the obfuscation of trans people in Indigenous activist rhetoric through the rise of "Two-Spirit" as adjunct to "women" is an intervention aligned to my concerns

in this chapter, and I take this up below. On the emergence of Two-Spirit see also Wesley 2014; Wilson 1996. See also below note on the term "Indigiqueer."

8   There is a sense that while all Indigenous feminisms may be considered decolonial not all decolonial feminisms are Indigenous, though they may be in coalition (e.g., as per Lugones 2010). Arvin et al. (2013) consider Indigenous feminisms (centred in present Turtle Island/Anglo-North America), as distinguished by a critical linking of ongoing settler-colonialism and (racialized) heteropatriarchy. While suggesting a conception of Indigenous feminist methods and analyses against "identity-driven labels," they forward a distinction from "Asian, black, Latina, third world, transnational, and queer feminisms" (2013, 10) drawn according to the matter of land. This is troubled by those who may stand in the interstices or indeed crosshairs between Indigenous and other identifications with their relative landed-ness, like myself.

9   Morgensen is here referring to the narrative formation of "non-Native and Native queer modernities" (2011, 22).

10 Storying and storywork as I present here is one form of storytelling among others in a vast and diverse array of Indigenous conceptions of story and "telling activity"; which as Leslie Marmon Silko relates is not limited to "old stories," sometimes does "not differentiate or fragment stories and experiences" nor narrowly circumscribes settings or occasions for storytelling (Silko 1981, 56,59). Likewise, Simon Ortiz reminds that oral tradition need not be simply defined as "vocal-verbal manifestations" (Ortiz 1992, 7) and Justice (2018) that story may be "embodied" as well as "inscribed."

11 Regarding the heuristic rather than prescriptive role of political theorists as commentators in complementary positions to other storyworkers, I distinguish storying for self-determination and its witnessing function, from narrativizing phenomena or events as imposing uniform meaning and linear causality, as though we are its (sole) authors (authorship as authoritarian). In articulating this ethos for the kinds of written scholarship I do on and in what Audra Simpson calls the settler-colonial and public "theatre of apprehension," I've turned to Maracle and Hannah Arendt. This includes aligned concepts of "concatenations" and "correspondences" in their work for my thinking on the role of critical theorists in re-membering.

12 The ostensibly Euro-Modern theory/practice division and "abstracting distraction" or commodifying inflation of theory's "use value" (Million 2014, 34) in relation to Indigenous decolonial movements has been long debated, see Simpson and Smith (2014), de Sousa Santos (2016), and Deloria Jr. (1998).

13 This despite possible disidentifications as such by those who've subsequently been described as Indigenous feminists like Patricia Monture-Angus and Beth Brant — as Anderson puts it Brant "theorized and practiced Indigenous feminism before we had a language for it" (2021). I would add of Brant against her assimilation to feminism alone, queer–Two-Spirit theory and practice.

14 This coding defers to an array of dichotomous registers that bifurcate and prioritize concepts like mind/body (Cartesian dualism), reason/emotion, human/animal, theory/practice, politics/culture, civilization/savagery, individual/collective, productive/unproductive, active/idle, literate/oral, public/private etc.

15 This might affirmatively be described as the "subjunctive quality of stories, their capacity to change our frame of reference — to make it so by saying it is so" (Lessard et al. 2011, 10).

16 And arguably, a (formerly coded white now brown, straight) masculine destroys (a coded brown, queer) feminine. Fanon's treatment of gendering and its interface with racialization has been widely discussed.

17 As Stark (2023, 3–20) contends, Indigenous resurgence is not a term exclusive to nor originating with Coulthard and Simpson among others, particularly Alfred and Corntassel. However, their definitions do suffuse the broader discourse and it is for this reason I emphasize their work as itself normative here.

18 Jaffee and John (2018, 1410) point out how "Indigenous interventions in academic scholarship, challenge some of the widely-accepted divisions and binaries in Western/settler philosophy" and that not only do Indigenous onto-epistemologies "question the inherent separation of such concepts, but they also challenge scholars to think differently about binaries at large."

19 Starblanket (2017) has addressed the recursion of cis heteronorms in models of authenticity or what "being Indigenous" entails within resurgence discourse.

20 Noting a similar "inclusion" of disability in Simpson's passing references to resurgence as "propelled by the diversity of Indigenous bodies of all ages, genders, races and abilities" (Simpson 2017, 21), I've recently begun to consider ableism within resurgence discourse. This is also informed by my own experiences as an autistic person (see Aguirre et al. 2024). Extant work by scholars in and adjacent to critical disability studies has focused on concepts of colonial "disablement" and "settler ableism" in analyses of violence to Indigenous lands and bodyminds (e.g., Hutcheon and Lashewicz 2020; Cowing 2020; Jaffee and John 2018). Critiques on analogizing in such analyses have been longstanding however (Sherry 2017; Grech and Soldatic 2015; Barker and Murray 2010). Areas of my interest include: assumptions of requisite staminas or "fitness" for participation in "land-based practices" narrowly defined; contributions assessed and impelled by metrics of accessibility and utility to "community" (including being sensible or easy to understand), and productivity (if not from within a neoliberal or capitalist logic); conceptions of those dislocated from land as impaired or afflicted, and decolonization as a therapeutic, curative, rehabilitative, or eugenic process to resolve imperfection, trauma, damage, etc. Here there is alignment to Byrd's concern on the straightening of queerness to rebuild healthy and "strong societies of best selves" (Byrd 2020, 117). Following work in queer disability and neurodiversity justice (Piepzna-Samarasinha 2018; Yergeau 2017; Egner 2019), I'm interested in moving beyond critiques of ableism in favour of access or inclusion to a normalcy that may be assimilative, toward articulating disabled and neurodiverse decolonial imaginaries and futurities. What would it mean if as Cowing put it, we move beyond formulating justice as simply those normatively positioned "communicat[ing] to disabled, chronically ill and/or neurodivergent people that their presence is anticipated and expected"? (2020, 10).

21 Joshua Whitehead has discussed "Indigiqueer" as a braiding and alternative to Two-Spirit that he's often credited with coining but that rather it has been "floating in digital spaces on social media," describing its connective power as "working like a hyperlink" (Whitehead quoted in Wilbur and Keene 2019).

22 Lugones describes a feminist imperative toward emphasizing the "praxical" or lived "grassroots" experiences, with *ground* understood as "historicized incarnate intersubjectivity" (2010, 246). This is part of a move away from logocentrism, or "against the privileging of language by attending to the embodied practices of everyday life" (Stahl 2002, 827). I'm not forwarding an

anti-foundationalist or poststructuralist critique redux of this imperative but rather of the straight-thinking around which and how certain subjects and bodies are made to matter as such. As Bronwyn Carlson and Ryan Frazer put it, I'm here also evoking affect but beyond "the clearly felt or easily articulable dimensions of everyday experience to consider what bodies can and cannot do, say, and sense," to ask, "how bodies are connected to other bodies and what capacities these connections might produce or preclude" (Carlson and Frazer 2020, 2).

23 I here want to acknowledge my former student at the University of Victoria Q Roxas for their enlivening conversations on their brilliant undergraduate honours thesis. The thesis considered the storying possibilities in Lugones' concept of the "fractured locus" at/in which resistant subjects dwell or people, evading totalizing capture by coloniality. Particularly to locate women's and trans and gender-non-conforming subjectivities, as well as possibilities for feminist and queer-of-colour coalition building.

24 Posthumanist feminist Astrida Neimanis has forwarded reflections on watery embodiment (2012, 2013, 2016).

25 As Fiske put it here the "social foundations of matrilineal groups" and "honorific gender-segregated roles in both matrilineal and patrilineal nations" were the "texts" from which both drew "the metaphors of their envisioned nationhood" (1996, 73).

26 As I considered in relation to Idle No More (Aguirre 2018). The idea of "women as the first environment" (Cook quoted in Barker 2019, 5) has informed scholarship and activism on Indigenous reproductive justice and environmental violence (e.g., Violence on the Land, Violence on Our Bodies Toolkit [Women's Earth Alliance, and Native Youth Sexual Health Network 2016]). Commentaries on the #NoDAPL movement for example, have recently emphasized the gendered dimensions of violence and the role of water-protectors, see for example Anderson et al. 2013; Jewett and Garavan 2019; Dennis and Bell 2020; Privott 2019; Christiansen 2021.

27 Here we might consider how embodying the symbolic redolence of menstruation and birthing blood may have never been tied to womb-having in some ceremonial contexts (see Lang 1998, 133–141). Thanks again here to Jamey Jesperson for the reference.

28 Alex Wilson has also reflected on disparagements of queer–Two-Spirit experiences in ceremony and the refiguration of traditional protocols she experienced through work with Elder Mae Louise Campbell (2018).

29 As Boon et al. (2018a) relate, fluidity as both a feminist and queer analytic is not contain/able to Indigenous engagements. Particularly notable regarding "bodies of water" are conceptions of excess, flood, etc. in contrast with scripts of "masculine corporeality," e.g., Elizabeth Grosz on women's "seepage" (cited 59).

30 As Kim TallBear suggests, there is a "need for precise languages to talk about precise ideas that have derived from specific histories of work" (TallBear 2017, 17). Yet there is always ambivalence. Jacques Derrida describes the indeterminacy of "medicine" as poison or remedy (with reference to the Greek concept pharmakon) and applies this notion to the practice of writing (Derrida 1981). While medicine is a complex concept in many Indigenous intellectual and spiritual systems and is entangled with notions of the curative through translation, that medicine can heal or harm (Justice 2018, 4) is a way to think on

attempts to control the received meaning of our words, and stories once uttered. Particularly as an issue of ethics in anticipation of this indeterminacy.
31 Though Million elsewhere is like Tuck and Yang concerned about the violence of "dematerialization" — how "Indigenous peoples suffer harms that stem from the killing and abstraction of their embodied, affective existences" (2021, 402).
32 Boon et al. (2018b) consider the shoreline as a "contact zone" between land and water from which to theorize (pressing on the solidity of "landed" concepts like borderlands per Gloria Anzaldúa and others). The metaphor of wetland for such liminality, like muskeg or chinampas is one I'm increasingly interested in. Tiffany Lethabo King's Black Shoals (2019) offers a similar metaphor for Black and Indigenous encounter.

REFERENCES

Aguirre, Kelly. 2018. "Re-Storying Political Theory: Indigenous Resurgence, Idle No More and Colonial Apprehension." Doctoral dissertation, University of Victoria. dspace.library.uvic.ca:8443/handle/1828/10455.

———. 2021 "Apprehending Indigenous Decolonial Movements: Questions on Recursivity in Critical Theory Scholarship." In "Robert Nichols in Conversation with Kelly Aguirre, Phil Henderson, Cressida J. Heyes, Alana Lentin, and Corey Snelgrove." *Journal of World Philosophies* 6, 2.

Aguirre, Kelly, et al. 2024. "Your Absence Is Not an Accident: Storying Feminist Friendship from Dissonance to Dissidence." In *Feministing in Political Science: A Manifesta for Change in the Academy,* edited by N. Nath, S. Paterson, A. Cattapan et al. Edmonton: University of Alberta Press.

Alfred, Taiaiake, and Jeff Corntassel. 2005. "Being Indigenous: Resurgences against Contemporary Colonialism." *Government and Opposition* 40.

Anderson, Kim. 2000. *A Recognition of Being: Reconstructing Native Womanhood.* Toronto: Sumach Press.

———. 2021 "Multi-Generational Indigenous Feminisms: From F Word to What Ifs." In *Routledge Handbook of Critical Indigenous Studies,* edited by B. Hokowhitu, A. Moreton-Robinson, L. Tuhiwai-Smith et al. London: Routledge.

Anderson, Kim, et al. 2013. "Carriers of Water: Aboriginal Women's Experiences, Relationships, and Reflections." *Journal of Cleaner Production* 60. doi.org/10.1016/j.jclepro.2011.10.023.

Archibald, Jo-Ann, et al. (eds.). 2019. *Decolonizing Research: Indigenous Storywork as Methodology.* London: Zed Books Ltd.

Archibald, Q'um Q'um Xiiem Jo-Ann. 2008. *Indigenous Storywork: Educating the Heart, Mind, Body and Spirit.* Vancouver: UBC Press.

Arvin, Maile, et al. 2013. "Decolonizing Feminism: Challenging Connections between Settler Colonialism and Heteropatriarchy." *Feminist Formations.* Baltimore: Johns Hopkins University Press.

Barker, Clare, and Stuart Murray. 2010. "Disabling Postcolonialism: Global Disability Cultures and Democratic Criticism." *Journal of Literary & Cultural Disability Studies* 4, 3.

Barker, Joanne. 2005. "For Whom Sovereignty Matters." In *Sovereignty Matters: Locations of Contestation and Possibility in Indigenous Struggles for Self-Determination,* edited by J. Barker. Lincoln: University of Nebraska Press.

___. 2019. "Confluence: Water as an Analytic of Indigenous Feminisms." *American Indian Culture and Research Journal* 43, 3.

Belcourt, Billy-Ray. 2016. "Can the Other of Native Studies Speak?" *Decolonization: Indigeneity, Education, and Society*. February 1. decolonization.wordpress.com/2016/02/01/can-the-other-of-native-studies-speak/.

___. 2017a. *This Wound Is a World*. Okotoks, AB: Frontenac House Poetry.

___. 2017b. "To Be Unbodied." *Canadian Art* 49 (Summer).

___. 2017c. "Indigenous Studies Beside Itself." *Somatechnics* 7, 2.

Boon, Sonja, et al. 2018a. "Water: Flooding Memory." In *Autoethnography and Feminist Theory at the Water's Edge: Unsettled Islands*, edited by Sonja Boon, Lesley Butler, and Daze Jefferies. Cham: Palgrave Macmillan.

Boon, Sonja, et al. 2018b. "Introduction: Islands of the Imagination." In *Autoethnography and Feminist Theory at the Water's Edge: Unsettled Islands*, edited by Sonja Boon, Lesley Butler, and Daze Jefferies. Cham: Palgrave Macmillan

Brant, Beth. 1994. *Writing as Witness: Essay and Talk*. Toronto: Women's Press.

Byrd, Jodi. 2020. "What's Normative Got to Do with It? Toward Indigenous Queer Relationality." *Social Text* 38, 4.

Carlson, Bronwyn, and Ryan Frazer. 2020. "'They Got Filters': Indigenous Social Media, the Settler Gaze, and a Politics of Hope." *Social Media + Society* 6, 2.

Chambers-Letson, Joshua, et al. 2019. "Foreword." In *Cruising Utopia: The Then and There of Queer Futurity*, 10th anniversary edition, by José Esteban Muñoz. New York: New York University Press.

Christiansen, Jordan. 2021. "The Water Protectors at Standing Rock: Survivance Strategies for Gendered Relinking." *Women's Studies in Communication* 44, 3.

Coulthard, Glen Sean. 2014. *Red Skin, White Masks: Rejecting the Colonial Politics of Recognition*. Minneapolis: University of Minnesota Press.

Coulthard, Glen, and Leanne Betasamosake Simpson. 2016. "Grounded Normativity/Place-Based Solidarity." *American Quarterly* 68, 2.

Cowing, Jess. 2020. "Occupied Land Is an Access Issue: Interventions in Feminist Disability Studies and Narratives of Indigenous Activism." *Journal of Feminist Scholarship* 17.

de Sousa Santos, Boaventura. 2016. "Introduction: Creating a Distance in Relation to Western-Centric Political Imagination and Critical Theory." In *Epistemologies of the South: Justice against Epistemicide*. London: Routledge.

Deloria Jr., Vine. 1998. "Intellectual Self-Determination and Sovereignty: Looking at the Windmills in Our Minds." *Wicazo Sa Review* 13, 1.

Dennis, Mary Kate, and Finn McLafferty Bell. 2020. "Indigenous Women, Water Protectors, and Reciprocal Responsibilities." *Social Work* 65, 4.

Derrida, Jacques. 1981. *Dissemination*. Trans. Barbara Johnson. London: Athone Press.

Egner, Justine E. 2019. "'The Disability Rights Community Was Never Mine': Neuroqueer Disidentification." *Gender and Society* 33.

Ellasante, Ian Khara. 2021. "Radical Sovereignty, Rhetorical Borders, and the Everyday Decolonial Praxis of Indigenous Peoplehood and Two-Spirit Reclamation." *Ethnic and Racial Studies* 44, 9. doi.org/10.1080/01419870.2021.1906437.

Fanon, Frantz. 2004 [1961/1963]. *The Wretched of the Earth*. Trans. Richard Philcox. New York: Grove Press.

Fiske, Jo-Anne. 1996. "The Womb Is to the Nation as the Heart Is to the Body: Ethnopolitical Discourses of the Canadian Indigenous Women's Movement." *Studies in Political Economy* 51, 1.

Garba, Tapji, and Sara-Maria Sorentino. 2020. "Slavery Is a Metaphor: A Critical Commentary on Eve Tuck and K. Wayne Yang's 'Decolonization Is Not a Metaphor.'" [In English]. *Antipode* 52, 3. doi.org/10.1111/anti.12615.

Goeman, Mishuana. 2015. "Land as Life: Unsettling the Logics of Containment." In *Native Studies Keywords*, edited by S. Nohelani Teves, A. Smith, and M.H. Raheja. Tucson: University of Arizona Press.

Grech, Shaun, and Karen Soldatic. 2015. "Disability and Colonialism: (Dis) Encounters and Anxious Intersectionalities." *Social Identities* 21, 1.

Haraway, Donna. 1994. "A Game of Cat's Cradle: Science Studies, Feminist Theory, Cultural Studies." *Configurations* 2, 1.

Hunt, Sarah Elizabeth. 2014. "Witnessing the Colonialscape: Lighting the Intimate Fires of Indigenous Legal Pluralism." Doctoral dissertation, Simon Fraser University. summit.sfu.ca/item/14145.

Hutcheon, Emily J., and Bonnie Lashewicz. 2020. "Tracing and Troubling Continuities between Ableism and Colonialism in Canada." *Disability & Society* 35, 5.

Jackson, Michael. 2002. *The Politics of Storytelling: Violence, Transgression and Intersubjectivity*. Copenhagen: Museum Tusculanum Press.

Jaffee, Laura, and Kelsey John. 2018. "Disabling Bodies of/and Land: Reframing Disability Justice in Conversation with Indigenous Theory and Activism." *Open Access* 5, 2.

Jewett, Chas, and Mark Garavan. 2019. "Water Is Life: An Indigenous Perspective from a Standing Rock Water Protector." *Community Development Journal* 54, 1.

Justice, Daniel Heath. 2018. *Why Indigenous Literatures Matter*. Indigenous Studies Series. Waterloo, ON: Wilfrid Laurier University Press.

Kelly, Casey Ryan, and Jason Edward Black. 2018. *Decolonizing Native American Rhetoric: Communicating Self-Determination*. New York: Peter Lang.

King, Tiffany Lethabo. 2019. *The Black Shoals: Offshore Formations of Black and Native Studies*. Durham, NC: Duke University Press.

King, Thomas. 2003. *The Truth About Stories: A Native Narrative*. Toronto: Anansi Press.

Klein, Naomi. 2013. "Dancing the World into Being: A Conversation with Idle No More's Leanne Simpson." *Yes! Magazine*, March 6, 2013. yesmagazine.org/social-justice/2013/03/06/dancing-the-world-into-being-a-conversation-with-idle-no-more-leanne-simpson.

Lang, Sabine. 1998. *Men as Women, Women as Men: Changing Gender in Native American Cultures*. Austin: University of Texas Press.

Lessard, Hester, et al. 2011. "Introduction." In *Storied Communities: Narratives of Contact and Arrival in the Constitution of Political Community*, edited by H. Lessard, R. Johnson, and J. Webber. Vancouver: UBC Press.

Longman, Nickita, et al. 2020. "'Land Back' Is More Than the Sum of Its Parts: Letter from the Land Back Editorial Collective." *Briarpatch Magazine*, September/

October. briarpatchmagazine.com/articles/view/land-back-is-more-than-the-sum-of-its-parts.

Lugones, Maria. 2010. "Toward a Decolonial Feminism." *Hypatia* 25, 4.

Mack, Johnny. 2011. "Hoquotist: Reorienting Through Storied Practice." In *Storied Communities: Narratives of Contact and Arrival in the Constitution of Political Community*, edited by H. Lessard, R. Johnson, and J. Webber. Vancouver: UBC Press.

Maracle, Lee. 2015. *Memory Serves: Oratories*. Edmonton: NeWest Press.

Million, Dian. 2009. "Felt Theory: An Indigenous Feminist Approach to Affect and History." *Wicazo Sa Review* 24, 2.

———. 2014. "There Is a River in Me: Theory from Life." In *Theorizing Native Studies*, edited by A. Simpson and A. Smith. Durham: Duke University Press.

———. 2015. "Epistemology." In *Native Studies Keywords*, edited by S.N. Teves, A. Smith, and M.H. Raheja. Tucson: University of Arizona Press.

———. 2021. "Resurgent Kinships: Indigenous relations of Well-Being vs. Humanitarian Health Economies." In *Routledge Handbook of Critical Indigenous Studies*, edited by B. Hokowhitu, A. Moreton-Robinson, L. Tuhiwai-Smith et al. London: Routledge.

Moreton-Robinson, Aileen. 2007. *Sovereign Subjects: Indigenous Sovereignty Matters*. Crows Nest, N.S.W: Allen & Unwin.

———. 2011. "The White Man's Burden: Patriarchal White Epistemic Violence and Aboriginal Women's Knowledges within the Academy." *Australian Feminist Studies* 26, 70.

Morgan, Jas M. 2016. "My Pronouns Are Kiy/Kin." *Red Rising Magazine*, May 13.

Morgensen, Scott Lauria. 2011. *Spaces Between Us: Queer Settler Colonialism and Indigenous Decolonization*. Minneapolis: University of Minnesota Press.

Neimanis, Astrida. 2012. "Hydrofeminism: Or, on Becoming a Body of Water." In *Undutiful Daughters: New Directions in Feminist Thought and Practice*, edited by H. Gunkel, C. Nigianni, and F. Söderbäck. New York: Palgrave Macmillan.

———. 2013. "Feminist Subjectivity, Watered." *Feminist Review* 103.

———. 2016. *Bodies of Water: Posthuman Feminist Phenomenology*. Environmental Cultures. London: Bloomsbury Academic.

Ortiz, Simon J. 1992. *Woven Stone*. Tucson: University of Arizona Press.

Pasternak, Shiri. 2016. "The Fiscal Body of Sovereignty: To 'Make Live' in Indian Country." *Settler Colonial Studies* 6, 4.

Piepzna-Samarasinha, Leah Lakshmi. 2018. *Care Work: Dreaming Disability Justice*. Vancouver: Arsenal Pulp Press.

Privott, Meredith. 2019. "An Ethos of Responsibility and Indigenous Women Water Protectors in the #Nodapl Movement." *American Indian Quarterly* 43, 1.

Pyle, Kai. 2019. "'Women and 2spirits': On the Marginalization of Transgender Indigenous People in Activist Rhetoric." *American Indian Culture and Research Journal* 43, 3.

———. 2020. "Reclaiming Traditional Gender Roles: A Two-Spirit Critique." In *In Good Relation: History, Gender, and Kinship in Indigenous Feminisms*, edited by S. Nickel and A. Fehr. Winnipeg: University of Manitoba Press.

Sherry, Mark. 2017. "(Post)Colonising Disability." *Wagadu* 4, 1.

Silko, Leslie Marmon. 1981. "Language and Literature from a Pueblo Indian

Perspective." In *English Literature: Opening up the Canon*, edited by L.A. Fiedler and H.A. Baker. Baltimore: Johns Hopkins University Press.

Simpson, Audra. 2016. "The State Is a Man: Theresa Spence, Loretta Saunders and the Gender of Settler Sovereignty." *Theory & Event* 19, 4.

Simpson, Audra, and Andrea Smith. 2014. "Introduction." In *Theorizing Native Studies*, edited by A. Simpson and A. Smith. Durham: Duke University Press.

Simpson, Leanne Betasamosake. 2011. *Dancing on Our Turtle's Back: Stories of Nishnaabeg Re-Creation, Resurgence, and a New Emergence*. Winnipeg: Arbeiter Ring Publishing.

———. 2014. "Land as Pedagogy: Nishnaabeg Intelligence and Rebellious Transformation." *Decolonization: Indigeneity, Education and Society* 3, 3.

———. 2017. *As We Have Always Done: Indigenous Freedom through Radical Resistance*. Indigenous Americas. Minneapolis: University of Minnesota Press.

Sium, Aman, and Eric Ritskes. 2013. "Speaking Truth to Power: Indigenous Storytelling as an Act of Living Resistance." *Decolonization: Indigeneity, Education & Society* 2, 1.

Stahl, Ann Brower. 2002. "Colonial Entanglements and the Practices of Taste: An Alternative to Logocentric Approaches." *American Anthropologist* 104, 3.

Starblanket, Gina. 2017. "Being Indigenous Feminists: Resurgences Against Contemporary Patriarchy." In *Making Space for Indigenous Feminism*, second ed., edited by J. Green. Black Point, NS: Fernwood Publishing.

Starblanket, Gina, and Dallas Hunt. 2020. *Storying Violence: Unravelling Colonial Narratives in the Stanley Trial*. Semaphore Series. Winnipeg: Arbeiter Ring Publishing.

Stark, Heidi Kiiwetinepinesiik. 2023. "Generating a Critical Resurgence Together." In *Indigenous Resurgence in an Age of Reconciliation*, edited by H. Kiiwetinepinesiik Stark, A. Craft, and H.K. Aikau. Toronto: University of Toronto Press.

Strakosch, Elizabeth, and Alissa Macoun. 2020. "The Violence of Analogy: Abstraction, Neoliberalism and Settler Colonial Possession." *Postcolonial Studies* 23, 4. doi.org/10.1080/13688790.2020.1834930.

TallBear, Kim. 2017. "Standing With and Speaking as Faith: A Feminist-Indigenous Approach to Inquiry." In *Sources and Methods in Indigenous Studies*, edited by C. Andersen and J. O'Brien. New York: Routledge.

Todd, Zoe. 2017. "Refracting Colonialism in Canada: Fish Tales, Text, and Insistent Public Grief." In *Coloniality, Ontology, and the Question of the Posthuman*, edited by M. Jackson. London: Routledge.

Tuck, Eve, and K. Wayne Yang. 2012. "Decolonization Is Not a Metaphor." *Decolonization: Indigeneity, Education and Society* 1, 1.

Voyles, Traci Brynne. 2015. *Wastelanding: Legacies of Uranium Mining in Navajo Country*. Minneapolis: University of Minnesota Press.

Walcott, Rinaldo N. 2020. "Diaspora, Transnationalism and the Decolonial Project." In *Otherwise Worlds: Against Settler Colonialism and Anti-Blackness*, edited by Tiffany Lethabo King, Jenell Navarro, and Andrea Smith. Durham: Duke University Press.

Watts, Vanessa. 2013. "Indigenous Place-Thought and Agency Amongst Humans and Non Humans (First Woman and Sky Woman Go on a European World Tour!)." *Decolonization: Indigeneity, Education and Society* 2, 1.

Wesley, Saylesh. 2014. "Twin-Spirited Woman: Sts'iyóye Smestíyexw Slhá:Li." *TSQ: Transgender Studies Quarterly* 1, 3.

Wilbur, Matika, and Adrienne Keene. 2019. "Indigiqueer." *All My Relations Podcast*. April 2. allmyrelationspodcast.com/post/ep-6-indigiqueer.

Wilson, Alex. 1996. "How We Find Ourselves: Identity Development and Two-Spirit People." *Harvard Educational Review* 66, 2.

———. 2018. "Skirting the Issues: Indigenous Myths, Misses and Misogyny." In *Keetsahnak/Our Missing and Murdered Indigenous Sisters*, edited by K. Anderson, M. Campbell, and C. Belcourt. Edmonton: University of Alberta Press.

Women's Earth Alliance and Native Youth Sexual Health Network. 2016. *Violence on the Land, Violence on Our Bodies: Building an Indigenous Response to Environmental Violence*. Berkeley.

Wynter, Sylvia. 1995. "1492: A New World View." In *Race, Discourse, and the Origin of the Americas: A New World View*, edited by Vera Lawrence Hyatt and Rex Nettleford. Smithsonian Institution.

Yergeau, Melanie. 2017. *Authoring Autism: On Rhetoric and Neurological Queerness*. Durham: Duke University Press.

About the Contributors

KELLY AGUIRRE (SHE/THEY) is an assistant professor in the Department of Political Science at the University of Victoria. A queer and autistic mestiza of Nahua, ñuu savi, German-Russian, and Welsh ancestry, she was born in Mexico City Tenochtitlan and grew up in Winnipeg, Manitoba, Treaty 1 Anishinaabeg, Cree, Oji-Cree, Dakota, and Dene territories and Métis homelands. Kelly's areas of research are Indigenous politics, decolonial and critical theory, methodological ethics, rhetorics and poetics, and the roles of theorists as witnesses and storytellers of political life. Recently she has begun work considering the interventions on normativity and entanglements of Indigiqueer and neuroqueer lifeworlds, storywork, and otherwise political imaginaries.

HŌKŪLANI K. AIKAU (SHE/HER/ʻO IA) is a Kanaka ʻŌiwi professor in the School of Indigenous Governance at the University of Victoria. She is the author of *A Chosen People, a Promised Land: Mormonism and Race in Hawaiʻi* (University of Minnesota Press 2012) and co-editor of *Feminist Waves, Feminist Generations: Life Stories from the Academy* (with Erickson and Pierce, University of Minnesota Press 2007), *Detours: A Decolonial Guide to Hawaiʻi* (with Gonzalez, Duke University Press 2019), and *Indigenous Resurgence in the Age of Reconciliation* (with Stark and Craft, Toronto, University of Toronto Press 2023).

ISABEL ALTAMIRANO-JIMÉNEZ is Zapotec or Binizá, and is a member of the community of Ixtaltepec in the the Isthmus of Tehuantepec, Mexico. Isabel is professor of political science and Canada Research Chair in Comparative Indigenous Feminist Studies at the University of Alberta. Her scholarly work focuses on Indigenous feminisms in relation to the politics of land and resource extraction, capital, and Indigenous ontologies. By examining Canada and Mexico, her research bridges discussions on Indigeneity, capitalism, and the state in Latin America versus Anglophone/Francophone North America, theorizing Indigenous feminisms transnationally.

BILLY-RAY BELCOURT (HE/HIM) is from the Driftpile Cree Nation. He is an assistant professor and Canada Research Chair in the School of Creative Writing at the University of British Columbia. He is the author of five books: *This Wound is a World*, *NDN Coping Mechanisms*, *A History of My Brief Body*, *A Minor Chorus* and *Coexistence*.

ROBYN BOURGEOIS (LAUGHING OTTER CARING WOMAN) is a mixed-race nehiyaw iskwew (Cree woman) whose Cree family comes from Treaty 8 (Lesser Slave Lake) Territory. She was born and raised in Syilx and Splats'in territories of British Columbia and is connected through her three children to the Six Nations of the Grand River. She is an associate professor in the Centre for Women's and Gender Studies at Brock, where her scholarly work focuses on Indigenous feminisms, violence against Indigenous women and girls, and Indigenous women's political activism and leadership. In addition to being an academic, Robyn is also as activist, author, and artist.

LEANNE BETASAMOSAKE SIMPSON is a Michi Saagiig Nishnaabeg writer, musician, independent scholar, and member of Alderville First Nation. She is the author of eight previous books including the novel *Noopiming: The Cure for White Ladies,* and *Rehearsals for Living*, co-authored with Robyn Maynard.

SHELAGH DAY is an international authority on women's human rights. A prolific author, she is an expert on anti-discrimination law, constitutional equality rights, and social and economic rights. A driving force behind ensuring that women can use their rights, she was the first president of the Women's Legal Education and Action Fund and a founder of the Court Challenges Program. Shelagh is a Member of the Order of Canada and founder of the Canadian Feminist Alliance for International Action and chair of its Human Rights Committee.

MARY EBERTS helped develop the equality provisions enshrined in the Canadian Charter of Rights and Freedoms. She is a co-founder of the Women's Legal Education and Action Fund and served as litigation counsel to the Native Women's Association of Canada from 1981 to 2016. With her legal expertise she has performed a lifetime of allyship and solidarity with Indigenous women. Recognition for her work includes the Governor General's Award in Honour of the Persons'

Case, the Law Society of Upper Canada Medal, the YWCA Woman of Distinction Award, the Distinguished Service Award of the Canadian Bar Association–Ontario, the Women's Law Association of Ontario President's Award, and several honorary doctorates. In 2017, Mary was awarded the Order of Canada "for her visionary leadership as an advocate and litigator advancing equality and women's rights."

JOYCE GREEN is professor emerita in the Department of Politics and International Studies at the University of Regina. Her research has focused on Indigenous-state relations; Indigenous feminism; citizenship; identity and racism in Canada's political culture; Indigenous human rights, and the notion of *reconciliation*. More recently she has focused on Ktunaxa Nation matters, such as its contemporary constitution and its cultural and political problematics since colonization. She is the editor of *Making Space for Indigenous Feminism* (Fernwood Publishing and Zed Books 2007; second ed. 2017) and of *Indivisible: Indigenous Human Rights* (Fernwood Publishing 2014). Joyce is English, Ktunaxa, and Cree-Scottish Métis. She now lives in ʔa·kiskaqǂiʔit, in ʔamakis Ktunaxa (Cranbrook, BC, in Ktunaxa Territory).

EVA JEWELL (SHE/HER/HERS) is Anishinaabe from Deshkan Ziibiing and a member of Chippewas of the Thames First Nation in Southwestern Ontario with paternal lineage from Oneida Nation of the Thames. Her research is in areas of Anishinaabe cultural and political reclamation, Indigenous experiences of work and care, and accountability in reconciliation. She is the research director at Yellowhead Institute and an assistant professor of sociology at Toronto Metropolitan University.

EMMA LAROCQUE is a Plains Cree Métis scholar, writer, poet, and professor in the Department of Native Studies, University of Manitoba. Emma is the department's longest service faculty member and has been with the department since 1976. She is a 2005 recipient of an Indspire Aboriginal Achievement Award. Professor LaRocque is the author of *Defeathering the Indian* (1975) and *When the Other is Me: Native Resistance Discourse, 1850-1990* (2010), and has also written numerous scholarly and popular articles on images of "Indians" in the media and marketplace, Canadian historiography, Native literature, education, racism, and violence against women. Her poetry has appeared in numerous national and international journals and anthologies.

ROBYN MAYNARD is an author and scholar based in Toronto, where she holds the position of assistant professor of Black Feminisms in Canada at the University of Toronto-Scarborough in the Department of Historical and Cultural Studies. Her writing on borders, policing, abolition, and Black feminism is taught widely in universities across Canada, the United States, and Europe. Maynard is the author of two books — *Policing Black Lives: State Violence in Canada from Slavery to the Present* (Fernwood 2017) and *Rehearsals for Living* (Knopt/Haymarket 2022).

SHARON McIVOR is an activist and academic. She is a member of the Lower Nicola Indian Band located outside of Merritt, British Columbia. Sharon is a lawyer, and has a master of laws degree from Queens University and an honorary doctor of laws from the University of Victoria. She teaches Indigenous studies at Nicola Valley Institute of Technology. As the plaintiff in one of the leading challenges to the sex discrimination in the Indian Act (McIvor v. Canada) and the author of a successful petition to the United Nations Human Rights Committee, Sharon has established the right of First Nations women to equal status and membership in their communities and to reparations for the discrimination they have experienced. Sharon speaks and writes on prison reform, violence against women, disability rights, Aboriginal rights, and equality rights.

CARA PEACOCK (SHE/THEY) is a political philosophy PhD student at the University of Toronto. She is Nehiyaw from Treaty 8, where she was born and raised, and N'bissing Anishinaabe from the Robinson-Huron Treaty. Her research focuses on Indigenous political thought and Western political thought at the nexus of race and colonialism, taking up questions related to gender, decolonization, and time.

MEGAN SCRIBE (SHE/HER/HERS) is Ininiw iskwew from Norway House Cree Nation. She is an interdisciplinary Indigenous feminist researcher, writer, and educator. Scribe's research interests include Indigeneity, gender and sexuality, systems of power and oppression, and Indigenous worlding through speculative fiction and poetic inquiry. Scribe is an assistant professor in the Department of Sociology at Toronto Metropolitan University, the education director with Yellowhead Institute, and a council member for Aboriginal Legal Services' Community Council Diversion Program.

Acknowledgements

THIS BOOK WOULD NOT HAVE been possible without many key relations and supports. First, I want to begin by thanking all the contributors to this edition for sharing their brilliance and their gifts, insights, experiences, and selves. I also want to express my deep gratitude towards the authors of chapters from previous editions of *Making Space* that are not reproduced in this edition but that nonetheless continue to be widely read and remain enormously impactful. The chapters in this volume indicate a continuity and advancement of Indigenous feminist thought and practice, and evidence just how deeply important your ideas and interventions have been to the trajectory of the movement.

I want to offer special thanks to my co-PI and compañera, Kelly Aguirre, for helping secure and manage multiple grants for the 2022 Indigenous Feminisms Symposium that preceded this edition, and for standing with me as I've navigated the many twists and turns of editorship personally and professionally. I also want to acknowledge Alex Wilson and Emily Riddle for sharing their work at the symposium, along with Rita Dhamoon and Christine Sy for speaking on the significance of Joyce Green's work. I also want to thank Danette Starblanket, Shalene Jobin, Daniel Voth, Mandee McDonald, Heidi Kiiwetinepinesiik Stark, and Kaia Lamothe for their love, support, and insights shared along the way.

I also want to extend my profuse appreciation to Fazeela Jiwa of Fernwood Publishing. You are an exceptionally supportive, diligent, and generous editor, and I am deeply grateful for the time, thought, and expertise that you brought to this project. This volume, my thinking, and the ideas and interventions of each of the contributors have been immeasurably advanced by your insights, experience, and conscientiousness. I cannot thank you enough.

The 2022 Indigenous Feminisms Symposium that preceded this book was resourced by a small grant from the Social Sciences and Humanities Research Council of Canada and generous financial contributions from the Yellowhead Institute, UVic's Centre for Indigenous Research and Community-Led Engagement, and UVic's School of Indigenous Governance. The University of Victoria also provided conference supports and a subvention grant supporting the publication of this book. I want to recognize Jas Morgan's work curating *Protect the Sacred,* an exhibition of artwork by Indigenous women and 2SLGBTQIA+ folks that formed part of the symposium and was well received by those in attendance. I extend my gratitude to all the students who assisted with this project along the way, including Ariane Wilson, Q Roxas, Emily Hiser, Peyton Juhnke, Sadee Lamothe, Taeja Liu, and the 2021/22 IGov cohort. And I'd like to thank Christi Belcourt for her beautiful art, which is featured on the cover of this book.

Lastly, I want to recognize Joyce Green, my colleague, friend, and editor of the first two *Making Space* volumes, for entrusting me to carry on this project and for the seemingly endless encouragement, kindness, and respect that you've exercised along the way. As is common with relations that lie close to the heart, ours is complex, incredibly meaningful, imperfect, and always growing. It entails feelings of trust and connection so rare they become difficult to capture or represent in form. Anyone in your orbit knows that the high expectations you hold for yourself also extend outwards, and thanks to your unrelenting encouragement I've been able to travel down paths that seemed unimaginable when I walked into your classroom nearly two decades ago. The challenges that we've faced have not been identical, at least professionally, and there are many I will never have to suffer thanks to the work of feminists of your generation.

From your location, making space isn't a neutral project. Yet you've carried on crucially important work while enduring, troubling, and resisting nearly every sexist and racist trope about Indigenous women imaginable. You've shown so many of your students and colleagues how to navigate and challenge an academic structure that actively excludes our subjectivities, histories, identities, and interventions. You've problematized the foundations and assumptions of your discipline, its association, and its canons, producing well-researched, critical scholarship despite gatekeeping in promotion, tenure, peer review, and publication processes. You've inspired a relational ethos and practice for so many of us, cultivating and growing networks of solidarity and activism among your racialized and Indigenous colleagues. Through you, we have learned the importance of careful, conscientious, and critical research and analysis to intellectual and activist dialogue and movement. You've shown us how to maintain boundaries, perseverance, and self-worth in the face of efforts designed to minimize the legitimacy and significance of our work. You've taught us all how to advance principled, transformative perspectives in the face of entrenched power structures and dynamics. Above all, you've modelled how to live the worlds we want to bring forward.

This work has not been in vain; it is recognized, it is valued, and it is generative. On behalf of all who have been educated and inspired by you, I thank you for the possibilities and opportunities that you have opened and held for us with such deep care.

Index

2SLGBTQIA+ people,
   Indigenous feminist inclusion and valuing of, 11, 16, 18, 140
   settler state oppression/violence, 138–9, 146, 217
2SQ/Q2S analysis/experiences, 215–17, 224–5, 232–3, 301n7
   grounded normativity, 227–8, 230–2, 287–9, 291–5, 300
   storywork, 289–90, 295–301

ableism, 138, 294, 303n20
abolitionism, 270–2, 277, 280, 283–5
Aboriginal Women's Action Network, 125
abuse, 258
   child welfare system and, 153, 158–60
   men's, 31–2
   residential school, 131
   silence about, 31–2, 265
academia, 4, 102
   citations, 40, 284, 287
   coloniality and, 36, 41–5, 102
   Indigenous women, invisibility/condemnation of, 4, 27, 33–7, 40, 43–5
   hostility to feminism, 7, 33, 36–8, 41–2
   knowledge production in, 41–3, 45–7
   no neutral position in, 38, 40, 45
   as patriarchal, 33, 36, 173, 275
   remaining in/negotiating, 42–7
   threefold harms of, 43
   training in, 6, 29, 36, 41, 275
accountability, 18, 40, 299
   calls for community, 21–2, 172
   discourses of, 181–2
   settler state lack of, 30, 151
   violent men's personal, 10, 67, 69
activism, Indigenous feminist, 18, 100, 291, 301n7
   characteristics of, 11, 13–14, 68, 272
   on gender/territorial violence, 200–7, 246, 304n26
   growth of, 2–8, 22, 41, 204
   against heteropatriarchy, 216–17
   on Indian Act/Indigenous rights, 106–7, 110
   on MMIWG inquiry, 122, 125, 137
   personal experiences driving, 29, 46–8, 53–5, 200–4
   relevance of, 281, 288
   representations of, 103, 106–7, 200, 207, 289, 296
advocacy, 3, 42, 293
   child welfare, 132, 146, 149, 162, 182
   gender-focused, 18, 146–7
   human rights, 53–4
   Indigenous feminist, 124
   Indigenous women's self-, 30
   organizations, 22n4, 152, 154
   theory development alongside, 11–12
   treaty rights, 108, 110–11
Africa, 271, 282
Ahmed, Sara, 104, 170
'Aikapu religion, 220
'āina (land),
   experiences with, 216, 219, 230–1
   spiritual power of, 215, 227, 233n6
'Āina Momona (AM, non-profit organization),
   operation of, 217–18, 222–3
   wetland taro farming restoration, 214–15
Alberta, 261, 265
   historical Métis life in, 56–8, 62
   MMIWG in, 126–7
   Red Ticket Women in, 108, 113
alcohol use, 58–9, 62–3, 73
Alderson, Aedan, 10–11
"all our relations," meanings of, 8, 14, 19, 48, 63, 67
Anderson, Kim, 188, 289, 296, 302n13
Anishinaabe, 188
   language, 261–2, 266n2
   perspective/ways of life, 170–2, 179, 183, 273
   women/femmes, 77, 83, 170–1, 251, 265
anti-Black racism/anti-Blackness, 138–9, 180, 274, 292, 299

anti-capitalism, 205, 274, 281
anti-colonial analysis, 15, 291, 294
    of academic canons, 42
    cross-movement, 277, 280, 282–3
    feminist care ethics, 170, 178, 184–5, 188
    frameworks for, 123, 164, 178, 288
    land defence, 205, 282
anti-oppression framework, 123–5, 138
anti-racism, 271
    critical, 124
    need to engage in work of, 39, 42, 140
    theory/analysis, 5, 69, 123
anti-violence efforts,
    colonization of, 135–7, 139
    government-sponsored, 123, 128, 138–40
    Indigenous women's, 135–7, 281
Aotearoa/New Zealand, 4, 221
Archibald, Jo-Ann, 289–90, 299
Assembly of First Nations (AFN), 22n5, 131, 140, 295
assimilation,
    child welfare system, 133, 149, 154
    enfranchisement as, 75–6
    forced, 75, 87, 265
    institutions of, 131–3, 256, 259–60
    narratives of, 177, 221
    Q2S disrupting, 289, 297, 302n13
    settler state goals of, 72–3, 87, 131–3, 287
asylums, *see* mental hospitals/asylums
Australia, 4, 195

Backhouse, Constance, 43
bands, Indian Act,
    denial of Indigenous women's experiences, 9, 13, 76, 131
    identity problematics, 4, 17, 35, 90, 130–1
    policing/critiquing Indigenous women, 3–4, 148
    reinstatement/acceptance of Indigenous women, 38, 47, 86–8
    removal of women's status by, 76, 81, 90, 105, 148
    resource scarcity narratives of, 89, 109
Barker, Joanne, 297, 299, 301n2
Bear, Shirley, 3
Bedard, Yvonne, 77
Belcourt, Billy-Ray, 169, 240–1, 245–6, 294–5, 297, 301n4
Bezanson, Kate, 180

Bhargava, Rajeev, 252
Bill C-3: 82, 86
Bill C-31: 86
    "all the way" amendment, 84–5
    court challenges to, 81–4
    new forms of sex discrimination, 79–81, 130
    Red Ticket Women and, 105
Bill C-38: 85–6
Bill of Rights, 77
Bill S-3: 84–6
birth alerts, 153–5, 160, 163, 264
Black feminism, 180–1, 269, 271–4, 277–8, 281
Black power/liberation movements, 270, 280, 285
Blackstock, Cindy, 42, 182
Black women,
    experiences of, 12, 280, 278–80, 283–4, 291
    Indigenous shared histories, 138, 175–6, 180, 188
    movements of, 112, 270, 277–80, 284
    see also anti-Black racism
Blaney, Fay (Xwemalhkwu), 122
Bourdieu, Pierre, 179
British Columbia, 48n1, 88, 257
    feminist organizing in, 3, 134–5, 137
    missing women commission of inquiry, 134, 136–7
    MMIWG in, 126–7, 134–7
    provincial court cases, 81–2
British North America Act, 148, 154
Byrd, Jodi, 197, 298, 303n20
    queer normativity, 245, 287–8, 294
    subjectless queer critique, 240–1

Calder et al. v. Attorney General of British Columbia, 88
Campbell, Maria, 115
Canada,
    as colonial settler state, 5, 83, 87–8, 128–30
    dominant narratives of, 100–1, 140, 185
    ignoring UN recommendations, 78–9, 83
    Indigenous genocide, 43, 73–4, 83–7, 137–8
    ongoing violence of, 68, 121–3, 131–5, 183
    sex discrimination by, *see* Indian Act
canons, disciplinary,

dominant colonial/white, 28, 37, 41
Indigenous feminist critiques of, 36, 44–5, 118
teaching against, 38, 42, 173
capitalism,
anti-, *see* anti-capitalism
environmental destruction of, 9, 278, 282, 296
Indigenous feminist/2SQ critiques of, 36, 217, 223, 271–2
Indigenous integration in, 113
oppressive systems of, 138, 185, 197, 205, 216
racial, 47, 197, 277–82
settler colonial, 184, 296
capitalist class, 10, 303n20
accumulation, 198, 203
Captive Maternal, 175, 180
carceral systems, 43
child welfare and, 152
Indigenous women/2SQ in, 259, 282–3
overthrowing/growing beyond, 270, 280
care ethics/work, 168, 171–4
colourblind theorizing, 175–6
feminist killjoy critique of, 170, 187
as pluralist project, 178–9
social/cultural reproduction, 110, 170, 175–89, 197, 204–6
Carlson, Keith, 256
Carlson, Nellie, 100, 107, 114–16
Catholic Church, 30, 59, 261
ceremonies, 263
body-land, 195, 271–2
criminalization of, 133–4, 256
intimacy of, 273–4, 298
menstruation/coming-of-age, 3, 284, 296, 304n27
Charter of Rights and Freedoms, 22n4, 89
section 15 challenges, 79, 82–3, 85–6
Chesler, Phyllis, 258
Child and Family Services (CFS), Manitoba,
absconding, 158–9
caregiving arrangements, 155, 157–8
emphasis on family reunification, 156–7
foster home versus group home, 156–9, 162
independent living programs, 160–2
legislation and policy manuals for, 151, 154, 156–9, 163–4
treatment centres, 156–7
victimization, 158–9
children, 278
abandonment, 160–1
adoption in non-Indigenous homes, 132, 149–50, 155–6, 185, 188
birth alerts for, 153–5, 160, 163, 264
conferral or loss of Indian status, 74–83, 89, 108, 111, 148
constructions of Indigenous people as, 168–9, 176, 179, 258
cultural deprivation, 31, 48n5, 108, 153, 181
forced separation from, 30, 47, 73, 130, 185
graves for, 182–4
Hawaiian storytelling and, 223, 225
institutionalization of, 20, 131, 148–9, 183, 258–62
residential schools, *see* residential schools
responsibilities to, 115–17, 127, 203, 216–17, 265, 270
right to have or not have, 17, 41
violence/death facing, 20, 30, 43, 131, 151
witnessing familial (gender) roles, 28, 55–6, 60–3, 260–1
see also girls; missing and murdered Indigenous women and girls
child welfare system,
aging out of, 154, 160–3
Agreements with Young Adults (AYA), 160–2
apprehension of children, 30, 58, 132–3, 151, 153
cis-heteropatriarchal policies and practices, 146–7, 156, 159–60, 163–4
compensation for child seizures, 86
First Nations and Metis services in, 151, 154
foster care, 132, 152–3, 155–60
harms of, 32, 132–3, 151–3
Millennial Scoop, *see* Millennial Scoop
narratives of, 146–9, 159–64
racism in, 150–3, 155, 163
rates of Indigenous children in, 148–50, 153
reforms, 149–53
Sixties Scoop, *see* Sixties Scoop
Christianity, 4, 177, 220

class, 182
    capitalist/elite/political, 10, 16, 30, 111, 280
    feminist movement addressing, 12, 54, 179–80, 204–5
    intersectionality and, 14–16, 280
    white, middle-class, 173–4, 280–1
classification,
    of identities, 11, 105, 240
    sex/gender, 147–8
    violence of, 11, 117, 124
colonialism,
    academia's complicity in, 36, 41–5, 102
    care work, notions of, 169, 175–7, 274
    choice, removal of, 65–8
    dehumanization and, 53, 65–6, 129, 205–6, 265
    fur trade, 30–1, 48n2, 57
    gendered impacts of, 29–30, 64–5, 129, 154–5, 215, 282
    gender and sexuality norms, 200–3, 207–8, 239–42, 247–8, 263
    harms from, 43, 47, 66, 73, 101, 170, 291
    heteropatriarchy, 4–5, 10–14, 66, 252–3, 259–65
    Indigenous feminist critiques of, 15–16, 41, 53–4, 104, 164, 286
    Indigenous feminist preoccupation with, 2–5, 7–14, 19
    Indigenous feminist resistance to, 8–9, 27–9, 187, 209, 243, 258, 277
    Indigenous mobilizing against, 105–7, 199–200, 232–3, 280, 291
    Indigenous women's experiences with, 3, 10–16, 66, 73, 101, 262–4
    madness/sanism and, 252, 260, 262–5
    myths of, 15, 36, 41–3, 129
    narratives of, 58, 69n5, 100–1, 159–60, 199, 294–5
    psychiatry and, 251–3, 256–60, 263
    Red Ticket Women in, 107, 111, 117
    resource extraction, 178, 199–200, 206
    Spanish, 196, 201
    violence of, see genocide; violence
    see also Indian Act; settler colonialism
colonial-straight thinking, 287–9, 294–7, 301n4
Combahee River Collective, 277–8, 281
Confederation, 57
    assimilatory goals of, 72–5

consciousness, 262, 290
    Indigenous historical, 256
    lack of, 14, 246
    of land-body relations, 14, 195
    raising political, 15, 32–3, 170
Constitution, 295
    Acts (1867 and 1982): 10, 22n4, 72, 81
    Mexican, 196–8
Convention on the Elimination of All Forms of Discrimination Against Women (CEDAW), 78–9, 84–5, 89
Convention on the Prevention and Punishment of the Crime of Genocide, 73–4, 138
Coulthard, Glen, 4–5, 292, 303n17
Cree, 59, 247
    language, 57–8, 61–3, 261, 295
    people, 28, 47–9, 134, 150, 241
    Wehsakehcha stories, 60–1
Crenshaw, Kimberlé, 14
critical race theory, 21, 36
Crown, 11
    lands, 9
    Indigenous relations with the, 88, 101

Daniels v. Canada, 72–3, 130–1
daughters, 59, 261, 298
    cultivating mana wahine, 215–18, 224, 231–2
    loss of Indian status, 35, 83
Davis, Angela Y., 271, 280
Dawes Act (United States), 168–9
day schools, 84, 148, 261
deaths, 32, 47, 248, 283
    child welfare system, 132, 150–3
    colonial systems of care and, 169, 177, 183, 264
    familial, 42, 58, 62
    Indigenous girls', 62, 126–7, 136, 140, 150–3
    Indigenous women's, 126–8, 134–7, 140, 253
    premature Indigenous, 252–3, 256–8, 262
    social, 177, 301n4
    see also genocide; missing and murdered Indigenous women and girls
Dechinta Centre for Research and Learning, 273, 275
decolonization,
    bodily/gendered impacts of, 207–8, 215–17, 232–3, 244

colonial-straight thinking in, *see* colonial-straight thinking
critiquing notions of, 67, 207–8, 216–17, 296, 299–301
grounded normativity, 230–2, 287–9, 291–5, 300
Indigenous feminist objectives and, 9, 14, 102–3, 123, 181, 281
land, relationships to, 288–9, 291–300
movements, 102–3, 283
Q2S storywork in, 286, 288–91, 298
queer notions of, 232, 238–42, 245–8
settler state violence and, 140, 147
dehumanization, 131–2
colonization and, 65–6
Indigenous people refusing, 53, 55, 265
Indigenous women, 75, 129
"squaw" namecalling, 29, 114, 129
Descheneaux, Stephane, 81, 83–4, 86
Dhamoon, Rita, 15, 37
Diaz, Natalie, 242–5, 248
disability, 46, 279, 294, 303n20
discourses, 185, 199
accountability, 181–2
care, 149, 176
colonialism and, 15, 107, 133, 241, 260, 294
deficiency, 176, 197
gender-neutral, 146–7
Indigenous feminist critical, 18, 21, 41, 288, 294–5
on Indigenous women's political presence, 104, 117
resurgence, 248, 288, 291–7, 303n20
violence in, 101, 104, 117, 133, 207
dispossession, Indigenous, 8–9, 44, 87
bodily/care relationships to, 179–80, 200, 253, 293, 300
familial impacts of, 59, 66, 184–6
Indigenous feminist analysis of, 17, 100–1, 111, 240
Indigenous resistance to, 55, 270, 293
resource extraction and, 168–9, 198–200, 203–5
schools and, 57–8
settler state goals of, 30, 69n5, 72–4, 168–9
Doucet, Andrea, 170–2
Driskill, Qwo-Li, 206–7

Earley, Mary Two-Axe, 77
Eberts, Mary, 10, 130–1
Echaquan, Joyce, 264
ecofeminism, 8, 32–3
Edelman, Lee, 239–40
Elders, 32, 108
feminist, 3
Ktunaxa, 34, 46
relationships with, 275–6, 284, 304n28
electro-convulsive therapy (ECT), 258
Elliott, Alicia, 184, 263
enfranchisement, 79, 107
assimilation through, 75–6, 85–6, 148
environmental degradation, 9, 19
colonialism and, 200, 282
feminist struggles against, 8, 14, 17, 296, 304n26
epistemic justice, 251–2
erasure, Indigenous women's/2SQ, 243
in academia, 17, 36, 171, 178
Indigenous combatting of, 8–9, 17, 53, 107–8, 181, 207
in law, 35, 46, 74–6
violence fuelling, 133, 177, 182, 193, 252, 294
Erickson, Lesley, 134
erotic, the, 239, 245
sovereignty and, 241, 206–8
exploitation, colonizer, 124, 158, 270, 280
of Indigenous identities, 18, 39–40, 75, 140
of Indigenous women and land, 9, 17, 128, 136, 203
ongoing economic, 9, 15, 128–9, 132, 175, 180
extractive industries, 9–11, 199–200, 203, 206
extractivism, 9, 206–8, 296
extractive labour, 175, 301n5
accountability for, 21, 178, 193

Fanon, Frantz, 291, 303n16
fatherhood,
accounts of, 260–2, 171, 257
community models of Indigenous, 59, 63–4, 265
enfranchisement/loss of status through, 59, 76, 79, 85–6
gentle/assistive, 56, 59–60, 62–4, 67
Indian Act status through, 57, 74–6, 80, 83–4
paid work, 28, 61
violent, 59, 62, 258
federal government, 11, 90, 182

child welfare approaches, 148, 150–1
denial of Indigenous women's experiences, 13, 121
funding for MMIWG initiatives, 125–6, 136, 140
Indian Act discrimination, 69n4, 77, 113, 169
paternalism of, 129–30, 148, 154–5
Fellows, Mary Louise, 124
femininity, 60, 174, 257
discourses on Indigenous, 55, 133–4, 290, 301n5
Muxes'/2SQ, 201–2, 215, 220–8, 239–40, 276
water and, 296, 298
see also mana wahine
feminism, 17, 269
alliances and solidarity, 7, 11–14, 33, 177–9, 187–9, 278, 282
Black, *see* Black feminism
care ethics, 168, 170–82, 184–9
class analysis, 12, 54, 179–80, 204–5
conceptualizations of, 54–5, 64–5, 69, 123–5
discussions of race, 12, 53–4, 175–6
emergence of theory, 8
hostility toward, 5, 7, 33, 36–8, 40–2, 53–5
importance of, 3, 12, 65–6, 106–7, 178, 207
Indigenous, *see* Indigenous feminism
Indigenous cultures versus, 3–4, 13, 207–8
labelling one's, 52, 55, 64–5
lack of identification with, 52–3, 65, 226, 289
white, *see* white feminism
feminist ear, listening with, 104
First Nations,
child welfare services, 151, 154
denial of women's experiences, 9, 13, 17, 34–5, 53, 89–90, 131
impacts of Indian Act on, 86–90, 181
inclusion of views from women/2SQ, 122, 138, 140
use of term, 69n1, 141n1
Fiske, Jo-Anne, 295, 304n25
Fletcher, Alice, 168–9
Flowers, Rachel, 184, 187
foster care, 132, 152–3, 155–60
Foucault, Michel, 180, 253
freedom,
bodily/erotic, 208, 239–40, 242
to choose, 65–6, 69, 208
collective/movement-focused notions of, 125, 270–5, 278–80, 283
enfranchisement's lack of, 75–7, 79
gendered notions of, 56, 59–60, 64, 112, 116
imagining, 240, 242, 292
lack of Indigenous Peoples', 101, 104, 217

Garba, Tapji, 291–2, 299
Gary, M.E., 178–9, 189
Gehl, Lynn, 83–4
George, Pamela, 134
gender,
colonial/Western notions of, 147–8, 233n7, 242, 247, 251
expression, 59, 109, 224–6, 301n7
Indian Act discrimination, 46, 79–82, 100, 103–7, 113, 148
inequality, 15, 52–6, 59–60, 111
madness and, 256–8
need for analysis based on, 4–7, 204, 232, 280
power and, *see* power relations
resurgence movements and, 276, 280–3, 288
socialization, 33, 147–8, 173–4, 214–15
third, 193, 200–1
traditional Indigenous notions of, 28, 52, 215–17, 228, 245–7, 295
violence, *see* gendered violence
gender binaries, 28, 30–1, 55–61, 287
colonial/hegemonic, 201–2, 214–15, 220–1, 228, 253
dismantling, 147–8, 230, 240, 258
Indigenous women challenging, 253, 258, 262, 274
troubling, 18, 59–60, 63, 204–6, 223–4
gender-diverse people, 164, 301n7, 304n23
challenging notions of gender violence, 193–4
feminist support for, 12, 16, 18
mana wahine, 214–17, 223–8, 231–2, 233n6
troubling constructions of sex/gender, 16, 18, 215, 225–7
see also Muxes
gendered labour,
care-based, 170–6, 182, 188, 274–6

divisions of, 55–6, 214–16, 220–4, 228–30, 233n4
in Hawaiian culture, 219–25, 233n4
paid versus unpaid, 57–8, 61, 63, 74, 175
reproductive, 175, 178–81, 204, 276, 296, 298
in storywork, 228–9, 289–91, 299–300
gendered oppression,
Indigenous feminism confronting, 9–13, 19, 21, 223–4
government policymaking/discourse, 140, 146–7, 152–4, 163–4
settler state, 4, 13–15, 46, 122–3, 252–3
gendered violence,
body-land, notions, 194, 199–200, 203–8, 289, 294–300
colonial, 2, 46, 107–8, 129, 260
community impacts of, 66–8, 137–8, 202, 206–7
Indigenous feminist critiques of, 21, 54, 208–9, 282
Indigenous women and girls facing, 63–8, 134, 159–63, 193, 204, 283
as self-determination issue, 9, 14
state sanctioning/justification of, 63–8, 134, 140, 202
technologies of, 259–60
gender-non-conforming people, *see* gender-diverse people
gender studies/theory, 4, 11, 16
genocide, 9, 241, 270
Canadian policies of, 74, 83–7, 137–9, 149, 182–6
care as, 169, 175–9, 188
cultural, 73, 83, 137–8
definitions of, 73
gender-specific, 46, 83–7, 137–8, 296
settler colonialism and, 44, 73, 83, 139, 175–7, 188
Gilligan, Carol, 172–5
Gilmore, Ruth Wilson, 140, 270–1
girls, 278
biases against, 56, 59–60, 63–4, 159–64, 174
in child welfare system, 146–7, 150–3, 159–64
expectation to find men, 28, 30–1, 59, 62
Indigenous feminist support for, 16, 52–4, 64–7, 89, 296

missing and murdered, 30, 46, 53–4, 121–8, 135–8, 150–3
racialized misogyny on, 10, 68–9, 129–35, 138–40
Gladue, Cindy, 134
Goeman, Mishuana, 188, 203, 292–3
Gordon, Avery, 247–8
Goulding, Warren, 126
governments,
band, *see* bands, Indian Act
federal, *see* federal government
provincial, *see* provincial governments
grandmothers, 48n3, 62–4, 82–3, 183–4, 232, 298–9
Green, Joyce, 2–3, 6
Grindr, tribal fetish on, 241
Grismer, Jacob, 81–3, 89
Groberman, Harvey, 83, 89
grounded normativity, 227–8, 230–2, 287–95, 300

Haida Nation v. British Columbia (Minister of Forests), 88
Haida people, 85, 125
Halberstam, Jack, 164n1, 239–40, 287
"half-breed," as term, 28, 31, 48n4, 57
Hāloanākalaukapalili (Hāloa, taro), 217, 224–32
queerness of, 224, 227–32
story of, 225–7, 228–9
see also kalo (Hāloa, taro)
Harper, Stephen, 121, 136
Haudenosaunee, 77, 171, 178
Haumea (Hawaiian deity), 224, 226–7, 230–2; *see also* Papahānaumoku
health care systems, 43
access to, 62, 148, 162
heteronormativity, 297
Indigenous feminist theory on, 13, 217
policymaking, 169
social movement, 204, 283, 303n19
societal, 56, 61, 159, 220
storywork interrogation of, 215–16, 224, 228, 231–2
heteropatriarchy, 186
assumptions, 8, 228, 239, 258
continued oppression from, 10, 21–2, 138, 202, 282–3
decolonization and, 241–2, 289, 300, 302n8
gender-neutral discourse issues in, 146–7, 152–4, 163–4

Index 325

Indigenous feminism versus, 7, 215–16, 231–2, 276–7
Indigenous traditionalism and, 214–17, 221–4, 228–30, 234n13
psychiatry/sanism and, 252–3, 258–60, 262–5
see also patriarchy
hierarchies, 39
gendered, 10, 124–5, 129, 205, 287
Indian Act, 72–9, 82–6, 89–90
institutional, 42, 45
refusal of, 209, 220
Hokowhitu, Brendan, 220–1, 228
homophobia, 28, 45
assumptions and relations of, 8, 36, 41
Indigenous traditionalism and, 214, 217, 219–24, 228, 284
structural violence of, 202, 206–8, 247–8
hooks, bell, 54, 112
human rights, 124
advocacy, 52–5, 159, 202
Canada's violation of international, 78–9, 83, 89, 136
treaties, 78–9
Human Rights Act, 78
Hunt, Sarah, 300–1

identity, 240, 263, 302n8
Canadian, 155, 183
claiming one's, 29–31, 38–9, 42, 46–8, 66, 171, 297–9
cultural, 109–10, 205, 112, 205
feminism and, 11–12, 54, 174–5, 281
gender/sexual, 7, 147, 180, 207, 215, 224, 301n7
intersectionality of, 14–15
labelling with fraudulent, 37–9
politics, 11, 102, 105–7, 276–8
problematic of Indigenous, 3–4, 17–18, 27–9, 37–40, 115–17
state denial of Indigenous, 9, 17, 47, 76, 83, 87–90
tensions within, 29, 43
Idle No More, 187, 304n26
imperialism, 36, 101, 180, 278
challenging, 9, 69, 292, 301n4
incarceration, 256–60, 278, 285
settler state goals of Indigenous, 73, 133, 136
Indian Act,
bands, *see* bands, Indian Act

"Indian," who counts as, 69n4, 77, 113, 129–31, 169
Indigenous genocide through, 73–4, 83–7, 137–9, 149, 182–6
legal challenges to, 74–83, 89, 108, 111, 148
section 12(1)(b), impacts of, 77–8, 100
sex discrimination in, 72–9, 82–6, 89–90, 100, 103–7, 113, 148
status, *see* status, Indian
Indian Rights for Indian Women (IRIW), 77, 90, 101–8, 110–16
Indigeneity, 221
claiming in academia, 38–9, 47, 294
denigration of, 42, 253
mitigating essentialization of, 15–17, 103, 110–11, 294
queerness and 245–6, 300
regulation of, 100, 107–9, 126, 240–1
reticence about, 28, 33, 39–40
Indigenous feminism,
anti-oppression framework, 123–5, 138
conference on (U of Victoria), 5–6
dimensions of resurgence, 8–9, 13–14, 18–19, 41, 215, 273–7
identification with, 29, 46–8, 52–5, 64–5, 200–4
other feminisms versus, 9, 11–16, 170, 174–80, 188, 207–8, 297
relevance of, 10, 21, 64, 281, 288–9
representations of, 103, 106–7, 200, 207, 289, 296
signal characteristics of, 2, 7–9, 11–15, 68, 272
theory, *see* theory, Indigenous feminist
transformative interventions of, 12–14, 41, 102–4, 111, 114, 215, 290
Indigenous men, 46
bias toward, 74, 108–12, 255
denial of Indigenous women's experiences, 13, 28–30, 106, 173
disapproving presence of, 34, 202
enfranchisement, 59, 75–6, 79, 85–6, 148
Indian Act status through, 57, 74–6, 80, 83–4, 130–1
Indigenous feminist approaches to, 12, 16, 54–5
notions of resource scarcity, 28, 113–14

social dominance of, 8–9, 14, 43, 204–5, 220–3
violence by, *see* violence
women's demands for, 10, 216
see also gendered labour
Indigenous Peoples,
academic treatment of, 39, 44, 102, 131–6
adoption of European gender norms, 221
asylum treatment, 255–7
care, colonizer notions of, 168–70, 176–8, 181, 185–9
colonialism and, *see* colonialism
land, relationships to, 8, 11, 48, 194–9, 203, 206–8, 291
mainstream feminism versus, 3, 11, 53–5
queer, 241–2, 245, 248
racist narratives of, 5, 69n5, 103, 126–9, 152–5, 251
resurgence/resistance, 55, 187, 194, 197, 203–5, 283, 286
rights of, 89, 137
settler state genocide of, 42–3, 72–3, 100–1, 122–3, 138
sovereignty, *see* sovereignty
systemic oppression of, 8, 13, 89, 181, 305n32
tensions among, 105–11, 115–18
see also United Nations Declaration on the Rights of Indigenous Peoples (UNDRIP)
Indigenous politics, 291
binary notions of, 102–3, 109–11, 117–18, 295
Canadian versus, 101–2
historical periods of heightened, 105–7
Indigenous women's/Q2S presence in, 3, 106–7, 238, 300
Red Ticket Woman in, *see* Red Ticket Women
Indigenous self-government, 52, 154
confronting gender oppression, 10, 111, 115
Indigenous feminist goals of, 14, 90
movements toward, 88, 106–7, 110–11, 115
Indigenous studies, 246, 289
feminism in, 4, 33
Indigenous women,
academic invisibility/erasure, 4, 27, 33–7, 40, 43–5, 171, 178

anti-violence efforts, 135–7, 281
condemnation of, 3–4, 34–6, 44, 75, 129, 148
criminalization of, 133–4, 259, 282–3
exploitation of land and, 9, 17, 128, 136, 203
as haunted by loss, 46–7, 62
Indian Act discrimination, see Indian Act
male disapproval of, 34, 202
missing and murdered, *see* missing and murdered Indigenous women and girls
re-centring of, 9, 104, 117
societal invisibility, 30–1, 102–4, 133, 177, 182, 193, 252, 294
university presence, 34–40, 42–7
voice, finding one's, 31, 38–40, 46, 69
Indigiqueer, notion of, 247, 294, 301n7, 303n20
institutionalization, 200
children's, 20, 131, 148–9, 183, 258–62
experiences of Indigenous, 251, 254–62, 265
gender regimes in, 10–11, 28
of misogyny, 65
settler state goals of Indigenous, 73
institutions,
accountability, lack of, 39, 122
of assimilation, 131–3, 256, 259–60
child welfare, *see* child welfare system
endemic racism in, 17, 45–6
hierarchies, 42, 45
Indigenous feminists/women versus, 11–14, 42, 106–7
Indigenous self-government, 90
patriarchal, *see* male-dominated institutions
penal, *see* prisons
psychiatric, *see* mental hospitals/asylums; psychiatry
queerness in, 241, 246–8
reproducing themselves/culture, 36, 42–3, 179
settler state, 4, 42–3, 121–3, 148–9, 198
violence of, 73, 122–3, 129–32, 140, 256–62
intergenerational trauma, 86
harmful impacts of, 33, 67, 127, 131–2, 169
Indigenous feminist theory on, 11–12, 36, 204

International Covenant on Civil and
    Political Rights (ICCPR), 78, 83, 89
intersectionality, 14–15, 104, 252, 269
Inuit, 69n1, 130, 141n1
    community denial of women's experiences, 13, 17, 43
    women's representation, 122, 138, 140
Irlbacher-Fox, Stephanie, 187
Isthmus of Tehuantepec,
    development plans, 196–200, 208–9
    ejido system, 195–8
    Interoceanic Corridor, 193, 196, 199–203
    land, wind, water of, 194–5, 208–9
    matriarchal societies of, 193, 200–5
    see also Muxes; Nguius

James, Joy, 175, 180
Jamieson, Kathleen, 76
Jilek-Aall, Louise, 257, 264
Johnson, Breya, 175
Juchitán, 193, 200–1

Kainai (Blood Tribe), 34–5
Kaʻiulani (āina momona farm worker), 218–19, 222–3
kalo (Hāloa, taro), 233n4
    a daughter's relationship with, 216–18, 231–2
    gendered labour in farming, 214, 222, 227–30
    as gender-non-conforming beings, 224–8
    see also Hāloanākalaukapalili (Hāloa, taro)
Kameʻeleihiwa, Lilikalā, 220, 234nn14,15
Kamloops Indian Residential School, 182–3
Kāne Kuahiwinui, Makana, 229, 234n13
killjoy, feminist, 170, 187
Kimelman, Edwin C., 150
Kitchen Table Collective, 2, 40
Kohlberg, Lawrence, 172–3
Ktunaxa Nation, 27–8, 33–4, 38, 46–8, 49nn7,8
Kuokkanen, Rauna, 9–10, 28

labour, 132, 293
    care, 170–6, 180–2, 186–8, 274–6
    emotional, 204, 222–4, 230
    gendered, *see* gendered labour
    intellectual, 42, 216, 283–4, 290
    paid versus unpaid, 57–8, 61, 63, 74, 175
    reproductive, 175, 178–81, 204, 276, 296, 298
land, 113
    bodily relationships with, 193–6, 199–209, 271–3, 293–301
    communal/collective, 195–8, 201, 204–8
    defence, 193–4, 197–200, 203–5, 208, 279, 282
    extractive relations with, *see* extractive industries; extractivism
    forced removal from, 47, 73, 87, 132–3
    lack of ownership of, 57–9, 67, 148
    living off the, 56–8, 61
    protectors, 8, 13, 19, 90, 296
    reclamation of, 9, 17, 106, 206, 265, 288, 292–4
    reconciliation and, 88, 185–6
    reserve, *see* reserves
    responsibilities to, 186
    restoration, 214–18, 232
    scrip, 57, 59, 62, 69n4
    settler state assertions of sovereignty, 72–3, 88, 100–1
    theft, 9–15, 69, 169, 176–7, 203, 292
    title, 13, 73, 75, 88
    violence against, 186, 199–200, 205–6
    wind and water, relationships with, 193–5, 198–9, 203, 289
    see also dispossession, Indigenous; loʻi kalo (wetland taro farming) restoration; terra nullius
land back, 14, 181, 185, 291, 300
language, 18, 34, 75, 169, 221, 298
    deprivation of, 31, 57
    reclamation, 14–17, 48, 58, 181, 184, 204
Lavell, Jeanette Corbiere, 77
law, 72, 102, 174
    challenges to Canadian, 77–8, 79, 81–7, 100
    child welfare, 147–8, 156
    enforcement, *see* police
    faculty condemnation, 45–6
    Indigenous, 13, 177–8, 189, 197, 298–9
    Indigenous women's invisibility in, 4, 46
    international versus Canadian, 138
    settler state, 43, 74, 163, 197–8, 283

legal system, Canadian, 37, 43
    dispossession and exclusion in, 57, 73, 75, 85, 130
    Indigenous criminalization in, 133–4
    Indigenous women in, 54, 68, 131, 133–4, 296
    rights in, *see* rights
    violence, *see* violence
    see also incarceration
Lemkin, Raphael, 73–4
lesbianism, 28, 138, 200–1, 278
    used as epithet, 36
letter-writing, 270, 272–5
liberal feminism, 16, 32
liberalism, 61
    Indigenous, 240–1
    settler state, 100–1, 181
Liberal Party of Canada, 182
liberatory efforts, 21
    addressing gendered oppression in, 5, 9, 280–3, 285, 288
    alliances and solidarity in, 7, 11–12, 17, 269, 278
    critiques of, 111, 116, 252, 294
    envisioning notions of, 269–70, 273–5, 278, 285
    Indigenous feminist, 8, 13–14, 18–19, 41, 215
    Indigenous women's, 9, 21, 27
    national, 5, 280, 288, 291
    white feminist, 177–9, 187–9
Lindberg, Tracey, 184–5
literature, Indigenous feminist, 58, 290
    absence/growth of, 4–6, 11, 255–6, 260, 275
    academic cannon versus, 36, 41, 194, 253–4
    care ethics and, 172, 179, 188
    on gendered violence, 54, 193
    on psychiatric experiences, 255–6, 260, 263
lo'i kalo (wetland taro farming) restoration, 217, 224–6, 231–2
    gendered labour in, 214, 222, 227–30
López Obrador, Andrés Manuel, 199
Lorde, Audre, 239, 275, 234n9
love, 66, 227
    grief and, 243–4
    of the land, 214, 233n6
    queer Indigenous, 207, 242–3, 245, 297
    relational practices of, 32, 187, 205, 209

Lovelace, Sandra, 78, 83, 89
Lugones, Maria, 287, 303n22
Luther, Martin, 254–5

madness,
    Indigenous women and, 251, 257–60, 262–5
    relations of power/violence and, 251–4, 262
Maihi, Renee, 225
Mailhot, Terese Marie, 263
making space, 47, 316
    continuous conversation in, 2, 7, 282–4
male-dominated environments,
    exclusionary, 4, 13, 33, 168
    Indigenous women as challenging, 12, 106–8, 111
    romanticizing pre-contact, 14
    social movements, 106–8
    women's oppression in, 7–8, 11–12, 22n5
Maliseet, 3, 78
mana wahine (female generative power/authority), 233n4
    concept of, 214, 225
    lo'i as site of, 214–18, 223–4, 228, 232–3
    passing onto children, 215–18, 224, 231–2
    pono (duality) of spirit and, 224–6, 228
    queer, 214–16, 223–6, 233
Manitoba,
    birth alerts in, 153–5
    child welfare system in, *see* Child and Family Services (CFS), Manitoba
    Millennial/Sixties Scoop, 147, 149–50
    MMIWG in, 54, 126–7, 150–2
Māori, 220, 225
Maracle, Lee, 216, 263, 287, 290, 299, 301n3
Maracle, Sylvia, 296
Margetts, Jenny, 113, 115
marriage, 46, 265
    "mixed," 34, 48n2
    pressure on girls for, 31, 63–4, 154–5, 282
    sexual activity outside of, 28
    tribal membership through, 34, 80, 130, 148
    women's loss of Indian status through, 75–81, 83–6, 105

see also Red Ticket Women
marrying out, 109, 130
  impacts of, 107–8, 110–11
masculinity,
  adoption of toxic, 10, 68, 202–3, 220–2
  gendered expectations, 55–6, 60, 220–1, 303n16
  Indigenous, 60, 116, 216, 221, 246
  queer, 201, 214–16, 224, 246, 296–7
  in political movements, 273–4, 296
matriarchal societies, 296, 299
  Isthmus of Tehuantepec, 193, 200–2
  settler undermining of Indigenous, 74, 130–1
matrifocal culture, 201, 204
matrilineal Indigenous societies, 56, 304n25
  denial of status in, 84–5
  imposition of patrilineality on, 129–31
McIvor, Sharon, 35, 46, 48n6, 81–3, 89, 131
McLachlin, Beverley, 88
men, non-Indigenous, 55
  as abusive, 31–2
  Indigenous women marrying, 108, 112, 265
  see also Indigenous men
menstruation, 3, 304n27
  taboos around, 59–60, 228–31, 234nn11,13,15, 284, 296
mental health, Indigenous, 140, 251
  women's re-storying of, 263–4
mental hospitals/asylums, 251, 254
  Indigenous women in, 256–62
Métis,
  as Apeetowgusanuk, 57–9, 69n3
  community denial of women's experiences, 13, 43, 60–1, 130
  government consultation with, 122, 138, 150–1
  identity, 28, 31, 35, 38, 47–9, 141n1
  railroad line community life and history, 55–8, 60–3
  scrip, 57, 59, 62, 69n4
  women, 17, 22n5, 53, 56–61
Mexico, 193–4
  development plans, 196–200, 203, 206–9
  ejido system, 195–8
  Isthmus, *see* Isthmus of Tehuantepec
  McLane-Ocampo Treaty, 196

Revolution, 195, 197
  see also Zapotec people
Millennial Scoop, 149, 155, 184–5
Million, Dian, 171, 188, 224, 289, 300
misogyny, 5, 8–10
  in child welfare system, 146, 150
  Indigenous feminist analysis of, 8–12, 18–19, 65
  prevalence/impunity of, 64, 202
  racialized, 8–10, 30, 36, 46, 150, 264
  violence of, 69, 202, 206, 288
missing and murdered Indigenous women and girls,
  documented cases, 125–8, 135, 159–60
  intergenerational impact, 127
  memorials and marches for, 122, 135
  National Action Plan on, 140
  National Inquiry, *see* National Inquiry into Missing and Murdered Indigenous Women and Girls
  phenomenon of disproportionate violence, 121–3, 127–8, 131–4, 277
  public reports, 53–4, 134–40, 153
  settler state narratives about, 30, 69n2, 136, 279
Monture-Angus, Patricia, 45, 302n13
Moreton-Robinson, Aileen, 203, 290–1, 301n2
Morgan, Jas, 298
motherhood, 296
  absence of romanticizing, 60, 63
  accounts of, 59–64, 217–18
  commitments, 215–16, 231–2
  Earth versus women's, 204–5, 220, 225, 301n5
  facing oppression/violence in, 30–1, 127, 131, 155, 163
  Indian status and, 80–4, 110
  institutionalization and, 258, 265
  labour in, 55–8, 61, 63, 74, 217–18
  notion of "strong," 200–1
  white, 168, 174, 177–8
  see also daughters; fatherhood; grandmothers
movements,
  Black feminist/Lives, 112, 270–4, 277, 284–5
  collective/self-government, 14, 107, 110
  critiques within and across, 21, 104, 186, 270–80, 283
  decolonial/nationalist, 102–3, 283

feminist (mainstream), 4, 12, 65, 106–7, 178, 207
gendered dynamics in, 204, 208, 304n26
giving love to, 205, 209
Indian Rights for Indian Women (IRIW), 77, 90, 101, 103–8, 110–16
Indigenous feminist, 6–8, 16, 18, 273–7
land defence/reclamation, 193–4, 197, 208, 304n26
liberatory, 7–8, 12, 252, 269–75, 285
political, 20, 107, 274
queer, 7, 277, 279, 284–5
resurgence/resistance, 55, 187, 194, 197, 203–5, 283, 286
social, *see* social movements
solidarities across, 7, 11, 205, 269–72, 285
Treaty Rights, 106–7, 111
Muñoz, José Esteban, 239–42, 247–8
Muxes, 193, 200–8

Narayan, Uma, 176
National Action Committee on the Status of Women (NAC), 12, 22n4
National Day for Truth and Reconciliation (Orange Shirt Day), 183–4
National Inquiry into Missing and Murdered Indigenous Women and Girls, 53, 121, 135
anti-oppression analysis in, 138
on child welfare system, 146, 153
documentation of genocide, 46, 137–9
limitations of, 122–3, 138–9
settler state lack of reparations, 139–40
testifying for, 136–9
see also missing and murdered Indigenous women and girls
Native studies, *see* Indigenous studies
Native Women's Association of Canada (NWAC), 35, 90, 295
MMIWG database of cases versus RCMP files, 125–8, 135
Sisters in Spirit initiative, 53–4, 132, 135–6
neoliberalism, 303n20
narratives of, 42, 183–4, 197, 199
queer countering of, 241, 247
Nguius, 200–3, 205–8
non-binary people,
feminist inclusion of, 12, 16, 297–9
fluid understandings of gender, 18, 206
non-Indigenous feminists, 3–4
Indigenous alignments with, 7, 18, 55
Indigenous feminists versus, 13, 207–8
see also Indigenous feminism
non-Indigenous scholars, 301n5
Indigenous alliances with, 5, 7, 102, 123, 187
North American Free Trade Agreement (NAFTA), 197–8

Oʻahu, Hawaiʻi, 214–15
ʻohana (non-heteropatriarchal, non-heteronormative family), 230–2
ʻŌiwi people, 233nn2
feminist theorizing on, 215–17, 227, 230, 233n6
traditionalization of invader masculinity, 220–2
Ontario, 84
institutionalization in, 251, 258, 261
oppression,
2SLGBTQIA+ people's, 138–9, 146, 217
in capitalism, 138, 185, 197, 205, 216
colonial/settler state, 4, 8–9, 16, 44–5, 53–4, 65, 233
confronting/dismantling, 10–11, 36, 138, 147, 170, 186, 262
continued, 6–7, 53, 114, 173, 278
gendered, *see* gendered oppression
heteropatriarchal, 10, 21–2, 138, 202, 282–3
Indigenous feminist analysis of, 8–13, 41, 53–4, 104, 164, 278, 286
Indigenous women facing, 8–13, 33, 89, 129–31, 181, 289
intersecting systems of, 10–15, 124–5, 138, 203
liberation from, 14, 269, 276, 280
in liberatory movements, 5, 9, 280–3, 285, 288
racialized, 18–19, 28, 67, 112, 252–3
systemic, 8, 33, 42–4, 68, 175, 281–2, 290
see also anti-oppression framework
Orange Shirt Day, *see* National Day for Truth and Reconciliation (Orange Shirt Day)
Osborne, Helen Betty, 30, 54, 150, 159
Overall, Christine, 54

Palmater, Pam, 90
Papahānaumoku (Hawaiian deity), 220, 224–5, 227; *see also* Haumea (Hawaiian deity)
Pasternak, Shiri, 181, 294
patriarchy,
   in academia, 33, 36, 173, 275
   care work, denigration under, 173–4, 179, 185–8, 276
   colonial, 4–5, 10–14, 66, 252–3, 259–65
   harms from, 59, 66–8, 174
   Indigenous feminist analysis of, 8–9, 55, 65, 123–4, 208, 258
   Indigenous male leadership, 107, 113–15
   Indigenous women/2SQ facing, 36, 53, 179, 202–6
   settler state imposition of, 74, 123, 129–31, 169
personal context, 252
   in academia/scholarship, 38–9, 42, 290
   driving force of, 29, 123, 207, 246
   feminist identification and, 52, 65, 226
   as political, 13, 35, 104, 215–16, 274
Picton, Robert, 30, 135, 137
Pierre, Sophie, 34, 37, 49n7
police,
   adversarial relationship with Indigenous women, 134–5, 159
   complacency about violence, 30, 64, 121, 126, 133, 150–1
   political mobilizing for abolishing, 271, 277–80
   racism, 31, 133
   Royal Canadian Mounted, *see* RCMP (Royal Canadian Mounted Police)
   violence by, 43, 66, 159–60, 279–81, 284
political science, 30, 34
   Indigenous, 101–4
   white male elite perspective in, 28, 41–4, 47, 102
   see also Indigenous politics
positionality, awareness of, 38, 52, 69, 281
post-colonial analysis, 10, 243, 282–3
   feminist work on, 5, 15, 36, 39, 69, 176, 245
post-traumatic stress disorder (PTSD), 65, 139

poverty, 198, 278
   as feminist issue, 52, 66
   Indigenous/Métis community, 57–9, 62, 111, 134
   Indigenous women facing, 17, 31, 68, 162–3, 259
Povinelli, Elizabeth, 195
power relations, 61, 199, 287–9, 297
   academic, 36–9, 44, 47
   focus on, 8, 107, 209
   gendered, 2, 10–12, 28–31, 181, 204–8, 221
   intersectionality in, 14, 107, 113, 203
   psychiatric, 252–4
   relevance of Indigenous feminism in, 10, 21, 28, 107
   settler state–Indigenous, 35, 113–17, 151, 184–9, 206–8
praxis, Indigenous feminist, 11, 34
   anti-colonial, 178, 184
   intersectionality in, 14–15
   reliance on feminist processes, 12, 34, 172
   in storywork, 290–1
pre-contact Indigenous societies, 241
   responses to violence in, 129
   romanticizing male dominance in, 14, 108
   women's self-determination in, 108–9, 253
prisons, 135, 172–3, 274
   settler-colonial reliance on, 256–60
   structural racism in, 151
   see also incarceration
privilege, 11–12, 15
   care ethicist, 173–5, 187
   educational, 42, 44–5
   examining one's, 16, 42, 56–8, 124–5
   gendered, 8, 28, 36, 205, 240
   Indigenous feminist interrogation of, 13, 18, 54–5
   obliviousness to one's, 12–13, 16, 33, 38, 175
   structural, 16, 44–5, 111–13
   white, 10, 16–18, 36–8, 45, 173–5
prostitution, 128, 283
   narratives on Indigenous promiscuity and, 68, 133–5
provincial governments,
   child welfare management, 148–53, 156, 160–1
   concern for MMIWG, 54, 121, 126–8, 136–7, 140

denial of Indigenous women's experiences, 13, 75, 121
Indigenous feminist struggles against, 14
psychiatry,
colonial heteropatriarchal character of, 251–3, 256–60, 263–5
Indigenous women's experiences with, 252, 254–6, 260–3, 265
institutions, 251, 254, 256–62
racialization and, 253, 255–6, 259–60
violence of, 252–4, 256–65
Puxley, Peter, 65
Pyle, Kai, 298, 301n7

Q2S storywork, 289–90, 295–301
Quebec Superior Court, 81, 83–4, 86
queerness,
decolonization and, see decolonization
Indigeneity and, 238, 245–6
mana wahine, 214–16, 223–6, 233n4
negativity, theories of, 238–40, 242–4
subjectless critique and, 240–2
queer Indigenous people, 138, 233
care ethics and, 179, 186–8
erasure/absence of, 200, 207, 223
troubling normative gender/sexuality, 18, 201
Two-Spirit, see 2SQ/Q2S analysis/experiences; Two-Spirit people
writers/poets, 238–9, 241–5

race, 73, 150
equality, 12, 281
feminist discussions of, 12, 53–4, 175–6
intersectional notions of, 14–15, 31, 124, 182
in movement building, 112, 280
psychiatry and, 253, 255–60
settler colonial narratives of, 31, 130, 137, 153
racial capitalism, 277, 279, 281
racialization,
care work and, 169, 175–6, 180
division of labour, 276
Indigenous feminist analyses of, 2, 10–13, 28, 302n8, 303n16
settler colonial narratives of, 5, 133, 197
structures of power, 13, 37, 107–8
violence, 15, 159, 200, 252–3, 280–1

racism,
in academia, 7, 27, 36–7, 41–7, 316–17
anti-Black, 138–9, 180, 274, 292, 299
anti-Indigenous, 5, 69n5, 103, 126–9, 152–5, 251
child welfare system, 150–3, 155, 163
colonial, 4, 8–9, 16, 44–5, 53–4, 65, 138, 233
confronting/dismantling, 31, 33, 122, 138, 147, 170, 186, 262
Indigenous feminist analyses of, 2, 8–12, 52–4, 65
Indigenous women's experiences with, 3–8, 11, 17, 107–8
intersectional notions of, 14–15, 123–4
misogyny, 8–10, 30, 36, 46, 69, 150, 264
obliviousness to, 7, 12–13, 16, 33
rural, 28–30, 127
settler state, 5, 34–5, 46–7, 57, 133, 197
structural/systemic, 9, 12, 18–19, 28, 66–9, 112, 252–3
see also anti-racism
Radek, Gladys, 125
Razack, Sherene, 15, 74–5, 124–5, 134
RCMP (Royal Canadian Mounted Police), 136, 261
MMIWG case files versus NWAC database, 125–8
Reclaiming Power and Place: The Final Report of the National Inquiry into Missing and Murdered Indigenous Women and Girls, 53, 153
reconciliation, 16, 30
Canadian genocidal policies versus, 88, 148, 183–8
care ethics and, 182, 184–9
Indigenous versus settler state forms of, 184–7
see also Truth and Reconciliation Commission (TRC)
Red River settlement, 31, 48n5, 57, 59n3
Red Ticket Women,
in Canadian legislation, 106
concept of, 105, 107–9, 116–18
economic critiques of, 111–13
political conflict with, 108–15
self-determination of, 108–9
relationality, 100
feminist analysis and, 12, 15, 21, 123, 174

Indigenous community, 104, 114–18,
171–2, 176, 186
to the land, 11, 181, 185, 194–5, 200,
207, 292
liberation/resurgence and, 215, 273,
276, 284
with non-Indigenous people, 31, 39,
57, 177–9, 187–8
queer theory and, 242–6
radical, 67
Red Ticket Woman and, 110, 113–18
reparations,
calls for, 9, 14, 140
Canada's lack of considering, 89
reserves,
experiences on, 248, 261–2, 266, 271
forced relocation to, 47, 72–4, 132–3,
169, 256–7
inadequate food, housing, medicine
on, 73, 86, 113, 181
Indian status and living on, 17, 57,
74–5, 81
land for, 87, 90, 132–3, 148, 181
legislation on, 74–5, 131, 148, 154
MMIWG on, 121, 127
overcrowding on, 73, 109, 112–13
women's return to, 77–8, 85, 109,
112–14
residential schools, 68, 86
honouring instigators of, 43–4
operation of, 43–4, 148–9, 253,
258–61
violence and trauma from, 89, 131–3,
137, 176, 182–5
rights,
2SLGBTQIA+, 11, 279
activism for Indigenous women's, 47,
54, 88–90, 106–7, 110, 202
collective, 89, 102, 109, 112, 115–16
cultural, 78, 83, 89, 109, 112, 116
curtailing of, 43, 73, 78–83, 89, 105,
148
equality, 35, 65, 78, 296
to have or not have children, 17, 41,
185
human, *see* human rights
of Indigenous Peoples, 86–9, 137
individual, 89, 102–3, 109, 116, 281
land, 69n4, 74, 186, 196, 197
legal, 16, 72–4, 148, 154
political, 16, 78, 102
self-determination, 29, 46, 89, 109
status, 35, 84, 109, 112

treaty, 106–11
see also Bill of Rights; Charter of
Rights and Freedoms
Rollo, Toby, 176
Royal Commission on Aboriginal
Peoples, 128
Royal Commission on the Status of
Women, 77

Said, Edward, 42, 48
sanism, heteropatriarchal, 252, 262–5
Sápmi, 4, 10
Saskatchewan, 40, 125–7
scholars, feminist, 55
care ethics, 168, 170–82, 185–9
experiences of, 29, 33–5, 38–40, 53,
123, 296
Indigenous, 4, 11, 13–15, 46–8, 169,
206, 217
marginalization of Indigenous, 7, 27,
37–8, 42–5
non-Indigenous, 4, 124, 170–82,
185–9, 291, 301n5
scholarship, Indigenous, 288, 303n18
absence of, 2, 36, 100–2
growth of feminist, 4–6, 18, 21, 40–1,
171–2, 289–90
schooling, public, 184, 216, 280
loss of culture/language in, 57–8
Schuller, Kyla, 168
Scribe, Megan, 169
self-determination, 231, 302n11
collective versus individual, 89, 109,
115
Indigenous feminist goals of, 9,
14–17, 65, 108–9
national, 44, 101, 140
see also Indigenous self-government
settler colonialism,
care theory/work and, 168–70,
176–82, 186–9
cis-heteropatriarchy and, 146–7, 164,
176–7, 224, 302n8
child welfare system, 146–7, 153, 164
domination, systems of, 88, 122–4,
128–33
harm to Indigenous women and girls,
122–3, 128–9
Indigenous critiques of, 5, 88, 102
process of, 72–3
psychiatry and, 251–3, 256–60, 263–5
queer/2SQ challenging of, 215–17,
228, 289

reconciliation and, 182–6
    violence of, 72–3, 83, 101, 139, 175–
        81, 188, 292
settler state, 10
    assimilatory goals of, 72–3, 87, 131–3,
        287
    Canada as, 5, 83, 87–8, 128–30
    denial of Indigenous identity, 9, 13,
        17, 47, 76, 83, 87–90
    discrimination, 4, 8–9, 16, 44–5,
        53–4, 65, 233
    dispossession, 30, 69n5, 72–4, 168–9
    gendered oppression, 4, 13–15, 46,
        122–3, 140, 146–7, 152–4, 252–3
    as genocidal, 42–3, 72–3, 100–1,
        122–3, 138
    inaction on violence, 134–5, 137
    institutions, 4, 42–3, 121–3, 148–9,
        198
    laws, 43, 74, 163, 197–8, 283
    as patriarchal, 74, 123, 129–31, 169
    policing of Indigenous feminists, 3–4,
        27
    racism, 5, 34–5, 46–7, 57, 133, 197
    reconciliation, notions of, 184–7
    sovereignty, assertions of, 72–3, 88,
        100–1
    violence, 63–8, 122–3, 128–9, 133–5,
        139–40, 202
    uncritical teaching about, 43–4
sex, 18
    binary assignment at birth, 146–8,
        154, 233n7, 295
    discrimination in Indian Act, 35, 46,
        72–9, 82–6, 89–90, 130
    kalo (plant), 226
    queer Indigenous, 238, 241–4, 282,
        297
    trafficking, 137, 139
sexism,
    in academia, 37, 44–5, 316
    in child welfare system, 146–7,
        159–60, 163–4
    colonialism and, 8, 10–11, 31–5,
        66–7, 129–31
    Indigenous feminist analyses of, 2,
        8–16, 52–4, 66–7, 214
    Indigenous men's mimicry of invader,
        220–2, 228
    Indigenous women facing, 5, 10–11,
        31–5, 122, 220–1
    privilege of obliviousness to, 16, 36
    racism and, 10–14, 33–7, 44

sex work, see prostitution
Simpson, Audra, 104, 253, 296, 300,
    302n11
Simpson, George, 29, 31
Simpson, Leanne Betasamosake, 217, 224,
    228, 292–4, 303n20
Sinclair (Joyce Green's maternal) family,
    30–1, 38, 48n3
Sinclair, Phoenix Hope, 151–3
Sinclair, Raven, 155
*Sisters in Spirit: What their Stories Tell
    Us*, 53; *see also* Native Women's
    Association of Canada (NWAC)
Sixties Scoop, 58, 86, 149–50, 184–5
Skeets, Jake, 238, 244–5, 247–8
social movements, 270, 276
    transformative action focus, 12, 14
solidarity, 35, 40
    commodified, 184
    cross-movement, 7, 11, 21, 187
    feminist, 2–3, 12–14, 33, 282
    gatherings, 135, 273
    vigilance about, 187, 276–7, 280
Sorentino, Sara-Maria, 291–2, 299
sovereignty, 9, 196
    bodily/land/food, 203, 206, 208, 215,
        272, 300
    Indigenous women/people as threat-
        ening state, 251–3, 259–60
    notions of self-, 238, 241, 297, 300
    settler colonial assertions versus
        Indigenous, 72–3, 88, 100–1, 140,
        169, 296
Starblanket, Gina, 37, 303n19
    conference organizing, 5–6
    Indigenous resurgence, 8, 186, 205
status, Indian,
    conferral or loss to children, 74–83,
        89, 108, 111, 148
    via fatherhood, 57, 74–6, 80, 83–4,
        130–1
    living on reserves and, 17, 57, 74–5,
        81
    persons with, 76, 80–8, 105, 111, 148,
        169
    problematic of, 3–4, 17
    registration process inadequacies,
        85–7
    removal of women's, 34–5, 75–81,
        83–6, 90, 105, 148
    rights, 35, 84, 109, 112
St. Denis, Verna, 43
Steinhauer, Kathleen, 100, 107, 113–16

Stevenson, Lisa, 169
Stolen Sisters: A Human Rights Response to Discrimination and Violence Against Indigenous Women in Canada, 53, 136
Stó:lō people, 216, 263, 289, 298
Supreme Court of Canada cases,
  Aboriginal title, 73, 88
  Indian Act sex discrimination, 48n6, 77, 81–2, 130–1
survivors, 140, 181, 285
  child welfare system, 146, 149
  residential school/sanitorium, 58, 182–3
  women as, 37, 53, 123, 137, 296
Symposium on Aboriginal Feminism (2002): 2–6, 40, 300

terra nullius, 73, 88, 199, 245
theory, Indigenous feminist, 283
  criticisms of, 34, 102–3, 293
  distinctiveness/power of, 4–5, 11–12, 21, 118, 290
  as emancipatory/liberatory, 13–17, 47, 272
  as embodied/lived, 15–16, 245–7, 252, 297
  focus on praxis, 11–12, 302n13
  intersectionality in, 14–15, 206, 215, 269
  liberal/white feminisms versus, 15–16, 170, 174–80, 188, 297
  queer, 214, 224, 241, 287
  set of tools in, 11, 14, 55, 65, 118, 305n32
Todd, Zoe, 286
Toronto, 44, 135, 270, 277–9
traditionalism, Indigenous, 197, 206
  confronting forms of, 10, 18–19, 39, 215, 228–9, 304n28
  family practices of, 59–60
  gender role, 52, 201, 228–9, 289, 296–8
  heteropatriarchal, 214, 220–4, 228–9, 232–3, 234n13
  Indian Act versus, 108, 117, 131
  Indigenous feminist critiques of, 3, 108, 117, 289
  queer notions of, 289, 294–8, 300
  settler state oppression of, 256, 259
trafficking, human, 123, 128, 130–2, 137–40
trans Indigenous people, 164n1
  cis-heteropatriarchal oppression, 146–7, 159–60, 164
  community presence of, 194, 200–1, 207
  in decolonization, 244, 289, 298–9
  feminist inclusion of, 7, 138, 297–9, 301n7
  feminist political action for, 12, 164, 285, 304n23
  violence facing, 194, 205–6, 278–9
transphobia, 206
  rejection of, 208, 214, 228
  settler colonial traditionalism and, 146, 206, 214, 228, 284
  systemic, 8, 159, 247
trauma,
  growing beyond, 180, 245, 248, 303n20
  impacts of, 63, 139, 161–3
  intergenerational, 11, 67, 131–2
  see also post-traumatic stress disorder (PTSD)
treaties, 186
  Canada's refusal to comply with, 78–9, 86, 133, 177
  comprehensive claim or self-government agreements versus, 88
  imperialist process of making, 101, 148, 196
  Indigenous mobilizing around, 106–11, 116
  rights access to, 77, 106–11, 148
  United Nations, 78
  women, impacts on, 77, 130; *see also* Red Ticket Women
"treaty Indian," notion of, 100, 105, 110, 130
Tronto, Joan, 177
Trudeau, Justin, 121, 136, 182
Truth and Reconciliation Commission (TRC), 131, 149
  final report and Calls to Action, 182
  see also National Day for Truth and Reconciliation (Orange Shirt Day)
Tsilhqot'in Nation v. British Columbia, 88
Tuck, Eve, 286–8, 291–2, 299–300
Turtle Island, 121, 216, 282, 302n8
  colonial invasion of, 15, 48n2, 176
  use of term, 141n2
Two-Spirit people, 179, 301n7
  cis-heteropatriarchal oppression, 146–7, 164
  community presence of, 194, 200, 207, 215–16, 298

feminist inclusion of, 7, 18, 138
storywork, 286, 289–90, 295–301
violence facing, 188, 193–4, 205–6, 247, 277

United Nations Declaration on the Rights of Indigenous Peoples (UNDRIP), 72, 87
United Nations Declaration on the Rights of Indigenous Peoples Act (UNDA), 87
United Nations Human Rights Committee, 78–9, 82–3, 89
United States, 216, 280
    colonialism and gender oppression in, 4, 278
    Indigenous children to families in, 149–50
    Indigenous dispossession in, 168–9, 180, 196

Vancouver,
    Downtown Eastside (DTES) MMIWG, 134–5, 137
    political organizing in, 121–2, 125
Van Kirk, Sylvia, 29–30, 48n5
victimization,
    of abusers, 67–8
    blame for, 63, 132
    children's, 158–9
    colonial/cis-heteropatriarchal, 53, 122
    prevalence of Indigenous women's, 64, 122, 128
    silence about, 32, 126
    white women's, 112
violence,
    accountability for male, 10, 67, 69
    activism on, 122, 125, 137, 200–7, 246, 304n26
    anti-2SLGBTQIA+, 138–9, 146, 194, 205–6, 217, 278–9
    child welfare system, 32, 132–3, 148–9, 151–3
    choices about, 65–7
    of classification, 11, 117, 124
    demands for freedom from, 14, 124
    discursive, 101, 104, 117, 133, 207
    familial, 30–1, 58–60, 127–8, 131, 155, 163
    gendered, *see* gendered violence
    Indigenous male leadership, 113–15
    Indigenous women facing disproportionate, 17, 30–2, 52–4, 64–9, 121–8, 131–4, 277
    institutional, 73, 122–3, 129–32, 140, 256–62
    intimate partner, 68, 128, 285
    men's, 28, 31–2, 59, 62–9, 104, 258
    misogynistic, 69, 202, 206, 288
    against nonhuman beings, 100, 129, 186, 199–200, 205–6
    police, 43, 66, 159–60, 279–81, 284
    psychiatric, 252–4, 256–65
    racist, 15, 46, 159, 200, 252–3, 280–1
    residential school, 89, 131–3, 136–8, 176, 182–5
    settler colonial, 2, 45–6, 72–3, 83, 175–81, 188, 260, 292
    settler need for remediation of, 9, 122, 139–40
    sexual, 21, 74–5, 122, 128, 132
    silence about, 30–2, 63, 66, 163, 202, 220
    state, 34, 63–8, 100–1, 107–8, 128–35, 202
    state minimizing of, 42, 122–3, 133–5, 138–40
    systemic, 122, 125, 129–32
    threats of, 113–14
    toleration of, 28, 63, 66, 128
    treaty entitlements and, 100–1, 104, 109–17
    see also abuse; anti-violence efforts; missing and murdered Indigenous women and girls
vulnerability, 129–30, 259
    awareness of, 65, 275
    Indigenous children's, 146, 153–5, 160, 163
    Indigenous women's and queer, 64, 75, 122, 136, 140, 262

Waldron, Ingrid, 8–9, 257
water,
    contamination/violations, 100, 185, 203–4, 208
    defence of, 199–200, 208
    impure on-reserve, 86
    relationships with, 194–5, 199–208, 217–18, 241, 245
water protectors, women as, 8, 13, 296, 304n26
Webstad, Phyllis, 183–4
Wesley, Saylesh, 298–9

wetland restoration, *see* loʻi kalo (wetland taro farming) restoration
white feminism, 12, 66
    accusing Indigenous women of adopting, 35, 102–3
    care ethics, 170, 177–80, 188
    Indigenous women's critiques of, 34, 53
    Indigenous women's erasure from, 9, 106–7, 178, 189
    support for Indigenous women, 40
Whitehead, Joshua, 247–8, 303n21
whiteness, 112
    critiques of, 7, 18, 175, 263, 280–1
    privilege, 16, 36–8, 113
    thinking beyond replicating/reifying, 217, 240, 290–1
white supremacy, 31, 277
    Indian Act assertions of, 73–4
    relevance of Indigenous feminism in, 9–10, 215–17, 232
    systemic, 41, 123, 138, 186, 253–4
Williams, Bernie (Skundaal), 125
Wilson, Alex, 247, 304n28
wind power generation, 198, 203
womanhood, Indigenous, 15, 295–6, 298
    conceptions of, 18–19, 63, 116, 204, 264
    mocking/pathologizing, 60, 253, 258–60
    see also motherhood
Womb Theory, 180
women,
    Black, 112, 175, 180, 280, 283–4
    Indigenous, *see* Indigenous women
    questioning prohibitions on, 3, 111–12, 131
    white, 33, 112, 169, 175–8, 188–9, 253, 260

Yang, K. Wayne, 286–8, 291–2, 299–300
Yantha, Susan, 83
Yellowhead Institute, 5, 182

Zapotec people, 193–7, 200–9